Intranet Resource Kit

Intranet Resource Kit

Edited by Dr. Prakash Ambegaonkar

OSBORNE

Berkeley New York St. Louis San Francisco
Auckland Bogot Hamburg London Madrid
Mexico City Milan Montreal New Delhi Panama City
Paris São Paulo Singapore Sydney
Tokyo Toronto

Osborne **McGraw-Hill**
2600 Tenth Street
Berkeley, California 94710
U.S.A.

For information on translations or book distributors outside the U.S.A., or to arrange bulk purchase discounts for sales promotions, premiums, or fundraisers, please contact Osborne/**McGraw-Hill** at the above address.

Intranet Resource Kit

1234567890 DOC 9987

ISBN 0-07-882262-9

Publisher Brandon A. Nordin	**Proofreader** Linda Medoff
Editor in Chief Scott Rogers	**Indexer** David Heiret
Accquisitions Editor Wendy Rinaldi	**Computer Designer** Roberta Steele
Project Editor Emily Rader	**Series Design** Marcela V. Hancik
Associate Project Editor Cynthia Douglas	**Illustrator** Lance Ravella
Editorial Assistant Ann Sellers	**Quality Control Specialist** Joe Scuderi
Technical Editor Michael Erwin	**Cover Design** Timm Sinclair
Copy Editors Alex Miloradovich Judith Brown	**Cover Illustration** Matthew Nielsen

About the Editor ...

Dr. Prakash Ambegaonkar, known as Dr. P throughout the industry, came to the United States from India as a graduate student and launched Frontier Technologies Corporation, a successful global company focusing on Internet-, Intranet-, and TCP/IP-related software products, in 1982.

Since Dr. P first started Frontier Technologies in Milwaukee, Wisconsin, he has built the company to a recognized world leader, with product lines represented in almost every country. In the past three years, the company has been invited by the Governor's trade mission to China, Japan, Argentina, Brazil, Peru, and Chile. Frontier Technologies has more than 35 strategic partnerships, including value added resellers, distributors, and OEMs.

Because of his vision, Dr. P has gained international recognition and has won several prestigious awards including *Inc.* magazine's Entrepreneur of the Year award, *Information Week's* Top 25 Intranet Companies, and honored as one of *Upside* magazine's Hottest 100 Private Companies. In the past three years, Dr. P's expertise has enabled Frontier's product lines to win more than 30 awards, including *Communications Week's* Max Award, *LAN Magazine's* Product of the Year award (three-time winner), Motorola's MOTsan Gold Certificate of Excellence, *Data Communications'* Tester's Choice award (two-time winner), and *Network Computing's* Paradigm award.

Dr. P has been active in IEEE, ACM, and other professional organizations, and has spoken at various business and technical conferences.

Contributing Authors

Susan Archer has been a technical writer for the past ten years covering mainframe, PC, and Internet software. She has authored online help and manual documentation for a wide variety of Internet tools. Susan has a B.S. in History Education from the University of Wisconsin, Madison, and an M.A. in Mass Media from Marquette University.

Michael Beirne is a technical writer for Frontier Technologies. He has led several training sessions and seminars on TCP/IP and the Internet. Mike is highly versed in base Intranet technologies and Intranet security issues. He started working for Frontier in 1995 after graduating from the University of Wisconsin, Milwaukee.

Erv Bluemner is Vice President of Engineering at Frontier Technologies. From 1978 to 1995, he managed computer engineering groups responsible for the development of diagnostic scanners at GE Medical Systems. He has been an invited speaker at the IEEE conference of fault-tolerant computing and has presented papers on visualization, software engineering, and software documentation for various health industry organizations (ACR/NEMA, HIMA). Since joining Frontier Technologies in mid-1995, Mr. Bluemner has been responsible for the development of Internet- and Intranet-oriented products, including TCP/IP, Web browsers, HTML content-creation tools, e-mail, security, search, and other Intranet applications. Mr. Bluemner received a B.S. in Mathematics in 1978 and an M.S. in Digital Systems Engineering in 1980 from the University of Wisconsin, Milwaukee.

Lorraine Potter Kalal is Senior Product Manager at Frontier Technologies for the SuperTCP Suite and CyberJunction products. Prior to her association with Frontier, Lorraine taught economics and finance at The King's College, after 12 years in the telecommunications and satellite video communications fields. Lorraine received her B.S. in Computer Science from Duke University and her MBA in Finance and Entrepreneurial Management from the Wharton School at the University of Pennsylvania.

Ann M. Krauss, Public Relations Manager, has led creative and strategic marketing and public relations for Frontier Technologies for the past seven years. She has extensive expertise in Intranet and Internet products. Ann attended the University of Arizona, Tucson, and graduated from the

University of Wisconsin, Milwaukee, with a BBA and a double major in Marketing and Personnel Management.

Kia LaBracke joined Frontier Technologies in 1995. She has worked extensively with Web applications for the Intranet, Extranet, and Internet. She is Product Manager for Frontier's Intranet Genie and CyberSearch product lines. Ms. LaBracke is a graduate of Ripon College and of the Université de Paris, Sorbonne.

Ray Langford holds a B.S. in Engineering with minors in Math and Computer Science from the University of Wisconsin, Stout. Ray is the Engineering Manager for Advanced Products at Frontier Technologies and is responsible for defining and planning the future product directions for Frontier Technologies' Engineering Department.

John A. Luoma has been a manager in the finance and information systems fields for more than ten years. He graduated from the University of Wisconsin, Milwaukee in 1985, with a BBA in Information Systems. John is currently the IS Manager at Frontier Technologies, where he helps to design Internet software products for other IS departments.

Susan Moore is currently a technical writer for Frontier Technologies. She has led the effort at Frontier to document Web-centric technologies and customer applications. Susan graduated from St. Norbert College, where she majored in English and Math/Computer Science.

Nicole E. Rogers is a Public Relations Specialist for Frontier Technologies. She is an expert in both media and public relations, as well as in the application of Intranet technologies in those areas. She graduated from Marquette University in 1995 with a B.A. in Broadcast Journalism and a B.S. in Criminology and Law Studies.

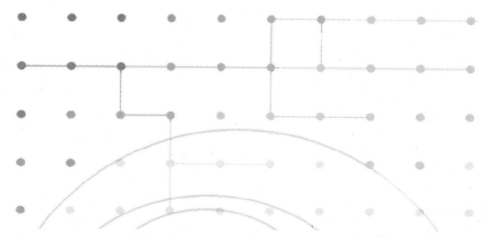

Contents at a Glance

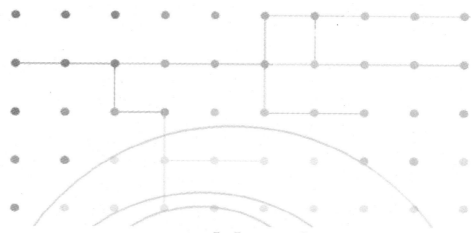

Table of Contents

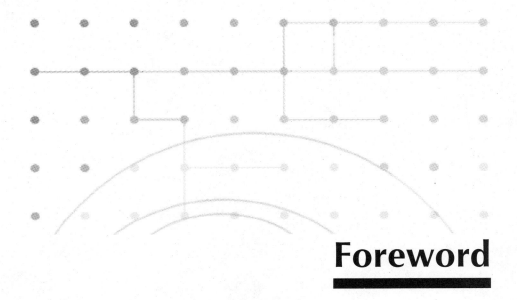

Foreword

Looking forward to the end of this century and beyond, we see several major changes that should transform standard business activities. The emergence of a "digital economy" will place a burden on corporations to compete and interact in an information-rich yet security-sensitive paradigm. Information will flow seamlessly between vendors and suppliers in digital packets. The exchange of goods and services between corporations and to end-customers will be facilitated by the corresponding exchange of digital "cybercash." Just-in-time inventory and product distribution practices will be coordinated with digital speed. In addition, nationalistic barriers and borders of trade will come crashing down as information and commerce-related transactions occur ubiquitously around the world. Critical information exchange takes on a global nature. Just as in the automotive industry today, where automobiles are assembled with components from all corners of the globe, the corporate data bank will dynamically link information as it is created and stored in data warehouses located anywhere in the world. The fabric of the corporate office structure will take on a dramatic new dimension as more and more employees work at home, pushing the need for effective online digital information exchange to even higher levels.

Corporations engaged in providing tools and platforms to enable this vision must address several barriers to its realization. For example, the bandwidth of the Internet is receiving widespread attention. New network carrier technologies must incorporate higher performance and lower cost to achieve the network interchange of larger informational units, including multimedia, sound, and video. A growing gap exists between the emerging Intranet/Extranet technologies and the applications that use these technologies. Users and vendors have barely begun to exploit the new capabilities of these technologies, such as sophisticated search algorithms, encryption and security, distributed object OS platforms, network computers, and VRML/3-D user interfaces. These technologies demand software applications that can innovatively take advantage of their capabilities in a meaningful way to effectively solve user problems. Such solutions must be easy to use, and standards must evolve so that various applications will work seamlessly together.

Over the last 15 years, many of the basic problems of the corporate office worker were addressed by the computational tools of the PC and the emergence of desktop computing. Moving beyond the desktop, information access and management are quickly evolving into the weapons of corporate victory or defeat in the intellectual and competitive battlefield of the future. In this scenario, information overload and the problem of securing exposed information are minefields to manage. Intranets linked with the global Internet comprise the basic technologies for waging that war. It is our hope that by examining the application of the Intranet/Internet technologies to current corporate needs, this book will serve as a bridge to this highly competitive future. In Web terms, we trust that the book presents a "hyperlink" examination of present technologies that will let you navigate your corporation toward a future with significantly higher levels of productivity and competitiveness.

The book provides a variety of vantage points from which to consider the application and implementation of Intranet solutions, including suggestions for applying the software supplied with the book to introduce Intranet capability to your company.

The *Intranet Resource Kit* has been written by a number of dedicated professionals with expertise in developing and applying Intranet technologies. Just as a health book is, appropriately, written by doctors, this book is written by members of Frontier Technologies' staff who are working every day to help create the necessary solutions to enable companies to construct easy-to-use and easy-to-manage Intranets. Frontier Technologies pioneered software solutions for the TCP/IP arena and now is doing the same for the Internet and Intranet. Because Frontier Technologies has been working with these technologies for some time and has helped other companies to successfully implement Intranets, we feel qualified to share our knowledge with those who are attempting to understand and apply these technologies.

Intranet technologies are dynamic and ever changing; therefore, we recognize that we cannot possibly cover every Intranet-related topic. As such, we attempt to focus on the most important angles of the Intranet revolution and present them here for your benefit. For example, at the time this book was going to print, a new terminology called "Extranet" was just beginning to surface. While Extranets are discussed briefly in this book, we may need to write a new book to follow this one in order to provide you with in-depth information about this new concept.

Enjoy reading and have fun with the Frontier Technologies Intranet Genie sampler software included. We hope you will find the book and CD useful and will recommend it to friends and colleagues.

Dr. Prakash Ambegaonkar
Chairman and CEO
Frontier Technologies Corporation

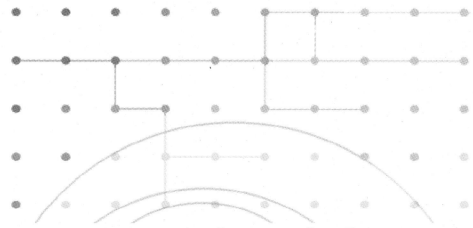

Acknowledgments

The authors thank the following people for their willingness to share their time and technical expertise: Bruce Backman; Jack Bishop, The Word Machinery Company; John O. Borchardt II; Lori Crawford, Wisconsin Asset Management; Mark Crawford, Wisconsin Asset Management; Ron Daggett, Tao Computer Services; Nishant Dani; Savithri Dani; Leon Davis, First Bank; Robin Faehling; Paul Feider, Wisconsin Asset Management; Tracey Grund; Jason E. Harder; Allen Klumpp; Cecil Murray; Laura Peck; Michael G. Phillips; Chad Plautz; Denise Radzins; Kris K. Saunders; Aniruddha Shrotri; Todd T. Tower; Yuliya Tsukerman; William Trotman; Nicholas Wagner; and David Yunck.

Special thanks for the preparation and development of the Intranet Genie Light CD-ROM goes to Allen Klumpp, Leon Milbeck, Jr., Susan Moore, and David Yunck.

We would also like to recognize the patience and persistence of those we worked with at Osborne/McGraw-Hill, especially Wendy Rinaldi, Acquisitions Editor, Emily Rader, Project Editor, and Cynthia Douglas, Associate Project Editor. Their professionalism and top-notch assistance has impressed us all!

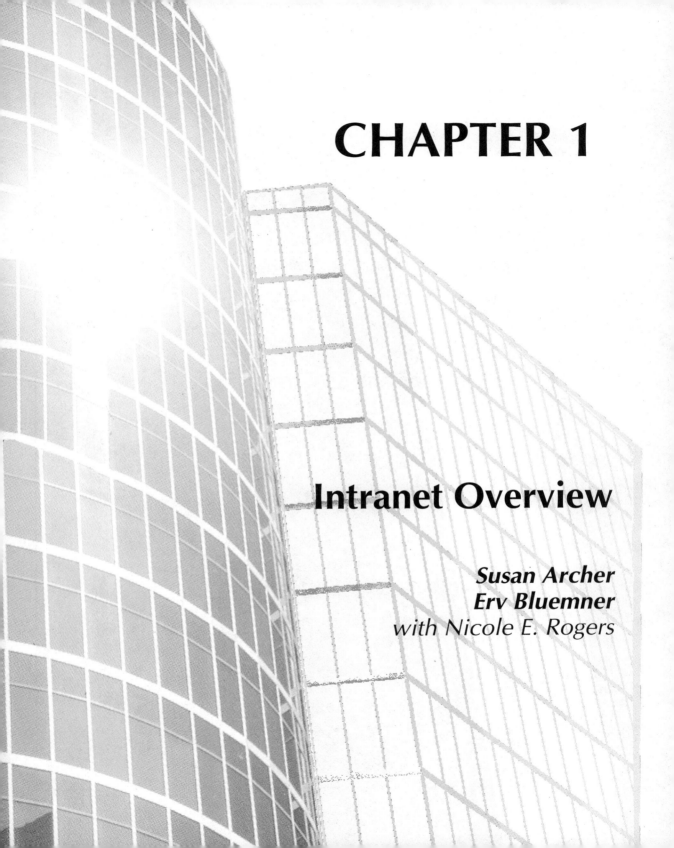

CHAPTER 1

Intranet Overview

Susan Archer
Erv Bluemner
with Nicole E. Rogers

Chapter Objectives

◆ Learn what an Intranet is

◆ Identify problems that can be solved by using
an Intranet

◆ Learn how Intranet applications can provide solutions

◆ Begin to understand how an Intranet can help your
corporation improve its productivity

Many people have heard of the Internet, the electronic global network that is changing the way people communicate, and also about the World Wide Web, which has brought forward a dynamic, globally connected information structure that can be viewed from any desktop browser. This book is about *Intranets*, which let you use the technology of the Internet and the World Wide Web within your organization, often behind a secure firewall, to revolutionize the way your organization does business. You can have an Intranet on your organization's *local area network* (LAN) that does not connect to the Internet, or you can have an Internet connection to your Intranet. This chapter illustrates the kinds of issues an Intranet can help your organization solve and will lay the groundwork for understanding a new paradigm for information exchange and management that can significantly increase your company's level of productivity.

Many organizations today use a LAN to connect personal computers (PCs) to shared resources such as file servers and network printers. An Intranet extends the resources an organization can easily share to include documents, databases, images, videos, sound, and multimedia. These resources can be shared securely within your LAN or around the world over the Internet. Additionally, with the availability of "browser" interfaces, the ability to have a common graphical interface for information creation, management, and access becomes a reality. Training time is greatly reduced, and new applications can be distributed across the entire organization instantly, as they become available. Within the paradigm of the Intranets, new generations of tools are springing up to provide links to existing corporate information databases and to provide assisted keyword access to information in a variety of formats (word processing files, graphics, databases, HTML, presentations) anywhere within your corporate computer environment, from local PCs to corporate file servers and mainframes.

With the addition of a security infrastructure, often including a firewall, corporations can dramatically improve the productivity of their workers with the confidence of being protected against malicious attacks. Information exchanges can be securely encrypted and even authenticated with digital signatures for validating the identity of the communicators. Secure electronic transfers make it possible for corporations to establish online order placement and allow other intercompany financial exchanges.

In this chapter, we'll take a very high-level look at how the capabilities of the Intranet might be applied in a corporate setting. We'll get into the details in later chapters. And if the Internet terms "server," "URL," "browser," or "newsgroups" are new to you, you'll want to skip ahead to Chapter 2 to gain a basic understanding of the Internet and Web technology. To get started, this chapter illustrates how the fictitious ABC Pharmaceutical Company becomes more effective by using Intranet technologies to improve decision making and information sharing within the company. As you're reading about the ABC Pharmaceutical Company, try to identify similar problem areas in your organization. Think about how an Intranet could help your organization.

Before Implementation of a Web-Based Intranet

The ABC Pharmaceutical Company makes aspirin and other over-the-counter medications. The 15 plants that make the different medications are spread across the United States, and the home office for the company is in Cincinnati, Ohio. Most administrative activity and the corporate information structure are centralized at the home office. Products are distributed either via a network of intermediate distributors to small drugstores or direct to the larger pharmaceutical store chains. Timely availability and order processing are critical factors in meeting customer demands.

Inside the company, the supervisory and administrative staff at the plants all have voice mail and a few PCs running spreadsheet programs and word processing software. The PCs also have terminal emulators for dial-up access to the company's mainframe, which has database applications used to process orders, handle inventory, and take care of accounting. The company has four dial-up lines to the mainframe, so remote or traveling plant personnel sometimes try dialing in several times before they are actually able to connect to the mainframe. The yearly cost of dial-up connections, in long-distance phone call charges, runs well into six figures.

Everyone at the home office has a PC with the same software as the PCs in the plants. The PCs at the home office are all on a LAN that connects the PCs to the central file servers, various printers, and the mainframe. The corporate LAN provides for sharing of disk storage space, sharing of printers, and access to several company databases on the mainframe. Being on the LAN simplifies getting access to the mainframe, because the mainframe connection is always available. Dial-in service runs at appreciably slower rates.

The upper management of the ABC Pharmaceutical Company has noticed that information doesn't flow as smoothly as it could within the organization. The following are some examples of the issues that have come to these decision makers' attention.

Impaired Decision Making

Because of the imperative to meet customer requirements promptly, many people in the company at all levels make decisions on their own, based on

1

incomplete information, and too often wind up guessing wrong. The painful thing about this is that often, after a problem has become a burning customer issue, upper management finds that someone knew the correct information. If the person who made the decision could have received the needed information, a major problem could have been prevented.

The fact that the 15 plants are dispersed geographically across four time zones compounds the problem. To get all of the internal experts on a given issue into a meeting, several people have to travel. While these internal experts are traveling, other issues and responsibilities are piling up on their desks and need to be taken care of after these experts get back to their offices.

Unfortunately, the number and location of plants also makes the logistics of managing meetings a major headache. Key players may be traveling, they may forget about the meeting, or they don't get the memo or fax that tells them the meeting is going on. By the time these experts are brought into the issue, mistakes have been made, which makes it even more difficult to straighten things out and get back on track. In addition, no clear-cut system exists for managing meetings and assigning responsibilities. All attendees of the meetings keep track of agenda items and action responsibilities individually, so anyone who wants to know what happened has to talk to someone who was there. This wastes more time and causes misunderstandings because different people remember different things about the meeting.

The results of this impaired process weigh everyone down. Many people at the satellite plants frequently feel left out of the decision making, while people at the home office feel the plant people don't try to communicate. Senior managers are trying to get products made and delivered to customers in a timely manner, but the details that aren't handled at a lower level seem to consistently cause major problems.

Employees at all levels feel like they don't matter. With the information and decision glut, supervisors seem to have very little time to get involved in the details of their employees' day-to-day activities. It's just that the supervisor gets wrapped up in too many other, "bigger" issues to handle. Of course, this is a self-feeding situation, as the employee details/issues escalate into these managerial problems. If employees try to get information they need from other departments, they also get little attention, because other departments are too busy taking care of their problems to give anything more than superficial or limited help. Real information is at a premium, and the mechanisms to distribute the information to all who have a need to know are seriously lacking. Mostly, this is because too many things are handled by a paper system, or the tools don't allow for rapid creation and universal distribution.

Difficulties Sharing Information

The customer service staff at ABC Pharmaceutical answer questions about the different products the company provides. Hospitals, doctors' offices, and consumers often call asking about the side effects of different medications and how the medications interact with other prescription drugs the patient is taking. Most of the information may be found in the many volumes of printed manuals located in the customer service area. The binders are big and hard to use in the limited desk area available to the customer service representatives. When new products are released or updates are required in the customer service manual, the new information gets added, but not always in a very organized way. It's time consuming to remove all the old pages and references and replace them with the current materials. The result is that the information is hard to find or sometimes out of date. Customer service representatives often need to call customers back after they find the information, and a significant amount of time is wasted.

The sales representatives for ABC Pharmaceutical Company travel all over the U.S. selling the company's products. A customer transaction starts with a sales quote. When the sales representatives get an order, the organization that is buying the product has to send a purchase order. The sales representatives receive the purchase order, usually by fax, write up the order on an order form, and fax the purchase order and the order form to the home office.

The accounting department receives the purchase order and the order form and goes through an approval process for each purchase. An order from a long-term customer is usually automatic, but the accounting department runs a credit check on new customers to make sure they are a good risk. After approval, the accounting department enters the order, and the shipping department sends the order out. If a purchase is denied, the accounting department gets back to the sales representative about why the purchase was denied.

The sales representatives never know where a purchase order is in the approval process and whether an order is being shipped. The sales representatives are tired of having to ask accounting and shipping about their orders, and these departments are tired of dealing with pushy salespeople.

Hidden Costs

The costs associated with the impaired decision making and difficulties of sharing information at ABC Pharmaceutical Company are often hidden. For example, significant effort is spent in attempts to keep information flowing through manual systems. Systems specialists do their best to install the latest software and tools on each desktop. But this manual process must be repeated for each and every employee for each and every revision of the software used. Product information is created with the best intent of timely distribution, but the addition of new information can frequently invalidate the usefulness of information in the field. Information such as pricing and delivery can change by the week or day in some industries. Of course, the printing costs are exacerbated when the product information is dynamic and continual updates need to be integrated. And there is the human factor of inserting the new material into the existing binders. Reprocessing costs for actions taken on the wrong information cannot even be estimated, but frequently appear on customer complaint cards.

Coordination of new product introductions across multiple plants is another major headache. There are both significant internal project costs and customer/market costs of lost sales when a major project runs a month past its deadline because of minor issues that weren't addressed in a timely manner, but could have been averted if the details were known or the right flags were raised at the right time.

Lost sales or erosion of customer confidence occurs when customers have to wait to receive products because of a complicated purchase approval process. It would take an expert in organizational cost analysis to figure out the exact cost of issues like these. But these are the kinds of hidden costs that make the difference between organizations that do all right and organizations that have superior performance.

After Implementation of an Intranet

Realistically, an Intranet is not a one-size-fits-all solution to every organizational problem. However, an Intranet can ease problems of ineffective information creation and exchange. Intranets also enhance collaboration among workgroups. Corporate America is moving at an incredible pace. Many companies are refocusing their identities or reengineering their processes to compete effectively, or they are moving into new product spaces as the marketplace dictates. Those that move slowly will often cease to exist. In some situations, a major change in corporate culture or technology is necessary to compete in the marketplace, and it will be important to change or provide new tools for the workforce. The trick is to achieve a simplicity of operation and internal cooperation while the product technologies and marketplaces are becoming more complex. Adoption of an Intranet paradigm can give good people better technology to manage the information infrastructure that will be required to compete and improve overall corporate productivity.

To some extent, the impaired decision making and difficulties in sharing information at the ABC Pharmaceutical Company are people issues. If people work well together, some of these issues can be overcome with conscientious communication efforts. People who don't want to collaborate and who don't want to change and grow are probably going to be bottlenecks in an organization whether or not you have an Intranet. You can't use a technological solution to completely fix a people problem. However, the Intranet technologies are aimed at improving some fundamental people processes. An Intranet provides a tool kit for significantly easier and more intuitive information sharing across organizations and individuals. The ability of the people in an organization to work effectively together is greatly improved when the desktop inherently supports collaborative interaction. Intranets provide facilities for online meetings, activity/task scheduling, calendering, document sharing and updating, and messaging.

The presentation of information can also promote efficiency. Intranets allow a common user interface for the display of rich multimedia-oriented content, including diagrams, graphics, video, audio, and animated displays. Commonly used information sources can be cataloged for easy follow-up retrieval, and monitoring agents can be set into action so that the availability of specified content can be automatically forwarded to interested users. For instance, all salespeople involved in the sales and promotion of a particular group of pharmaceuticals will receive the pertinent product information as it is released to the corporate Web servers.

Every organization has people in it who are creative, conscientious, reliable, and eager to embrace new technology that can improve or automate their daily activities. These leaders take new technology like an Intranet and make it a springboard for growth and improved performance in their organizations. Fortunately, others will see this progress and, with the natural appeal and ease of the Intranet browser interface, will follow along quickly.

There are times when people have to get together to bring their full expertise to bear on a problem, but this isn't required for every small issue. Being able to make decisions based on information exchanged electronically speeds decision making and shortens the response time within your organization.

The remainder of this chapter shows how an Intranet provides new technology you can use to make your organization more successful. This overview doesn't go into technical detail, but provides a framework for understanding how an Intranet can release powerful forces for change and growth within your organization.

1

Improved Decision Making (the Ground Floor)

As a first step to improve the decision-making process and information flow, ABC Pharmaceutical Company installed e-mail and newsreaders on users' desktop computers. E-mail has been around for a long time in both proprietary and more open standards-based incarnations. Modern Intranet e-mail is based on open communication standards and often works seamlessly with emerging browser technology by integrating messaging with advanced information-viewing capability. Newsreaders provide online interactive discussion threads. These basic capabilities can be the foundation for better collaboration within your corporation. The following shows some of the ways these applications helped to improve the decision making at ABC Pharmaceutical.

Using E-mail (the First Tool to Implement)

Figure 1-1 shows a screen capture of an e-mail application. If you look closely at the To field, you can see that the first part of the e-mail address is "arthritis." Obviously, no one has a first name of "arthritis," so what is this? It's a mailing list set up at ABC Pharmaceutical that includes all the decision makers, across all the plants, who are responsible for getting a new arthritis pain medication to market. In this e-mail, Sharon is arguing for a different product name. The e-mail capability coordinates the delivery of common information to a linked group of individuals. Everyone receives the same timely information online without any of the handling associated with manual interoffice memos or external post office handling of letters and postage costs.

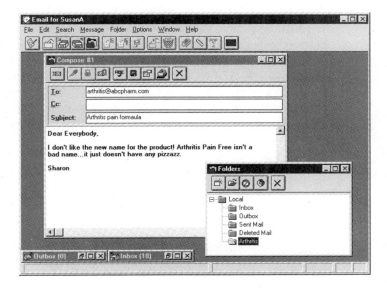

Example of an
e-mail
application
Figure 1-1.

The first benefit of using e-mail to handle issues such as naming a product is that you don't have to schedule a meeting, create and distribute memos, or enter into a series of phone calls. You can argue about it over e-mail, and everyone can see all the comments and discussion! In this e-mail application, you just click Message, Reply All to send your reply to all of the people in the arthritis mailing list. This way, everyone can respond when they have a free minute. Information is exchanged openly, and you have an electronic record you can save to an electronic folder or print on paper. If anyone comes back to you in six months complaining about the product name, you have a record of what you did. The whole process means decisions are made faster and at a lower cost to the organization.

With the pressures of competition on the Internet, the e-mail of yesterday has grown into several major new capabilities. Internet mail allows users to attach other information objects, such as word processing documents, graphics, audio, or even video clips. Incoming mail can be automatically sorted into the appropriate folders for later viewing based on urgency/priority, who sent the message, the title, or even key content phrases or search keywords. The content of messages can support hyperlink jumping to World Wide Web HTML pages at locations anywhere on the Internet around the world.

Using Newsreaders

Figure 1-2 illustrates a newsreader displaying an Internet Usenet newsgroup where people ask and answer questions about arthritis. The company's news server has a newsfeed to the Internet and downloads this and other Internet newsgroups once a day. In addition, the company's news server uploads postings by internal users once a day.

In addition to this public newsgroup, the company has internal technical support newsgroups. The people at the plants and at the home office use the newsgroups on a regular basis to ask and answer questions. The newsgroups serve as a record of what has happened within the company in support of resolving specific customer issues. Many new employees read the newsgroups when they start their jobs and learn in-depth technical information about the company's products. The company also has set up newsgroups for its large customer accounts, so that at any time, the customer and employees can find out the status of that customer's account.

Wider Sharing of Information

ABC Pharmaceutical has now installed more advanced World Wide Web (Web or WWW) technology on their Intranet and uses the "Web-centric" technology to provide up-to-date, easily accessible information for their customer service staff and sales representatives. The key components to this

1

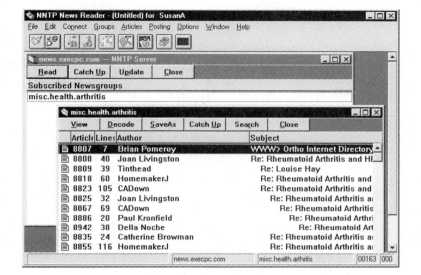

Example of an
Internet
newsgroup
Figure 1-2.

technology are the Web-based information structure (based on HTML Web
pages linked through hyperlinks); a Web browser for display of text,
graphics, or other multimedia content; and the Web server, which provides a
convenient administration center for storing and managing a variety of
information sources and applications. The Web server responds to the
commands of a client (computer) by returning requested information, often
in the form of Web pages but not limited to that format.

A Web page is like a magazine page that includes text, graphics, and pictures
with the inherent ability to be linked to any other Web page regardless of
what computer that Web page is on. Tool kits for creating Web content
make it easy to generate new Web-based documents (these documents
adhere to the HTML or Hypertext Markup Language format) or to convert
existing documents, such as word processing-based text/graphics documents,
into Web-based content. Advanced browsers/servers support the ability to
index the company's entire collection of Web (and even non-HTML)
information. Information can then be retrieved through keyword or natural
language queries.

Even more advanced Web software makes information residing in
SQL/ODBC-compliant databases available to the users of a browser. All
information access can be accomplished with complete security. Digital
certificates can be used to authenticate any user's identity before allowing
access to the server and its information store. Chapter 3 covers the details of
these tools and capabilities.

Using a Browser to Search for Information

Suppose a hospital calls in and wants to know about the side effects of taking the company's generic aspirin, ABC Aspirin. As shown in Figure 1-3, the customer service representative opens the search application on the Intranet, enters **ABC Aspirin**, and chooses to search the Aspirin information. To start the search, the customer service representative clicks the Submit button.

In about a second, a new page of search results displays. The customer service representative skims the search results, consisting of a list of the best possible matches to the keyword in ranked order of potential relevancy, and clicks on the document that seems most likely to have the information. The browser interface is immediately invoked, providing a windowed screen area for the display of the document with any enclosed graphics or text. After skimming the document, the customer service representative tells the hospital representative the possible side effects for taking ABC Aspirin. With a quick point-and-click selection, the rep saves the document's address (URL) to her bookmark organizer so the next time this issue occurs she can immediately go to that information source. With another quick selection, she enters the mail utility, attaches the retrieved document, and forwards the information to the hospital representative as a thoughtful substantiating follow-up, which might be printed later for a patient.

Using a Database with a Web Server

The company decided there would be fewer problems with orders if the sales representatives entered their own orders in the mainframe database. To do

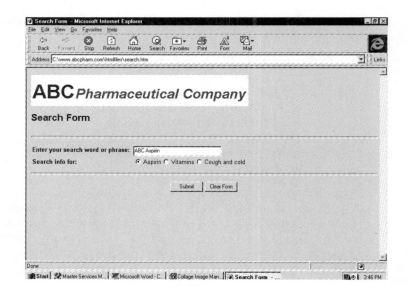

Using a search
form in a
browser
Figure 1-3.

1

this, the company hired a new employee to create Web pages like the one in Figure 1-4 for the sales representatives to use. With the new tools, construction of the Web form does not require any programming background. The tools allow text and graphics to be laid out by directly typing or using the mouse to point, click, and drop elements onto the form's workspace. Entry fields can be quickly defined and the rules for checking legal values or ranges easily specified. A program (called a *back end*) must be developed to process the form's input and communicate with the database (typically an SQL/ODBC-compliant database such as those offered by Sybase, Oracle, or Informix) located on the Web server. A template for construction is included in the Web server tool kit and is used to provide the general framework for the application. In a couple of hours, the order form is ready.

Sales representatives have a copy of the Web page shown in Figure 1-4 on their laptops or PCs. To create an order, the reps fill out the order when they have time and then dial in to the company's Intranet when they have a minute. They connect to the company's Intranet Web site over a secure connection and then submit the form they want. The Web application on the Intranet lets them know if the form is out of date and automatically downloads a new form if the current one is old. After receiving the correct form, the Web server transmits the form to the accounting department.

The sales representatives still have to send the accounting department a purchase order along with the order form. The accounting department has a new fax server that stores incoming faxes electronically, so the reps fax the

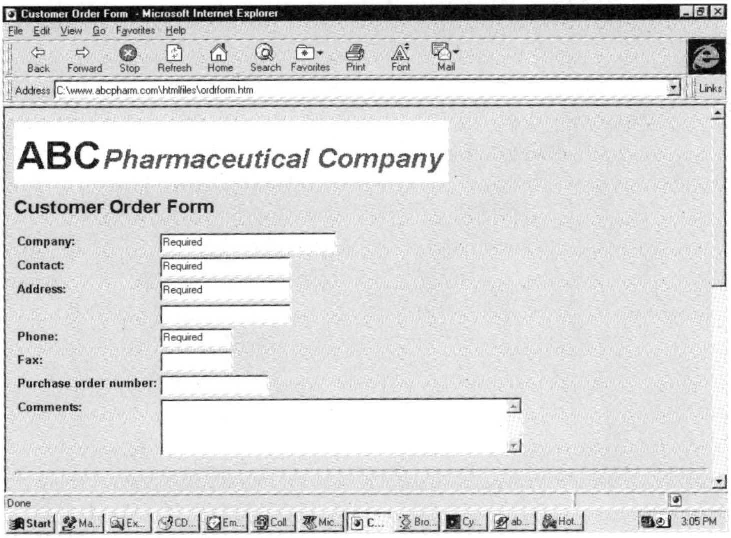

Order form in
a Web browser

Figure 1-4.

purchase order to the new fax server, and an accounting clerk matches the purchase orders with the order forms. The accountant who is responsible for approving the purchase orders opens her Web browser and goes to the approval page. In this page, she enters the approval. The Web application automatically generates a shipping order and delivers it electronically to a shipping clerk. In addition, the Web application sends the sales representative an e-mail message saying the order was approved. If the accountant denies the purchase order, an e-mail message is automatically sent to the rep telling him the reason for denial. If the sales representative doesn't get any response after a period of time, he calls the accountant and asks about the status of the approval, or he can search online to see who in the line of approvals has been most recently electronically forwarded the order.

Other Collaborative Applications

At the root of the implementation of ABC Pharmaceutical's Intranet is the underlying network technology of the Internet—TCP/IP. The TCP/IP communication protocol provides for the addressing and safe delivery of networked messages between computers and subnetworks around the world. A backbone of interconnectivity is available at a fraction of the cost of linking remote dial-in users to a central facility. ABC made use of this fact to ensure that each remote or traveling user would be provided an account with a nationally distributed ISP (Internet service provider). These companies provide local linkage to the worldwide Internet. By making local calls to the provider rather than using regular phone lines for data access, ABC was able to eliminate 70 percent of its phone costs.

As a next step, ABC implemented Web conferencing and meeting software that allows groups to interact in electronic meetings between remote company locations. This software has greatly reduced travel time in the ABC company. The software works within the browser window (in fact, it's a browser downloadable application). The software interfaces with calendering and messaging facilities to automate the logistics of meeting management. Any user can schedule an online meeting with any other group of individuals within ABC. The software checks for common available time slots from each participant's online calendar. An agenda can be constructed by conferring with participants via e-mail. The agenda and notification are automatically routed to participants. Attendees can request that reminders be electronically delivered a day before the meeting.

The online meeting sports several onscreen components from Web technology. The active agenda item occupies a portion of the screen along with a meeting clock. A pop-up window for displaying action items is available. A small, optional window with a video display of participants can be utilized, though bandwidth does not effectively support the remote dial-in users at 28.8Kbps. Workstations are equipped to handle an audio stream between sites (headphone optional), which essentially delivers the phone-conferencing capability.

The central meeting component is the whiteboard space for showing documents or a notepad. Anyone in the meeting can update or sketch on the whiteboard, and all participants see the updates. Because each workstation is connected to the corporate Web server, at any time, individual participants can initiate a retrieval of any pertinent information or document for other attendees to see. After the meeting, action items and meeting notes can be automatically forwarded via e-mail to all participants.

Others Are Implementing Their Intranets

If the benefits and improvements that the Intranet promises apply to your company, you'll need to put together a game plan for gaining approval and implementing the technology. There are many ways to proceed. Some of the vendors are offering all-in-one solutions that allow you to get an integrated environment established in a short period with a consistency of both "look and feel" and functionality across the applications. In other cases, you'll want to look at some specialized components that uniquely address your problems. We'll explore these options in later chapters, but the leaders who would implement an Intranet in their organizations need to identify their goals and vigorously pursue them. You're going to have naysayers around you with all kinds of "reasons" why an Intranet won't work. You're also going to have the normal frustrations of learning a new technology and implementing it. On the other hand, this is exciting stuff, and the reality is that your competition is moving forward into this paradigm. Here are some examples:

♦ Many companies have implemented an Intranet to open communications among geographically dispersed locations. For example, according to Ted Meyer, public relations spokesman for General Electric in Fairfield, Connecticut, the company uses its Intranet to get employees more information at their desktops and more convenient ways of accessing information. "We're looking at putting benefits information online to consolidate a lot of information for employees," Meyer says. The company's Intranet contains annual reports and other financial and business information that employee stockholders can use to manage their investments. The company's Intranet also offers a travel center so that employees can easily book their own business trips. General Electric plans to link all 220,000 employees worldwide to the company's Intranet, Meyer says.

♦ According to Chiron's Boyd Waters, a Macintosh systems analyst who developed the Intranet at this pharmaceuticals manufacturer based in Emeryville, California, the company is using an Intranet to circulate a database of graphical images of molecular structures of chemicals. "With an Intranet, we can easily add to the database and have the graphics of the chemical structure available for everyone, whether they're using a Mac, a PC, or a Silicon Graphics machine . . . . Before . . . we didn't have any database applications that could effectively deal with graphical information on multiple platforms," Waters says. According to Waters, Chiron has doubled in size because of acquisitions and mergers. Each company acquired has its own set of computing standards and platforms, Waters says. Because Chiron consists of a multitude of disparate systems, the ability to use the Intranet has become more valuable.

♦ To enhance customer service mechanisms, Federal Express recently implemented an Intranet solution to keep track of customers' packages in all phases of the delivery process. For years, FedEx relied on mainframe systems to locate tracking information while customers waited on the phone. FedEx installed its own Macintosh and Windows software to query its mainframes, and developed an interactive interface so that users could easily dial in and connect to the company's Intranet tracking system. This package tracking system was originally developed for internal use only. However, FedEx has opened it to the public—cutting down on the flood of incoming customer phone calls. The tracking information still resides on FedEx's mainframes, but a customer with a browser and Internet access can easily access the company's site to locate tracking information.

♦ Bay Networks simplifies many administrative activities for employees by letting them perform daily tasks on the Intranet. Prior to implementing an Intranet, the company had several forms available for employees to fill out manually when necessary. Now Bay Networks offers these forms on the Intranet, including travel requests, move and change requests, facilities requests, payroll forms, travel advances, accounting forms, Information Systems work requests, engineering-approval vendors, human resources benefits forms, and marketing project requests.

More and more corporations are becoming familiar with the Intranet and what it has to offer. Chapter 6 includes more case studies of actual Intranet implementations. The Intranet delivers what is most important to a company: cost effectiveness, increased productivity, and efficient information delivery. Because of these benefits, corporations increasingly turn to Intranets to address many of their business needs. According to Forrester Research, 40 percent of today's corporations plan to consider or are considering an Intranet. Forrester also predicts the Intranet server business will reach $1 billion in sales by the year 2000.

Putting It All Together

The examples in this chapter are just a few of the ways actual organizations are using an Intranet. Common Intranet applications such as e-mail, newsreaders, browsers, and Web servers make information available electronically, so good decisions can be made more quickly. Use your imagination and think of ways an Intranet can improve decision making and information sharing in your organization. If you're not familiar with these Internet/Intranet applications, Chapter 2 provides a basic overview of the Internet and World Wide Web technologies. The remainder of this book provides in-depth technical information and know-how to help you make wise decisions about your own Intranet. It tells you what to look for, where the potholes are on the Information Superhighway, and what you can do to make your Intranet implementation successful.

Frequently Asked Questions

◆ **What is an Intranet?**

An Intranet is like a small Internet coupled with the information management and access tools of the World Wide Web, all on your organization's network. The applications used on an Intranet, such as e-mail, newsreaders, and Web browsers, can all be used on the Internet as well. You can choose to connect your Intranet to the Internet, or you can decide to keep your Intranet local and never connect to the Internet.

◆ **What kinds of problems can Intranets solve?**

Intranets give you new ways to make decisions based on information that is exchanged electronically instead of on paper, on the phone, or in face-to-face meetings. Electronic publishing of information gives you complete, easily accessible information, as well as forums you can use to ask and answer questions within your organization. Collaborative capabilities help to promote more effective interaction between groups. Advanced features provide for presentation of multimedia information and time-saving search capabilities for effective information retrieval.

◆ **What applications are available on Intranets?**

Intranet applications provide different ways to create, access, and exchange information electronically. These applications include e-mail, newsreaders, Web browsers, back ends, file transfer software, and terminal emulators.

CHAPTER 2

The Internet and the World Wide Web

Lorraine Potter Kalal,
Nicole E. Rogers

Chapter Objectives

♦ Gain a basic understanding of the Internet and the World Wide Web, including their histories

♦ Learn about the technology and tools of the Internet and the World Wide Web

♦ Learn how the Internet and Web can help businesses and organizations become more competitive and effective on a global scale

♦ Find out how to access and provide information on the Internet and the World Wide Web

♦ Learn the concerns people have about the Internet and World Wide Web technology

♦ Understand how the Internet and World Wide Web technologies and applications translate to an Intranet

2

Without the Internet and the World Wide Web, Intranets would not exist. Just as companies utilize the Internet and the World Wide Web (from now on referred to as the "Web") for external, intercorporate communications, they have started to adopt the same tools for internal, intracorporate interactions. Tools pioneered for use on the Internet now form the basis for internal communications on an *Intra*net. The tools of *inter*corporate "net" communications have become *intra*corporate "net" communications tools.

This chapter takes you through an overview of the inception of the Internet and the Web, their building blocks, business and organizational uses of the Internet and the Web, concerns about using these communications vehicles, and how the Internet and Web paradigms can facilitate internal communications via an Intranet.

Although the Web exploded onto the country's consciousness in the past few years, the Internet, in one form or another, has enhanced communications in the educational, governmental, and technical spheres for 25 years. Today, both the Internet and the Web provide businesses and educational, governmental, and nonprofit organizations with such benefits as an immediate international presence, improved circulation of new information and current events, immediate and relatively inexpensive advertising, cost-effective product order processing and delivery, and global research, to name just a few.

Hundreds of organizations a week still discover for the first time the advantages of the Internet, a worldwide network of 13 million interconnecting computers and 35 million users (Source: CyberAtlas). Organizations publish, share, and find information, and conduct business over the Internet using a variety of tools—the most popular of which is e-mail and the most recent of which is the World Wide Web. Yes, the Web is a tool, not a network. The Web is not a subnetwork of the Internet, but a means of traversing the Internet itself.

History and Overview of the Internet and the World Wide Web

A couple of years ago (ancient history in the software world), most folks didn't know a URL from a UFO. A URL was just another high-tech acronym that included a bunch of letters and slashes—http://web.whatzitzname.com. Now, almost all ads include an organization's *universal resource locator* or *URL*—the address of their home page or site on the Web. What is the Web? And how does it relate to the Internet? The answer to these questions starts best with a history and overview of the Internet.

Origins of the Internet

The Internet's roots reach back into the Cold War and the former Soviet Union's *Sputnik* launch in 1957. The U.S. government was understandably concerned about the perceived loss of ground in defense research. Consequently, the government initiated the Advanced Research Projects Agency (ARPA) to effectively speed up defense and related research. ARPA's projects utilized the expertise of major U.S. universities. To facilitate joint research activities, the government developed a plan in 1968 to link four of the universities through an experimental computer network, ARPANET.

The government selected a communications technology for ARPANET called *packet switching,* which allowed transferred data to be broken down into smaller packets tagged with destination addresses. Since the packets were so small and required little bandwidth, they could be transmitted via simple telephone lines. These packets were sent out on the network to bounce around from computer to computer, looking for their final destination. They were directed by routing computers in the network. Linking the university networks was no mean feat since the computers at each site differed. IBM, DEC, and various other mainframes at the universities ran different operating systems. As a consequence, the computers had to be modified to package, address, and receive data using the same set of rules, known as a *protocol.* A protocol is a detailed description of messages that need to be exchanged and rules that need to be followed by two or more systems in order to exchange information.

The original ARPANET protocols were defined by graduate students at the four pilot universities. Convinced that a group of professionals would take over this project at any time, the students were careful not to be assertive in the early specification language, for fear of offending the professionals. Therefore, early specification documents were labeled as Request For Comment (RFC), indicating that anyone could contribute to the specification and nothing was official. When no professionals took over, the RFCs became the defining documents, setting the standards for the Internet protocol suite. Because these RFC protocol definitions were openly published, any software developer could use them and program a computer to speak the protocol. As a consequence, ARPANET grew. The experiment was a success. By 1972, the ARPANET linked most major universities in the U.S.

Establishment of the TCP/IP Standard

In 1972, the U.S. government officially adopted ARPANET as the Defense Data Network (DDN). A year later, the government required that all *nodes* (private networks or computers) on ARPANET utilize Transmission Control Protocol/Internet Protocol (TCP/IP) as the official standard protocol.

The TCP/IP protocol now had to be placed on each Internet machine as a software-based TCP/IP "stack" or "kernel," which acts as a TCP/IP translator for each machine, as illustrated in Figure 2-1.

For transmission of messages, a *stack* takes the data to be sent, breaks it apart into packets, addresses each packet, adds error-checking bits, and sends the packets on their way to the addressed host machine. Along the way, router machines in the Internet guide the packets to their final destinations using address tables that are updated each time a new host machine or network connects to the Internet. Each machine or network is identified with a unique Internet Protocol (IP) address when it registers with the U.S. government as part of the Internet. The receiving system's stack reassembles the individual packets into a single data file. Individuals accessing the Internet can communicate with other users on the Internet as long as both computers' operating systems can communicate via this protocol.

Those operating systems that don't run off of TCP/IP cannot connect to the Internet or communicate with others outside their environment unless a *gateway* (a conversion process) is in place. For instance, users on a Novell NetWare local area network communicate via Novell's proprietary protocol known as IPX (Internet Packet Exchange). In order for computers in a Novell

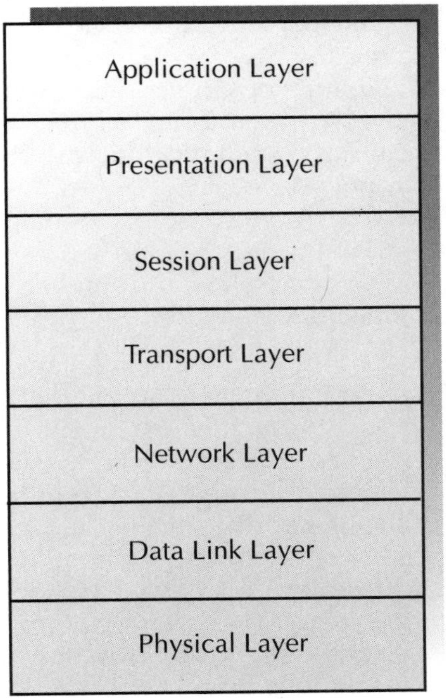

2

A TCP/IP
stack provides
protocols for
each layer
of data
communications

Figure 2-1.

| Application Layer |
| Presentation Layer |
| Session Layer |
| Transport Layer |
| Network Layer |
| Data Link Layer |
| Physical Layer |

NetWare environment to access the Internet or communicate with other computers running TCP/IP, a conversion from IPX to TCP/IP has to take place. Several software and hardware companies provide Internet gateways that accomplish private protocol conversion to TCP/IP.

The open standards of the TCP/IP RFCs, coupled with the low communications cost, spurred Internet growth beyond the walls of government and the universities, to commercial laboratories, libraries, and eventually, to businesses the world over. The Internet today is essentially a network of networks, which utilizes the existing telecommunications infrastructure to allow PCs and *host computers* (the TCP/IP name for system computers) around the world to communicate by publishing, accessing, sending, and sharing information. All computers that connect to the Internet, from PC to mainframe hosts, still communicate via TCP/IP. Frontier Technologies was among the companies that pioneered the development of a TCP/IP stack for use on the PC. Now Macintoshes and IBM PCs also communicate by means of TCP/IP.

Other Internet Protocols

Basic real-world requirements, such as sending electronic mail or accessing a computer at another university location, drove early development efforts to add applications protocols to the basic TCP/IP protocol. RFCs that defined "e-mail" and "Telnet" communications thus arose. These and other protocols provide standards for communication between server and client machines. Servers, typically larger computers, provide information. Servers perform background functions in response to client requests. Clients, typically PCs today, get or receive information. The client provides an end-user interface and a means of communicating with the server. For example, the Simple Mail Transport Protocol (SMTP) defines how an e-mail message should be addressed and delivered to a client machine over the lower-level TCP/IP protocol. Computer users around the world now communicate via Internet e-mail (see Figure 2-2), sending and receiving electronic letters addressed to their unique Internet addresses.

File Transfer Protocol (FTP) is the standard TCP/IP protocol for transferring files from one computer to another. FTP defines the protocol rules by which a host or server computer can provide data files for others to use and by which a client computer or PC can locate and download these files. With FTP, a user logs on to an FTP site on the Internet and is allowed access to some of the files at that site with proper authentication. (Users may often access an FTP site as "guest.") Using FTP, for example, Frontier Technologies can make its software programs available for download from its FTP server. A customer with an FTP client logs on to Frontier's FTP server, gains access permission through user and password authentication, and transfers a file to his or her computer's hard drive, as illustrated in Figure 2-3.

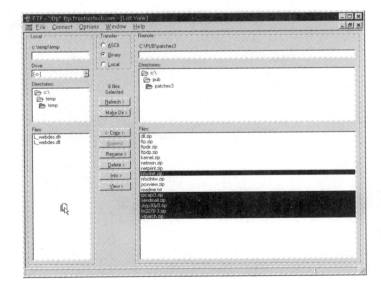

The graphical interface to an e-mail application. The user is viewing the Inbox and composing a new e-mail.
Figure 2-2.

2

The Telnet protocol allows a client computer to log on to and interact with a distant server computer. The remote system, or host, is usually a Unix system. When using Telnet, a login command is entered in order to access the host. Once access is allowed, users enter text commands to interact with known applications and information.

A user dragging a file for download through a graphical FTP interface
Figure 2-3.

News servers allow host computers to set up a service whereby client computers with newsreaders can access the host, post comments electronically, and read the comments of others. Figuratively, the result looks like a bulletin board where many users' comments and responses are posted on 3 × 5 cards under various topics. Threaded discussions show the links between comments about a topic, as illustrated in Figure 2-4. News servers allow groups of users to gather together and discuss shared topics of interest. These groups, called *Usenet newsgroups,* discuss technologies, religion, finance, sports, UFOs, and much more. Over 24,000 Usenet newsgroups now exist. A user searches a small subset of Usenet groups using newsreader client software, as in Figure 2-5. Once users find a newsgroup they are interested in joining, they must subscribe and then view the newsgroup posts via the newsreader.

Initially, Internet users shared their e-mail addresses, the locations of FTP sites, news servers, and Telnet hosts by electronic word-of-mouth. Eventually, a number of methods arose for finding this information. Gopher and its siblings—Veronica, Jughead, and WAIS—began as a way to let users query host computers that searched the Internet for the locations of various Internet servers that might provide important articles and other information relative to academic or governmental research. These host computers frequently indexed the locations of FTP, news, and Telnet sites by topic or organization. Whereas FTP allows users to download data files whose addresses they know, Gopher enables users to search for and view image, text, and sound files from Gopher servers on the Internet. The Gopher protocol was developed at the University of Minnesota, home of the Golden Gophers football team.

A user posts to the threaded discussion in the "genie" newsgroup
Figure 2-4.

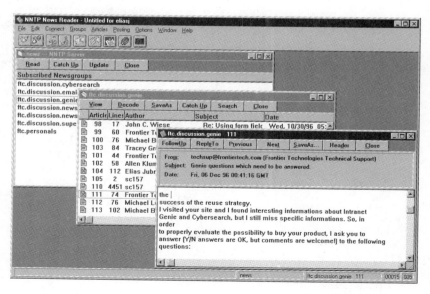

The World Wide Web: The Internet Goes Mainstream

In the early years, users interfaced with the Internet using Unix text-based commands from Unix machines such as DEC mainframes. Eventually, PCs and other hosts gained the ability to access the Internet with the addition of a TCP/IP stack. However, communication still took place via Unix-type commands or text-driven menus.

It took the most recent development in Internet protocols, the World Wide Web, to change the entire face of the Internet. Timothy Berners-Lee, a physicist for the European Particle Physics Laboratory (CERN) in Geneva, Switzerland, created a plan for the Web back in 1989. Berners-Lee decided physicists separated by distance needed the ability to easily collaborate on their projects. Berners-Lee proposed a *hyperlink* system, a network of links that would allow users on client computers to move easily from one host computer to another on the Internet in search of related topics of information. Documents would be written in an open language, the Hypertext Markup Language (HTML), that any type of computer could interpret, independent of the operating system. More significantly, documents included embedded "hyperlinks" to other documents. From the user's perspective, a highlighted word, when selected by pressing TAB or some other key, would immediately transfer him or her to another document linked to that word, perhaps on another machine on the Internet. Berners-Lee developed both the server and client specifications for this new Internet protocol. Because individuals could use this protocol to move around the Internet from point to point, sites using HTML joined together in 1990 to form what Berners-Lee dubbed the "World Wide Web." Documents written in HTML (see Figure 2-5) were called "Web pages"; servers, "Web servers." Because the client software allowed users to move from Web page to Web page, much like browsing in the library, Berners-Lee called his text-based client a "browser." All of these components are described in more detail later in this chapter.

Initially, Web pages included only text. The real Web revolution occurred when Marc Andreeson, a student at the University of Illinois, developed a browser called Mosaic, which ran on a PC and read HTML pages via a graphical user interface (GUI) similar to that of Microsoft Windows (see Figure 2-6). In a brilliant marketing move, Netscape Corporation turned Andreeson's Mosaic design into the first version of the Netscape Navigator browser available for free download around the Internet in 1994, disseminating the graphical interface on the world. Of course, both the technical and "secular" press began to take notice of developments on the Internet. Once the purview of engineers, academics, and government employees who knew the Unix text commands by heart, the Internet

```
<HTML>
<HEAD>
</HEAD>
<META name="description" content="Frontier Technologies Corporation pioneers
Intranet / Internet applicaticationss making corporations and individuals
more productive and competitive in the global market.">
<META name="keywords" content="Intranet, intranet, superweb,
cyberjunction, intranet, cybersearch, intranet genie, intranet, internet,
 Milwaukee, Frontier Technologies">
<BODY bgcolor = "#ffffff" text = "#000000" link = "#0000ff" alink = "#0000ff" vlink = "#0000ff" >
<CENTER>
<A HREF="MAIN.HTM"><IMG SRC="/graphics/lionlgn.GIF" ALIGN=MIDDLE BORDER=0></A>
</CENTER>
<BR><BR><BR>
<TABLE BORDER=0  CELLPADDING=5  CELLSPACING=3  HEIGHT=20 WIDTH=100%>
<TR ALIGN = left VALIGN = top>
<TD>
Frontier Technologies Corporation is a proven technology leader in Intranet/ Internet networking
applications for Microsoft Windows 3.x, Win 95, and NT environments. Building on its core
competency in open systems networking, Frontier Technologies offers a range of innovative
software products suited for businesses of all sizes. A strong commitment to providing
easy-to-use, complete solutions, together with responsive customer service has won Frontier
Technologies a loyal customer base spanning across Fortune 500 corporations, small-to-medium
size businesses and the government.
<BR><BR><BR>
<CENTER>
<TABLE BORDER=0  CELLPADDING=3  CELLSPACING=3 HEIGHT=20>
<TR ALIGN = LEFT VALIGN = top>
<TD bgcolor="#ffffff" bordercolor="#ff7373">
<BR>
<IMG SRC="/graphics/NEW-PILL.GIF"> What's New
<HR>
<BR>
Frontier Technologies, an industry leader in Intranet technology, just released the latest
version of WebDesigner, version 1.2, for <A HREF="/shareware/free.htm">free download from
Frontier's web site at http://www.frontiertech.com.</A> Frontier's WebDesigner is an easy-to-use
```

Raw HTML code of a Web page
Figure 2-5.

became available to the faint-hearted through a simple PC-based graphical interface. The press could smell a revolution. And the press added fuel to the fire. A graphical interface—Microsoft's Windows operating system—had achieved wider popularity for the PC. Perhaps a graphical Internet interface—the Netscape browser—would do the same for the Internet.

The same Web page as viewed through a graphical browser
Figure 2-6.

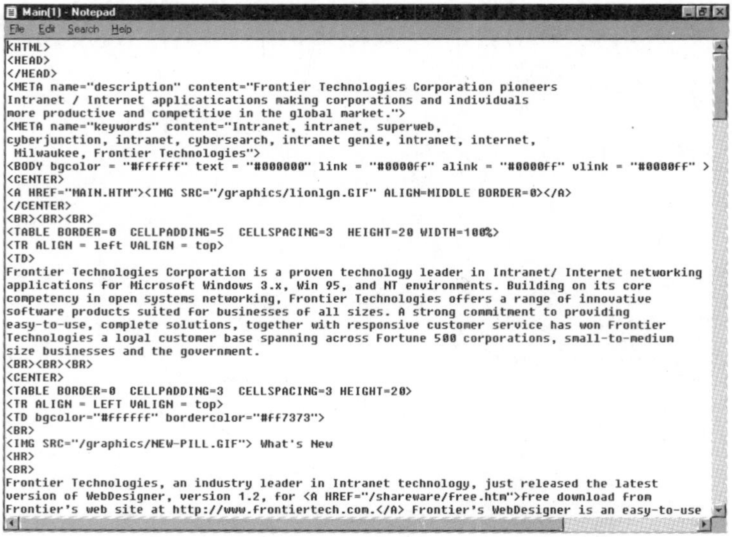

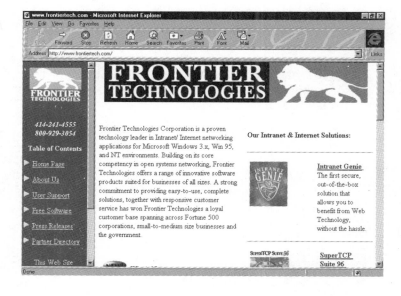

Businesses took notice and began to develop interesting Web sites. More and more users started to browse out of curiosity, which led to an increased corporate presence to reach these users. The spiral started upward.

Once the spiral began, Web pages didn't stay static for long. Organizations soon desired not only to present text and graphics, but to identify how many users accessed their Web pages and to receive user information, including sales orders with credit card numbers. To accomplish these interactive capabilities, Web server software was enhanced to allow developers to write Visual Basic or C++ programs that interact with Web pages via an application program interface (API). Called *back ends,* these programs provide an increasing number of applications. Back ends interact with the server to count the number of home page "hits" per day. They allow users to fill in forms on a Web page, from sales orders to service requests. Other back ends enable a user to fill out and send an e-mail to the organization right from the Web page. In fact, any interaction with a Web page is accomplished via a back end. This type of programming is more fully discussed in Chapter 8.

2

As browsers started to become widely available and HTML programmers developed Web pages with graphics and back ends, organizations increased the speed with which they developed Web pages using HTML. Today, browsers read Web pages developed with text, graphics, pictures, moving graphics, interactive forms, and more.

Another current added to the exponential growth of the Web. Many users had their first exposure to the Internet and Web through one of the commercial online services, most notably America Online (AOL), CompuServe, and Prodigy. In fact, the contribution of these services to the growth of the Internet and Web is often overlooked. While CompuServe has been providing services to the computer industry for some time and Prodigy was the first to direct its efforts toward the consumer, it took AOL (see Figure 2-7) to perfect the user interface and blitz the market with free software bundled in PCs and mailed nonstop to PC users. These services introduced users to the Internet and Web in two ways. First, they each provided users with a private mini-Internet. Those who subscribed to AOL, for example, had their own Usenet groups, called *message boards*; AOL's private e-mail system; access to information with Web page–like graphics; and the ability to interact with one another in "chat" rooms—graphical copies of the Internet's Internet Relay Chat (IRC) locations. Without entering the Internet directly at all (besides e-mailing out of their service over the Internet), subscribers began to understand what the Internet was all about. And then the services provided direct Internet access. Via easy graphical interfaces, users could search for Gopher sites, FTP documents, and browse the Web. The Internet had gone mainstream.

America Online windows, including the index of "channels"

Figure 2-7.

Web Technologies

Before discovering how corporations benefit from using the Internet and the Web, we will discuss Web technology and directions in a bit more detail. This technology includes not only Web servers and browsers, but the Hypertext Markup Language (HTML), the universal resource locator (URL), Internet search engines, and back-end server applications. We will also touch on future trends in Web technologies, such as Virtual Reality Markup Language (VRML) and Java.

As we've just discussed, the Web provided a new means of accessing information on the Internet. Initially, host computers published information via pages written in HTML, which displayed text and included hyperlinks. The *home page* is the first Web page that a user sees when accessing a site's Web server. The home page typically includes an index of additional pages on the server with hyperlinks to these pages. The home page may also include hyperlinks to other Web pages with associated information sources the author wishes to reference.

In the Web paradigm, the client machine accesses and views the server's Web page using a browser. From the browser user's perspective, a hyperlink is a highlighted word, which, when clicked on by the client machine's mouse, transfers the user to another Web page on that machine *or any other machine on the Internet*. This ability to link information pages among different computer systems on the Web is one of the Web's most important functions. Behind the Web page, HTML defines a host computer's Web address that is linked to the highlighted word. Clicking on the highlighted hyperlink accesses the computer and the specific file at that address, then downloads the information onto the user's computer.

Moving from link to link is called "browsing," because users follow hyperlinks from document to document. Since hyperlinks are not sequentially oriented, users may browse related information without regard to the order (or even location) in which the information is actually stored. The Web is like a book with references in it. When you read a textbook, for example, and see a reference to another book, you may go to the library and try to find that book. When you use the Web, the hyperlinks are your references. However, instead of going to the library to find out about the reference, you merely click on the hyperlink to access the information. For example, an article about the Milwaukee Zoo may include a hyperlink on the highlighted words "San Diego Zoo." When a user double-clicks on these words, his or her client machine automatically reconnects to the San Diego Zoo's computer home page, whose Web address is programmed in HTML to the words "San Diego Zoo."

Web Servers

Most Internet protocols involve a client/server pair. The server (for example, a news server) provides information. A client (for example, a newsreader) accesses information. Information in the Web paradigm is provided or published on a Web server. Web servers are principally used to maintain a directory of Web pages and sites and to respond to requests from Web browsers to view these pages and interact with the server.

A Web server is a Unix fileserver, mainframe, or NT server that is configured with the appropriate hardware and software to respond to requests from the client's, or user's, computer via a browser. Essentially, Web servers download Web pages and applications to users. If the server breaks down, users are unable to access the Web page or site until the server is available again.

Before a user's browser can download and view the site(s) requested, the Web server waits and listens for requests from Web browsers. Once the Web server receives a download request, or "hit," from a browser, it will find the requested document, or site, and send it back to the browser so the user can view the file. In this instance, the Web server's function is to respond to the browser by obtaining the requested site or sites.

Web Browsers

As previously discussed, a Web browser is the vehicle that allows users to browse the World Wide Web. Users simply type in the address of a specific

Web server's Web page (the URL, discussed in more detail next), in the designated retrieve area, and the Web browser locates the Web server to request the Web page addressed. The Web browser then waits, usually only seconds, until the requested information is sent back from the Web server. The user can then view the information through the Web browser.

Following Netscape's lead, several other companies have developed browsers and released them to the market, for example, Microsoft's Internet Explorer, GNN's GNNWorks, and Frontier Technologies' WinTapestry. All of these browsers offer a suite of functions that assist users' everyday needs, including bookmark catalogs for organizing the addresses of frequently visited Web sites, e-mail, a newsreader, and setup scripts for Internet service providers (discussed later in the chapter).

Along with the growth of the Web, Web server usage has risen dramatically. According to CyberAtlas, Web servers currently number more than 450,000, up from 130 in 1993 (Source: International Data Corporation). Frontier Technologies, however, believes these figures will more than triple by the end of 1997 as servers move in-house with Intranets.

Universal Resource Locator (URL)

As mentioned at the beginning of the chapter, the universal resource locator or URL (pronounced "you are el"), such as the one shown below, is the address of a Web page or file, database, query, or other location on a server anywhere in the world:

    http://www.frontiertech.com/prodinfo.htm

The URL guides a browser request to the appropriate server through the various components in the address.

For example, the first part of the URL, "http:", indicates that the browser is sending a request via the Hypertext Transfer Protocol (HTTP), the protocol of the Web. HTTP allows the transfer of a network request to a Web server. Use of the introductory command string "http:" (as opposed to "ftp:" or "gopher:") indicates that the data package is being sent to a Web server (as opposed to an FTP or Gopher server). Of course, only Web servers will be able to decode the rest of the URL string. In the case of the URL above, the personal computer is asking a server to allow the user to access an HTTP document. HTTP documents are written in Hypertext Markup Language, which is described in more detail in the next section. The second part of a URL string is a double forward slash "//", which indicates that a machine name follows.

The third part of the URL string indicates the type of host machine sought. Any remote Web server will be identified with the now nearly ubiquitous "www" identification. Since the URL has already indicated the use of HTTP, it follows that the machine is a Web server; thus, when accessing Web files on remote hosts, the URL typically begins "http://www".

A company's Web *domain name* is registered with the U.S. government and associated with a numerical address. Web names make up the next part of a URL string and identify the exact server the URL addresses. Frontier Technologies' domain name, for example, is "frontiertech".

2

The rest of the URL indicates the file path to an individual Web page located on the Web server—the exact area on the Web site where the specified document can be found. This portion of the URL is similar to file-naming conventions in Unix, not unlike DOS names. With the URL above, the name of the Web page is "prodinfo.htm" and likely includes product information provided by Frontier Technologies. The "htm" tag or *extension* indicates that the file is written in HTML and is a hypertext markup (.HTM) file, which can only be read by a Web browser. The browser finds the document and downloads it from the server to the user's browser viewer.

Typically, when browsing a Web site for the first time, users first encounter the organization's home page. URLs to the home page typically follow the format http://www.frontiertech.*com*, where the "com" portion of the string represents the type of domain in which the organization is registered. The organization's name and domain make up the IP address of an organization and are common to all protocol addresses: FTP, e-mail, and Gopher. Frontier Technologies' FTP server is therefore located at ftp.frontiertech.com. All Internet addresses fall under one of several domains, including "com" for commercial organizations, "gov" for government, and "org" for nonprofit organizations. In our example, frontiertech is a member of the commercial domain. Home page URLs bring up the server's home page or directory index. A home page, such as Frontier's home page shown in Figure 2-8, typically includes links to other pages on the Web server. A directory index is a site where users can search for other pages on the Web server based on keyword(s) included in these documents.

By now you know that Web pages are written in HTML, but what is Hypertext Markup Language? It is an open systems language that uses tags, or symbols, to identify the various parts of a Web page. HTML describes the structure of a document, where text begins and ends, how text is presented, where graphics are located, and, most importantly, where hyperlinks are presented. For example, the bold print command is specified by the symbols <b> and </b>. Each machine that reads or interprets HTML is free to translate these tags as best as it is able. Some machines, unable

Part of
Frontier
Technologies'
home page
with a
directory of
hyperlinks on
the left side
Figure 2-8.

to read graphics, for example, can simply present a symbol to represent missing graphics.

In HTML, a hyperlink is composed of a graphic or word that is then associated with a URL. The URL is that of another Web page on the same Web server or on another server located elsewhere on the Internet. The user simply sees a highlighted word or an illustration with text directing the user to "double-click" with a mouse. After clicking on the word or graphic, the user's browser is redirected to the associated URL, as in the San Diego Zoo illustration discussed earlier.

Because the majority of users don't know HTML coding or would prefer not to program, tools for creating HTML content that operate like word processors have emerged. These tools generate the HTML tags associated with language construction, such as highlighted text, tables, and frames. One such tool is HTML Edit, which operates in WYSIWYG (What You See Is What You Get) mode. HTML Edit provides the icons necessary for a user to point and click when building a Web page. For instance, instead of typing **<b>** to make text bold, a user simply clicks on the bold icon. These icons are set up similar to those in Microsoft's word processing program, Word.

Search Engines

The proliferation of Web servers and browsers allows users to locate information worldwide, but how? Finding information on the Web can be difficult. Many companies and universities recognize this and have responded by developing search sites and search engines. The better-known search sites include Lycos, Yahoo!, InfoSeek, AltaVista, and Web Crawler. Users connect to a search site the same way they connect to any other site. For example, to access Lycos, developed by Carnegie Mellon University, users type the site's address in the browser's "connect to" section: **http://www.lycos.com**.

Once at the search site, users simply type in a keyword or keywords that pertain to the subject of interest, as illustrated in Figure 2-9. For example, if the user wants to find Italian food recipes, keywords such as "Italian food," "pasta," or "Italian recipes" would locate hundreds of sites about these topics. Search sites include powerful search engines that store giant indexes of Web sites, brief descriptions, and the associated URLs. After the user clicks the search button, the search engine retrieves and displays the URLs of sites whose descriptions contain the keywords. Search engines typically display a 50-to-100-word description about each site to assist users in narrowing their search. As shown in Figure 2-10, 36,365 Lycos database sites include the terms "Italian food." Abstracts about each of these sites are given, making it easier for users to choose which sites to access.

2

Technology Trends

The Internet grew because of Berners-Lee's World Wide Web invention, enhanced by the Mosaic GUI and the addition of graphics and back ends to Web sites. New technology continues to enhance what the user sees in a Web page. Netscape recently developed the first tables programmed in

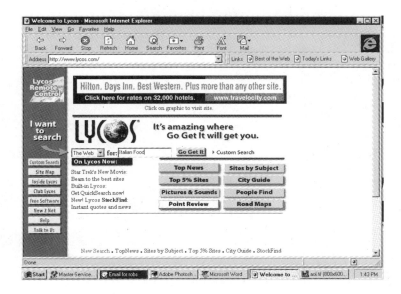

Entering a search request in the Lycos search site
Figure 2-9.

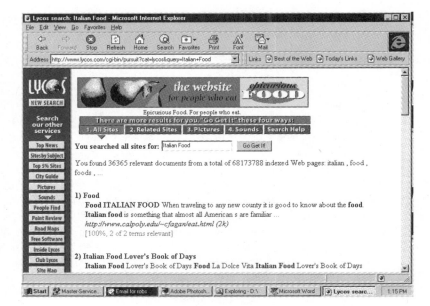

Results of the
Lycos search
shown in
Figure 2-9
Figure 2-10.

HTML and viewed by browsers, as illustrated in Figure 2-11. Soon, "frames"
allowed users to scroll through two pages simultaneously, an index on one
side of the screen and the home page text on the other side, as illustrated
in Figure 2-12.

In 1995, Sun Microsystems developed a new programming language, Java,
that enabled programmers to write small programs or *applets* that could be
incorporated in an HTML document. Today, programmers use Java mostly to
design the moving graphics seen in many Web sites and to provide simple

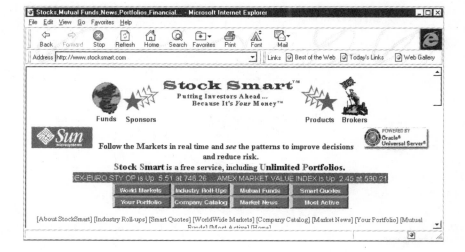

An HTML
table allows
users to view
tabular data
like these
eight links to
various Stock
Smart pages
Figure 2-11.

An HTML frame breaks the Web page into multiple graphical windows that scroll independently
Figure 2-12.

applications that client machines can download and execute, but Java's potential is far-reaching, as discussed more fully in Chapter 8. When both servers and browsers eventually include the Virtual Reality Markup Language (VRML), users will be able to view Web sites in 3-D. Three-dimensional companions, known as *avatars,* will interact with and lead users through 3-D worlds of shops and information. As these innovations come to market and prove beneficial, others won't be far behind.

Business Uses and Benefits of the Internet and the World Wide Web

As increasing numbers of individuals browsed the Web, increasing numbers of businesses saw this as a marketing and sales opportunity, and increasing numbers created Web home pages. Then, these same businesses began to publish their URLs—everywhere. When your competitor has a URL, what can you do but create your own Web page and publish your URL? The marketing potential of the Internet fueled even faster Web growth. Today, over 450,000 Web servers populate the World Wide Web. But having a Web presence because your competitors do isn't the only rationale for using the Web and other Internet technologies. In 1995, $436 million in sales was generated on the Web; by 2000, that figure is projected to exceed $23 billion (Source: CyberAtlas). In addition to supporting market presence and sales efforts, businesses use the Web and other Internet tools for advertising, product promotions, enhancing their corporate image, communications, customer service, research, and posting job listings.

According to Intelliquest, a research firm, more than 35 million Americans currently use the Internet. By 1999, International Data Corporation predicts the number of users will increase to 199 million. The typical Internet user is male (70 percent), in his 30s, and has a higher-than-average income, which means the Internet can only expand to new markets. The majority of users (75 percent) are located in the U.S., which means the Internet can only continue to grow in its global reach.

These individuals use the Internet tools and the Web for communications plus shopping, research, games, and building online communities. For example, nearly everyone who uses the Internet communicates by e-mail. Sports lovers access the Web to find out the outcome of a key game or batting averages on a specific ball player. Hobbyists browse thousands of newsgroups and Web sites on specific interests to gather new ideas and meet other hobbyists. News junkies discover a plethora of newsgroups that talk about all sorts of issues including world, national, and local events. The Web supports those interested in financial listings, stock market prices, and financial recommendations. Even children access sites for downloading or participating in interactive games.

This huge market continues to entice businesses to join the Internet and the Web. Businesses use the Web, e-mail, and newsgroups, plus other Internet protocols, to accomplish a variety of beneficial activities that affect every department, from sales to human resources. Corporate uses of the Internet and Web technologies range anywhere from advertising products and services to posting current job openings. Other corporate uses include publishing information, such as product white papers and executive biographies, and processing information, including sales orders and customer requests.

Since corporations first constructed their Web sites, many have noticed an increase in public awareness and sales. AviON Science Museum in London relies on their Web site to promote the museum, display their latest exhibits, and educate the public. After AviON first inaugurated their Web site in February of 1995, they noticed an increase in visitors attending exhibits along with an increase in public awareness. The amount of traffic at their Web site also gradually increased over the months. When AviON's site was first available, a few thousand people on a weekly basis accessed their site. By October, 1996, the museum tracked over 24,000 users a week accessing the Web site. Internet and Web technologies also benefit various corporate departments, including marketing, advertising and sales, technical and customer support, research, and human resources.

Marketing, Advertising, and Sales

Internet and Web communications support marketing, advertising, and sales in a variety of ways. For example, potential customers might access a company's Web site before taking the time to make a phone call or otherwise find product information. Such customers find it easier to view corporate information online. To meet these customers' needs, marketing and sales departments utilize the Web to deliver both corporate and product messages, display product and service descriptions, advertise their products and/or services, offer downloadable product demonstrations for potential customers, display current product promotions and discounts, and offer interactive forms for purchasing products and services. Providing this information on the Web page saves marketing departments the cost of producing and mailing product specification sheets, catalogs, manuals, and brochures to those customers who prefer browsing to calling or receiving *snail mail* (the online world's nickname for U.S. mail). And the Internet's global reach allows companies to reach customers around the world.

Users may first discover a company's Web site after searching on a particular topic of interest. In this case, the search engine acts as a type of Yellow Pages. Once the individual finds several companies offering a service of interest via a search engine, he simply double-clicks to the home pages of some or all of these companies to gain more information, without ever leaving his seat. Marketing and advertising departments now ensure that their companies' home pages are listed on each of the most popular search sites.

Of course, companies don't want to sit back and wait for users to come to their Web sites. One of the most popular ways to ensure that users visit a home page is to place an advertisement on Web sites with very high hit rates, such as search sites, financial pages, and entertainment sites. Interested users simply click on the advertisement and are automatically linked to the advertiser's home page. Online advertisements include full-color graphics, artwork, and text. Many software advertisements and Web pages include a demonstration of the offering for users to download, as illustrated in Figure 2-13.

In a groundbreaking agreement, Proctor and Gamble arranged such an advertisement deal with the Yahoo! search site. The groundbreaking part of the deal was not the advertisement, but the fact that P&G would only pay Yahoo! when users linked to its site from Yahoo!, not for simply having a presence on the site. In the print world, an equivalent arrangement would allow advertisers to pay the magazine only when they received an 800 number call as a result of an ad running in that magazine! Some companies utilize newsgroups and e-mail to encourage Web site visits. Marketing personnel visit newsgroups that discuss topics related to their company's

2

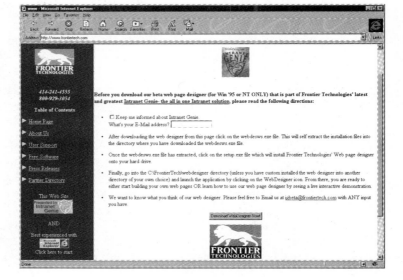

Frontier
Technologies
allows users to
download free
software from
its Web pages
Figure 2-13.

product or service. Occasionally (and when not offensive), these personnel
may announce a new product or the availability of free evaluation software
in the newsgroups, encouraging readers to visit the company Web site.
Marketing personnel may also host ad hoc market research questionnaires
and focus groups through newsgroup discussions. Finally, company
marketers mass mail e-mails, inviting users to visit their Web site for more
information. Like most junk mail, however, many of these e-mails wind up
in the recycle bin.

The Web also provides a convenient sales medium. Direct mail and other
companies have started to place catalogs online as well, offering potential
customers full-color graphics and pictures plus easy ordering procedures.
People wanting to purchase items online can easily do so, perhaps to avoid
the Christmas crowds of shoppers. From wine cellars, to clothing stores,
hobby shops, or sports and recreation stores, users can find all they need
on the Web. Like any other paper catalogs, online catalogs offer users
full-color pictures and text on the latest products. Once an item or items
of interest are found, the user simply fills out an online request form (see
Figure 2-14), submits the appropriate information and credit card numbers,
and clicks the submit button. After the order has been processed, usually
within seconds, a receipt is sent back to the customer, and shortly thereafter,
the product is shipped.

As more and more people access the Internet and Web, marketing and
sales departments utilize these avenues to deliver marketing messages, and
advertise new products and services, as well as sell these products and

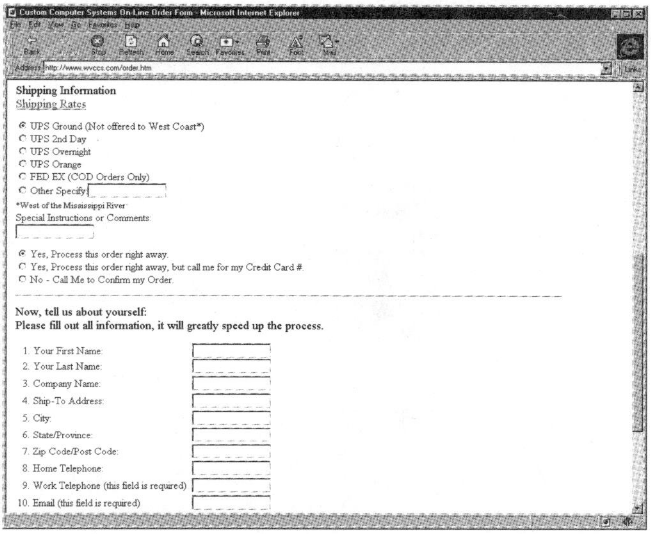

Users enter
order data
through
online forms
programmed
as "back-end"
applications
Figure 2-14.

2

services. Because of the number and global scope of users surfing the
Internet and Web, companies can promote themselves effectively to a wide
variety of people.

Technical and Customer Support

Technical and customer support are fundamental to gaining new customers
and retaining existing customers. Without good service, people go elsewhere
to purchase products and do business. Since increasing numbers of
individuals have Internet and Web access and experience, companies now
offer support services online. Such services include newsgroups, e-mail
newsletters, and interactive Frequently Asked Questions (FAQs). Software
vendors use Web and FTP sites to provide both product updates and bug
patches for quick and easy download by customers.

For example, a company's customer support department can offer a
newsgroup for each one of their products and services. This allows both the
customers and the support department to talk about the latest offerings,
current problems, how to solve these problems, and upcoming company
offerings. The newsgroup environment allows the customer to freely express
opinions and share feedback with companies. Given this information,
companies can more rapidly act on customer demands, advice, and
complaints, if necessary. Customers, in turn, can use the information found

in newsgroups to solve problems, avoid any potential problems, and receive advice from both their peers and the support department.

Posting lists of Frequently Asked Questions (FAQs) also assists customers who come across problems that need to be addressed immediately. In this case, frequent problems or concerns are posted and discussed in online interactive FAQs. Users don't have to wade through manuals or wait for new manuals that include the latest product information. At the same time, these customers can avoid telephoning company reps, only to wait on hold for several minutes or receive the rep's voice mail. By accessing the online FAQs, a customer receives immediate support. Because FAQs are interactive, the customer can view a scenario on how the product works and how it can help solve current or potential in-house problems.

Software customers may find themselves frustrated because of frequent product updates or the occasional bug. In either of these scenarios, online product updates and *patches* (product fixes for defective features) are offered online. Customers can download the latest offerings in a matter of minutes. Traditionally, customers would have to wait a day, or several days, to receive a software update or replacement for the defective product, and companies bore the burden of product and shipping costs.

Chapter 1 describes an excellent example of service via the Web, in which Federal Express set up a customer service page that lists all the package requests and mailing dates. The page also includes the name of the recipient, whether the person received the package, and if received, what time the package was delivered. This setup allows FedEx customers to instantly view their order, and cuts down on the number of service calls the company receives.

Offering quick and high-quality customer service is essential. Because the Internet and Web offer many accommodating support services to a wide variety of people, businesses are able to comfortably rely on these technologies to solve day-to-day problems. Now that many support services are offered online, customers save on phone costs, and companies' incoming support calls have decreased.

Research

The Internet and Web are robust mediums for gathering information for performing market, product, or competitive research; writing a thesis or book; or understanding market trends. Instead of going to a library and spending hours trying to locate the correct information, which is often out of date by the time it's published, users can access the most current information in a matter of minutes.

For example, a financial analyst researching a company pursuing an initial public stock offering (IPO) can quickly and easily obtain product and service information, corporate and product strategies, current customer lists, and any third party or distributor relationships. The financial analyst can also learn more about company personnel and executive management by reading available biographies.

Because newsgroups offer an excellent source of customer feedback on products and services, developers can get a feel for what types of new products and services are required in order to maintain or gain new audiences. Developers can easily tap into the newsgroups and share conversations on what is important and what future services are needed.

For instance, a travel agency's product manager has been asked to research and develop a new vacation package in the Pacific Rim, gathering information on various tourist attractions in the area, flights offered to the area, competitors' package offerings, hotels that can accommodate tourists, and transportation. With the Internet and Web, the product manager can easily surf the Web for the appropriate information rather than making many long-distance phone calls and receiving high volumes of mail.

The Internet has always been an excellent tool for graduate students researching information on their theses. For example, a criminology student writing a paper on victimology can easily find a plethora of information regarding this subject in Web sites, newsgroups, FTP sites, and mail groups. Because students writing theses look for the most current and cutting edge information, the Internet and Web accommodate their needs, regardless of the subject. Also, because new information is constantly added to the Internet and Web, students don't need to worry about obsolete information.

Human Resources

Finding potential employees to fill job openings, researching new benefits and insurance policies, and sending and receiving résumés and references can all be time-consuming and costly processes. However, the Internet and Web technologies greatly assist the human resources (HR) department in alleviating burdensome administrative projects.

For instance, instead of posting current job openings in several newspapers around the country, HR can post these openings on the company's Web site and reduce the number of placements in publications. If a company seeks to fill several engineering and customer service positions, an HR rep can easily post the position descriptions on the company's Web site and in several commercial job listing sites. Because a company's site is available worldwide, current job openings receive maximum exposure.

Administering company benefits and insurance policies can be a hassle—especially if an insurance carrier decides to double premium costs. With the Web at hand, a rep can browse and view hundreds of potential policies rather than spending hours on the phone researching information. Finally, potential employees now frequently use e-mail to send a résumé and references to an HR department within minutes. Utilizing e-mail for sending information cuts down on the cost of mailing and the time it takes to receive information.

Frontier Technologies—A Case History

Frontier Technologies was founded in 1982 by Dr. Prakash Ambegaonkar, Chairman & CEO. The company entered the Internet and Intranet software world when it developed one of the first TCP/IP stacks for use with the Windows operating system. Today, products include a suite of TCP/IP applications (SuperTCP Suite), a one-stop Intranet package (Intranet Genie), and an Intranet information search tool (CyberSearch), and a NetWare to Internet gateway (CyberJunction).

Frontier Technologies' use of the Internet and Web illustrates some of the benefits of these new technologies for business. When a user visits Frontier Technologies' Web site, the home page links to pages that include company press releases, product awards, the latest company and product information, free downloadable software, Frontier's history, job listings, and who's who at the company. Companies who use the Web this way generally achieve success. Why? Because potential customers visiting the site get a "personal" sense of what the company is all about and what products and services are offered. While at the site, the potential customer can access product literature, competitive advantages, and what industry experts are saying about the company.

Financial and market analysts visit Frontier's site to find out company objectives, mission statement, and product offerings. This information assists analysts in projecting market trends and comparing products with those of the competition. Furthermore, students writing papers can access Frontier Technologies' Web site to learn more about current market technology and products.

Frontier's evaluation software can be downloaded from the Web site. If customers need software patches or the newest release of a product, they may visit the FTP site. Using both of these sites saves Frontier thousands of dollars a month in CD, jewel case, and shipping costs.

E-mail is an important tool for communications within Frontier and between Frontier and its customers, the press, strategic partners, and others. One employee recently conducted over 40 rounds of contract negotiations electronically. Both negotiators passed the document, with its changes, back and forth using e-mail. In fact, the negotiators never met in person! E-mail allows Frontier employees to send and receive messages without interrupting their workdays, while keeping an electronic trail of what they have written. Occasionally, Frontier sends mass e-mailings of press releases, questionnaires, and newsletters to its press contacts and customers.

Newsgroups provide both a communications and a marketing edge to Frontier. Internally, the technical support group, sales, and engineering post product issues and their resolution in a number of product-related newsgroups. Marketing visits newsgroups around the Internet that focus on the various technologies that Frontier incorporates in products, such as Web server or Web designer newsgroups. Participants are invited to visit Frontier's Web page when new information or downloads are available. In this way, Frontier can very specifically find its target market on the Internet.

2

Getting Started on the Internet and the Web

Individuals and companies wishing to access the Internet and the Web or to publish Web pages must invest in some degree of hardware and software plus find a means of physically connecting to the Internet. Various methods of accomplishing the goals of access and publishing are discussed below and illustrated in Figure 2-15. These options range from using an Online Service to installing a Web server on a company's premises.

Online Services

As discussed earlier, many users first access the Internet and the Web via one of the online services, such as Prodigy, CompuServe, and America Online. For a flat monthly fee (about $10 for five hours of access per week), users have access not just to the Internet, but also to the many private services offered by these providers, such as financial advice, online magazine subscriptions, and easy-to-access user communities. AOL provides individuals and organizations a Web page hosting service via its GNN subsidiary. For a startup fee ranging up to $350 and flat monthly fees up to $200, users can develop their own Web pages using GNN's HTML designer and then store the pages on GNN's Web server. In either case, client or server access, the user merely needs to have purchased a PC and a modem (see later sections for more details on equipment requirements).

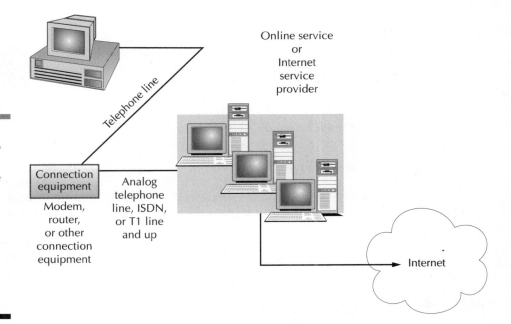

A user connecting to the Internet via an Online Service or an Internet Service Provider at various connection speeds
Figure 2-15.

Internet Service Providers

Use of an Internet service provider (ISP) is the next logical step when users wish to buy cheaper Internet access time and don't require the private services of an online service. Hundreds of ISPs exist across the country and are listed on the Web site http://www.thelist.com. Most ISPs have now discovered the Yellow Pages. And AT&T and other telecommunications providers now act as ISPs. The user or business simply signs up with an ISP in order to gain access to the Internet, but, in this case, the user's PC must also speak TCP/IP. Online service providers translate user commands to TCP/IP, but connection to an ISP assumes the existence of a TCP/IP stack on the user's machine, which is now available with Windows 95 and NT. Windows 3.x users can purchase a commercially available stack from Frontier Technologies or download a shareware stack.

Connect charges through an ISP are lower than those of online services, especially for unlimited usage. Typically, ISPs will charge a flat $20 to $30 a month for access. ISPs also provide Web page hosting services. Customers utilize the ISP's Web server and storage (for the Web page content), plus receive an e-mail account, for about $100 a month.

Software and Hardware

In addition to the TCP/IP stack software, users who access the Internet directly or through an ISP will need to buy browser, e-mail, and newsreader software at a minimum for Internet access. In order to publish on the Web, users must purchase Web server and HTML content creation software. ISPs often provide the browser software, and it is available with Windows 95 and NT as well. The options discussed thus far require only a typical PC setup (with processor, storage, and memory requirements determined by the user's overall needs). However, at some point, a company may wish to have its Web server operating in-house, rather than leasing time on an ISP's server. This option requires a more powerful PC or a mini-computer and additional server software. Since an Intranet requires the same configuration, this option will be discussed more fully in Chapter 3. Still, the company must physically connect to the Internet via an ISP.

2

Physical Connection

In order to access the Internet as either a client or server, a physical data line must be in place. Online services and basic ISP-provided services require only a modem and a direct dial line. Higher speeds or dedicated connections cost more and sometimes require additional hardware as discussed next.

Modem

Modems allow PCs to transmit data across a telephone line at speeds ranging from 14.4Kbps to 28.8Kbps. The higher the modem speed, the quicker the Web access, the less time spent online, and the lower the connection cost. Modems typically cost $100 and up, depending on speed and quality.

Direct Dial Line

A direct line is simply the analog Plain Old Telephone Service (POTS) provided by a local telephone company. Direct dial supports up to 28.8Kbps and costs the same as POTS usage. This type of access is optimal for a home user or a one- to two-person company.

ISDN Line

Higher speeds can be achieved by ordering an Integrated Services Digital Network (ISDN) line, which combines voice and digital network services in a single medium at speeds from 56Kbps to 128Kbps. The local telephone company can provide an ISDN line on a full- or part-time basis for somewhere between $300 and $1,500 a month. Instead of a modem, however, users must install a router, starting at $900. This type of line is optimal for companies of more than three users when a modem connection (dial-up) just isn't fast enough and faster options (such as T1, discussed next) are too expensive. The ISDN line is capable of handling a larger number of users and at speeds greater than a modem.

T1 Line

A T1 line is several phone lines that can carry large amounts of data quickly, up to 1.544 megabits per second. A T1 line can support hundreds of users and is typically purchased on a full-time basis for continual Internet access. Typically, companies that utilize T1 lines already have a local area network in place and use a router and other connectivity equipment to access the T1 line. The setup cost for all the hardware required is about $15,000. The T1 line is charged a flat monthly fee of about $3,000.

Because of the bandwidth of this line, most companies use this medium to access the Web. The T1 is most practical for businesses of all sizes because of the capacity and cost. With this type of service, a company can start out with a relatively low number of users and then increase the bandwidth as the number of employees increase by asking the ISP for greater bandwidth when necessary. However, an issue to consider when increasing bandwidth is to make sure the server (if an internal Web server is used) can handle this expansion, since the number of hits from outside browsers may increase.

Cable Line

Cable companies want to get a piece of the Internet business and now offer quicker access to the Web because of the inherent bandwidth advantage over phone lines.

Concerns of the Internet and the World Wide Web

The Web is an excellent medium to promote corporate image, drive sales, and disseminate information. Though the Web may be a wonderful business tool, several concerns surround this technology, some real and some not so real. The most visible concern is security, followed by the costs of accessing the Internet and having a presence on the Web, and the question of how Internet access affects productivity.

Security

Concerns about Internet and Web security include fear of people hacking into systems, software piracy, destruction of data warehouses, sending credit

2

card numbers out over the Web, copyright infringement and plagiarism, and viruses that can potentially damage systems. These issues now affect international trade and jurisdictions, since Web business is conducted globally. Software and hardware vendors have reacted by developing software protections and firewalls to reduce, if not eliminate, these security breaches. Security includes techniques that safeguard computer systems and information from unwanted access. The most common of these is authentication: requiring a password and/or a username in order to log on to a system. *Firewalls* deny access to those users dialing in from outside the network who are not identified by the system.

Encryption and Authentication

Because security issues are a major concern, many vendors design programs that protect sensitive transactions, databases, and access to private information. Three of the best-known security systems (although not yet implemented on a wide scale) include Secure Sockets Layer (SSL), Secure Hypertext Transfer Protocol (SHTTP), and Secure Multipurpose Internet Mail Extensions (S/MIME).

SSL provides a secure transaction between the client and server in a threefold process: (1) the user's PC identifies who it's talking to (*client identifying the server*); (2) the server identifies who it's talking to (*server identifying the client*); and (3) once the two have identified each other, data is exchanged and encrypted securely.

SHTTP is a simple authentication whereby a user enters a name and password in order to access a site, a document, or a server. S/MIME sends a user's e-mail attachment(s) encrypted and/or signed. Only e-mail recipients who hold the sender's "public key" can decode S/MIME e-mails. The signature is verified by a third party, such as Verisign, so that the recipient is sure that the sender is who he says he is.

All three protocols, SSL, SHTTP, and S/MIME, help conduct safe and secure business transactions over the Internet. All three of these security standards are discussed in more detail, along with firewalls, in Chapter 9.

Credit Cards

Sending credit card information across the Internet is really safer than leaving credit card receipts in the garbage can, and hardly less safe than giving out credit card numbers over the telephone (after all, is that really L. L. Bean on the other end of the line?)—even without additional security measures. However, where SSL has been implemented, users can be assured they are sending the credit card number to the correct Web server (SSL lets the visitor know this really *is* L. L. Bean's Web site). Anyone who handles the credit card number once it arrives at the destination Web site is no less a security scare than someone who handles credit card numbers at a direct merchant.

Plagiarism and Copyright Infringement

Another concern on the Web is plagiarism. With the vast array of information readily available, users access the Web to inspire new ideas and assist in research. However, Webmasters, those who administer Web sites and pages, and companies may discover that their ideas, slogans, artwork, or written documentation have been used by another individual or company. With so many millions of users worldwide viewing a site or page, it's easy for people to take information and claim themselves as the source. As in any other business endeavor, it's best to copyright and trademark information that is uniquely created for product or corporate promotions.

Viruses

One of the greatest concerns on the Web is the possibility of downloading or receiving by e-mail a software virus. When the e-mail is opened or the software installed, the virus attacks. Viruses can damage operating systems, hard drives, and software; they can erase documents and scramble configurations, attacking operating systems by scrambling, adding, or deleting code. New viruses are constantly being developed by hackers. Today there are hundreds of known viruses, including the Monkey and Simple viruses.

The Monkey virus infects the boot sectors of a computer. When the system is loaded with this virus, the virus will load itself into the memory. While loaded, the virus infects any accessed, unprotected disks. Once a PC is infected, the virus will scramble the partition table of the master boot record. If users try and boot from a clean floppy, the disk will be inaccessible because the partition table has been moved. The Simple virus, on the other hand, searches for .COM files in the current directory. When it finds a .COM file, it checks to see if the file was previously infected by the virus. If not, the virus will then infect all remaining .COM files in that directory.

Because it is impossible to know all existing viruses, users can maintain familiarity with the most common ones by talking with various Information Systems, Information Technologies (IT), and engineering professionals, as well as searching the Web for the latest virus news. Many vendors, including Macafee and Norton, offer software packages that can detect and correct viruses.

Costs of Hardware, Software, and Personnel

The cost of Internet access can range from the one-time cost of a PC, modem, and software plus a few dollars a month for e-mail and Internet access—to millions of dollars a year to host a high-tech Web presence. Many companies dove headlong into the Internet without a second thought about the cost-to-benefit ratio of their investment. And in many cases, the cost of hosting a Web site is well offset by the opportunity loss of *not* hosting, especially when every competitor has a URL. Now that the early adopters have sunk their Internet costs, newer entrants on the Internet scene rightly have concerns about the benefits of investing in hardware, software, and people.

2

Fortunately, the cost of accessing the Internet and hosting a Web site is dropping. Whereas the early adopters utilized large Unix machines for Web servers, Web server software now runs on NT servers. Along with Unix equipment costs, companies had to invest in a Unix guru's salary. This is no longer necessary. And HTML design no longer requires an HTML expert, since WYSIWYG-designers have entered the market. As Microsoft offers more and more access and server software with its operating systems and cable and telephone monopolies offer less expensive access, more and more companies will find Internet access and hosting a profitable enterprise. The savings, and even revenue generation, will more than offset the costs. For example, Frontier Technologies regularly provides software evaluation copies and patches via its Web and FTP sites. If, instead, Frontier mailed 50 evaluation copies or patches a week, the cost of goods (CD, jewel case) and shipping could easily exceed $20 a unit, or $4,000 a month—more than the cost of a T1 line.

Productivity

Some companies fear that Internet access will allow their employees to spend several hours a day surreptitiously browsing unsavory sites or reading prurient posts in nefarious newsgroups. The same employees could just as easily spend their days reading pornography at the desk, and the same means of curbing such behavior apply. However, to ensure that managers prevent productivity loss to employees lost in the Internet, software vendors have developed logging and filtering capabilities as part of firewall, NetWare-to-Internet gateways, or proxy server products (through which employees must pass on the way to the Internet). Logging features allow management to identify where users have ventured on the Internet and Web, while filters allow management to control Internet access rights.

Applying the Internet and World Wide Web Paradigms to the Intranet

Internet products have enabled businesses to be more competitive and individuals more productive on a global scale. Soon after businesses worldwide began migrating to Web technology, the question was raised: *why can't businesses utilize Internet and Web tools for internal communication and information processing?* Where e-mail facilitated intercorporate communication, it might facilitate internal information sharing. Internal newsgroups could foster interdepartmental communication, especially in cases where a history of past activities and communication matter—as in technical support issues. Various departments might benefit by publishing paperless memos on an internal Web site: from human resources policies to marketing and sales prices to engineering product plans. Instead of submitting information on a Web page back-end form to order software, employees could submit expense reports or purchase orders via internal back-end processes. And the search engine paradigm of the Web might be tailored to facilitate internal information searches across existing document directories on the LAN, as well as the internal Web server. Of course, many companies have already discovered the benefits of incorporating Internet and Web technologies internally on an Intranet.

These companies now benefit from both a Web presence and an Intranet implementation. For example, marketing posts competitors' products and features in one place on the internal Web server using the same technology used to post product information on the Web, except that only employees can access the internal server. An Intranet allows marketing to go a step further; people outside of the company, such as customers, resellers, and distributors, can have access to this information as well if they are given access rights when dialing in to the server. In another example, a human resources department posts current job openings internally before posting them outside of the company. Employees can discover a job fit in minutes or hours, well before it lands in the newspaper and an outsider is hired. An Intranet can clearly enhance corporate communication flow by hosting internal Web pages for each department. The departments then easily post critical information for easy and fast access by other employees. Chapter 6 describes several corporate case studies highlighting Intranet uses and benefits.

Without much effort, all the tools of the Internet—e-mail, newsreaders, and Web technology, including such advances as back ends, Java applets, and search technologies—can be applied to publishing, sharing, collaborating on, and finding information in the corporation. Applied to the corporation, these tools form the Intranet. And that is what the rest of this book is about.

Putting It All Together

What is an Intranet? An Intranet applies Internet and Web technologies to corporate networks to enhance activities across the corporation. The Internet itself arose from the Government's 1968 ARPANET experiment, which connected several universities and government organizations. E-mail, newsgroups, file transfer, and Telnet capabilities quickly became the means of facilitating communications as the Internet continued to grow. The advent of the World Wide Web, HTML, Web server, and browser technology in the late 1980s led eventually to the incredible expansion of the Internet and its extension well beyond the walls of academia and government. These tools now enhance the sales and marketing, research, technical support, intercorporate communications, and human resources activities of corporations around the world. And now these same tools, when applied to internal corporate communications, can enhance the way a business operates. Chapter 3 follows this introduction of Internet and Web history, technologies, and uses with a more detailed discussion of the technology components as applied to an Intranet.

2

Frequently Asked Questions

♦ **What is the World Wide Web?**

The World Wide Web is a means of accessing information on the Internet.
The Web consists of computers linked together through hyperlinks, allowing
users to browse from one Web site to another.

♦ **How can the Web and the Internet help corporations?**

For starters, the Web provides exposure for a corporation's image and product
to the world via Web sites. Through a Web site, a corporation can advertise
and promote new and existing products and conduct sales transactions.
Moreover, corporations use e-mail to communicate to customers, vendors, and
the press. Web sites enhance customer support activities, and the list goes on.

♦ **How easy is it to use Web technology?**

Web technology was designed for all users, from the novice to the technical
guru. Users can find a plethora of information, whether the latest NASDAQ
reports, FBI yearly crime statistics, or baseball batting averages, by pointing
and clicking on hyperlinks. Because the Web's tools are easy to administer
and customize, nontechnical users can set up and administer a Web site.

♦ **How costly is the technology?**

The cost of Internet and Web technology varies from several dollars a
month for access to millions of dollars a year for high-tech, high-volume Web
page publishing.

♦ **How do the Internet and Web enhance productivity?**

Both the Internet and the Web allow users and corporations to extend their
reach across the world, saving time and money compared to more expensive
communications. E-mail is far more convenient than "snail" mail and less
expensive than the telephone. Other Internet and Web technologies similarly
save time and money by allowing users to download software from a Web site
and by increasing the speed by which competitive research is accomplished.

◆ **What are some of the major concerns about the Internet and the Web?**

Issues and concerns include employee productivity, costs of access and publishing, outside intrusion, plagiarism and copyright infringement, security, and viruses.

◆ **What functions can Internet and Web technology perform?**

With e-mail, users and organizations can communicate around the globe. Usenet newsgroups allow users to post to electronic bulletin board discussion groups, sharing information on thousands of topics of interest. Telnet allows users to access distant computers to find information. FTP lets users download that information to their computer. The World Wide Web servers allow individuals and organizations to publish graphics and text about themselves, their companies and their products, plus add links to other topics of interest. Web browsers allow users to read these publications (Web "pages"), interact with the server computer, and link to related sites.

2

CHAPTER 3

What Makes Up a Web-Centric Intranet?

Susan L. Moore
John A. Luoma
with Susan Archer, Scott Kosloske,
Kia K. LaBracke, Ray Langford

Chapter Objectives

◆ Investigate the definition of a Web-centric Intranet and the advantages and disadvantages of such an architecture

◆ Learn what the key components are in a Web-centric Intranet

◆ Understand how these components work with your existing network configuration

◆ Find out about the latest platform development tools

◆ Discover how search tools can improve inform- ation management

Y ou may have heard the term "Web-centric" thrown around by computer magazines and Internet junkies who eagerly grab at the latest buzz words, anxious to look knowledgeable. But what does the term actually mean? What sets a Web-centric Intranet apart from a traditional local area network (LAN) is its devotion to Internet technologies. A Web-centric Intranet is centered around its Web server. Information is often passed between employees by posting Web pages on the server, which they then access through their browsers. This information might be restricted information, such as the payroll details, or it might be general information, such as the next set of shipping dates for a new product.

The Web-Centric Advantage

If the Intranet is connected to the Internet, then often the Web server plays a large role in the promotion of the company and its communication with the outside world. In progressive companies, the Web site is fully developed with product information and sales opportunities. The graphics are stunning, the functionality amazing, and the Hypertext Markup Language (HTML) code has clearly been pushed to its limits. Sites such as Microsoft's home page (http://www.microsoft.com) and Microsoft's Mungo Park (http://www.mungopark.msn.com) are constantly changing examples of what you can do with Web pages.

3

Web-centric Intranets have users who have become comfortable with the graphical user interface (GUI) provided by browsers and the Web server's remote administration tools. Therefore, the same look and feel is carried over into the other applications that are used in the Web-centric Intranet. Perhaps the employees use their browsers as newsreaders or e-mail viewers, or maybe the client applications simply have a consistent design philosophy behind them so that as the employees switch tools, they are shifting easily from one application to another. Commands appear with the same wording in many applications, and can be found under the same menu items, increasing productivity. Dialog boxes have frequently used buttons such as the OK and Cancel buttons, located in the same order all of the time, reducing mistakes by users who sometimes click before they read.

NOTE: Perhaps now you understand what a Web-centric Intranet is, but don't really see why having one is so important. Maybe you aren't that familiar with Web servers, and the thought of centering your company around such a mysterious piece of software makes you cringe. True, your Intranet does not need to be Web-centric. However, the enormous benefits such a setup provides should help you overcome any trepidation you might have.

The Graphical Interface

To put it simply, a Web-centric Intranet does for your network what Windows did for your desktop. If you already have an existing network setup, then you probably have some type of file server. You have a directory structure on the file server that attempts to fit the needs of all your employees, but even when you use File Manager or Windows Explorer, the file structure appears cryptic. If you can't use long filenames, then you are restricted to naming files and directories with just eight letters plus a three-letter extension. No matter how creative you are, there are times when eight letters just aren't enough to express a file's content. Those not familiar with your company (either new employees or consultants) often have difficulty picking up on the naming schemes used. For example, in the sample file server directory in Figure 3-1, you would have to be an employee for awhile in order to understand that CSREVG.PPT contains the CyberSearch Reviewers Guide, or that SPLION.GIF is the SuperWeb Server logo.

By implementing a Web-centric Intranet, you are using a graphical user interface to access and organize your network. It provides an easier means to publish, administer, and locate information than a traditional file server architecture alone. In Figure 3-2, you can see files stored on a Web server. Though you are seeing the same type of information as in Figure 3-1, it is presented in a much more coherent fashion. You don't have to guess at a file's contents because the title immediately tells you what the file contains. Employees waste much less time opening file after file, searching for the correct one.

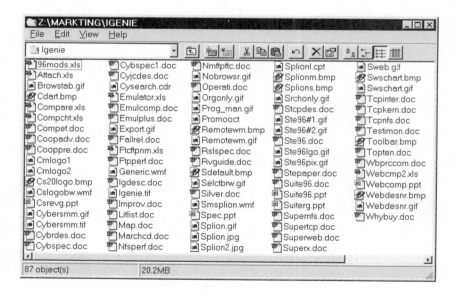

Example of a directory on a file server

Figure 3-1.

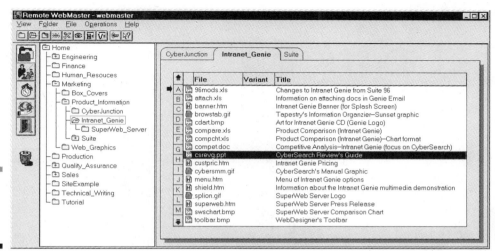

Example of a
folder on a
Web server
Figure 3-2.

Intuitive Data Linking

A Web-centric Intranet also presents a company with a unique, intuitive method of accessing all company information. The Web paradigm is based on hyperlinks to connect documents together. As more pages are linked, the bigger the "Web" becomes. In your company, you can apply the same architecture. By placing files on your Web server, you can link documents together using HTML.

For example, if you have added all of your product specification sheets to your Web server, you can also create a Web page that serves as an index to the sheets, as shown in Figure 3-3. Anyone in your company who has access to the area can then go to the index sheet using their browser and open the specification sheets one after the other. If the sheets are in HTML, then the HTML page is displayed. If the sheets are in a different format, then the appropriate application is launched, as long as it's on the client's computer. Employees no longer need to open up a separate application and then try to find the file they are looking for by browsing through nonintuitive directory structures.

The documents that are linked together can also be located on multiple servers of different types. You might have a Unix file server that you use in addition to your Windows news server. However, you can create hyperlinks to both data sources using HTML, so employees can easily find the information sources. They no longer need to map drives, searching

through strangely named directories and machine names trying desperately to find one piece of information!

Back-End Services

The Web-centric Intranet also presents employees with the opportunity to keep up with the latest technologies and useful applications that maximize their efficiency. On your Intranet's Web server, you can create *back-end services*—applications that run on your Web server and are accessed through a browser. The back ends may take data that employees enter on a form through their browsers, such as shipping requests, and enter it into a database. The back ends might be created by someone in your company to meet a particular need. The cost to the company is only the salary of the person working on the back end. The company doesn't need to purchase additional client software to run on each computer, as long as all of the employees have a browser. As browsers such as Microsoft's Internet Explorer are free, the cost is minimal or nonexistent, especially compared to systems such as Lotus Notes. You also get the added benefit of creating a custom application that truly fits your needs, as opposed to forcing another vendor's software to do what you want it to.

NOTE: See "Creating Back-End Services," later in this chapter, for more information about creating them.

Downloading Files

Another advantage of having a Web-centric Intranet is being able to download files. If you are not connected to the Internet, you might place files on your Web server for employees to download. You might have expense reports, vacation request forms, insurance claims, or other useful information available for downloading to employees' hard drives.

 CAUTION: Though downloading files can provide you with new (and fun!) software, be sure you are retrieving the files from a trusted source. If the files you download are infected with a virus, you could spread the virus not only to your computer, but to the whole company.

 NOTE: See Chapter 5 for tips on placing files on your Web server.

3

If you are connected to the Internet, you might download applications so that you have the most current software on your computers. For example, employees might download the latest version of Microsoft's Internet Explorer because it supports new HTML tags. You might also download a beta, or first, version of a new accounting software package. By previewing and testing the package, you can test it out immediately instead of waiting for diskettes or a CD or to be shipped to you.

 TIP: If you want to download files that will be for company-wide use (such as the latest version of Internet Explorer), you might want to have only one person download the file and copy it to a common location. Depending on your Internet connection, it could take you a half an hour or more to download a large file, so it makes no sense for more than one person in your company to do so.

Platform Independence

Another exciting benefit of the Web-centric Intranet is the flexibility it offers the people who are connecting to it. If you have a Web server, people in your Intranet (and on the Internet) can connect to it using the browser of their choice. They must have a browser to get to your Web server, but they don't have to use a browser from the same company because the software is designed around protocols that all vendors follow. A Macintosh browser can connect to a Windows NT-based Web server as seamlessly as a Windows browser can, because both of the browsers use the Hypertext Transfer Protocol (HTTP). E-mail can be sent between people all around the world, no matter what e-mail software they are using. E-mail messages created using a Unix-based package such as Pine or ELM can be received by someone using Frontier Technologies' or Microsoft's Windows-based e-mail software. Your Intranet is as scaleable as your business, and can accommodate in-house and remote users, regardless of which platform they are using on the client side.

NOTE: Though you can use almost any browser to connect to almost any Web server, keep in mind that different features are supported by different browsers. For example, if you have an internal Web site and people in your company are using different browsers, some of the browsers may not support all of the HTML extensions that your employees have incorporated into their Web pages.

The Value to Customers

Just as a Web-centric model must be valuable to your employees, it must also be valuable to your customers. If you are connected to the Internet, then you can connect with your customers using your Web tools. The growth and popularity of the Internet has spawned the rapid development of emerging technologies. The Internet experience is now faster and more realistic, allowing for more advanced forms of communication. It is no longer uncommon to see a company's external Web page and e-mail addresses included on business cards, letterhead, and advertisements. Many customers have come to expect companies to provide such information. People are at times disappointed when they want to find out about a company, only to discover that it doesn't have a Web site.

TIP: The Internet has become one of the first places many people look for information, so if your company doesn't have a Web site, you could be losing customers to companies who have adopted a Web-centric architecture.

Just as your Web-centric Intranet makes accessing information easier for employees, it makes accessing information easier for your customers and business partners. Web pages often provide easy, obligation-free ways of discovering information, giving the customer a chance to learn about your company without having to make a phone call or send a letter. The point-and-click design of Web pages makes them easy to use, especially for those customers who may not be completely comfortable with computers. People who don't understand File Transfer Protocol (FTP) can easily download files from your FTP server, because the steps are hidden behind a simple, clickable button to the customer in the code of the Web pages. Through firewall technology, you can even securely share your Intranet with business partners around the world, enhancing communication between the groups.

Some Potential Drawbacks

As with any technology, there are a few drawbacks to a Web-centric Intranet. However, with some planning and flexibility, you can overcome these problems and implement a successful Intranet!

3

Employee Resistance to Change

One of the largest obstacles may actually come from employees. Some may have just familiarized themselves with a traditional file server network. They've heard about Web pages, and they know about e-mail, but they are simply not interested in making any more changes. They have too many passwords and user names to remember and don't want to be bothered with learning more utilities, even though those utilities make their lives easier, increase their productivity, and boost sales. Some employees may also be frustrated with the introduction of a new structure. If your existing setup is working, why bother changing it? Who knows what problems might arise if you switch to a Web-centric Intranet?

 T IP: What you need to make clear to the employees who are resisting the change is that they are building on their knowledge, not learning something completely new. Present the Web tools as the next step, not a new step.

Taking the Next Step

Teach people what is involved in the next step. Yes, they may need another user name and password in order to access the Web server through their browsers. Yet, if they can just remember that user name and password, a new, easy-to-use method of information gathering is opened up to them. To help smooth the path, have hands-on training sessions before the software is installed on employees' computers so that the Management Information Systems (MIS) department or Information Systems (IS) department isn't flooded with calls. Break down the training into experience levels. Those who don't know how to use a mouse shouldn't be in the same session as those who spend three hours a night surfing the Internet on their home computers.

A New Way of Communicating

Your employees may need to learn new methods of communicating. For example, they may need to access the internal Web site and download a form to fill out their expense report instead of filling one out by hand. They may even be able to fill out their expense report from their browsers! Show them in the training how these changes can make their lives easier. For example, they can have an electronic copy of their expense report to refer back to at a later date. The information is legible to the people in the finance department, so they can process the report much more quickly, getting the money to the individual faster.

The New Skill Sets Required

The skills a Web-centric Intranet requires may be ones that you already have in-house, but there may be areas where your employees need a little help. For example, no one may know how to create Web pages. Maybe your network administrator is a Novell expert but doesn't know the first thing about configuring a Web server. By identifying the areas where your company may be lacking skills, you can plan to hire new individuals or train current employees.

 NOTE: Chapter 5 discusses in detail the roles you need to fill in a Web-centric Intranet.

As you investigate your weakest skill areas, keep in mind that software packages today are being developed more and more for the novice. Because many vendors are using *wizards*, or intuitive setup dialog boxes, to install and configure software, you may not need as much expertise as you think. In addition, many content-creation tools are being designed with a *WYSIWYG* (What You See Is What You Get) user interface that seeks to hide the lower-level functions such as writing HTML code. With such user-oriented tools, you may not need extensive employee training.

Exploring the Key Server Components

Servers are a crucial part of any Intranet. They help store and control the information your company uses internally and perhaps externally. These are the pieces the employees access with their client applications in order to better perform their jobs and meet their goals. The servers you need depend on the size of your company and its specific information structure needs. The servers discussed in this section are the most common ones that can assist you and your company.

TIP: If you have a small company, some of the services may be provided by an Internet service provider (ISP).

A Web Server

3

The key to the Web-centric Intranet is the Web server. By using a Web server (or Web servers), corporations can publish public and confidential information consisting of visually attractive, content-rich documents made up of text, graphics, video, and sound. Readers can access this information from their desktop computers using a Web browser. The most basic function of the Web server is to store Web documents, which are "served" on demand when a client (Web browser) requests the information. The Web server can also run back-end applications that interface with databases and other applications (to provide auto-notification of e-mail, for example). Through administration tools, information on the Web server can be managed and distributed.

NOTE: See Chapter 7 for specific features to look for in a Web server as you plan your Intranet.

Advanced Web server software often allows you to set up multilayered security and administration from any PC. In other words, you can set different types of access for different departments and individuals within and outside of the corporation. Read and write access should also be possible within the software's file manager, so that different folders and files can be configured to have varying levels of access. Being able to set such access helps you bring certain information into the reach of the general public, while protecting confidential information. With a typical LAN set up, you don't have this ability.

 NOTE: See Chapter 5 for tips on setting access levels to your Web server. Chapter 9 also has detailed information on securing your Web server.

How It Fits into Your Intranet

To help you better understand how a Web server fits into your Intranet, take a look at Figure 3-4. The figure shows how you might use your Web server to accept customer input and display information based on that input. You can also see the multiple locations from which the Web server administrator, or *webmaster*, can administer the server.

 NOTE: Administering the Web server might involve registering back-end applications; copying files to the server; creating groups, users, and folders on the server; or setting access restrictions to the information. The duties of the webmaster vary depending on the Web server software package you use.

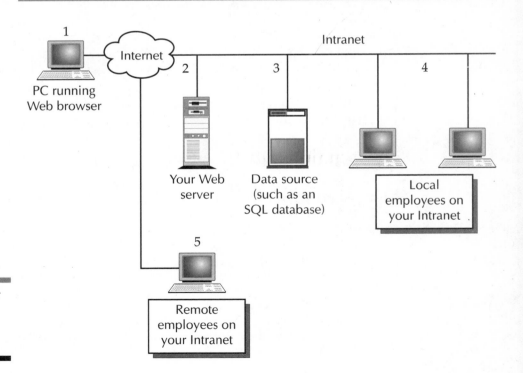

A Web server
on your
Intranet
Figure 3-4.

How It Works

The numbered labels in the following list refer to the numbers shown on the diagram in Figure 3-4.

1 Anyone who views your Web site through a browser is accessing your Web server. They are viewing your Web pages and possibly running a back-end service you have created. You may allow anyone on the Internet to access your site, or you may want to restrict access to your Intranet.

2 Your Web server resides on a computer in your company. You might have a Windows-based Web server, or you might have the Web server on a Unix box, a Macintosh, a mainframe, or an OS/2 computer.

3 On a computer within your company, you may, for example, have a database you want to update. People using a browser fill out the forms that provide the database with information when they access the Web server.

4 Employees on your Intranet can access your Web server to view documents, download files, or run back-end services. They might also be able to perform administration, if your Web server software allows it.

5 Employees anywhere on your Intranet can access your Web server if they can connect to your network. They can use a browser to view Web pages on the server, or they can use the Web server software's remote administration tools, if the software has the capability.

As you can see, the Web server is accessed both from a browser and from administrative tools (which might also be browser-centered). The access to the server can be restricted to your Intranet, or you may develop an external Web site and invite people from the Internet to stop in and see what your Web site has to offer them.

A Domain Name System (DNS) Server

Before you are able to mail someone a letter, you must know their street address. Your Intranet is similar to the postal system; the addressing scheme used throughout the Internet and on Intranets is contained in a distributed database called the Domain Name System. The database for domains in the United States is administered by InterNIC, an organization responsible for registering domain names and providing database services to Internet users. In its entirety, this database describes every host, somewhat like a large telephone book, giving information such as each host's Internet Protocol (IP) address and alias, and mail server information for each domain. Because the overall database is distributed, small sections can be managed on individual networks throughout the world. Client applications, such as e-mail packages and browsers, can access the entire database through a client-server protocol.

How It Fits into Your Intranet

On your Intranet, a DNS server would contain information about a section of the overall network and know how to communicate with other DNS servers to provide IP addresses in response to client queries. *Resolvers* are the client applications that send the queries for IP addresses to the DNS servers. For many TCP/IP (Transmission Control Protocol/Internet Protocol) implementations, including Windows 95 and Windows NT, the resolver is built into the TCP/IP stack and is not seen by the user.

For example, suppose your customer wants to view your company's new home page, opens a browser, and enters **www.acme.com** in the Connect To dialog box. While an IP address is like a specific street address to your Web server, the host name www.acme.com only provides information that is like a building name, such as the Empire State building. The host name uniquely identifies the destination, but doesn't provide the direction for getting there. Therefore, domain name resolution steps in, and the following events occur, as illustrated in Figure 3-5.

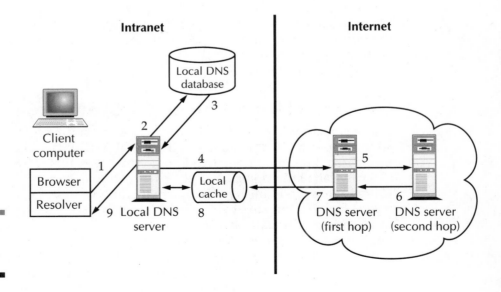

How a DNS server works

Figure 3-5.

How It Works

The numbered labels in the following list refer to the numbers shown on the diagram in Figure 3-5.

1 The browser consults its internal resolver. The resolver issues a query to the DNS server on the same network. The client's TCP/IP configuration includes the IP address of this DNS server.

2 The DNS server checks its local database for www.acme.com. It may also check its local cache for the name.

3 If the record is found in the database, the record is returned to the client. The record contains the IP address, and the browser can retrieve your home page.

4 If the record can not be found on the local DNS server and is configured as a *forwarder*, or a computer that passes the request on to another computer, it simply sends the query to another DNS server and waits for the response.

3

NOTE: If the DNS server is not configured as a forwarder, it consults its databases to determine what to do next. Hopefully, the cache contains information about DNS servers in the *acme.com* domain or the *com* domain. Otherwise, the *Root Name Servers*, or stable Internet forwards that don't change often and can be used as default forwarders, must be used.

5 This computer (the second hop) may, in turn, forward the request again, until the name can be resolved.

6 When the record is found, the second hop (or whichever hop resolved the name) passes the information back to the previous DNS server.

7 The first DNS server passes the name back to your Intranet's DNS server.

8 The record is added to your DNS server's local cache so it doesn't need to forward the request next time it is received from a client computer.

9 The client resolver receives the answer. Some resolvers also cache answers locally so they don't need to repeat the lookup process. The resolver returns the IP address to the browser and the browser now has the information it needs to retrieve your company's home page!

NOTE: Though there are many steps involved, the entire process takes places in under a second and is normally totally transparent to you.

Do You Really Need a DNS Server?

If you are connecting to the Internet, you must have a DNS server. You won't be able to connect to other hosts on the Internet if you don't have a DNS server either on your network or at your Internet Service Provider. If your organization is connected to the Internet, your Internet service provider (ISP) may provide a service in which the ISP maintains your domain. There are also advantages to maintaining your domain in-house. You can easily make changes to your domain without the intervention of your ISP. Also, host lookups for local records or records that are cached on a DNS server are faster when the DNS server is on your local network.

NOTE: You also need to know the IP address of a server in order to connect to it—having a DNS server isn't enough.

Other Options

If you are setting up an Intranet that doesn't connect to the Internet, there are two possible ways to resolve Intranet addresses on your network:

♦   **A hosts table**   Name resolution can be done by having a hosts table on each computer in your Intranet. Hosts files contain the names and IP address of all other hosts on the network. However, any change in the domain necessitates updating the hosts file on each computer.

♦   **A DNS server**   Keeping a single database on a DNS server simplifies maintenance.

The choice is yours. If your Intranet is fairly stable (few people coming and going), then you might be able to easily maintain your hosts table. Your network administrator may be able to update all of the PCs easily. However, if you are at a larger or less stable company, then a DNS server is probably your best option.

NOTE: Chapter 7 also discusses issues surrounding DNS servers.

A Mail Server

E-mail has become an integral part of corporate life. People are tired of playing phone tag and need a way to store the interaction with coworkers until a time when it is convenient to review the information. E-mail has filled the gap between personal interaction and a busy schedule.

NOTE: Though some people may feel resentful that e-mail has taken the place of person-to-person communication, it truly has become a part of everyday corporate life.

Your mail server, which acts like an electronic postal worker to send and deliver e-mail, should have flexible security options and remote administration capabilities. While software offerings vary, your mail server should allow you to grant direct access based on domain name or the host name of a specific computer. A critical feature is multithreading, which allows multiple incoming connections to the server. On a busy mail server, you need the ability for many people to connect to the server at the same time. Depending upon the number of users you need to support, you may elect to devote one server machine to your mail or load the mail server onto the same computer used for your Web server.

How It Fits into Your Intranet

The Simple Mail Transfer Protocol (SMTP), Post Office Protocol 3 (POP3), and Internet Message Access Protocol, Version 4 (IMAP4) are three popular means of message delivery. SMTP stores e-mail on the user's computer, not on a remote server. Therefore, if the PC is disconnected from the supporting TCP/IP network, mail can't be delivered during that time.

CAUTION: If you decide to use a mail server that keeps the messages on the server instead of on the client, be sure you instruct people about the importance of deleting unnecessary messages, so they are not taking up valuable server space.

In contrast, POP3 mail accounts allow messages to be stored on a network server, so that users can "POP" their e-mail messages from the server when they open their e-mail applications. You would typically set the e-mail configuration to delete the message from the server once it has been delivered to the client. IMAP4 actually allows the messages to reside on the server, so the client PCs simply view the messages living on the server.

T IP: If the messages live on the server, as with IMAP4, then they can be retrieved multiple times. For example, if you read your e-mail at work but want access to the same messages when you get home, the messages would still be on the server and thus accessible to you.

How It Works
Figure 3-6 gives you two different scenarios. They both show SMTP clients sending mail to each other, but one scenario doesn't use a mail server.

The SMTP Scenario   In the left picture of Figure 3-6, the following is happening:

1 In order to send a message, the SMTP client computer sends e-mail. On its way to its destination, the e-mail first stops on the Intranet's mail server.

2 The mail server asks a DNS server to perform a mail exchange (MX) lookup, which translates the e-mail address the person entered in the To field into a machine name. The DNS server finds the machine name, as described in the section on how a DNS server works, earlier in this chapter.

3 Once the DNS server has found the address, it sends the machine name back to the mail server.

4 The mail server sends the e-mail to the correct machine name.

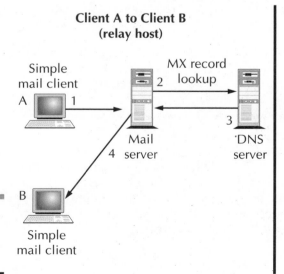

Sending a
message to
SMTP clients

Figure 3-6.

In the right picture of Figure 3-6, there is no mail server to show you that you don't need one. In this situation, mail is sent as follows:

1 The SMTP client sends a message. In the background, the computer sends a request to the Intranet's DNS server to perform an MX lookup to find the machine name of the destination.

2 Once the DNS server finds the machine name (which it might have found in its own database, or it may have searched other DNS servers' databases), it returns the machine name to the client's computer.

3 The SMTP client sends the message directly to another SMTP mail client, which could be on your Intranet or somewhere on the Internet.

CAUTION: Though you don't need a mail server (see the right half of Figure 3-6), your computer needs to directly connect to another computer or to someone else's mail server every time you send a message. Doing so can slow your computer down. Your computer also needs to handle the rescheduling of undelivered mail and possibly handle a large number of hits, if many people send you mail.

3

The POP and IMAP4 Scenario   Figure 3-7 shows you how messages are sent to POP and IMAP4 clients. Because POP and IMAP4 e-mail must be

Client A to POP Client B

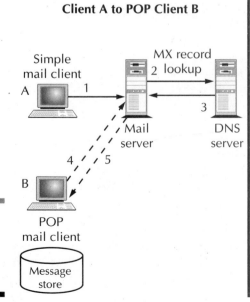

Client A to IMAP4 Client B

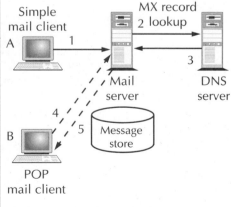

Sending a message to POP and IMAP4 clients
Figure 3-7.

retrieved from a mail server, the client sending the mail must communicate either directly or indirectly with the receiver's mail server at some point.

NOTE: The only difference between the POP and IMAP4 clients is the message retrieval and storage after the message has been delivered. POP clients remove their messages from the mail server, while IMAP4 clients can choose to store their messages in folders on the mail server, instead of on their own computers.

1 The client computer sends the e-mail message. Its first stop is at the Intranet's mail server.

2 The mail server asks the DNS server to do an MX lookup.

3 The DNS server sends back the machine name to the mail server. If the recipient is on the same LAN as the sender, then the e-mail message sits on the mail server. If the recipient is located outside of the LAN, the message would be sent to the recipient's mail server.

4 The POP or IMAP4 client requests the message from the mail server.

5 The message is sent to the client. If the person is using POP, on the left side of Figure 3-7, the message is physically copied to the person's computer. If the person is using IMAP4, on the right side of Figure 3-7, the message remains on the mail server.

A News (Discussion) Server

A news server distributes bulletins, discussion groups, and similar information under the name Usenet. The information is commonly called *news* and is divided into newsgroups that deal with a particular topic or set of topics. Internet newsgroups provide forums for discussions about topics ranging from versions of Unix to movie reviews or comments on current social or political issues.

How It Fits into Your Intranet

The protocol used by the news server is the Network News Transfer Protocol (NNTP). After you install and set up a news server, users on your Intranet or on the Internet can visit your newsgroups, post questions, and read information. There are tens of thousands of public newsgroups existing on the Internet. Newsgroups are popular because they provide an excellent means of sharing ideas. Within an Intranet, discussion groups facilitate communication among workgroups, regardless of where the user is located.

Discussions are facilitated by using threading, so that users who subscribe to a particular newsgroup can easily follow the progression of multiple topics within the newsgroup. Any time a new comment is posted, adjunct replies are threaded onto the original message, usually seen in an indent format, so you can quickly identify where the thought began and what the latest update is. Most newsreaders allow you to also sort the messages for even easier viewing, and provide a catch-up mode, so you can use a view that shows you what is new in the group.

NOTE: Chapter 7 discusses features you might want to look for in a news server.

How It Works

3

The two main actions you perform with your newsreader are posting and viewing messages. Figure 3-8 shows how newsreaders interact with news servers so that posted messages are stored for later viewing. The numbered labels shown in the following list correspond to the labels in Figure 3-8.

1 Your Intranet's news server receives information that has been posted to a news server on the Internet (such as one at an Internet service provider). The Intranet's news server must receive a feed from the news server. It can't request an update.

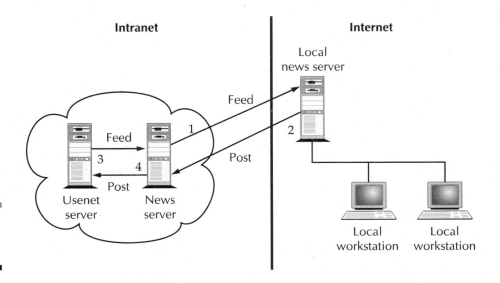

How a news
server works
Figure 3-8.

NOTE: If you are not connected to the Internet, then you simply post messages to your own news server and view the messages residing on it. The messages are never copied to a news server outside of your Intranet.

2   When the feed is received from an Internet news server, the Internet server simultaneously grabs any new posts made to your Intranet's news server.

3   One of the main Usenet news servers feeds the other Internet news servers new messages.

4   Any news posts that the Internet news servers have gathered are also collected at this time and saved to one of the main Usenet news servers.

TIP: By copying all of the posts back to the main Usenet servers, if you post a message to a national newsgroup through your ISP's news server, it is seen by everyone across the country.

A Firewall

One of the biggest challenges of setting up a corporate, Web-centric Intranet is ensuring the security and integrity of the network and the sensitive information contained within that system. Firewall software is another means of securing data stored within your Intranet. This software also provides the flexibility needed with any security mechanism.

How It Fits into Your Intranet

A company's network no longer means simply their in-house LAN; instead, the mobile and global nature of today's work force implies any number of needs beyond sitting at a PC in the home office. You might have employees working out of their homes, or traveling around the world, who need to connect to the Intranet. In some cases, companies even rely on third parties to host their Intranets, if they determine that they simply cannot afford to manage the content in-house. This extended network concept, or "extranet," requires serious consideration to security and protection of information.

A firewall lets you control who is allowed in or out of the network. It acts as a sort of security guard, controlling access to your Intranet. When you are looking for firewall software, be sure that you can easily configure it. You want to be able to fully control people's access. You should be able to specify which IP addresses are allowed in and out. For example, you may want to allow only the IP addresses of remote employees through the firewall.

NOTE: For more information about firewalls, see Chapters 7 and 9.

How It Works

A firewall can be a combination of hardware and software that essentially wraps a computer or computers within a network, as shown in Figure 3-9. You can place computers, such as your external Web server, outside of your firewall, but you would probably place most of your employees and any internal servers inside the firewall to protect them.

Going further than simple packet filtering, or monitoring the headers of the information packets sent between hosts, firewalls can act on the application level to further mask internal systems information. The network manager has firm control over even the types of access that these users can have,

3

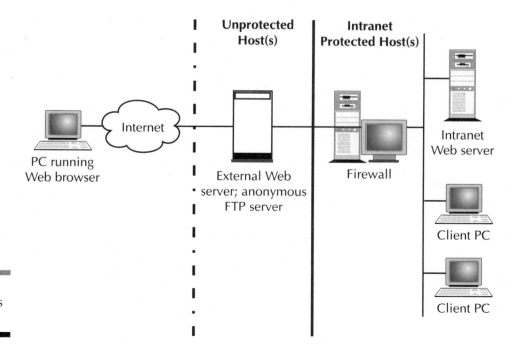

How a
firewall works
Figure 3-9.

whether it be an HTTP or an FTP call. Of course, with this added security layer comes the need to carefully plan where you want sensitive information stored, and how you want your users to be configured. Access to the Internet, for example, becomes a more difficult user configuration when that PC is "behind the firewall."

A Proxy Server

A proxy is another type of server. It's mainly used as a poor-man's firewall to control the use of network resources and to limit access to the Internet. Some companies that are connected to the Internet have problems with employees spending too much time surfing the Internet for non-work-related information. By using a proxy server, you can restrict access to the Internet to as few or as many sites as you deem appropriate.

TIP: You may not want to restrict Internet access unless it becomes absolutely necessary. The Internet is a great place for employees to discover information about competitors and potential customers, so restricting access may also restrict your profits!

How It Fits into Your Intranet

Instead of users sending HTTP, FTP, Gopher, WAIS, or security requests directly to the remote server outside of their domain, the request is sent to the proxy server, which then forwards the request outside the firewall if this access is permitted. Similarly, the reply from the remote host is not delivered directly to the user but sent first to the proxy server, which then delivers the reply to the client.

NOTE: See Chapter 2 for information about HTTP, FTP, Gopher, and WAIS.

This intermediary action and chaperoning by the proxy server can be steadfastly controlled by the network administrator, or Webmaster, who can use the proxy server to deny access to certain resources both inside and outside the firewall. Often, the proxy server is also used to cache (replicate) frequently visited sites, so that users do not have to traverse the Internet each time they want to access the information. The control mechanisms for this type of use vary from server to server, but providing this intermediary cache can indeed improve performance on your network. The proxy server is also a mechanism for logging activity through your Intranet/Internet. This information can be invisible to the end users, if you choose to monitor their activities without their knowledge. Proxy servers can also be used to map to a single externally viewable IP address, shielding others and giving some IP assignment flexibility.

How It Works

As you can see in Figure 3-10, a proxy server exists inside of a firewall. A proxy server is more configurable than a firewall. Generally, firewalls decide only whether or not a packet of information is allowed in or out of the Intranet. A proxy server can be configured to accept particular types of connections. The proxy server and firewall may reside on the same or different computers.

NOTE: See Chapter 9 for more information about proxy servers.

3

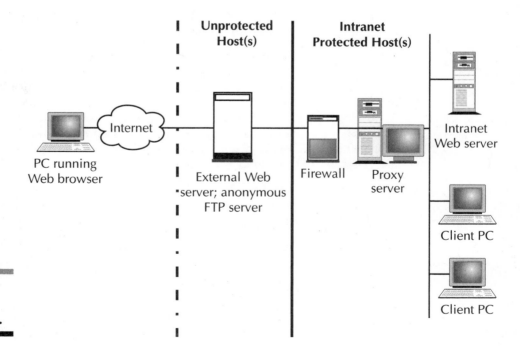

How a proxy
server works
Figure 3-10.

Making Platform Choices

Now that you know about the servers you might want to use in your Intranet, you also need to decide what platform you want to use. In this book, we focus on a Windows NT platform for servers and a Windows 3.1x, 95 or NT platform for the clients. Although these are popular choices for small- to medium-sized companies, using the open standards of TCP/IP you are not tied to one specific platform. You may have a mixture of Intel, Macintosh, and RISC-based machines throughout your Intranet, and they can interact without a problem.

 T IP: You probably want to stick to a platform with which you are comfortable. If you have all Intel-based servers, install an Intel-based Web server. If your servers are RISC-based machines running Unix, install a Unix-based Web server. Fortunately, there are excellent software offerings in all arenas.

Exploring the Key Client Components

Client software makes your servers valuable. After all, what's the point of having a Web server if no one has a browser to access it? The client components of a Web-centric Intranet allow employees to explore the latest technology while using time-saving, productive tools that help them find, sort, and deliver information quickly and effectively.

You want to be sure to purchase the client components that best match your servers, and give the best possible performance to your employees. Though you may purchase the client component from the same vendor as you purchased your server, the open standards of TCP/IP, and the developing standards of the Internet and World Wide Web, make it possible to purchase any vendor's software that complies with the standards. In other words, you can use one vendor's server, another's browser, and still another's HTML editor.

 T IP: All-in-one solutions give the user a common look and feel that may lower training costs and increase productivity.

Web Browsers

A Web browser is a client application used to retrieve and display documents. Most documents, called Web pages, are written using HTML, which is the standard language for Web page creation. There are a number of different Web browsers available. They all share the capability of retrieving and displaying HTML documents; but beyond that basic capability, the features of each browser may vary widely. Web browsers are available for a variety of different hardware platforms such as PC's, Apple, and RISC, and operating systems such as Microsoft Windows, Mac OS, and Unix. Because of the wide variety of options, it is fairly easy to add browser technology to an existing computer environment or obtain one for a new environment.

The Browser Advantage

Because Web browsers are so readily available and can so easily fit into almost any Intranet environment, they are an ideal tool for users to find and display information on your Intranet. Even if you have many different kinds of computers and operating systems in your Intranet, you can probably find a browser that works on each one. This means that your Intranet is accessible from anywhere, not just from a few computers that must be shared by everyone. If each user has a PC or workstation on his or her desktop, they can have a Web browser and access the information available on your Intranet.

3

NOTE: The history of browsers is covered in Chapter 2.

Internet Explorer and Netscape Navigator

Two popular browsers in the PC environment are Microsoft's Internet Explorer, shown in Figure 3-11, and Netscape's Navigator, shown in Figure 3-12. Both applications offer many features above and beyond basic document retrieval, display, and navigation. They support the advanced display features of HTML, such as tables and frames, and other advanced features, like ActiveX, Java, JavaScript, and security. Navigator is available for more hardware platforms and for more operating systems, although there are plans to make versions of Internet Explorer for more platforms as well.

TIP: A key advantage of Internet Explorer is that it is free, and the final (as opposed to beta) releases of Navigator are not. In a PC environment, using Windows 95 or Windows NT, either one of these browsers can be sure to support all of the latest features, providing you with the latest technology. Therefore, the real decision may come down to price and availability.

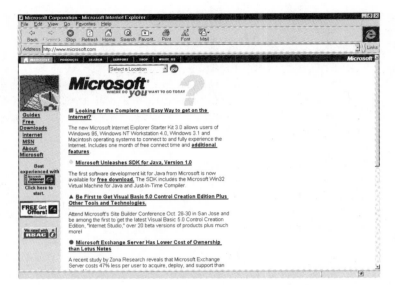

Microsoft's
Internet
Explorer
Figure 3-11.

Browsers from Other Vendors

Besides these two Web browsers, there are many other less well-known
browsers available. Other companies have created their own browsers,
perhaps for inclusion in a suite of Internet or Intranet applications or to fill
some particular niche in the market. Generally, they do not have all of the
graphic display features available in Internet Explorer or Navigator, but they
may have other features that appeal to users. For example, Frontier

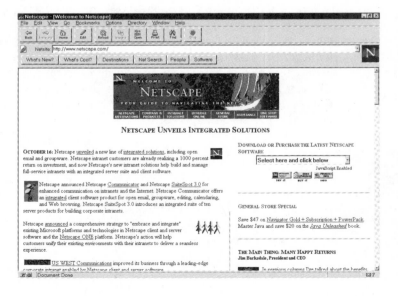

Netscape's
Navigator
Gold
Figure 3-12.

Technologies' Tapestry browser has a feature called the Internet Organizer, shown in Figure 3-13, which allows users to easily organize and catalog their favorite sites in an intuitive and logical way. While Tapestry does not offer the range of functionality and support that Internet Explorer and Navigator do, it does offer a great organizational feature that has kept people using it even when these more popular browsers are available.

Using Multiple Browsers

With all of these choices, it is not necessary to restrict yourself to a single browser. Some of the more popular browsers are available for free, eliminating any cost factor when deciding which browsers to use. Just as you may have multiple text editors available on your desktop, such as Notepad, WordPad, and Microsoft Word, each of which serves different functions, you may decide to have multiple browsers available to you, each filling a specific need. Find the browsers you like, and stay tuned to all of the competitors' Web sites. In a changing browser market, the major players are constantly updating their products, making new options available every day.

Electronic Mail (E-Mail)

E-mail applications, such as the one shown in Figure 3-14, are used to compose, send, view, and manage electronic mail messages. A typical session involves reviewing any new messages that are in your in-box, responding to them, and creating and sending any new messages.

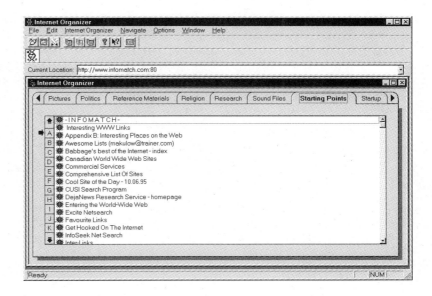

The Internet
Organizer in
Tapestry
Figure 3-13.

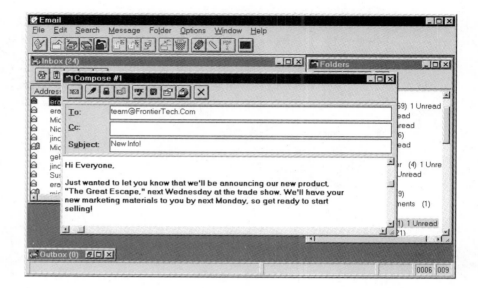

An e-mail
application
from Frontier
Technologies
Figure 3-14.

The SMTP Protocol

Current e-mail clients support the SMTP mail protocol which, in turn, can
support Multipurpose Internet Mail Extension (MIME) file attachments,
which allow you to attach a variety of special files to your messages. Special
files may include spreadsheet files, database files, and even digital audio and
video files.

S/MIME E-Mail

If you want to send and receive secure e-mail, you can use S/MIME. S/MIME
provides the means for e-mail to be encrypted from the time it leaves
the sender's computer until the time it reaches the recipient's computer.
In its current configuration, S/MIME allows you to send someone who is
using an e-mail application that supports S/MIME a signed message. Once a
person has received this message from you, they can send you encrypted
messages. You can also send encrypted messages once someone sends you
a signed message.

NOTE: Chapter 9 discusses the details of S/MIME security.

Newsreaders

Usenet, the Internet news system, is made up of news and information databases around the world. Internal discussion groups can function as a central meeting place of ideas on a wide range of topics. The application the user employs to connect to the NNTP news server is called a newsreader, shown in Figure 3-15. You can use the newsreader to read, reply, or post new messages to a specific group. The interface typically resembles an e-mail interface, but unlike a user's e-mail in-box, newsreader postings are not stored on the client computer but rather on the server. Newsreaders also provide the functions of including attachments and checking spelling.

Working with Content-Creation Tools

3

In order to make your Intranet truly useful, you need to have solid content for your employees to use. To help you with the creation of this content, you can turn to many of the tools already on the market. Some of these tools have been designed specifically for a Web-centric Intranet, while others are old favorites that fit smoothly into your new Intranet.

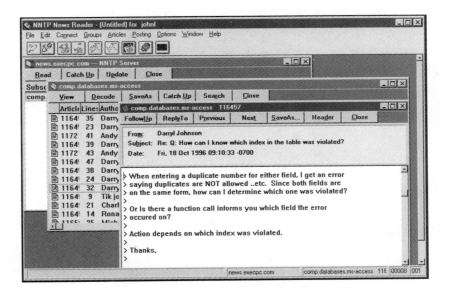

A newsreader application from Frontier Technologies

Figure 3-15.

TIP: When you are looking for content-creation tools, be sure to ask your employees what capabilities they think they need, and why the software they mention is the ideal product. Though you may not be able to supply them with everything on their wish list, you can at least determine what features your employees think are crucial in their software.

HTML Editors

Hypertext Markup Language (HTML) is used to create Web pages stored on the Web server and viewed by the Web browser. In the early days of the World Wide Web, HTML was written in longhand code, and many enthusiasts still prefer this method to the new breed of editors available on the market today. Because the standards for this format change so rapidly, the ability to code in raw mode HTML remains a plus, so that the latest and greatest *tags*, or codes, can be included in a document. In that way, even if your current authoring tool doesn't support a new tag, you can still add the tag into the HTML file so the browser recognizes it (provided the browser also supports the tag!).

WYSIWYG Solutions

In addition to products that help you code in HTML, there are an ever-increasing number of applications that support the idea that the HTML code should be invisible to the user. These WYSIWYG solutions make creating a Web page less intimidating. WYSIWYG editors, such as the one shown in Figure 3-16, act similar to word processing software, such as Microsoft Word. The users don't even have to know the tag name; they simply need to know that they want to draw a line across the page, for example. With a click of a button, the line appears on the page. The code that created the line is completely invisible.

NOTE: You can find WebDesigner on the CD-ROM with this book.

The Interactive Nature of HTML

So what is it that makes HTML documents on the Web server different than, say, word processing documents in a traditional file manager? The most exciting difference is the interactive nature of HTML. Links within documents, whether plain text or graphical, can connect to other documents on the server, allowing users to quickly access exactly what

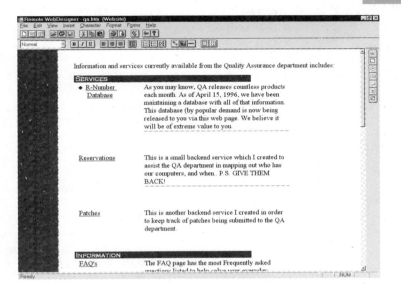

A WYSIWYG HTML editor called WebDesigner
Figure 3-16.

3

they want. HTML pages can also include forms that users fill out and submit to a database via a back-end service on the server.

Document-Conversion Tools

Less ubiquitous than HTML authoring tools are document filters, which allow you to take an existing document and convert it into HTML format. Document conversion prevents the reinventing-the-wheel syndrome: you need HTML content, but you don't want to lose all the time you've invested with other electronic document creation. You can simply convert the document using the software, instantly creating an HTML page.

TIP: Be sure to select the appropriate converter. For example, Blue Sky Software has a product that converts Help files into HTML files, but it would not be appropriate for spreadsheets.

The Hyperlink Solution

Not all documents necessarily need to be converted into HTML. Instead, you can create a hyperlink from another HTML page to a spreadsheet or word processing document. When users click on the link, the file is opened in the appropriate viewer if the users have one on their computers.

Formatting Issues

HTML does lend itself nicely to linking and a more graphical representation of information, so converting, for example, your employee manual from a word processing to an HTML format certainly makes sense. Some documents may be better kept in their native format. Perhaps you have a document consisting of many specially formatted tables. Though this document can be converted to HTML, you might lose some of the special formatting.

Graphics Editors

Various graphics formats are supported by today's browsers, including Graphics Interchange Format (GIF), Joint Photographic Experts Group (JPEG), Bitmap (BMP), Tagged Image File Format (TIFF), and others. Of all of these, GIFs and JPEGs are the most common formats that you can find on the Intranet. There are many excellent graphics editors that can be used to construct the visual components. The expression that "a picture is worth a thousand words" is especially true when organizing your Intranet. When used wisely, graphics can make your site more interesting and more functional.

Traditional Graphics Tools

There are traditional tools like CorelDRAW, Corel PhotoPaint, Adobe Illustrator, and Adobe Photoshop that have been standards in the graphics industry for years. Most have enhanced their capability to accommodate Web graphic development.

T IP: One useful feature of traditional graphics tools is their ability to save files in a GIF format. Using GIFs allows you to choose a color within the graphic that is considered transparent by browsers. In other words, the background color or image on the Web page is displayed in the transparent areas of the GIF. You can also animate GIFs with programs such as Microsoft's GIF Animator, found at their Web site (http://www.microsoft.com). Browsers that support animated GIFs cycle through a series of images contained in one GIF file, giving the illusion of animation.

Raster Versus Vector Editors

Graphics editors are generally broken up into two types, raster and vector image editors. CorelDRAW, shown in Figure 3-17, and Adobe Illustrator are examples of vector editors, while Corel PhotoPaint and Adobe Photoshop, shown in Figure 3-18, are examples of raster editors.

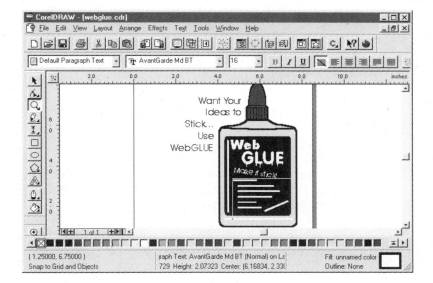

Editing a
vector image
in CorelDRAW
Figure 3-17.

3

How Vector Editors Work In the vector image editors, the drawing is
composed of objects that can be represented by geometric formulas. Because
they are mathematical representations of a square, line, or other shape, you
can re-size the graphics by stretching them on the screen and letting the
program recalculate the formulas. You always get perfectly shaped objects,
no matter what size you choose.

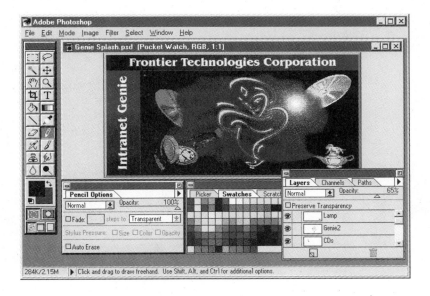

Editing a raster
image in
Photoshop
Figure 3-18.

TIP: Vector image editors are good for creating graphics such as logos or line art. You can scale your logo to the appropriate size without distorting the image. Vector editors are also helpful when there is a large amount of text incorporated into your graphic. Because the text is an independent object, you can always reopen the graphic and edit the text.

The Raster Image Advantage   Although vector editors give you the advantage of scalability, you probably want to use a raster editor to give you the power to express your creativity. Raster editors view the image as a series of colored dots. Since there are no underlying mathematical formulas, when you shrink or stretch an image, the program can only make its best attempt to make the image fit the new size. You can generally get acceptable results if you attempt to shrink an image. When you stretch an image, you probably get a pixelated appearance, where the original smooth lines and curves have a jagged look to them. The advantage is that there is a huge array of special effects you can achieve using some of the filters and plug-ins available for most raster editors. Some more common filters blur the image or adjust the contrast and brightness. Some filters allow you to show different light sources pointed on the image.

TIP: In many cases, you may want to begin your image in a vector editor and cut and paste the image to a raster editor to add the final touches.

Saving in GIF or JPEG

When you are satisfied with your graphic, you should save your masterpiece as either a GIF or a JPEG. Both of these file formats are actual raster formats, so in the process of saving your images, they are converted to raster images. Make sure you save a copy of your graphic in the program's native format (.CDR for CorelDRAW, .AI for Adobe Illustrator) before you save it as a GIF or JPEG. If you intend to alter the graphic at a later date, you need the native vector format to alter the individual objects.

NOTE: You can also save your files in either TIFF or BMP format. However, the majority of Web page creators today use GIF or JPEG files. Also, more browsers support GIF and JPEG files than they do TIFF and BMP.

Image Map Editors

Have you even been surfing the Internet and run across a Web page that has a picture you can click on? Even more exciting, have you seen images that link you to different pages depending on which area of the image you click on? You can add such user-friendly, visually appealing images to your own HTML documents by using an image map editor, such as the one in Figure 3-19.

NOTE: The CD-ROM, included with this book, comes with ImageMaster. Your Web server software also might come with an image map editor, as might HTML editors.

3

A map file works with the image file to make clickable areas. The map file is a text file that contains definitions of image regions along with their corresponding universal resource locators (URLs). The displayed regions are geometrical figures such as circles, polygons, or triangles. For example, you might see *circle (50, 50) 70 \some.htm* in a map file, which tells you the image has a circle defined on it. If users see the image in a browser and click on this area, the page *some.htm* is displayed. One map file can contain many definitions such as this one.

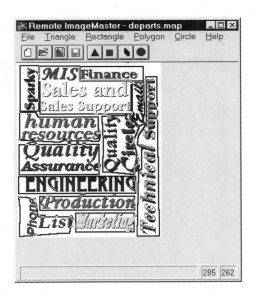

An image map editor called ImageMaster
Figure 3-19.

Hyperlink Checkers

To ensure that all links in your HTML files work properly, you can use a hyperlink checker application. You can easily check all of your links so that your Web users won't encounter links that don't connect properly. Bad links can be caused by someone entering in a link incorrectly, or perhaps someone unintentionally deleting the referenced page.

TIP: You might want to check the hyperlinks in all of your Web site's pages as a part of routine maintenance. Often, hyperlinks, especially external links, may be altered without your knowledge. To ensure that people accessing your Web pages (especially customers) don't ever encounter bad hyperlinks, you can run a hyperlink checker once a week or once a month on all of your Web site's pages.

Most hyperlink checker applications also allow you to check external links. For example, in Figure 3-20, you can select whether or not to check external links. Because Web sites change so frequently, having an invalid link to someone else's Web site can easily happen.

NOTE: The CD-ROM, included with this book, comes with HyperCheck.

The hyperlink
checker
application
called
HyperCheck
Figure 3-20.

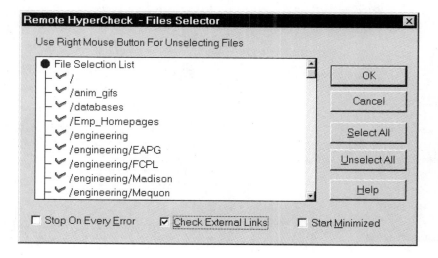

Creating Back-End Services

Maybe you have the basic client and server pieces on your Intranet. However, you want to make your company as efficient as possible, or perhaps you want customers accessing your Web site to be awestruck by the creativity and usefulness of the information. If you fall into any of these categories, then you are ready to begin customizing your Web-centric Intranet with back-end services.

TIP: If you don't have the time or don't want to learn how to program your own back-end services, try to get Web server software that includes ready-to-run or easy-to-customize back ends. You might also check on the Internet. Some companies offer free back-end services for you to download. They may call them by a different name, such as server extensions or server applications.

3

HTML pages can display images and text, and link to other Web pages. However, without creating back-end services, or executable programs, to run on the Web server, the development of your Web site is limited. Using back-end services created with Internet Server Application Programming Interface (ISAPI), Common Gateway/Windows Common Gateway Interface (CGI/WinCGI), Netscape Server Application Programming Interface (NSAPI), or other application program interfaces (APIs), you can make your Web site more interactive and useful for visitors.

NOTE: While CGI, ISAPI, and NSAPI represent the lion's share of server back-end interfaces, individual servers also may have additional APIs to help you extend that particular server's capabilities.

The HTML Form

Anything a C, C++, Pascal, or Visual Basic (VB) program can do, so too can a back-end service. The only limit is the HTML interface. How does HTML fit into the picture? In order to get data from a user, you need to create a form in HTML, like the one in Figure 3-21, so Web users can enter their data. Without the form, you can't get the data from the user to use in your back-end service. Conversely, without the back-end service, you can't do anything with the data you get from a user who fills out a form.

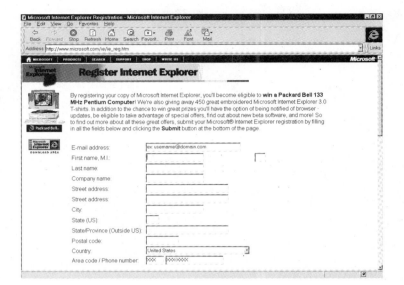

A sample
HTML form
Figure 3-21.

 TIP: You can use an HTML editor to help create a form, if you don't know HTML.

What Back-End Services Do

You might create a service to determine key information about a user and return a different page based on that information. Perhaps you have a database of product information that you want customers to be able to access. You could create a back-end service that helps customers who visit your Web site customize a database query. Suppose you own a software company and you want your Web site's visitors to find out what product is best for them. You can have them fill out a form answering specific questions about their needs. When they press the Submit button, then your back-end service could take over, querying a database using the criteria the visitor gave. The visitor would then see an HTML page with the appropriate products listed.

Using CGI

Standard CGI—which can be written in many languages, including Perl, Pascal, C, and C++—gets data from a user by means of protected or locked environment variables. The data is taken from a form and placed into these environment variables, as shown in Figure 3-22. The interface, in this case, is these variables.

Often times, people use CGI if they are bringing a program over from a Unix system. Standard CGI uses environment variables and *stdio*, or standard input and output, to transfer data to and from the CGI program. For example, you might have a form where the user enters query criteria to use on your database. Once the user has filled in the information and clicked the Query button, the data entered is placed into the environment variables. The program that performs the query on the database uses these variables when executing. After the query has been performed, the program creates an HTML document to send back to the user by using standard output (for example, by outputting one line of the HTML document at a time to the user).

3

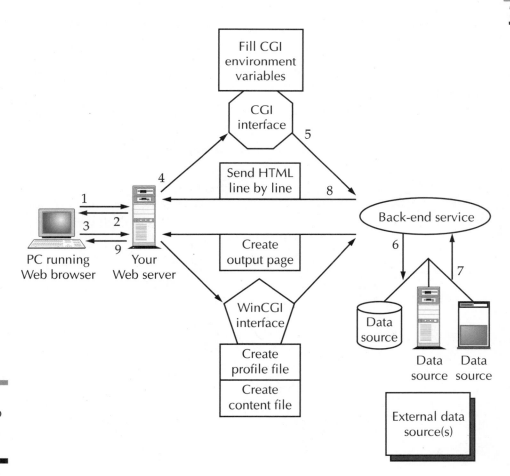

CGI/WinCGI
and your Web
server
Figure 3-22.

TIP: Standard CGI back ends can be written in any language that can create an executable file and can access environment variables.

WinCGI

Windows CGI (WinCGI) is used for many programs written for Windows platform Web servers because it is more closely related to Windows. You can write these CGI programs using any Windows programming environment, including but not limited to Visual Basic, C, or C++. WinCGI was originally developed to enable Visual Basic programmers to create back-end services. Visual Basic can't access environment variables, so a new interface needed to be created. WinCGI places data into temporary files instead of environment variables, as shown in Figure 3-22.

How CGI/WinCGI Works

Take a look at Figure 3-22 to see how a CGI or WinCGI back-end service interfaces with your Web server. The numbered labels in this list correspond to the labels shown in the figure.

1 A person running a Web browser on a computer enters, in the URL of a page on your Web server, an address such as:

http://www.frontiertech.com/demo.htm

2 The server transfers back the requested HTML page, which contains a form requesting the name, address, and request of the Web user.

3 The Web user enters the information into the form and clicks a Submit button, which sends the data to the Web server.

4 The server places the data into a storage area, which is dependent on the type of back-end service.

A WinCGI Program   For a WinCGI program, the server creates 2 files with the .TMP extension, which is the conceptual CGI interface. The two files are

♦ The profile file, which contains data from, or file pointers to, the HTML form.

♦ The content file, which can contain custom data from the specific server implementations according to the CGI standard. In addition, if the form data normally placed in the profile file exceeds 64K, then it is placed into the content file.

A CGI Program   For a CGI program, the data is placed into environment variables.

5 From this point on, the server has no knowledge of what occurs. The server simply waits for the service to return data. The data is sent to the back-end service. When the back-end service receives this file, it selects the data it needs from it.

6 The back-end service may interface to an external data source (for example, an SQL call to a database or a local user-defined file access).

7 In the event of an external data source interaction, data might be retrieved from this external data source.

8 The back-end service creates data that is returned to the user via the interface. The interface delivers the back-end-service-created data from step 8 (shown in Figure 3-22) to the Web server.

NOTE: With a CGI service, the data is returned line by line, or standard output. With a WinCGI service, the data is returned in one file.

9 The server sends the output data from the service to the Web user. For example, the Web user might see an HTML page that thanks the person for filling out the form.

Using ISAPI

Developed by Microsoft and Process software, the Internet Server Application Programming Interface (ISAPI) is quickly becoming a Web server standard for back-end service development. Faster and more efficient than CGI or WinCGI, ISAPI extensions offer developers a chance to push the performance of back-end services even further.

NOTE: CGI and WinCGI programs are actually executable programs that run on the same computer as your Web server. Every time a Web user clicks, for example, the Submit button on a form, the executable runs. If another Web user clicked the Submit button, another instance of the program would run.

3

Dynamic Link Libraries

In contrast, ISAPI extensions are dynamic link libraries (DLLs), not executables. The DLLs actually function as a part of the Web server. They are ready to run on command! If a request isn't made for them within a certain time frame, then the DLL is unloaded from memory to free up space. An ISAPI program should be *thread-safe*, which means that the DLL can be called by multiple threads. When multiple threads are used on your Web server, a new instance does *not* have to be opened every time a request for the back-end service is made. The same process is used—just a new thread. With CGI, a new process is started with every request. Thus, ISAPI involves less overhead than CGI programming, making it more efficient with respect to speed and memory.

Creating an ISAPI Extension

ISAPI extensions are more complicated to write than CGI or WinCGI back ends. Because you are creating a DLL than runs within the Web server, you need to be extra careful about cleaning up after yourself. If you don't properly terminate an ISAPI extension, it can crash your Web server! Therefore, test your extension thoroughly before running it on your live server. Use the debugging utilities included with your programming tools.

TIP: Some Web server software comes with special debugging applications, such as the SuperWeb Debug Server on the CD-ROM included with this book, that allow you to run your extension on a Web server, other than your live server, for testing purposes.

You can use any programming tool to create an ISAPI extension that allows you to create a DLL including, but not limited to, C, C++, and Pascal.

NOTE: If you are familiar with Visual Basic, you may be wondering how you can use it to create an ISAPI extension. Though it is possible, you would have to obtain the OLE ISAPI extension from Microsoft.

The Files You Need

There are also special files you need to download from the Microsoft Web site at http://www.microsoft.com. Be sure to get the following files before starting on your first project. These files are standard and should not change often. Therefore, if you download them once, you probably only need to check back on Microsoft's site every couple of months or so.

♦ *HTTPEXT.H* The ISAPI header file that defines data structures that ISAPI uses. The file is required only for C and C++ programmers. Other languages have their own mechanisms for defining the ISAPI header.

♦ *HTML.H* A header file used for HTML output commands. You can use these commands to output HTML into your return document with little work (recommended).

♦ *HTML.CPP* The source file for the HTML commands previously mentioned (recommended).

♦ *KEYS.H* A header file used for key processing in an ISAPI back end. Keys in this case refer to data that the Web server gives you when it calls into the ISAPI back end (recommended).

♦ *KEYS.CPP* The source file for the key processing commands previously mentioned (recommended).

NOTE: Only the first file, HTTPEXT.H, is required in a C/C++ environment. The others are extras provided for enhancement of your programs. If you use the ISAPI wizards in Microsoft Visual C++ (MSVC) 4.2, then you probably don't need to use the extra files, because Microsoft Foundation Classes (MFC) provides better macros for extracting or outputting data in ISAPI.

Using NSAPI

The Netscape Server API (NSAPI) is an extension that allows you to extend and/or customize the core functionality of Netscape server products and is to Netscape's products what ISAPI is to Microsoft's. Like ISAPI, an extension written using NSAPI runs within the Web server instead of creating a separate application, saving the Web server's resources. Any client can connect to a Netscape Web server and run a NSAPI back end. However, a back end written using NSAPI only runs on a Netscape Web server, at this time. If you are comfortable with Netscape servers, and have no intention of switching to another, then writing back ends using NSAPI is to your advantage.

With NSAPI, you are using an API designed specifically to create back ends to run on your Netscape server, so the back ends can optimize the server's features. If you plan to use the back ends on more than one Web server, or you plan on switching to another Web server, then you probably want to use ISAPI to create your back ends simply because more Web servers support ISAPI.

TIP: If you own a Netscape Web server, and want to create customized back ends using NSAPI, then visit Netscape's Web site at http://www.netscape.com or http://Developer.netscape.com to learn about the header files you can use when creating the extensions.

Development Platform Technologies

The world of Web client/server development is rapidly advancing, and it may be difficult to keep up with all the new technological advancements. While you can't possibly know everything about every advancement, it is important to know the basics of those technologies that are here to stay. While the development field continues to shake out, let's identify some core development platform technologies.

Working with ActiveX

Though HTML continues to expand more and more each day, it still does not satisfy the needs of all Web users. For example, what if you have created a flashy PowerPoint slide show that took you weeks to get just right? You can always convert the demonstration to HTML, but you may lose some of your great formatting. Ideally, you want people browsing on your Web site to open the demonstration. You can do so by creating a link to the PowerPoint file. If the user has the application on his or her system, then PowerPoint opens. What if someone doesn't have PowerPoint, or what if someone gets confused by having to move between two applications instead of staying inside of the browser? This is where ActiveX comes in!

Running Applications Within Browsers

Using ActiveX, you can actually launch an application inside of a browser. The application doesn't need to be installed on the client's computer; it only needs to be present on the Web server. In the example shown in Figure 3-23, you could actually launch PowerPoint inside of someone's browser. They would even see the toolbars. This not only means that users don't have to open up another application, it also means that they don't even need the application on their computers! No longer do you have to limit the content on your HTML pages because Web users may not have a particular image file viewer on their computer. As long as you have the application on the Web server, you can create or use an existing ActiveX control to send the application over the Internet to the Web users' browser, allowing users to interact with the application.

A PowerPoint
demonstration
viewed in
Internet
Explorer
Figure 3-23.

3

NOTE: ActiveX can be used inside applications other than a browser.
Microsoft Binder is a great example. When you use Binder, you can open a
document from any of the Microsoft Office applications and save documents
of different file types—but related information—into virtual binders.

What Is ActiveX?

ActiveX controls are a somewhat stripped-down version of Microsoft's
Object Linking and Embedding (OLE) controls called *Component Object Model*
(COM) controls. The controls act as a wrapper around your code, as shown
in Figure 3-24. The controls interface between your code and the container
(such as a browser) in which it is running.

NOTE: At the time of this writing, Microsoft is using Windows
controls for ActiveX. This means that ActiveX controls will not run on
other platforms. However, keep your eyes open, because Microsoft has
released ActiveX to an open standards body, allowing it to be ported
to other platforms.

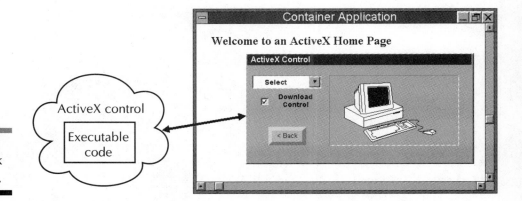

How ActiveX
controls work
Figure 3-24.

Running an ActiveX Control

When you encounter an ActiveX control on a Web page, certain files are
automatically downloaded to your hard drive. This means that you need to
endure the download time, which may be significant if you have a slow
Internet connection. Once you have these files on your computer, the next
time you view the same Web page, you can immediately run the ActiveX
control because you have already downloaded it.

CAUTION: Because files are being copied to your hard drive, you
need to be absolutely certain that you can trust the site you are visiting.
You should configure your browser to prompt you when you encounter
any ActiveX controls, so that you can decide if the site is trustworthy
enough to download a file. People could create controls that wreak havoc
on your computer!

If you visit another Web page, you may or may not need to download the
control. If the Web site is using a control that you happen to have
downloaded already, then no additional files are copied to your hard drive,
so you don't have to wait. The control can run as quickly as if you had the
application installed on your hard drive, depending on the speed of your
Internet connection.

TIP: For more information about ActiveX, visit Microsoft's Web site at
http://www.microsoft.com or http:// microsoft.com/devonly/.

Working with Java

Another name you'll be hearing a lot of is Java. Introduced by Sun Microsystems, Inc., Java is quickly becoming the hottest new programming language on the market. Developed by a group of people who wanted a language similar to C++—but stripped of redundancy and cumbersome features (such as pointers)—Java is for those who want to create programs (called *applets*) that are robust, secure, and platform independent.

 NOTE: People sometimes confuse Java and ActiveX because they both let users run programs from their browsers. Java is a programming *language* like C or Pascal. You use it to write code. ActiveX, on the other hand, is a programming *interface*. You don't actually write code in ActiveX; rather, it is a wrapper around the code that acts as the translator between the code and the container, which is an application such as a browser.

3

Common Usage

What many people are using Java for today is to create applets for the Internet. The applets are either inserted onto the Web pages and run when the user accesses the page, or they are accessed by a hyperlink that starts the applet. One of the most common examples of a Java applet is having a scrolling banner run across the top of your Web page. You can also create much more complex programs using Java. Sun is working on network administrative tools written in Java. Chat applications are also being created in Java.

Compiling Java

When Java code is compiled, you don't have a ready-to-run executable file. Instead, you have what is called *bytecode*. This code is one level higher than the *binary* compiled code created by traditional compilers used in, for example, C and C++. When you create binary compiled code, you need to compile it for each platform you are going to run the application on. If you want an application to run on Windows, Unix, and Macintosh, then you need to compile the code three separate times, creating three separate executable files, as shown in Figure 3-25.

Java code is compiled only to the bytecode stage. When you run the code, the Java interpreter, sometimes known as the *Virtual Machine*, essentially finishes the compiling job based on the platform on which you are attempting to run the application. This means that the exact same file can

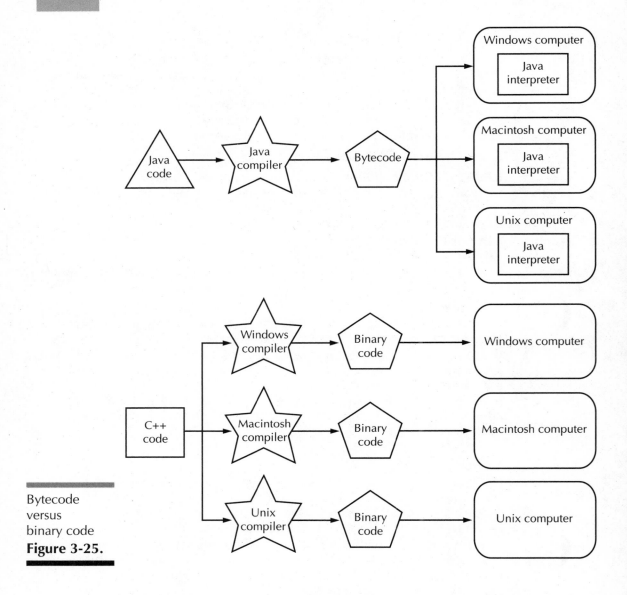

Bytecode
versus
binary code
Figure 3-25.

be used no matter what the platform. Those using a Web browser on a
Macintosh computer are running the same file as those browsing from a
Windows platform. It is just interpreted differently at run time.

NOTE: Java interpreters can be included with software. For example, browsers that support Java have built-in interpreters. If your company were to create a Java application to sell to others, then you could include a Java interpreter that would be copied to the person's hard drive and configured so that when your Java-written application runs, it finds and uses your interpreter.

Compiling at run time also means that only the classes (objects) that are needed are loaded into memory. When calls are made to classes, then they are loaded into memory. If you were to create a DLL file, such as is traditionally used by Windows applications, then you would need to load all of the classes into memory at once, since they are all contained in the DLL. Even if you only needed to use one of the classes, the entire DLL is loaded into memory.

3

NOTE: Though this architecture allows you to create platform-independent applications, some may run slightly slower than a traditional executable file because part of the compiling is done at run time instead of before the application ever reaches the end user.

Automatic Garbage Collecting

One of Java's features is automatic garbage collecting. Those using C and C++ run into problems when trying to handle how their programs utilize memory. They have to be sure to write code that explicitly cleans up after itself or frees up any memory it uses while running. Java avoids this problem by creating a low-priority background thread that automatically frees the memory when it is no longer in use.

CAUTION: Some programmers might run into problems if they are writing code in Java that is CPU (Central Processing Unit) intensive. Because you can no longer explicitly direct the program to free up memory, the program might run out of memory before the automatic garbage collector runs. However, Java was not created for writing programs of this nature, so keep this in mind when deciding in what language to develop a project.

An Object-Oriented Language

Java is an *object-oriented* language. This paradigm, which users of C++ are familiar with, allows software engineers to create blocks of code that can be reused in different applications. The objects are not a part of the source file. Instead, they are loaded into memory only when the program calls the object, saving the memory resources of the computer running the Java application. Unlike C++, Java forces you to use object-oriented design in your programs. Though C++ allows you to use object-oriented design, the language doesn't force you to use it like Java does.

NOTE: Object-oriented programming is centered around the data instead of the tools used to manipulate the data. Code is broken into objects, or small sections, which can be called on to perform tasks when needed. For example, you might have an object that computes the summation of a group of numbers. You can call this object with code written to add up sales totals, and you can also call the object with code used to add up the weights of fish. The final programs are used for totally unrelated tasks, but the object is created to manipulate data in a particular fashion.

Java-Enabled Browsers

Browsers such as Sun's HotJava, Netscape Navigator, and Microsoft's Internet Explorer have built-in support for the Java language. In order to run Java applets, you must be using a browser that has such support. If you try to run an applet in a browser that doesn't support Java, then you are basically using an English-speaking browser to communicate with a Greek applet. The two simply can't understand each other! A browser needs to recognize the HTML tags for Java applets, or the applet can't run.

TIP: Visit Sun Microsystem's JavaSoft Web site at http://www.java.sun. com for lots of detailed information about Java and Java-enabled browsers.

Working with JavaScript

JavaScript is for those who have little to no programming experience, yet want to make their Web pages more functional and exciting. As the name implies, JavaScript is actually a scripting language. It is similar to a programming language, but there are some differences. Scripting languages are not compiled into either bytecode or binary code. Instead, the code itself is sent, which is then interpreted by the application using the script. In the

3

case of JavaScript, the code is actually embedded in HTML pages between HTML <SCRIPT> tags, as shown in the following HTML sample. The code flags the browser, indicating the presence of code that needs to be translated.

```
<HTML>
<HEAD>
<TITLE>Menu
</TITLE>
</HEAD>
<BASE TARGET="BODY">

<script language="JavaScript">

<!-- Begin code
//
function scrollit_r21(seed)
{
var m1 = "Welcome to Frontier's Finance department home page! ";
 var m2 = "Please look around and tell us what you think of our new digs.
";
var m3 = "Coming soon...Solomon on-line!!!!!! ";

var m4 = "Send your comments to webmaster@frontiertech.com ";

var msg=m1+m2+m3+m4;
var out = " ";
var c = 1;

if (seed > 100) {
seed--;
var cmd="scrollit_r21(" + seed + ")";
timerTwo=window.setTimeout(cmd,100);
}
else if (seed <= 100 && seed > 0) {
for (c=0 ; c < seed ; c++) {
out+=" ";
}
out+=msg;
seed--;
var cmd="scrollit_r21(" + seed + ")";
window.status=out;
timerTwo=window.setTimeout(cmd,100);

}
else if (seed <= 0) {
if (-seed < msg.length) {
out+=msg.substring(-seed,msg.length);
seed--;
```

```
var cmd="scrollit_r21(" + seed + ")";
window.status=out;
timerTwo=window.setTimeout(cmd,100);
}
else {
window.status=" ";
timerTwo=window.setTimeout("scrollit_r21(100)",75);
}
}


}

// -- End code -->

</script>

</BODY>
</HTML>
```

 TIP: See Netscape's Web site at http://home.netscape.com/eng/mozilla/ 2.0/handbook/ javascript for more information about JavaScript. You can also search Netscape's site at http://www.netscape.com for more information.

JavaScript Versus Java

A programming language, such as Java, is more extensible than a scripting language. For example, you can use any objects you create in a Java applet. With a scripting language, you can only use the objects supplied to you by the container in which you are calling the language. For example, if you are using JavaScript in a browser, you can only use the objects supplied to you by the browser, such as those that deal with buttons, forms, frames, and anchors (hyperlinks).

Though their names sound similar, JavaScript differs from Java in the following ways:

♦ JavaScript is based on other scripting languages such as HyperTalk. Java is a full-blown programming language like C++.

♦ JavaScript supports global functions, while Java uses classes.

♦ JavaScript is object based, whereas Java is object oriented. This means that JavaScript can use objects provided by the container in which it is executing (such as a browser), but it can't create other classes like Java can.

♦ JavaScript isn't compiled, while Java is compiled into bytecode. However, they both need to use an interpreter in order to run.

Relational Database Connectivity

Integrating your Web server with an existing database on a PC, minicomputer, or mainframe adds powerful capabilities to your Intranet. Most companies keep important data in some form of a database. It may be a spreadsheet, text file, or an SQL database. The challenge is fast and easy delivery of the data. There are different ways of accessing database information with applications. The first implementations of database connectivity relied on a proprietary API provided by the database vendor or, in some cases, a third-party driver.

NOTE: This section provides more information about linking your Web server with a database on a PC. If you have a legacy database on a minicomputer or mainframe, see Chapter 10 for more information about integrating your Web server with your legacy database.

3

Open Database Connectivity (ODBC)

ODBC was developed by Microsoft and has become a standard. ODBC provides a common way for an application to access a wide range of relational databases.

Setting Up an ODBC Driver

To set up an ODBC driver, you define the database source. In essence, this is giving the database a nickname or alias that the host computer relates to the actual database location. The following steps show how easy it is to set up an ODBC driver in Windows 95 to an existing database:

1. In Windows 95, click Start, Settings, and then Control Panel.
2. Double-click on the ODBC icon shown in the following dialog box.

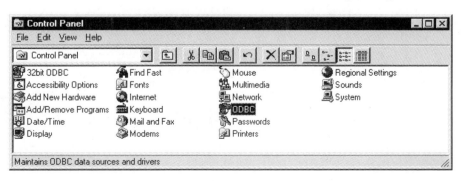

3. Highlight the type of database you want to add. If you have a proprietary ODBC driver, click the Drivers button and choose your driver. Click Add in the Data Sources dialog box shown here.

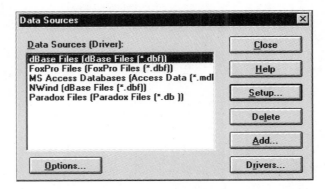

4. In the Add Data Source dialog box, shown here, click on the type of ODBC driver you want to add, and then click OK.

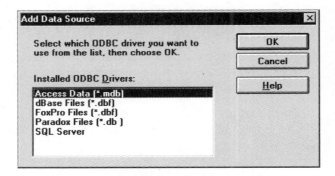

5. Enter the data source name and description in the ODBC Microsoft Access Setup dialog box, shown here, and click the Select Database button.

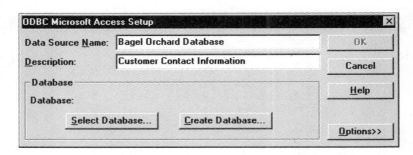

6. Click on the database dialog box, shown here, click on the database you want to use, and click OK.

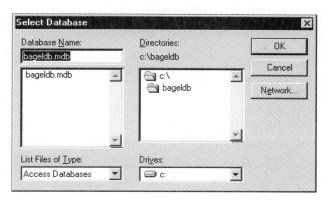

3

7. Click OK in the ODBC Microsoft Access Setup dialog box, shown here.

8. Click Close in the Data Sources dialog box, shown here.

Using an ODBC Driver

Once you have named your database, there is a list of standard commands that applications can send to your database through an ODBC driver to perform common database tasks. Since the requests to the database are made using the ODBC standard, it makes no difference to the application which database you are using. Your application simply refers to the database by the alias you have assigned it. For example, you can design your application using a desktop database and then substitute your enterprise database when the application goes online.

If your company outgrows its current database and switches to a different database engine, you should be able to use the same applications to access the data. The ODBC standard was established to eliminate code changes in applications when switching between databases.

 CAUTION: With different vendors developing ODBC drivers, there are some inconsistencies that may require you to edit your code.

Communicating with an ODBC Source

Communicating with an ODBC source is a four-tiered process, as shown in Figure 3-26. You have the application, the ODBC Driver Manager, the specific ODBC driver, and the database. The application makes calls to the ODBC Manager. These are standard calls that should work with any ODBC-compliant database, so your application does not have to know what database is connected behind the ODBC Driver Manager.

The ODBC Driver Manager loads the requested driver and sends the SQL requests through the ODBC driver to the database. Results are returned through the ODBC driver to the ODBC Driver Manager and back to the application. This whole process does incur a certain amount of processing overhead. But the benefit is that you are free to choose between databases without having to program proprietary calls into your application.

Types of ODBC Drivers

For every type of database, you must obtain a specific ODBC driver. A single driver can be used to connect to multiple instances of the same type of database. The driver contains all the proprietary information needed to manipulate that database. Most SQL (Structured Query Language) databases perform similar operations but may achieve that functionality in different ways. The ODBC driver allows you to access that functionality in a standard way. You must obtain an ODBC driver from the database developer or a third-party driver vendor. The more common SQL databases like Microsoft SQL Server, Oracle, and Sybase provide the drivers with their database software.

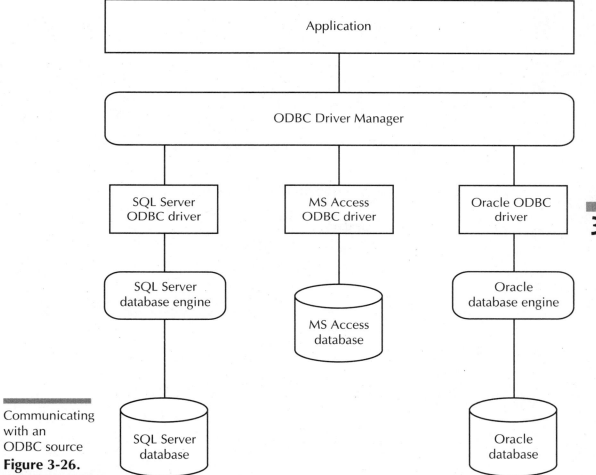

Communicating
with an
ODBC source
Figure 3-26.

Structured Query Language (SQL)

SQL gives you a standard method for selecting and retrieving records from a
database. SQL was developed by IBM in the 1970s as a means of retrieving
data from their developing database products. Since then, SQL has gone
through many revisions, but a standard has evolved guided by the American
National Standards Institute. Most database vendors adhere to the standard
SQL calls making it easier for the programmer to deal with databases.

NOTE: If database manipulation is crucial to the functioning of your business, you are probably very familiar with SQL. If you have not worked with databases in the past, you may need to do a little research on the commands used to select the data you want to display on your Intranet.

The SQL statement *SELECT * FROM INVOICES WHERE CUST_ID = "12982"* means *show me all the records from the INVOICE table where the customer ID is equal to "12982"*. Each word or symbol defines a key piece of the query as follows:

◆   SELECT is a keyword that begins the statement.

◆   "*" is a wild card that means to select all fields in the table. A table is a type of database data structure.

◆   FROM INVOICES defines the table to use.

◆   WHERE CUST_ID = "12982" says to check the field called CUST_ID for values equal to "12982".

This is a relatively simple example, but more complex statements can be used to join multiple tables and include multiple-criteria fields after the WHERE clause.

TIP: There are also statements for data manipulation such as INSERT, DELETE, and UPDATE. These commands can be used to make your database more dynamic by changing records in your database through Web pages.

Information Display Versus Database Updating

It is relatively easy to display information from your database on Web pages, but interaction between an application and a database is far more complex. Let's take accounting software as an example. Making customer information available to employees on a Web page is fairly easy to do. Allowing employees to add an invoice through a Web page may sound simple, but think of the interaction between the database tables that may go on behind the scenes. If you were entering an invoice within your accounting application, the simple act of pressing a Save button may set off a chain reaction of processes that adds records to many tables. Unless you have an intimate understanding of the relationships within your database, do not attempt to insert or delete records through your Intranet.

You also need to be sure that any alterations to your database are made over a secure channel. If the application resides on your Web server and your database is sitting elsewhere, is the channel between the two secure?

Working with Search Tools

Another of the extremely important aspects of a Web-centric Intranet includes the search capabilities that are opened up to you. You can use the search tools that come with your operating system, but those are often limited. The following sections show you how to take advantage of the latest search technology to make finding information on your Intranet much faster for your employees.

Internet Search Engines   3

There are a number of publicly available search engines accessible over the Internet that can be viewed through your Web browser. These engines attempt to provide different types of search services for Internet resources. The services offered vary from simple keyword searches over massive Internet indexes (such as AltaVista at http://www.altavista.com and Lycos at http://www.lycos.com) to attempts to provide a more cataloged and browsable interface (such as Yahoo! at http://www.yahoo.com and Lycos a2z at http://a2z.lycos.com).

Developing Search Sites Through Spidering

The sites that are indexed into these Internet search engines are found through a process called *spidering*. Spidering is a recursive operation where automatic programs (the spiders) running on fast computers begin by indexing the more popular Web sites (the roots). They then follow hyperlinks on Web pages to other sites, from there follow additional hyperlinks to other sites, and so on. Due to the interconnected structure of the Web, starting with just a handful of well-known roots and recursively following links lets the spiders reach almost every Web site on the Internet.

Internet Metasearching

Instead of going to many separate Internet search engines to find the results you are looking for, you can use applications that search many Internet search engines at once. Some applications have the ability to tap into the large number of indexes and search them in a more automated way known as *metasearching*. This functionality permits an information-organization application to automatically search the many different publicly available search services and combine the results into a single, relative list.

The search engine used to do a metasearch performs a slightly different task than those that use spidering to create indexes. As shown in Figure 3-27, search engines used in metasearching search already created indexes. Instead of using spidering to do the work of creating the indexes, they search what is already available for searching on the Internet.

NOTE: For an example, see the MetaCrawler site at http://www.metacrawler.com.

Processing the Results

There are a number of methods used to process and analyze the search results from the different Internet search engines. At a minimum, an application can check for and remove any duplicate search results. It might process the search results data returned by the Internet search engine, or, for

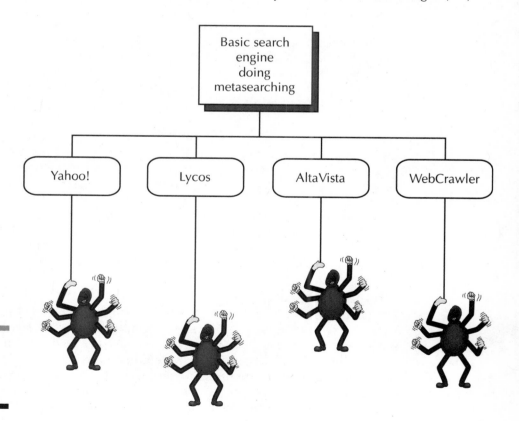

How a
metasearch
works
Figure 3-27.

each search result, it might also retrieve and analyze the content to display it in an intuitive and organized manner.

When results are given back to you, they have probably been assigned a value so you can assess their usefulness. Each engine handles value assignments differently. Some might place more importance on how often a search term appears, or some might place more value on a document where the search term appears in the first as opposed to the third paragraph. When you get your results back, consider how the engine normalized the values. Is the best document found given a perfect rating and all other results scored in relation to this "perfect" document? This means that a document that isn't a good match might be rated as a 1.0 (on a 1.0 scale), which is deceiving. Your search engine might instead assign straight values to your results. For example, the best result may only have .3 rating on a 1.0 scale.

More Intelligent Search Engines

3

Search engines today need to become more and more intelligent as Web page creators try to outsmart them, to weigh the search results in their favor. If a search engine selects a page based solely on the number of times the search term occurs in the document, then people can outwit the engine by placing a keyword on their Web page 500 times in small or invisible font in order to attract customers to their site. Consumers then see the Web site listed as the best match in their search results, when it really isn't. The more advanced search engines are able to compensate for such deception, and return an accurate rating of the site.

Search Agents

If your Intranet is connected to the Internet, then taking advantage of all of the information available to you is crucial. However, there is so much information out there that you can easily become overwhelmed. Despite all of the search engines on the Internet, it often takes too long to find what you're looking for. If you could use an application that independently retrieved Web pages of interest to you and cached them while you're working on something else, a search agent may be what you're looking for.

Though search agents haven't been around long enough to come up with a standard definition, you can assume that any intelligent application that can go to other sources of information (such as Web servers, hard drive space, or newsgroups) to find and retrieve information of interest can be considered a search agent. The parameters of a desired search can be defined. The agent then watches for new information that satisfies the search criteria, which it then forwards to the user. A search agent is intelligent. As you surf the Internet, it remembers the sites you've visited so that it begins to learn your preferences. As it learns more about you, it begins to anticipate what Web pages you might be most interested in, and presents them to you.

On Your Intranet

Search agents may run on your computer, or they may run on another Web server. You can use them to retrieve pages before you need them, or you might use the search agents to follow your movements as your surf the Web. Consider the following scenario. You need to do research for a presentation that you are to give next week. However, you must leave by three o'clock today in order to get home to look after your children. It's now two o'clock. What should you do?

If you had a search agent, you might be in the clear. If your search agent is configurable, you could set it to follow your movements as you quickly surf the Internet and your Intranet looking for information to help you out. Don't bother reading the information in detail. Just keep jumping to other hyperlinks so that you have a wide sample of information. When it's almost time for you to leave, have your search agent dump all of the pages you have found into a *container*, such as your Windows 95 Briefcase. You can then copy the pages to your laptop to bring home with you. Once you are at home, you can slow down and surf the pages on your hard drive, getting the information.

TIP: At work, you are probably connected to the Internet with a much faster link than you are at home. If you download the pages at work instead of waiting until you get home, you don't have to connect to the Internet using your home computer's slow modem. Instead, when you are at home, you can jump from hyperlink to hyperlink just as quickly as when you are at work, because the pages are stored on your hard drive.

When you return to work the next day, the search agent knows what information you loaded onto your laptop. The agent can visit the sites again to let you know if any information on them has changed, so you know if you want to revisit them.

NOTE: This scenario shows you the potential searching agents have, but not all search agents have these capabilities.

On the Internet

Search agents can also run on remote servers. For example, firefly has hooked up with Yahoo! to let users set up a customized Web page on Yahoo! To do so, all you need to do is visit Yahoo!'s Web site at http://www.yahoo.com and follow their simple instructions. You then create a page by checking boxes indicating your areas of interest. Recent pages found by Yahoo! that match with your interests are displayed with hyperlinks, as shown in Figure 3-28. The search agent is working on a remote server to intelligently find Web pages that might be of interest to you, making the Web page a quick reference area.

Indexing Your Search

Let's say your are searching for something, such as canned mushrooms, in a grocery store. What is the easiest way for you to find the mushrooms? You could go through the entire store, aisle by aisle, shelf by shelf, until you found the mushrooms, or you could find the mushrooms more quickly if you first looked at the list above each aisle. An index helps you in the same way. Instead of searching the entire contents of an information source, such as a Web site, for a search term, you can search the index of the site's contents, drastically cutting down on your search time.

3

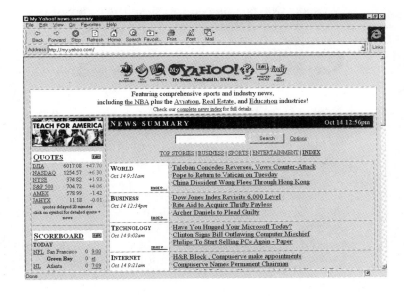

A personalized Yahoo! page

Figure 3-28.

One fast way for your employees to find information on your Intranet is by indexing it. Once an index is created, they can search this smaller block of information rather than the entire document structure. There are many indexing tools available for your Intranet. As you look for a tool, consider the following:

♦ What type of files does the indexer work with? Some document indexers may be designed especially for HTML files, while other indexers can index a much wider variety of file types. Record the file types used by most people in your company, and be sure that the indexer supports these types.

♦ Can the indexer update the index automatically? Can you configure how often the indexer runs? Does the indexer update the index immediately when a document is changed, added, or deleted?

♦ On what type of information structures can the indexer run? Where is the information you want to index? It may be on a file server or a Web server. Maybe you want to index newsgroups on your news server, or maybe you want employees to index their hard drives. Be sure that the indexer you are considering lets you index multiple information sources, and that it concatenates the results.

♦ Where do you want to store the indexer? Does the indexer allow you to store the index in a location other than where the information source is kept? Maybe you want to store the index of your file server on your Web server. Does the software let you do so?

CAUTION: If you are creating indexes, you might want to store them in a location where you can control access, such as on a file or Web server. If you create an index of someone's hard drive, for example, the index itself might contain confidential or sensitive information. If the index contains long filenames or some keyword, it may contain more information than all of the employees in your company should have access to.

As a rule, the index file consumes about 30 percent of the original space of the information files. Depending on the granularity to which the index has been built, the range can be 15 to 50 percent of the file sizes. Understanding how large the index is going to be helps you determine the best place for it, because some locations may not have enough disk space. Searching a file of this size rather than searching an entire information structure greatly improves the time it takes to return search results to you.

Using Catalogs

Indexes are a great way of organizing information so that it can be quickly searched. However, viewing an index is not exactly user-friendly. What if you want to just look around on the Intranet or Internet and check out what topics can be found under particular categories? By grouping Internet sites together into particular categories, catalogs are created that help you search the Internet in a more intuitive way than simply entering a search term.

What Is a Catalog?

A catalog is a database of resources that can contain any type of resource from your Intranet or the Internet. The most common resource is probably a URL, with a Web URL being the most prevalent. A catalog can maintain a variety of information about each resource, including

♦ A title

♦ Some type of location information (such as the URL)

♦ When it was last accessed

♦ When the entry was created

♦ When it was last modified

♦ An abstract or summary

♦ Keywords

♦ Size

♦ Links from this resource to other resources

 TIP: More sophisticated applications allow the resources to be categorized by topics defined by the user. The topical categories allow the information to be easily browsable by the user.

The relationship and organization of these different information resources can be displayed to you in a variety of ways. You might use a simple tree view, such as the one shown in Figure 3-29, or you can use a catalog with more intuitive, full-featured custom controls like a hierarchical tab view, such as the one shown in Figure 3-30.

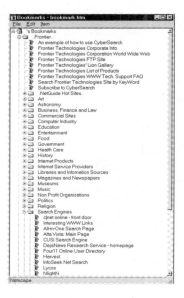

Catalog in
Netscape
Navigator
Gold using a
tree view
Figure 3-29.

On the Intranet

You can also develop catalogs of the information stored on your Intranet.
Certain software gives you predefined categories to create a catalog to
which you can add your own bookmarks. For example, CyberSearch,
shown in Figure 3-30, comes with many useful categories complete with

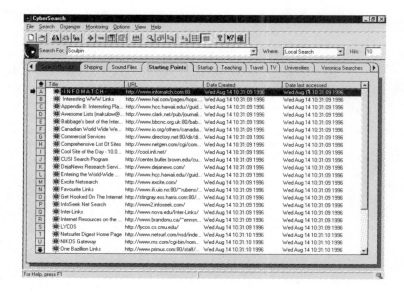

Catalog in
CyberSearch
using a
hierarchical
tab view
Figure 3-30.

bookmarks. As people surf the Intranet or Internet, they can mark certain locations (including e-mail address, Web servers, news servers, and FTP sites) as bookmarks. Other software solutions, such as Netscape's Catalog Server, automatically generate a catalog consisting of both Intranet and Internet information.

Giving the people on your Intranet cataloging tools helps them organize their information more logically. They can easily browse Intranet and Internet contents, which can spark ideas they never would have had if they only had an index to look at. They also are more likely to browse through a catalog than to keep entering search term after search term to find an item in an index, which means their research is more thorough and valuable.

On the Internet

There are some companies on the Internet creating catalogs for people to visit. Some find catalogs a more inviting place to stop and search rather than being presented with only one screen allowing you to enter one search query. For example, Yahoo! lets users either enter a search term or search one of the predefined categories, as shown in Figure 3-31. Lycos a2z is offering a catalog approach as well. Originally designed to be the largest database of Internet information, Lycos added a2z, which offers cataloged information for the users who want to look around for themselves, rather than being presented with search results, as shown in Figure 3-32.

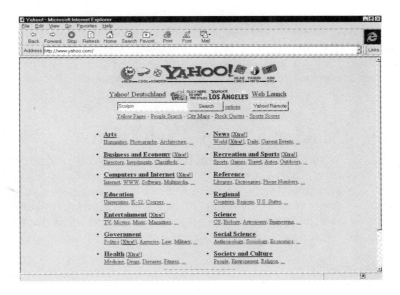

Yahoo!'s
search catalog
Figure 3-31.

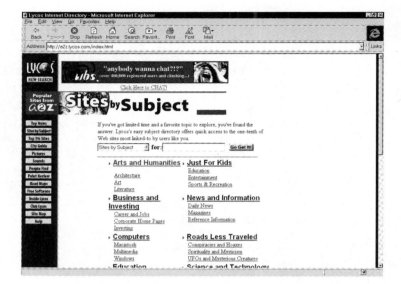

Lycos a2z's
search catalog
Figure 3-32.

Putting It All Together

As you have probably figured out by now, there are many pieces to a
Web-centric Intranet! You may have thought about the Web as being
something separate from your Intranet, something to be accessed by your
Intranet perhaps, but still a separate entity. However, the architecture of the
Web carries over nicely into the Intranet arena. For example, the easy-to-use,
graphical user interface provided by Web browsers can indeed translate into
a quicker, more user-friendly environment across corporate networks. The
point-and-click feel of the Web can be replicated on your Intranet,
integrating these two architectures to present employees with universal
methods of finding, creating, and sorting data. This can help prevent the
confusion that arises when employees must shift gears between applications
that feel differently from one another.

Making a Careful Selection

When you are selecting tools for your Web-centric Intranet, be sure you have
carefully researched the tools your Intranet can really use. All of the bells
and whistles that consumers crave are not necessarily required within the
context of an Intranet. In fact, many managers find the functionality they
require is far less than what is considered to be the latest technology. Decide
what you are trying to accomplish by implementing an Intranet.

♦   Are you doing simple document serving?

♦   Do you want to create back-end services that interface with databases?

♦   Do you want to implement search and index utilities?

CAUTION: As you begin to explore the options available with a Web-centric Intranet, remember to keep your eyes open for the newest technologies while keeping your feet planted in reality. Though some of the new tools may seem like the ultimate invention, don't leap to buy them before you have thoroughly looked at the functionality and reliability of the tool. Just because a product is announced as being Web-centric or Intranet-oriented doesn't necessarily mean that it's right for you!

3

The biggest issues are that the tools are robust, easy for the user to understand and utilize, and essential to making your business more productive. *Seamless integration* is a term often used to describe the way Web-centric tools should work with one another. Tools with a similar look and feel are much easier for your employees to accept and learn. Because the Intranet is based upon open standards, the administrator can implement more advanced tools once the need is identified.

Emerging Technologies

There are some other pieces you might want to consider adding to your Web-centric Intranet in the future. Most of these technologies are available on the market today but only in initial versions. There are more advanced pieces of software that are rapidly taking shape, and, although they may not be essential to your current Intranet, they may soon provide functionality you won't be able to do without!

Collaborative Work Tools

To ease communication between people distributed over many locations, many conferencing tools are being developed. Workflow applications can sequence tasks, send notifications, and provide automatic routing. For example, you might have a request for new software that needs to be approved by three people before you can actually purchase it. A workflow application can notify the three people that there is a request they need to approve, and it can actually send the request to each person in a particular order through e-mail.

Calendaring or scheduling tools assist in resolving personal and resource scheduling conflicts. If you want to schedule a meeting for two o'clock Tuesday afternoon, then you can use a calendaring tool to check the schedules of those you want present at the meeting. If they are busy at that time, the tool can reschedule the meeting for a time when everyone is free. If you have a conference room, the company can use a resource scheduling tool to reserve the room for a particular time.

Virtual Meetings

Web conferencing is starting to gain more popularity, allowing people to meet with each other despite being separated by long distances. At a minimum, Web conferencing tools can show a small video screen on your monitor that displays the person or persons with whom you are meeting. There may also be an audio feed so you can hear what everyone is saying. *White boarding* refers to the capability of sharing documents in your conference. If you are working on an advertising campaign with four people located in four different places, you can all be viewing the same document on your computer. When one of you marks an area on the document that needs an alteration, then all of you can see the spot as it is being marked.

If you add the ability to display multiple pieces of information to those attending the meeting, then you have what's referred to as a *Web meeting*. On your screen, you see more than the video feed and the white board. You can also see the meeting's agenda, along with action items that people have been assigned during the meeting. Web site information can also be displayed in the meeting space.

TIP: Chat applications provide a more informal means to have meetings with people in remote locations. As people type, others connected to their conversation see the text as it is entered. However, a chat application usually doesn't have audio or video capabilities. Once these features are added, the chat application becomes more of a Web meeting or conferencing utility.

Web Mapping

Traditionally, document structure on a Web server, file server, or any other data storage piece is shown in a hierarchical fashion. However, some vendors are trying a new approach to Web documents. By sending out spiders either on an entire Web site or on a selected portion of a Web site, the site can be mapped according to its hyperlinks. The spiders follow the hyperlinks until they reach an end. The linking between documents is then visually mapped out, showing which documents are related and connected to each other.

The Next Step

You now have a basic understanding of the components needed for a Web-centric Intranet, and you've learned about some of the unique and exciting applications of these tools. Now it's time to carry your ideas one step further. Chapter 4 tells you how to make your Intranet the most efficient strategy you can implement.

References and Further Reading

The following Web sites, articles, and books may help you on your journey:

3

http://java.sun.com

http://home.netscape.com/eng/mozilla/2.0/handbook/javascript/introd.html

http://zdnet.com/activexfiles/toolbox.htm

Brockschmidt, Kraig. *Inside OLE—Second Edition*. Microsoft Press, Redmond, WA: 1995.

Cornell, Gary and Cay S. Horstmann. *Core Java*. SunSoft Press, Upper Saddle River, NJ: 1996.

Denning, Adam. *OLE Controls Inside Out*. Microsoft Press, Redmond, WA: 1995.

Rauch, Stephen. "Unified Browsing with ActiveX Extensions Brings the Internet to Your Desktop." *Microsoft Systems Journal*. September, 1996, pp. 19–33.

Frequently Asked Questions

♦ What is a Web-centric Intranet?

A Web-centric Intranet centers around your Web server. The other tools in your Intranet, such as those used for content creation, reflect the graphic interface and intuitive architecture associated with Web sites.

♦ What are the advantages of a Web-centric Intranet?

The Web provides users with an easy-to-follow, point-and-click architecture. Basing your Intranet on this paradigm gives you the same advantages. Employees can find information because it is organized in a logical way. Customers can easily find out about your company while using the latest technology that shows your company is able to keep up with changing times.

♦ What are the disadvantages of a Web-centric Intranet?

As with any new architecture change, you may encounter resistance from current employees who are leery of change. You may also need to hire new people or train existing employees, so they become familiar with some of the skills unique to a Web-centric approach. For example, no one may understand how to configure a Web server or create HTML pages.

♦ What are the tools needed for a Web-centric Intranet?

The most important piece you need is a Web server. To place content on your Web server, you need tools such as HTML editors, image map editors, and graphics editors. If you want to extend the usefulness of your Web server, then you need to create back-end services using CGI, WinCGI, ISAPI, or NSAPI. You might also want to explore the potential of ActiveX, Java, and JavaScript. Finally, using proven search and information organizing tools can help you efficiently find and manage your information.

♦ What are my security concerns with a Web-centric Intranet?

Because your Intranet is centered around a Web server, the access to the server needs to be protected. Who do you want to let in? How can you create secure areas? Chapter 9 discusses the many ways in which you can secure your Web server and your Intranet.

♦ **How does search technology play into a Web-centric Intranet?**

Take advantage of available search technology to help you find and organize the information on your Intranet. There are search engines that can help you perform full-text searches on both your Intranet and the Internet. There are also indexing tools that can expedite your searches, and cataloging tools that can transform your search results into a browsable format.

3

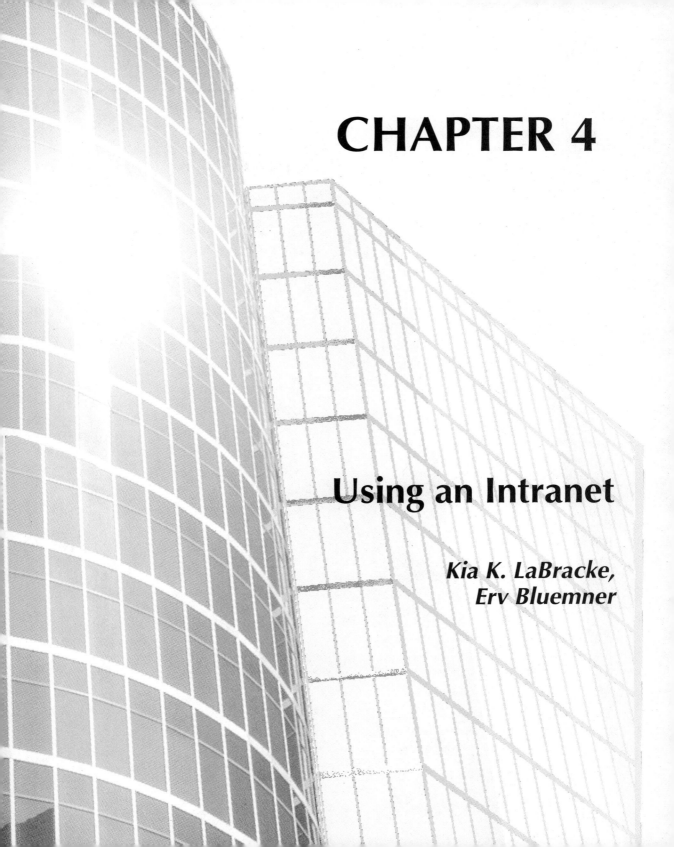

CHAPTER 4

Using an Intranet

Kia K. LaBracke,
Erv Bluemner

Chapter Objectives

◆ Understand how your company's culture may affect your approach to adopting an Intranet

◆ Become acquainted with a range of possible Intranet solutions by exploring some scenarios

◆ Explore how Intranet technologies can provide specific business solutions

In this chapter, we look at some Intranet usage scenarios. We explore how the tools and capabilities of the Intranet are applied in specific business situations. The chapter is devoted to developing an understanding of what is possible in terms of improving corporate and individual productivity and to make you aware of the kinds of things that are being accomplished with this new paradigm of desktop and collaborative capability. After you've read this chapter, you can journey into some of the technical details as they unfold in the remainder of the book.

Getting Started

With all the tools and applications available, the most daunting question users may have is, "Where do I start?" After all, Intranets don't spring up out of nowhere. They must be created and administered with careful attention to what makes sense for a particular community of users. In fact, identifying the culture of your particular company relative to the support of the Intranet paradigm shift is critical to your success. In order to deploy a productive Intranet, you have to choose what format is right for you—for your particular business needs. In addition, there are many different solutions to choose from. What one company elects to achieve via e-mail messaging may be better placed as a Web-based back-end service for another organization's business application. Finally, building an Intranet does not imply that every task is executed via Web technology; your Intranet should instead act as a bridge to resources already existing on your network. This is an extremely important point. We explore links to existing systems and the inherent opportunities/risks in Chapter 10.

4

Your Company's Culture

One of the biggest challenges you may face has nothing to do with the technology itself but rather the change in the cultural paradigm required to implement an Intranet. How close is your company to adopting an Intranet? Of course, you want to understand the business drivers and match a range of possible solutions to your specific needs and requirements. Beyond the technology and the business drivers, however, there are some major people and management issues to tackle. Does your corporate culture lend itself to change in general, let alone to embracing new technologies? You must test the waters of your organization in order to ensure that your implementation is a success.

NOTE: No two Intranets will be exactly the same, but any change in "business as usual" involves as a necessity the support of management and ultimately the user community.

At the risk of painting the canvas with too wide a brush, one might divide companies into two distinct and mightily opposite camps: the Demings and the Lemmings.

The Demings

Many of you have heard of W. Edwards Deming, the 20th century American statistician, philosopher, and innovator who coined the term "Total Quality Management." Deming revolutionized Japan's post-war economy by changing their manufacturing focus from quotas to quality (see http://www.siouxlan.com/initiative/smallbus/deming.html 9/26/96).

Deming's philosophy revolves around some fairly simple statistical principles. In particular, every process within a company can and should be measured against statistical process control limits to ensure that corrections to the process are made if it goes outside those limits. In plain English, every department or group in the company should have ways to measure the results of what they are doing and adjust their activities if results go astray from expectations. Deming also stressed the importance of empowering workers to take pride in the quality of the work they produce.

The Deming Philosophy

A Deming company, in the structure of their management organization, might extend these philosophies into their everyday culture as follows:

♦   Each management group should have a mission statement and each member of the team a clearly stated list of performance objectives, so that everyone is working toward a defined set of common goals.

♦   The workers on the base of the organization-chart pyramid must be involved in making informed decisions about company operations and infrastructure ("management from the ground up").

♦   Cross-departmental project teams are employed as a way to ensure that all involved parties contribute to solutions to everyday problems, with a "check your title at the door" approach.

♦ Information sharing is a primary way to improve the group's productivity rather than information hiding as a way to protect one's individual job by maintaining an information advantage over colleagues.

The Distributed Webmaster Approach

In the context of adopting an Intranet, a Deming company has no trouble adopting a distributed Webmaster approach, with many individuals within the organization creating and administering content for their department or project area. In this mode, information is created and distributed instantly to all who have a need to know. After all, a company with a "management from the bottom up" approach is already accustomed to its team members sharing in the responsibility for successes (and failures) and encourages creative suggestions from its employees.

TIP: Sharing information on an Intranet is a great way to have more employees take direct ownership of the communication process within their department and company. People gain enthusiasm for this approach when they see that not only can they help their fellow workers do their jobs better and faster, but increase their own productivity as well.

4

The Lemmings

On the opposite end of the management-style spectrum, we have the Lemmings. Lemmings seem to be driven by invisible but absolute forces. Management sets the path, the process, and the roles, and the employees act out the script. When circumstances change, these companies can be slow to react, waiting for "word from the top" to make adjustments to the game plan.

NOTE: Lemming companies can miss the opportunity to harvest the creative ideas of their employees and the lack of empowerment may drive employees to seek more satisfying positions in other companies.

We could have easily chosen another species for this example, but the legend about lemmings scurrying blindly to their death seems to fit this analogy especially well, although it is entirely the stuff of fiction! Lemmings (the real ones) tend to mass migrate when food supplies dwindle, sometimes delving into waters too deep for their swimming capabilities (see http://www.uab.edu/nusc/lemming.htm 9/26/96)

Some Lemming Symptoms

A Lemming company may lack knowledgeable leaders to guide them along the way, or they may have leaders who prefer not to delegate authority to their employees. Some symptoms are

- Traditional management from the top down, with little feedback from the base of the organizational chart
- Hierarchical communication across departments
- A general unwillingness to change that may make it difficult or impossible to implement new ideas or programs

The Autocratic Approach

A Lemming company likely adopts a more autocratic approach to Intranet implementation rather than the democratic, Web-administration approach of most implementations. They may feel more comfortable with a more traditional model: The Webmaster (one person, maybe two, usually from the MIS department) has control and knows the technology inside and out. All information passes through that gate and becomes an effective way to gain uniformity and control of the information hierarchy.

NOTE: The Webmaster(s) are in charge of training end users how to use the Intranet to browse and search for information, but they are unlikely to delegate responsibilities such as content creation and Web management.

The Webmaster becomes the "hub" for all Web-content delivery for the company. This ensures uniformity of Web page presentation format and, generally, assures that a highly skilled technical individual is responsible for creating dynamic content.

Potential Bottlenecks

But can't this approach effectively create a bottleneck? Yes it can, at the Webmaster level, since those one or two people manage the entire company's content, versus having a representative (or more) from each department. Depending upon the number of users and the enthusiasm to make the most out of the Intranet paradigm, managing an Intranet site could easily become a full-time job for the Webmasters.

NOTE: This may be the most comfortable implementation for a particular company, given that even having an Intranet is a pretty big step!

In reality, there are very few technical or experience barriers to a distributed Webmaster approach as opposed to the centralized Webmaster. The benefits of distributing the tools and responsibilities, as discussed later in this chapter, are facilitated by the fact that content-creation tools are relatively simple to use. Application tools are rapidly evolving to a level where programming skills are not necessary for customization and implementation. If users reap the benefits of increased productivity through the wealth of new information and content available to them on the Web site, that's at least a step in the right direction. For more details on the roles of different employees in building and maintaining an Intranet, see Chapter 5.

Gaining Management Support

4

You must have management support at all levels to make an Intranet work, so you should approach the situation realistically for your particular company. If your company's managers are not themselves accustomed to using a PC, imagine how intimidated they may feel granting control of corporate information to cyberspace Webmasters spouting Web-centric technobabble.

Positioning the Approach

Even the best managers tend to feel as though they need to have control over what is going on underneath their roofs (and under their rule), so there is often a fine line to walk in how to position your Intranet strategy to upper management. Be warned, however, that if you pursue an Intranet, the primary result is the availability of significantly more information for all users, local and remote. The adverse reaction may be a fundamental fear of inadvertently making sensitive corporate material available to the rest of the world, so you must determine which information is going to be housed where and what security measures and policies you have in place.

Selling the Concept

Mary Holland and Janell Picard, both librarians at National Semiconductor Corporation, write candidly about this phenomenon in their excellent article published in *WebMaster's* September 1996 issue, "Librarians at the Gate" (see *WebMaster*, September 1996, pp. 22 through 26, published by CIO Communications). Struggling to implement an Intranet to make their internal network more efficient, they quickly became aware of both the need to train other users to help share in the burden of creating and administering content, and the need to sell the concept to management once they'd already mustered plenty of grass roots support from users within the organization. "The first question from management was, 'Who told you to do this?' The answer was, 'No one....' Free-form information sharing was a foreign concept to managers, who preferred their information systems highly controlled."

Preparing for the Challenge

This is a common theme when we talk to customers about how they are implementing their Intranets. So prepare yourself for at least some uncertainty about the Intranet concept on the part of your upper management, because it can potentially pose fundamental challenges to how your company operates. If you do your homework (which is, after all, why you bought this book), you can have an arsenal of information to help you not only justify but correctly position how an Intranet can save your company time and money, regardless of the way your own particular implementation is ultimately managed.

 NOTE: The best news is that you can implement your first Intranet capabilities relatively quickly and with relatively low cost compared to proprietary solutions. We discuss these concepts in detail in later chapters.

The Intranet Usage Paradigm

So once you have made the management commitment and devoted the necessary dollars and personnel (see Chapter 5) to implementing an Intranet, what are the different ways to exploit this new resource? How do you actually use the different tools? What follows are some examples of general ideas on how you might use your Intranet, as well as some specific examples to guide you along the way. We look at real-life business case studies in Chapter 6.

The Information Management Role

At the heart of your Intranet information management system lies your Web server. Web servers are multipurpose vehicles for sharing and retrieving information internally and publishing information externally. Administrators can integrate their Web information with third-party or in-house applications, such as inventory systems or Electronic Data Interchange (EDI) systems.

In Publishing Information

On the Web server, corporations can publish public and confidential information on the Internet, as well as on their internal networks. Such information may consist of visually attractive, content-rich documents made up of text, graphics, video, and sound. Readers access this information from their desktop computers using a Web browser. Depending on the security that is put into place, at a minimum, users are able to view the Web pages registered with the server and, for example, enter data in an online, HTML Web form that can be processed by a back-end application. This back-end application can, for example, access a database for pricing, inventory, technical tips/troubleshooting, competitive information, or other strategic content. People using a browser fill out the forms that provide the database query information when they access the server. More sophisticated applications can be made available by using HTML forms-processing ability. Readers of your Web pages may interact with the information on the server to respond to a survey or place an order for your product.

4

In Allowing Access

You may allow anyone on the Internet or Intranet to access your site, or you may want to restrict access to people within your company. You might decide that employees accessing the server through a browser may not be able to perform any server information maintenance, such as creating groups or editing files. You might also make access conditional, depending on the software packages utilized and the permissions granted to users.

NOTE: Under circumstances of higher security, for instance, a client certificate (electronic authentication of a user's identity) may be required to access Web server applications. The Web server using advanced client authentication checks that the user has an electronic certificate that can be authenticated to ensure that the individual is a known person or represents a known corporation. Refer to Chapter 9 for more information on security.

Distributed Management

Webmasters are users who own groups or folders on your server. Using software packages that support remote administration allows distributed management of your Web site. With a distributed list of Webmasters, each owning a segment of your information-Web hierarchy, you can have Webmasters around the world who can perform maintenance such as creating groups or editing Web pages. They can connect remotely to the server by installing the client administration applications on their computers. If your organization is LAN-based, you can have Webmasters stationed throughout the company anywhere on your LAN, as shown in Figure 4-1.

The Web Server Function

So you have a better idea of how your Web server works, take a look at the diagram in Figure 4-2. Here's how a company might decide to distribute the

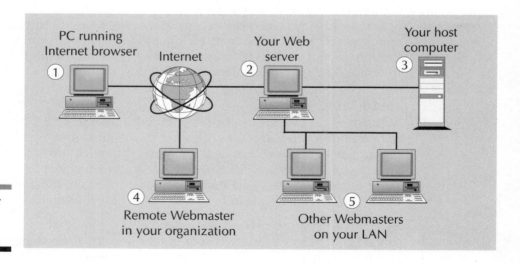

A Web server overview
Figure 4-1.

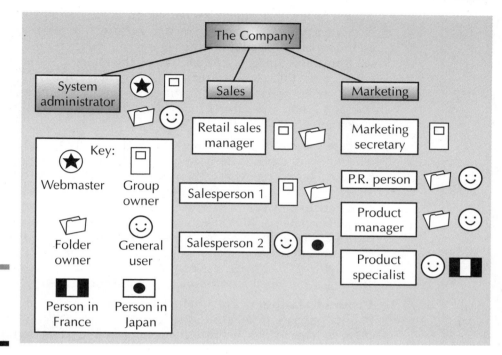

Distributing
Web site
maintenance
Figure 4-2.

responsibility of maintaining their Web site. (See Chapter 5 for more
information on management and administration of Web sites.)

♦ **The Company** The company is a large computer software retailer with
offices in the United States, Japan, and France. The systems
administrator at the company is in Chicago, Illinois. As the overall
company Webmaster, the system administrator sets up all group owners
and can also set up folder owners and general users. Workgroup
members can be participants in several system groups sharing common
sets of access privileges. The system administrator can also be a group
owner, folder owner, and a general user.

♦ **Retail Sales Manager**   A retail sales manager, who works in Chicago, is a folder owner and a group owner. Because sales information is confidential, the retail sales manager wants tight control over who can see the sales figures. As a folder owner, the retail sales manager controls who can see the sales information posted on the internal sales page. As a group owner, the retail sales manager determines who can be allowed in the sales group and defines the access privileges for specific folders and documents for the group.

♦ **Salesperson 2**   The retail sales manager recently hired salesperson 2 who works in Japan. Salesperson 2 provides monthly reports of sales in Japan, which salesperson 2 then adds to the sales folder on the SuperWeb server. On a weekly basis, the retail sales manager has a conference call with his sales team, including salesperson 2. By accessing the sales home page, *all* salespeople can see the most current information. Individuals see the latest pricing sheets, available quantities, delivery availability, product feature descriptions, special promotions, incentives, and commission structure. No time is wasted by asking people what version of a document they have.

♦ **Product Manager**   The product manager is responsible for maintaining all product information. As a general user, the product manager creates product information for public pages on the company's Web site.

♦ **Product Specialist**   The product specialist in France is a general user who creates French product information and then directly adds it to the product manager's folder.

Exploring Intranet Applications

Now that you've seen how a company's information can be effectively distributed and managed across its organization, let's continue on to some more detailed examples. Though only one (or none) may *directly* apply to you, they all can ignite new thoughts that lead to more exciting applications for your Intranet.

In Schools

People who are involved with the educational system know how important communication is. Teachers need to be in close contact with their students and vice versa. However, especially at large universities, communication often breaks down. Why not promote more effective interaction through your Web server? If professors at universities set up Web pages for their students to access, students can no longer claim they didn't hear the assignment. No more late-night phone calls would be made to a professor's home asking, "How long does that paper have to be that's due tomorrow?" All of this miscellaneous classroom information could be put on a teacher's Web page, so students could look at it any time, day or night.

Setting Up the System

How could such a system be set up? If a university has networked computers, it probably has an MIS director. This person could be the administrator. Each department could be a group, perhaps with one faculty member from each department volunteering to be the group's owner (and become a Webmaster). The other faculty members in the department then would be general users who could create their own Web pages. See Figure 4-3.

User Access Issues

Now the English student can sit in front of the PC in her dorm room and access the Web server through a browser to check out the latest assignments for her EN305 class. The Biology professor can use remote access to the server and update the BL320 page from his home office, which now points to three special research papers located at a Paris University doing complementary investigation to the class' current study. The students in the class can go to the university's computer lab to see what references their professor recommends they use for their next research project. Finally, the computer science professor adds some helpful hints for completing the next CS450 project from her office. How much easier the university life can become!

4

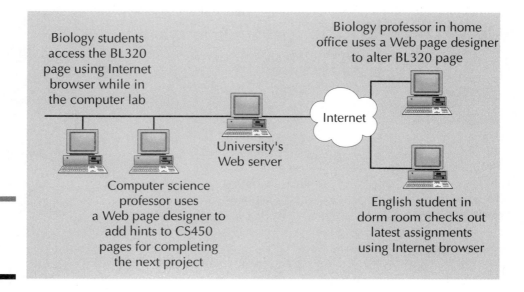

A university Intranet in action
Figure 4-3.

Biology students access the BL320 page using Internet browser while in the computer lab

University's Web server

Internet

Biology professor in home office uses a Web page designer to alter BL320 page

English student in dorm room checks out latest assignments using Internet browser

Computer science professor uses a Web page designer to add hints to CS450 pages for completing the next project

In Organizations

What if you are the president of an environmental group called
WE-R-CLEAN and have a membership list of only a couple of hundred
people? How can you make your membership list grow? Create a Web site,
as shown in Figure 4-4! You can ask other organizations to include your Web
page as a link on theirs, getting much needed attention for WE-R-CLEAN.

Linking Web Pages

The ability to link Web pages from around the Internet is one of the most
powerful aspects of constructing your information hierarchy. It also requires
tools that can check the integrity of hyperlinks between sites to make sure
they are still valid. It certainly wouldn't do to have the major links from
your company's home page pointing to a URL document or Web page that
no longer exists. With the right setup, interested WE-R-CLEAN users can
navigate to your site from many cooperating sites. Then you can amaze Web
surfers with eye-catching graphics and compelling information about
WE-R-CLEAN.

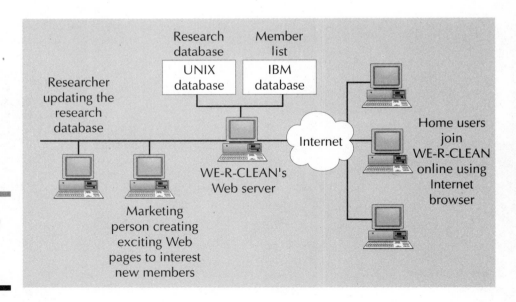

The
WE-R-CLEAN
Web site in
action

Figure 4-4.

TIP: You could even allow people to join WE-R-CLEAN online, by filling out a simple form you create. You can instantly have hundreds of new members added to your database. Think about the time you would save by not having to do the data entry by hand any more. Even if they decided not to join right away, they could enter their names and contact information through an HTML form, and you could capture this information for future promotional use or other follow-up.

Database Opportunities

Other opportunities for the organization could include keeping a database where you could enter the most recent research information. The people conducting the research could access the server through a browser, fill out a form, and enter in the pertinent information. Once they click a Submit button, the database is updated. Now the information is available to be used by the rest of the organization.

TIP: With the availability of search tools to index this information, it is an easy matter to retrieve by keyword search the specific information you are interested in.

4

The Intelligence Agent

Even more interesting is the ability to set in place an intelligent agent that can be directed to watch for emerging information on a particular topic of interest. For instance, as news of river pollution cleanup is added to the database, it can be automatically forwarded to WE-R-CLEAN individuals concerned with the progress of water purification in the state. The intelligent agent watches for new information that is posted to the Web server that matches the unique profile established by the user. The agent runs all the time, and any piece of information matching the search criteria is automatically forwarded. Agent technology is discussed in further detail in Chapter 11.

Content and Security Issues

Of course to be an effective organization, WE-R-CLEAN not only needs to process incoming information, but also to produce their own Web-centric content. To facilitate the WE-R-CLEAN organization, you, or perhaps an interested employee or volunteer of WE-R-CLEAN, could be the administrator.

Content Creators and Administrators   At first, a single person may want to do the design and creation of any Web pages for the group. As WE-R-CLEAN grows, there is more need to further distribute the administration, especially as the organization is geographically distributed. More people need to be added to the system, and thus more people become either Webmasters or general users.

Security Measures   The Web server knows no geographical limits, being able to support any remote user who can connect to the net. Of course, a firewall or online security measures may be mandated to maintain adequate access control to sensitive data on the server. By using address-restriction capabilities, you can set up your Web site to only allow access to the people belonging to your company, including Webmasters at home or a remote office. You can publish anything from birthday lists to confidential information on your Web site without worrying about people other than employees accessing it. You can even publish the names and e-mail addresses of all your employees without worrying about someone from outside your company seeing the list.

For Internal Communications

How many times have you been in a situation where one department is uncertain about the other's activities? Communication is an essential key to every company's success. Employees want to know what the current customer issues that need to be dealt with are. They also want to know the milestones that need to be met to get the next product out and any details that are changing that may affect their contribution to the effort. Most often, there is a need to provide details of organizational logistics, such as meeting schedules, budgeting information, processing needs between departments, setting calendars, and facilitating discussion on critical path activities.

Setting Up Internal Pages

With conscientious effort, it is possible to set up convenient, time-saving internal pages that greatly improve your company's communication (see Figure 4-5). If each department maintains its own Web page, then all employees can find out about the others' actions. Making the information so easy to find creates an environment more likely to keep the entire company working smoothly toward common objectives. It also helps to generate new ideas spurred by the work of other departments. You can further eliminate

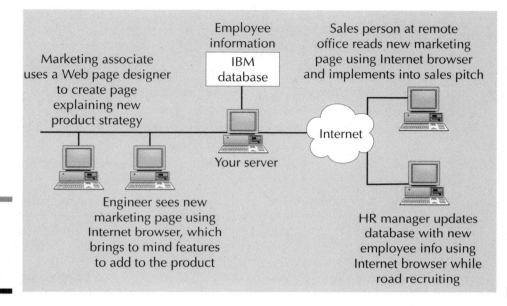

4

the burdensome problem of repeating an action that another department
has already completed.

Producing Timely Information

Like any other information center, a Web-centric Intranet is only as good as
the timeliness of the information it makes available. The great news is that
creating and distributing Web content is not difficult. Content-creation tools
have been designed to operate much like basic word processing software,
with additional capabilities for including rich, multimedia content and
inserting hyperlinks.

TIP: In some cases, traditional word processing tools can output
HTML-based Web pages as well as normal text data. Web pages can be
constructed in minutes and launched to the Web server with nearly
instant availability.

A Retail Example

Suppose a software retailer decides to set up an Intranet. What can they do
with it? Perhaps a better question would be, what *can't* they do?! The Sales
department's confidential information concerning the results of last

quarter's sales can be added and made available to the executive group defined by the SuperWeb master. By restricting access to the pages, no wandering eyes make their way into privileged information. Here's how this might work:

◆ Traveling sales personnel can enter their orders from remote Internet access points.

◆ The details can be uploaded into a database by way of a Web form-based entry.

◆ The results can be formatted and made available to the CFO and VP of Sales through a Web-based back-end application.

◆ An intelligent back-end application can monitor the pattern of specific product sales and deliver an analysis of shifting customer demand that can be fed to marketing and manufacturing personnel, helping to define next-step actions in advertising and raw material purchase.

Communication can be occurring in a timely and productivity-increasing manner, and sometimes without the initiation of a human being.

A "What's New" Page   You may have general information that everyone in the company should see. Each department could create a "What's New" page, explaining their most recent accomplishments.

TIP: By knowing exactly what another department is up to, people can take advantage of work already completed. If the marketing department has developed a unique strategy for pushing a new product, why not share it with the other departments, so everyone can implement it in their dealings with customers or product development?

Creating a Spirited Environment   Of course, an Intranet can also be fun! Why not have a competition to see which department can create the most informative Web page? Create company spirit by encouraging employees to raise their vision from the desk they're sitting at, so they can see and get involved with the overall company picture. At the same time, valuable information gains a vehicle for rapid and wide distribution.

NOTE: Workers who have a clear understanding of where the organization is headed and what is being done across the departments have a more intuitive understanding of what they themselves can contribute.

In Health Care

The StayWell Medical Center consists of a hospital, a clinic, several laboratories, a medical college, and an administrative building. StayWell wants to create an online information center to connect internal users, patients, other health care providers, and insurance companies, and to expand the range of available services. A highly localized Intranet, as discussed earlier, has clearly outgrown their needs. They need to allow Web users from all over the globe to access their Web server with Internet access availability, as shown in Figure 4-6.

Realizing the Potential

Once they are connected to the Internet, the potential is amazing! A medical student at the University of Iowa can access the center's Web server using a browser. By clicking on the appropriate hyperlinks, the student gains access to the summaries of procedures and success rates associated with age 50 and greater prostrate cancer patients in the StayWell Medical Center's research database. The indexed research study on the Web server allows the student to also see information links to associated studies at several other medical groups around the country. Key progress is shown in several of the articles with a particular pharmaceutical treatment series.

4

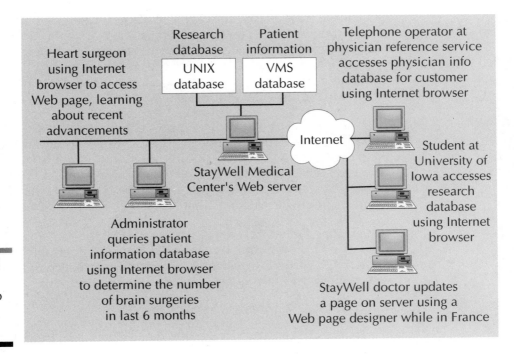

The StayWell Medical Center's Web site in action
Figure 4-6.

Online Connections   Using an online connection to several Internet search companies, executed simultaneously, an additional keyword search on the name of the drug links the student with the manufacturer of the drug. From the pharmaceutical company's home page, the student is able to find several more promising studies of utilization of the drug in other cancer sites. Information is available on the testing being conducted to satisfy the FDA (Federal Food and Drug Agency). The company indicates a likely commercial introduction in 1998. The student looks up the name of the product manager of this drug, again by browsing from the corporate home page.

E-mail and Newsgroup Follow-Ups   The student then forwards an e-mail requesting additional information using the e-mail address found within the company's Web pages. The product manager sends a reply e-mail with attached electronic documents including a multimedia presentation of the current benefits and potential side-effects associated with the new pharmaceutical. The product manager also indicates to the medical student that there is a world-wide, online newsgroup to follow treatment with the pharmaceutical. The student logs into the newsgroup and observes a threaded discussion on a new derivative of a chemically similar drug. As you can see, the possibilities are practically endless.

Promoting Services

From another perspective, the StayWell Medical Center's financial health is dependent on providing and promoting a range of quality services with a strong medical staff. Perhaps you've seen television commercials advertising physician-referral services. By calling the service, you receive information about doctors so you can make an educated decision about which doctor you want to entrust with your health.

The Database   The StayWell Medical Center has a database where they maintain information regarding all of their physicians. Referral services are able to use a browser to access this information through form-based queries to the StayWell Medical Center's Web server. Personnel at the referral service are able to search the Medical Center's database while on the phone with customers, finding the doctors that best match the patient's needs.

Disseminating the Information   Once selected, they are able to generate an online map of the appropriate center location and electronically attach it to a profile of the physician. This can be printed and mailed right in the office or given directly to the patient if he or she is on-site.

NOTE: As a further service, the referral service person may be able to link directly to the physician's online calendar appointment schedule. The patient is then scheduled immediately.

An Online Administrative Summary

To keep the StayWell Medical Center's doctors current on the latest reimbursement practices and laboratory facilities provided, the doctors can access an online administrative summary from the center's Web server. More interestingly, an intelligent search agent can be put into place that automatically posts a bulletin to the doctor when there is any new information related to center practices or other outside information in their specific areas of expertise.

NOTE: On the bleeding edge of research information sharing, surgical and other treatment sequences can be circulated via the media-rich format of the Web-centric paradigm. The information is made accessible via the browser using sound, video clips, graphics, and text to demonstrate some of the newest surgical procedures.

4

An Intranet at Work

The Bagel Orchard Company recently implemented their Intranet to facilitate communications with their resellers. The following sections detail how this innovative, if fictional, company implemented their Intranet.

The Home Page

The Bagel Orchard's home page features rotating bagels that disappear into crumbs before the users' very eyes! This animation is achieved using an animated graphics file activated by JavaScript to make the page come alive. The page is divided into three main areas of information (see Figure 4-7). By simply clicking on the appropriate bagel, visitors can see corporate, sales, or marketing information. The integration of images and hyperlink selection is intuitive and appealing and it gets customers to where they need to be fast.

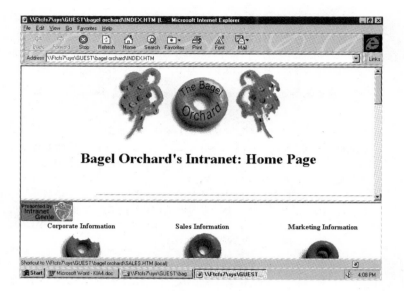

The Bagel
Orchard
home page
Figure 4-7.

The FAQ Site

In order to give resellers access to commonly needed information, the Bagel
Orchard folks established a popular Web site area, the FAQ (Frequently
Asked Questions), which provides front-line support and information
distribution on a variety of topics. For example, the FAQ area provides
remote sales staff the ability to download prepackaged information on
product offerings and company procedures, rather than having to phone the
office, locate the appropriate staff person, and then resolve the issue.

TIP: Since there are always a series of general and more detailed
questions that many people ask over and over, it makes sense to maintain
this information in a central location so that everyone can find it.

Discussion Groups

Another way to centralize information, in a less static manner, is through
using discussion groups. By creating a newsgroup around a certain subject
matter, users can log in to the news server and review postings or articles on
topics relative to that subject. For example, Bagel Orchard put up a
discussion group for its resellers on promotions, so that different resellers
could benefit from ideas on what works and doesn't work in promoting
bagels in their area. Discussions typically are threaded so that you can follow

not only the original post but also the replies. Another Bagel Orchard discussion group focuses on recipe variations from the standard bagel formula.

The Online Order Form

As an example of how the Bagel Orchard site operates, if a dealer clicks on the sales portion of the home page, they have the option to see an online order form (see Figure 4-8). This is simply an HTML form, where dealers can use simple drop-down menus to select quantities of various bagels and then submit their order any time of day. The information is then routed via a back-end script to an order database, and perhaps an e-mail confirmation to the dealer is sent to confirm the order.

NOTE: The beauty of this type of model is that if the order form changes, you can simply edit the HTML form, which is updated in real time, instead of worrying about printing costs and whether the customer has the most recent form. The reader always sees the most current form, whether you update it once per day or once per year.

4

Once the order has been placed in the system, users can easily track where the shipment stands by submitting a query to the database using another HTML form. This could be simply a view into the database residing on the

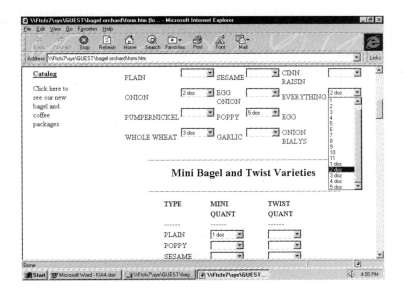

An online order form

Figure 4-8.

Web server or a connection to a third-party mainframe system. Many large shipping companies have tracking mechanisms online, so integration with popular modes of transport is made possible. Imagine the time and human resources you would save by not having to call someone to check up on the delivery of an order? No more waiting for return phone calls, reciting bill of lading numbers, and hoping that the person on the other end has the information you need. It's now automatic, and the query can be done any time of day.

Links to Other Information

As shown in Figure 4-9. The marketing section of the Bagel Orchard Intranet includes several links to useful information, including press releases, logo files for use in promotional artwork, case studies, quotes from satisfied customers, pricing information, and recipes for all the Bagel Orchard varieties.

NOTE: Not all this information is in HTML format. You can link to a spreadsheet, a word processing document, or any other document type that can be launched from a browser.

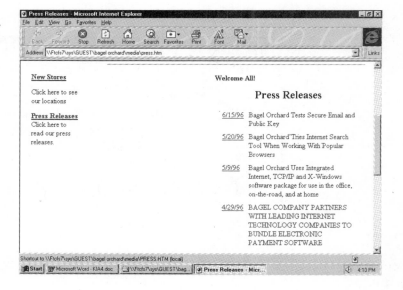

The marketing page on the Bagel Orchard Intranet

Figure 4-9.

Usually, within the Bagel Orchard community, the use of HTML-based content is favored to satisfy the users' desires and to give them the opportunity to navigate from that document to other information. HTML is an obvious choice because by using a browser, people can backtrack or skip to a new section immediately, whereas with other document formats, this generally isn't possible. (For more information on HTML, see Chapter 8).

Employee Policies and Communication

Bagel Orchard also uses online forms processing to deal with a variety of human resource and employee information issues. The following sections treat each of these concepts in detail.

Human Resources

Intelligent use of Intranet technology helps keep policy manuals completely up to date at all times, and, since human resources tends to be forms-intensive, the entire process is more streamlined. Users can go onto their internal Web to find 401(K) forms, medical and dental claims forms, change of employee status/information forms, etc. Provided you're using a secure interface, even sensitive information is safeguarded.

4

TIP: Using HTML forms allows you to maintain zero forms inventory, while providing users only what they need, when they need it. It also assures that your employees have the most up-to-the-minute forms.

The Employee Newsletter

What about the perennial employee newsletter? Most agree it's a good idea to provide a central communiqué from the company to its employees, particularly in larger companies where word may not travel quickly down the corridor. It improves morale to share news from other departments, even including announcements of birthdays and anniversaries. Unfortunately, by the time you gather all the information, typeset, and print the document, then pay for postage, you have an expensive and often out-of-date publication.

Electronic publishing of this type of information via the Human Resources home page makes more sense, from a cost and timeliness standpoint. By setting up a database of public user information—such as names, phone extensions, e-mail addresses, birthdays, and service anniversaries—employees can conduct a simple query to get only the information they want, not the whole listing.

TIP: Any new information can be published first under a "What's New" graphic or link, then archived for future reference by month, year, or however appropriate.

Searching the Intranet

As information accumulates on an Intranet, you can make use of a number of means to search the information you are managing. It is critical that users are able to find what they need quickly, with as little effort as possible. On the Web server side, you may be able to conduct a keyword search for information stored on the server. As shown in Figure 4-10, a Bagel Orchard dealer might type in the keyword "pricing" into an HTML form, and the search engine would return a list of pages where the term was found.

NOTE: Usually, there is a relevancy ranking (ordered by best fit to search criteria), document title, and brief description or abstract to assist users in selecting where they want to go. This is a good basic tool for locating information, and used with a good book-marking system, enables the users to keep track of information on the server.

Searching
your Web
server
Figure 4-10.

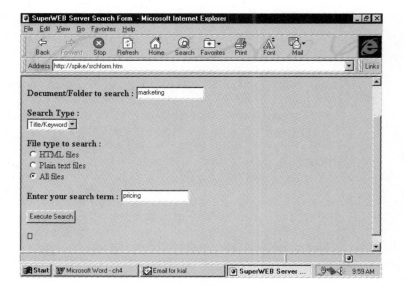

The information on your Intranet is not limited to HTML stores on the Web server, however. The same type of easy search can also be made available to the wider store of information residing on your network, whether the information lives on the Web server or in other directories. Information can be indexed periodically for eventual search by the user. Depending upon the type of package you are using, you may be able to have real-time updating, tuning of how and when the information is indexed, and a wide variety of file types, including spreadsheets, word processing documents, presentation formats, and databases.

Putting It All Together

This chapter has examined how a company's culture impacts the implementation of an Intranet. We saw how a distributed approach to information creation and management can invigorate the interaction of your organization. When everyone has a stake in ensuring that the content on your Intranet is reliable and dynamic, the entire organization benefits.

Any company in any industry (no matter what the size) can reap the cost- and time-saving rewards of sharing information in an easy-to-use graphical format. The emerging capabilities of the Intranet—including advanced search and retrieval, and database interfaces—provide springboards to next-generation levels of productivity and capability.

4

Frequently Asked Questions

♦ **What is the best way to sell the Intranet concept to my management?**

Determine the type of company culture in which you operate. If you are a progressive, management-from-the-ground-up type of organization, you may want to emphasize the load sharing that a distributed Intranet can provide. In other words, many people can contribute content to your Intranet, thereby lightening the load on any single Webmaster. If your company is resistant to change, new to Web technology, or more inclined to follow singular points of management control, you would be better off positioning the Intranet as a time and money saver that can still be controlled by a select few people, according to the wishes of upper management.

♦ **How can I reduce costs by using an Intranet?**

Just one example is putting human resources forms online. Instead of filling out a vacation request form on a piece of paper, the user browses the HR site and completes the information. More importantly, time- and version-sensitive documents—such as tax forms or policy manuals—are always up to date, because you update them online, and you don't have to print and distribute the revised forms to all your remote locations. You also save time, and therefore gain productivity, when your users can perform such tasks right from their desktops.

♦ **How can I make the most of my Web server?**

By making the Web server a dynamic source for corporate information— from pricing to technical tips to product information to financial and other business data—the organization is revitalized with current information. The multimedia aspect of Web information display via a browser presents data in a compelling and intuitive fashion. Back-end applications bring rich online services.

♦ **Does having an Intranet mean that I have to get rid of my e-mail package?**

No, your messaging program continues to play a key role in your Intranet. E-mail is a popular, though not exclusive, means to communicate over an Intranet. Once your users become familiar with discussion groups and online HTML forms, your e-mail usage may see a slight decline. On the other hand, many new collaborative software packages use e-mail as the vehicle for automatically forwarding notification and routing notices for workgroup task control.

4

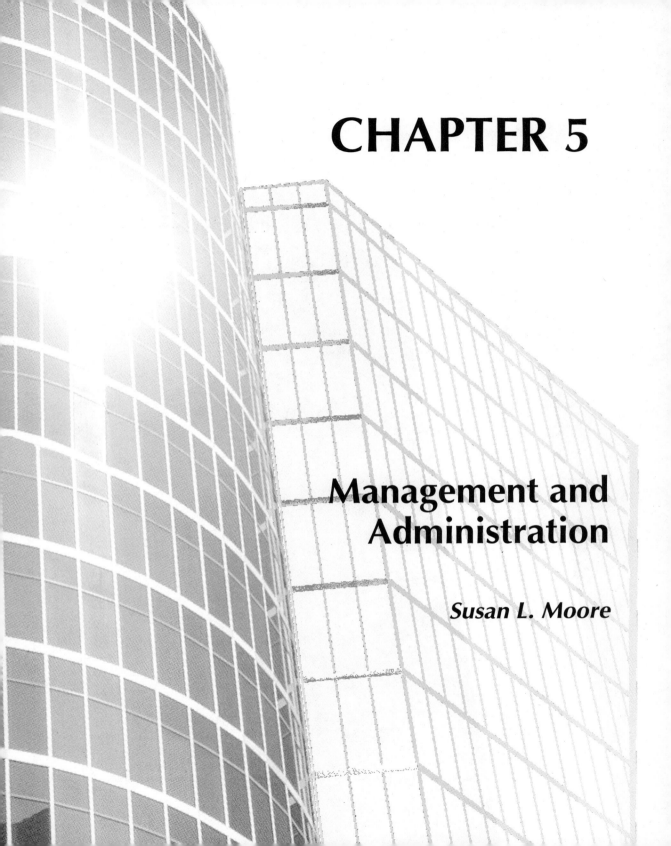

CHAPTER 5

Management and
Administration

Susan L. Moore

Chapter Objectives

♦ Learn what roles people will play in your Intranet

♦ Discover if you need to hire new people to fill the roles

♦ Learn how to set up your information structure

♦ Find out who should have access to which parts of your information structure

When you look at the Intranets in other companies, you might see smooth, efficient implementations: everyone in the company uses the many tools an Intranet provides to communicate more effectively with each other and the rest of the world. How do these companies do it? Will your Intranet run as smoothly? The answer is yes, if you take the time to plan! Before you can plan the tangible aspects of your Intranet, such as those discussed in Chapter 7, you need to iron out the conceptual details surrounding the management and administration.

Before You Begin

Before implementing your Intranet, consider the following basic concepts on how it should be managed:

♦ Define the roles people will play so that everyone has a clear understanding of what their responsibilities are before any hardware is configured or any software is installed. A typical Intranet needs people to fill the roles of one or more Webmasters, in addition to workgroup leaders, content creators, artists, and programmers.

♦ Decide the best way to administer the information on your Intranet. Construct your information and access structure so that each person can play the role with ease. The structure can, for example, mirror the organizational structure of the people who will interact with, administer, and configure the Intranet. Through effective Intranet organization, productive implementation is guaranteed!

5

 TIP: Though defining the roles and structure may sound too obvious to plan, doing so is crucial if you want your Intranet to run smoothly—and who doesn't want that?

The Roles People Play

In any Intranet, there are multiple people involved in setup and maintenance. One person cannot handle all of the technical and administrative issues associated with an Intranet site. Before you even install your Intranet, you should brainstorm about who needs to be involved and what exactly each person needs to do, so all of those who need to take part can at least be forewarned of their involvement. After all, no one likes new jobs sprung on them! Assignments can be driven by expectations of Intranet utilization. You can, for example, create a drawing of your expectations such as the one shown in Figure 5-1. You might create the drawing yourself or, better yet,

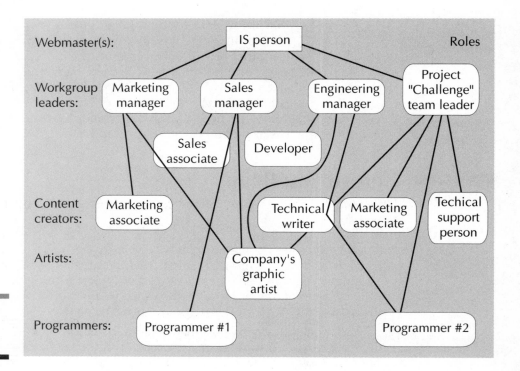

ask for input from other employees or people outside of your company who are already using an Intranet.

TIP: Creating a role map now for future use can help prevent mistakes as you implement your Intranet.

The Webmaster

As you can see in Figure 5-1, the *Webmaster* is the heart of your Intranet. This is the person who, minimally, takes care of other employees' problems with the Intranet's Web server, news server, mail server, or any other servers you might have. This person might also be responsible for installing and configuring the Intranet and posting all of the documents on the Web server. Depending on the size of your company and the experience of the employees, you might have one of two Webmaster types and any number of central Webmasters.

The Technical Webmaster

This person is usually one of the more technical people in your organization. In a smaller company where one person bears multiple responsibilities, the MIS (Management Information Systems) or IS (Information Systems) person often also becomes, by default, the technical Webmaster due to his or her experience. Though this person normally fields the questions posed by frustrated employees who have forgotten their password (yet again) or who can't figure out how to open their e-mail, he or she also installs and upgrades any Intranet-related software on employees' computers. The technical Webmaster may even handle hardware and software configuration issues surrounding employees' computers and the servers. When new employees start, the technical Webmaster is responsible for not only setting up the computers by loading software or specific capabilities, but also for getting the new employees set up on all of the servers. New employees need to be added to a computer "address book" such as exists on a DNS (Domain Name System) server or on a mail server. In addition, new employees need access rights established and accounts created on the servers.

Backing Up Information   One important detail the technical Webmaster may need to handle is creating backups of the Intranet's information. For example, if you have dynamic information stored on a file server, it should be backed up every night. If your file server happens to crash and all of the data is lost, you can spend twice as much time as you originally spent creating the information. Not only must you remember what you have done since the last backup, you must also re-create the information. Lost data can haunt you for months. Perhaps you created a small pricing document that was lost in the crash. You may not need it tomorrow, but when you look for it a month from now when you are under deadline pressure, you are going to be extremely frustrated by its absence!

5

CAUTION: If you do not back up your information, your company can be set back weeks trying to re-create lost data.

NOTE: For information about setting up DNS and mail servers, see Chapter 7.

Setting Up Remote Users   If you have remote employees accessing the Intranet, the technical Webmaster may need to configure their computers and set up accounts with Internet service providers (ISPs) in other cities. Often times, the employees carry laptop computers with them. If the Webmaster, or someone knowledgeable, doesn't install the software and configure the computer, the employee often gets to a remote location only to realize something isn't working right—and he or she can't figure out what that something is. Writing a small troubleshooting guide may also help with such problems. Give employees certain steps to take before they call the Webmaster when they think something is wrong with their laptops. Finally, if you have traveling salespeople who normally rotate through particular cities, the Webmaster can set up the accounts with ISPs local to those cities. The salespeople then have established accounts they can rely on whenever they return to the city. Again, guidelines for the employees to follow may help prevent questions. Tell them how to dial in to the ISP, and give them any necessary information about their e-mail account (such as address, username, and password), as well as any other information that is often asked of the Webmaster.

TIP: In the past, companies have often had remote employees dial directly in to the network. However, this was not only costly (as it was normally a long-distance phone call), but it also demanded that the technical Webmaster maintain the necessary servers, dial-up ports, and other hardware. If, instead, the remote employees use a local ISP to dial in to the Intranet, not only does the company save money, but also the time and sanity of the Webmaster! See Chapter 7 for information about some of the major ISPs in the United States.

Hyperlinks   More than likely, a Web server will be part of your Intranet. A problem unique to Web servers needs be addressed by the Webmaster. Web servers link information together in a unique way. Instead of people having to manually open file after file, HTML files (Web pages) are linked together by jumps known as *hyperlinks*. Using a browser, users can browse through an entire document set by simply following the links. However, if you have a large amount of information on your Web server, you need to be careful that it doesn't get lost. For example, suppose you have a large number of technical support documents that can only be accessed from an index page. What happens if someone moves the technical support documents, making all of the hyperlinks on the index page invalid? One way to prevent bad links on your Web site is to use a tool, such as the one shown in Figure 5-2, that checks the integrity of links. Often such utilities allow you not only to check the links on your site but also to be sure the links to other Web sites still exist.

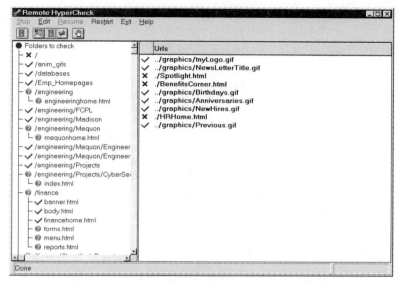

Checking the links of a site's HTML pages

Figure 5-2.

✗   The file or folder contains one or more invalid hyperlinks.

❷   A hyperlink in the file or folder could not be resolved (may be an external link).

✓   All of the hyperlinks in the file or folder were resolved.

Another problem you can encounter on your Web site is *floating* Web pages. These are pages that might be extremely valuable but no page points to them with a hyperlink, so no one knows they exist. The Webmaster is probably extremely familiar with the Web site; by looking through the information on the Web site—not through a browser but rather by viewing the Web server's actual information structure—he or she can see pages that look unfamiliar. If the Webmaster has never encountered a particular page when jumping through the Web site using a browser, odds are that the page has nothing pointing to it. The Webmaster can then inform the creator of the page, so that he or she can include a jump from another page to the floating page.

The Nontechnical Webmaster

Installing software is often not the nontechnical Webmaster's responsibility, nor is configuring the LAN. Instead, the nontechnical Webmaster begins to administer the Intranet after the technical people have the Intranet hardware and software installed and initially configured. While nontechnical Webmasters may look to the MIS or IS department for assistance when the technical jargon becomes too obscure, they are probably able to solve many problems on their own. This person probably has less

5

experience configuring hardware but has had enough experience to pick up on Intranet server configuration.

Nontechnical Webmasters may not even have to become involved in the administration and maintenance of any servers except the Web server. For example, the MIS department may want control over the mail server, DNS server, and news server, because they require an initial set up by an informed person but don't demand everyday maintenance. The Web server, on the other hand, may need someone to continually look after it. Some Web-server software restricts document manipulation to only one Webmaster. This means that every time a person wants to add, delete, or change a file, the Webmaster must do it. This is normally a job that technical people, such as those in an MIS department, don't have time to do. Therefore another, perhaps nontechnical, person may become the designated central Webmaster of the Intranet's Web site. This person is then required to perform the necessary administration of the Web site based on employee requests.

If you are using Web-server software that allows many people to add documents to the Web server, the Webmaster's tasks diminish significantly. He or she only needs to add users, set security options, or perform other infrequently requested tasks. Such tasks may involve a check once a month to ensure that the information others have placed on the Web server is useful company information and is organized into the appropriate folders. This type of check may need to be done more frequently at first, until employees are used to the Web server's administrative utilities. If the Webmaster catches user mistakes early on, people can avoid forming bad habits.

Having Multiple Webmasters

You might have more than one person who plays the role of the Webmaster. For example, all the employees in the MIS department might be considered Webmasters. With most software, having multiple Webmasters implies that more than one person knows the passwords for the administrative tools, and knows how to use them. Therefore, if one person is gone, no one has to wait; another Webmaster can answer questions and solve problems. The company's productivity, then, is not affected by the absence of one person.

A Potential Problem   Having multiple Webmasters can be problematic. If too many people have complete access to the administrative tools, one person might accidentally undo the actions of another. For example, suppose you have a Web server set up for internal use only. You also have a marketing person who works from home. Normally, the Webmaster restricts everyone outside of the company's domain from accessing the internal Web server, but the marketing person needs access. If one Webmaster gives the person's domain (or the person's Internet service provider's domain) access to the internal Web server, a second Webmaster may see that someone outside the company has been given access and take away the right, because he or she isn't aware of the special situation. When the marketing person can't get on the internal Web server, he or she is likely to make an angry call to one of the Webmasters to complain.

And Its Solution   To avoid falling into such a situation, one person can be designated as the central Webmaster. That way, others know the correct passwords and understand the administrative tools but are only allowed to configure the software if the central Webmaster isn't present, or if that Webmaster gives them permission to perform a specific function. To make decisions easy, Webmasters can have a written set of standards to which they adhere. The standards may define which sites are restricted from accessing the Intranet, which firewall application filters are to be used, which employees can be allocated what resources (such as file server space), and any other issues that are frequently addressed by the Webmaster. Of course, in an ideal situation, the Webmasters will work well together, keeping open lines of communication, so that they all know what the others are doing.

 CAUTION: If you are going to have more than one Webmaster, be sure each has a well-defined role and has a good understanding of what the others are doing.

5

Workgroup Leaders

Depending on the setup of your Intranet and the software you are using, workgroup leaders play different roles. Their main function, however, is to set up the standards for others in the group. Workgroup leaders need to show group members how to use Intranet tools such as newsreaders and e-mail. The workgroup leaders do not need to understand the technical issues of the Intranet. They just need to understand how to use the client software.

The General Role

Workgroup leaders, in general, provide direction for the other people in the group. These people may constitute an entire department, or they may belong to a project group composed of people from multiple departments. Workgroup leaders might be department heads or appointed project leaders. In either case, the leader is planning the workgroup's activities and keeping everyone on track with respect to their goals and deadlines.

Maintaining the Web Pages

In an Intranet, the role of the workgroup leader needs to be expanded. An Intranet provides the leader with exciting new ways of achieving business goals. Information can be made immediately available to all members of the project team or to external customers. Applications can use exciting, multimedia-rich browser front ends in combination with legacy database sources. Leaders can also have Web pages on the Intranet's Web server. These pages might explain to the company what the department or project group is working on or might be restricted to those in the group because they contain confidential information. In either case, the workgroup leader is the one who decides what should or should not be posted on the Web site. The leader can also decide who in the group should create and maintain the Web pages.

TIP: One fact leaders should emphasize to those creating content is the need to keep the pages fresh. If a page is created and dropped on the Web site, never to be touched again, others in the company stop visiting it after awhile because it contains the same, stale information.

Working with the Web Server

If you are using Web-server software that allows you to have one central Webmaster with access rights and multiple other Webmasters with fewer access rights, workgroup leaders play a more active role. Workgroup leaders can then take control of folders on the Web site, either making themselves or someone else in the workgroup the owner. If the software allows it, the workgroup leader and other workgroup members can then add, modify, and delete documents on the Web server without interrupting the central Webmaster. If your Web-server software allows one and only one Webmaster, the workgroup leader needs to get the documents to the Webmaster, or assign someone in the group to this task.

News Servers and Newsgroups

The workgroup leader may utilize other aspects of the Intranet. For example, if you have a news server, the workgroup leader might request that the Webmaster create a newsgroup for the group so that they can post questions or comments about the department or project in one central location. Technical support departments can ask questions of the engineers using a newsreader, as is shown in Figure 5-3. The newsgroup can also contain a Frequently Asked Questions list, called a *FAQ,* that the leader designates a group member to maintain. The person can then record questions commonly asked about the department or project. Having this information

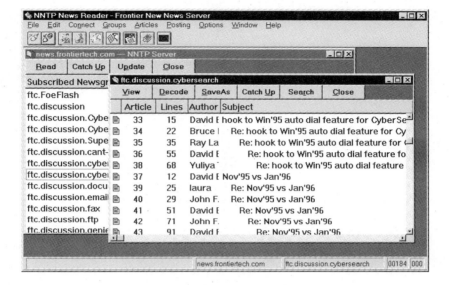

Technical support can use newsgroups to ask questions of engineers
Figure 5-3.

in a newsgroup for people to reference can save others the irritation of answering the same questions over and over again.

TIP: With a newsreader, the posts can be saved on the news server indefinitely without people in the group having to perform any special actions. New people, or people who are getting into a project late, can then easily be directed by the workgroup leader to the older FAQs and other posts.

5

E-mail Management

The workgroup leader might also request that an e-mail alias be created on the mail server so e-mailing everyone at once can be done quickly. If you don't have a news server, you can also use e-mail to ask questions of a large group at one time. However, if you are using e-mail to, for example, send and respond to FAQs, everyone needs to understand how to save messages so that they can refer back to them or send them to a new person. The messages might be saved in a particular folder that each group member creates in his or her e-mail application. The workgroup leader can define such a strategy for saving the messages, so that everyone is using the same method.

Administering Chat Applications

Chat applications are also useful tools that allow many people at a time to join in an electronic discussion. With news and mail groups, you don't see someone's response until they post or send it. With a chat application, many people can be logged on at once, and everyone can see responses as people type them. Meetings using chat applications can be set up by the workgroup leader. The workgroup leader can then start the chat by typing the agenda of the meeting and can direct the electronic discussion, thereby preventing others from veering off on a tangent.

T IP: Having virtual meetings with chat applications can help out in situations where person-to-person meetings or conference phone calls are impossible, such as when you are having a meeting with people scattered throughout the world.

An Educational Role

Explaining how these communication tools should be used is also extremely important for the workgroup leader to do. You can't simply tell the others in the group that a folder on the Web server or an e-mail alias on the mail server has been created. Instead, tell the group what sort of information should be passed on using the tool, how often the information should be updated, and what each person's specific responsibilities are. If you merely tell the group that a folder on the Web server has been created but tell no one what they should be adding to it, they probably either won't use it or will put the wrong information in it. Too many times communication tools are not used because people don't quite understand what they are supposed to do with them. Setting up a few simple guidelines for the group helps them understand the usefulness of the tools, making the group much more likely to use them.

T IP: The workgroup leader needs to instruct the group on how to use the proposed communication tool. Without such instruction, the tools are misused or unused.

Content Creators

Those in a department or project group who are not involved in the management often become content creators for the Intranet. These are the ones who make the Intranet valuable. They create useful information to place in well-thought-out locations for others in the workgroup, department, company, or outside world to access. Though everyone in your company is a content creator to some extent, the main content creators are the people who create the Web pages, post and respond to questions on the news server, and design documents, such as finance forms, which make communication and information tracking easier. They may also create charts, diagrams, tables, and other visuals that enhance comprehension of a concept or fact, helping to increase company productivity. These items may be embellished by an Intranet's artists, but the rough draft usually comes from a content creator. Content creators might only create information for one group or department, or they might create and pull together information for many areas.

Software Knowledge

The content creators do not necessarily need to be technically oriented people. They do, however, need to know how to use certain software tools. For example, if they are creating Web pages, they either need to know HyperText Markup Language (HTML), or how to use an HTML editor such as the one shown in Figure 5-4. If their job is to create Excel spreadsheets to place on the internal Web server, they need to know Excel, as well as the Web-server software. If they need to create a database, they need to learn database design and how to use a database program. Depending on their job, they might also need to know how to use a newsreader or an e-mail application. However, they do not need to understand how to configure an Intranet, or even how it works; they just need to make the information available to others.

Departmental Awareness

Perhaps just as important as knowledge of specific software is a content creator's knowledge of the group or department. Because they are the ones actually putting the information on your Intranet, content creators also need the ability to extract information from others with relative ease. They also need to be well-informed about the department or group. After all, you don't want an engineer creating the Marketing department's Web page, do you? Similarly, you don't want a person in Marketing who has little involvement with the rest of the department, or who is too timid to ask questions about the department's doings, to be in charge of the content creation for the department. If they are connected to the Internet, content creators should also be ambitious enough to look at other Web sites to continually find new, exciting ways of presenting information.

5

CAUTION: The content creator also needs to be dedicated to updating the company information. If information becomes stale, especially if it's on a Web page, people in the company will stop using it. Information has a useful half-life. When fresh, it has the power to make people more productive and competitive. Old information has a reverse effect. It is, therefore, imperative to set in place a policy to keep information up to date to energize the organization.

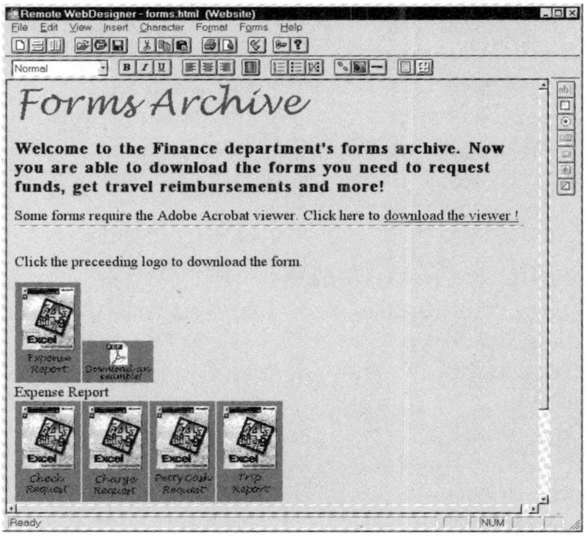

A forms
archive
designed
using an
HTML editor
Figure 5-4.

Knowledge of Display Methods

Content creators also need to understand the best method of displaying
their information. Though at times a workgroup leader may direct a content
creator to lead a discussion on the news server, it is also possible that the
content creator might just be asked to create an expense report form for
others to fill out. The creator's responsibility, then, is not only to construct
the form but also to decide how it should be given to the rest of the group,
department, or company.

T IP: Though forms can be e-mailed to everyone, people tend to delete
their e-mail if they don't need it right away. Maybe the better place for a
form is on the Web server. The creator can e-mail everyone to let them know
where the form is on the Web site. Making such judgment calls about
content placement can be as important as creating the actual content. What
good is the information if people can't easily find it?

Web Page Creators

Though you may not realize it, many content creators are probably already
hard at work in your company. They just need to be introduced to your new
Intranet so that they can understand how the Intranet's tools can take what
they do and truly distribute it to others. However, there is one specific type
of content creator who may not yet be in your midst: a Web page creator. To
find someone to fill this role, first check out your existing content creators,

and don't overlook others in your company who are excited about the Web and might be interested in creating Web pages. Ask around. You might be surprised at how many people will jump at the opportunity to tell others about their department's or group's doings, especially if it means they can test out the latest technology!

TIP: If you need someone to create your Web pages, don't overlook current employees. They may make the best content creators!

Intranet Artists

Though you might already have artists working in your company, creating an Intranet allows them to further expand their role. The most exciting new place where they can add a great deal of value is to your Web server. Artists are the people who add flashiness to your Web site, convincing people to stay a moment and making them want to come back. Whether your Web site is for internal use only or you allow people outside your company to access it, artists help make the site visually appealing, fun, and easy to use. If you look at other's Web sites, you can immediately see that text-based sites don't cut it anymore. You need strong, bold graphics in order to get your message across and have it be remembered.

Knowledge of Technical Basics

Artists do not need to be well versed in (or even aware of) the technical issues associated with your Intranet. They do, however, need to understand what file types (.GIF and .JPEG) they can use on your Web site. Making *image maps*—clickable graphics that hyperlink Web pages together with a point and click of the mouse—is another Web-specific skill artists might need. In addition, they need to know the proper tools to use. Rich multimedia toolkits are available to help artists, but such software demands more of an artist than does knowing how to draw. The artist needs to understand how to create and manipulate computer graphics, a skill set which may require training. It is crucial for artists to be aware of basic design principles, explained in Chapter 8, as well as to scout out the latest trends in graphics. The graphics an artist designed for your home page six months ago may have been unique then, but look old now. Web sites evolve so quickly that your Web pages can easily look old-fashioned.

5

NOTE: Though you don't necessarily want your graphics to look trendy, you also don't want them to look dated, especially if you have potential customers connecting to your Web site!

Make sure that your artists are also aware of the enormous libraries of ready-to-go clip art and easy-to-use creation tools available. High-quality, professional art can be costly, so starting with clip art and using the tools that accompany the clip art can cut down your costs. Starting from scratch takes longer than starting with clip art works. Your artists might be able to develop more pieces if they do not have to start over every time.

Understanding Graphic Limitations

Though graphics may make your pages really stand out, be sure your artists also research the problems associated with creating graphic-intensive pages. For example, not all browsers support graphics or particular graphic types. If anyone is connecting to the Web site with a modem, they may also turn the graphics off, especially if the artist has placed many large graphic files on the page, because they take too long (and thus cost too much) to download. The problems are fewer if you are not connected to the Internet, but they still apply if you have employees outside of your LAN connecting remotely to your Intranet. An alert artist will note such a fact, and consider it when designing graphics for your Web server.

Intranet Programmers

Programmers add yet more depth and usability to your Intranet. Though they are normally only involved with the Web server, what they can do in this area can really add to the productivity of your Intranet. For example, suppose you want to place a simple form on your Web server that employees can fill out to request vacation days. In order to create a form, you have to associate a back-end service, or application, with it. This is a program that executes once a person starts it, either by clicking a Submit button or by accessing the service directly through a browser. The programmer is the one who can write the back-end service, while the content creators design the form.

The Two Types of Programmers

There are probably two main divisions of programmers within a company. If your company produces any software or requires complicated, in-house applications, you probably have regular, experienced programmers. Writing back-end applications should be fairly easy for people with this kind of experience. These people might then be asked to write back-end applications as an infrequent side project. You might also have people who program less often for your company. For example, there might be a person in Technical Support who writes relatively simple Visual Basic programs for internal use. These programmers might also be able to handle writing back-end applications. In fact, they might enjoy the change of pace!

Adding Excitement

Programmers can also assist you in making your Web site more exciting. This is especially important if your Intranet is connected to the Internet and seen by potential customers. Programmers can write Java applets, for example, that rotate pictures and scroll text across your Web pages. Of course, Java can be used for a lot more than making pages glitzy, but looks do count! See Chapter 8 for more information about what your programmers can do with Java.

Using Vendors' Back-End Applications

Though many Web servers come with back-end services, they are probably rather generic. They are targeted for those who have no programming resources, and who must, therefore, resort to using canned back-end applications. Though many of these applications can be useful, if you want to customize any, or create your own, you probably need someone who can program.

NOTE: To learn about what tools these programmers need to have to create or customize back-end applications, see Chapters 3 and 8.

NOTE: Though you may need the help of an experienced programmer to write complicated back-end services, there are newly emerging tools that are putting the construction of these applications into the realm of the nonprogrammer. The idea is that a person with no programming experience will be able to create customized back-end services!

5

Unfilled Roles?

What if your company is extremely small—no artists, no programmers— what should you do? You always have the option of either sending current employees out for training or of hiring consultants or other outside agencies to help you out. Depending on your needs, one or both methods may work for you.

Training Current Employees

While training current employees can be costly and time consuming, the benefit is that you retain the expertise of those employees for as long as you employ them. If you pay to have one or two people trained, these individuals can take over the training of others within your company. Your employees will probably appreciate your efforts to train them. Too often, consultants are brought in when capable current employees are interested in learning the information, causing the employees to stand back and shake their heads in frustration.

Seeking Outside Help

If you would prefer to instead look for help outside of your company, especially consultants, there are a few items to consider first:

- Can the outside person train someone in your company at the same time?
- Remember that once the consultant is gone, you might be left high and dry. Can you find a company who is willing to support you after the consultant's contract is over?
- Can you get referrals from customers for the consulting firm?
- Can you get the URLs of any Web sites the consultant has created?

For Webmaster Duties   Outside resources can help you out in a number of ways. A person from a consulting company, for example, can play the role of the Webmaster, at least temporarily. This person may have set up other Intranets and can therefore do so much more quickly than someone within your company.

NOTE: Someone in your company should learn how to take over this role while the consultant is there, unless you can afford to have a permanent consultant in your midst.

For Content Creation   Though you can also hire outside resources to help you with content creation, think carefully before you do so. If you are publishing information strictly for your Intranet, you might want to keep the job internal—after all, no one knows your company's information better than someone who already works there! If you do decide to hire someone from the outside, be sure the person stays in close contact with one of your employees. This contact person should be in charge of updating the outside resource with the latest information and making sure what the resource creates is accurate and matches your corporate style.

For Artwork   You can also find outside sources to fill the role of an artist. Even large companies often seek outside sources for their artwork. There are many agencies around that can work with you to create graphics for your Web site. If your Web site is strictly an Intranet, you might not need to spend the time or money to have incredible graphics created. However, if customers are accessing your site, great graphics can help your site get noticed and be remembered.

For Programming   You can also enlist the aid of programmers from outside resources. There is no substitute for experience when speed to market is the major requirement. In addition, it might be less expensive to hire someone to program (and debug!) a back-end service than to hire a full-time programmer in your company. If you don't have enough work for a full-time programmer, hiring one from an outside resource might be the best investment of your time and money. Just be sure that the program is really working before you let the person go! Also be sure that the program has been fully documented. Once the consultant leaves, you want to be sure that any programmer can pick up the program and quickly understand the logic behind it.

TIP: To find outside resources, you can look in many places. Try phone books and newspapers. Look in magazines—not only computer magazines! Be sure to also look in trade journals, and if you have access to a browser, look around on the Web. Many sites have a note on their home page telling you who helped them design their site, which can lead you to programmers, artists, or content creators. Also look at nearby colleges and universities. College students are always looking for internships, and this might be a great way for them to gain experience and for you to obtain creative, cutting-edge work.

5

Structuring Your Information

Now that you have some ideas about who needs to be involved in managing and administering your Intranet, you need to decide how information should be stored and who should have access to it. Planning your information structure beforehand, or at least the skeleton of it, can save you a lot of future headaches. An effective, carefully constructed information structure will result in intuitive, efficient access and retrieval of your corporate knowledge base. What might be most helpful for you to do is sketch out an information chart, similar to the one in Figure 5-5.

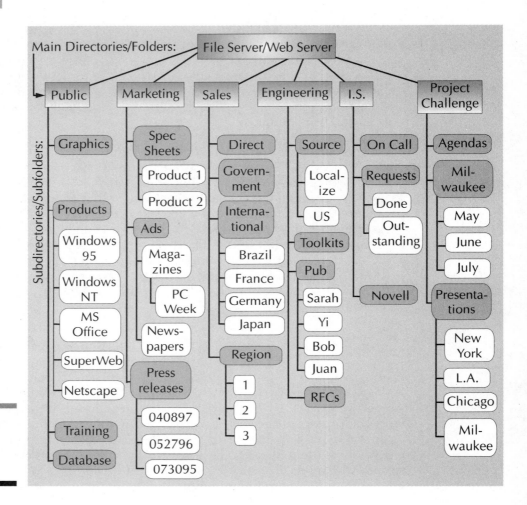

Sample
information
structure
Figure 5-5.

Departments and Folders

The most crucial point illustrated by the chart in Figure 5-5 is that you need to organize your information structure *before* you begin moving files around. The chart defines a hierarchical approach to the information organization. This method is probably the most intuitive one. When you organize your own loose papers, for example, you probably place related information into one folder. Then you probably group together the folders relating to each other and place them in a bigger folder with a more generalized name. The same idea applies here. To best organize your information, follow these steps:

1. Start with the big picture: your main divisions, such as departmental divisions (Marketing, for example). Make these divisions main directories.

2. Divide the main directories into subdirectories containing related pieces of information. Create as many subdirectories as necessary to neatly organize the information. For example, you may have a subdirectory that contains all specification sheets, or you may create subdirectories named for each product.

T IP: You can also create folders for project groups, either instead of, or in addition to, departmental folders. These types of folders are especially useful for projects being worked on by team members from multiple departments.

Storage Options

You need to define a strategy for the physical location of the various file types (HTML Web pages, text files, image maps, back-end applications, and so on) that comprise your corporate Intranet information warehouse. You have a few options for storing information, any of which fit the model of your information structure chart. Following are the most important items to consider:

♦ Who will need the information?

♦ What is the most intuitive and practical location for the information?

♦ Can the necessary people easily retrieve the information?

♦ Is there enough space at the location for the information?

♦ If the information is confidential or crucial, can access to it be restricted?

Using a File Server

If you have an existing file server, you can keep using it to store your information. Many people in your company may also be used to working with a file server, so keeping information on the file server is comfortingly familiar to them. Sometimes, files are best suited for your file server. For example, if you have programmers in your company, the best location for their source code is definitely on a file server. Programmers need a location for storing and compiling their code, and a file server is really the only location that can provide for both needs. File servers can also be used to

5

store and install software for people in the company to access. In addition, confidential information can be stored on a file server, if access to directories can be controlled by the Webmaster. Large document sets are also right at home on a file server, as shown in Figure 5-6. File servers generally have enough space to handle large bundles of information. If you run out of space, you can usually purchase more space with relative ease.

Using a Web Server

The Web server is an ideal location for placing files or pieces of information that many people in your company need to access. Any HTML pages will probably be stored on the Web server. The information on these pages can be anything from updates on employee benefits to the latest sales figures. These are small pieces of information that are important but that can often get lost on a file server. Using a Web server allows you to connect your Web pages with hyperlinks, letting people quickly browse through files to find the bits of information they need.

The amount of space available on your Web server depends on where you have installed it. For example, if you are using a Windows NT–based Web server, the amount of space available depends on the size of the server's hard drive. This space can always be increased by upgrading the computer.

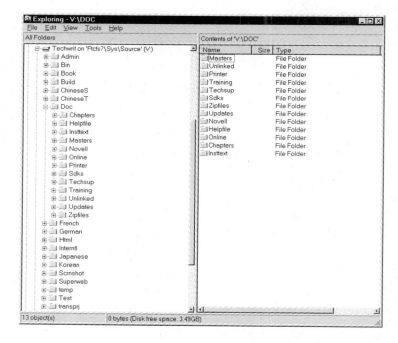

Example of a large document structure stored on a file server
Figure 5-6.

TIP: Depending on your Web-server software, you might be able to simply point to files on the file server that you also want registered with the Web server, which eliminates redundant file storage and saves space on your Web server.

Many Web-server software packages allow you to easily restrict access to areas you don't want others entering, making Web servers a fairly secure location for information. You might be required to enter a password to administer the Web server, and even then you might not have access to all of the documents. For example, in Figure 5-7, you can restrict folder access to only certain groups.

Using a News Server

If you are also interested in storing smaller bits of information, such as frequently asked questions, a news server might be an ideal location. You cannot store documents on a news server, but it is a good, central location for small pieces of information. For example, your technical support group could post customer questions to engineers, as shown in Figure 5-8, or your sales group could have discussions about next quarter's strategy.

5

Restricting
access to a
folder on a
Web server
using
Web-server
administrative
tools
Figure 5-7.

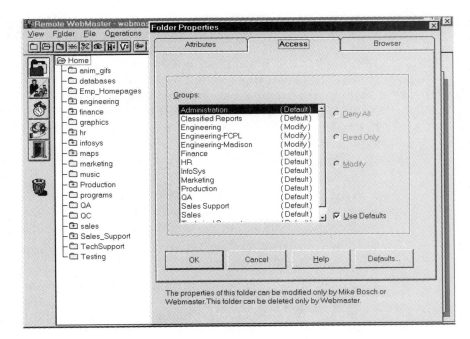

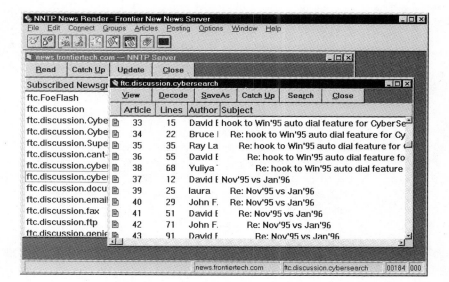

Posting
questions to
engineers
using a
newsreader
Figure 5-8.

Using FTP Servers

You can also store smaller pieces of information on an FTP server, as it can be readily accessed by those who use it the most. Your FTP server might be used by customers to download new versions of software, information about your product, or perhaps some catchy, multimedia demonstrations. This is not a place where you store files that are frequently needed by people inside your company. FTP sites are more useful to people outside your company who want to download files from you, as the Remote directory in Figure 5-9 shows. The easiest way to point to your FTP site is by using links on your Web site. For example, you can create links on your Web pages such as "Click here to download our newest software!" The link can then go to the FTP server. In this way, you limit access to your FTP server to those who first come through your Web server.

Be sure that

♦ One person is, or only a few specific people are, in charge of the FTP site—perhaps the Webmaster. This should prevent confidential or internal-use files from making their way into the outside world.

♦ The files placed on the FTP server are valuable to those in the outside world.

♦ If you have a *beta,* or first version, of your software on your FTP server, it runs. (This is not as silly a point as it might seem!) Have you included enough documentation with the software so that the phones in technical support won't be ringing off the hook? The documentation should clearly explain how to get the software up and running. It should also mention the known problems and where customers can call or send questions and comments.

◆ Before placing files on your FTP server, be sure that they are clean. Nothing irritates a customer more than downloading a file that is infected with a virus!

CAUTION: Before putting files on your FTP server for outside people to download, be sure they are of high quality. If a customer gets a defective file once from your server, the odds are they won't return.

Levels of Access

No matter which of the storage methods you select, there are always issues of access to consider. Who should have access to a particular directory on the Web server or file server? Who makes changes to the information? What information needs to be controlled, or restricted? Should any IP addresses be restricted from the news server? The way you assign access depends on what type of servers you are using and your software. Some server software allows you to determine who has read or write access to an area. You might also be able to allow people into an area if they supply the correct password. Different security options, such as those discussed in Chapter 9, may also

5

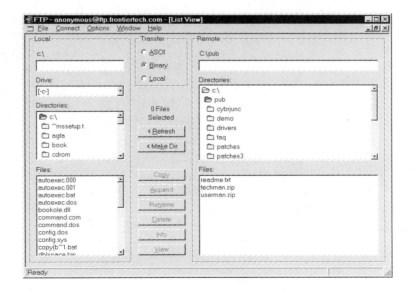

Possible setup of an FTP server

Figure 5-9.

help you restrict people from accessing, or permit people to access, your information.

Constructing an Access Chart

Whatever the method you use to assign access, you can construct an access chart, such as the one in Figure 5-10, that helps you define your access levels. You can start by designating the access levels of your most frequently used information structure, which is probably either a Web server or a file server. Once you have the access structure created, you can design structures for smaller areas, such as a news server or an FTP server.

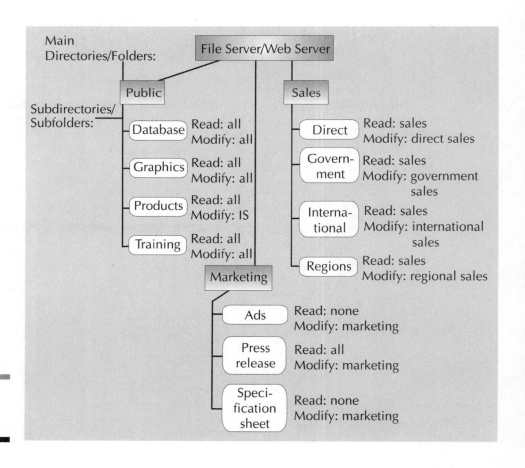

An Intranet
access chart
Figure 5-10.

Considering the Needs of People

To help you decide who should have access to what types of files, consider the needs of groups of people. It might help to divide your structure into the following main levels:

♦ Workgroup

♦ Corporate

♦ World Wide Web

Keep another idea in mind as you assign access levels: It's better to give people too little access at first than too much. You can always give people read access to a folder if they discover they need it, but you can't take away someone's memory if they see information that was not meant for them!

CAUTION: People might also accidentally delete or change files, losing the originals forever, if the information isn't backed up. Such mistakes can set a company back weeks.

Access at the Workgroup Level

A workgroup can either be a project group or a department. This is probably the lowest main-division level in your company, although there might be sublevels under workgroups. You can, for example, give workgroups their own folder on a Web server, their own drive on a file server, or their own group on a news server. These are locations where the members of the workgroup can share information they have created. If your workgroup is small, you might want to give the entire group the same access rights. However, if you have extremely large workgroups, you might give parts of the workgroups different access than others. For example, Government Sales might have write access to folders on your Web server that the rest of the Sales department does not.

Handling Revisions When people collaborate on projects, they are often accessing shared document sets. How do people avoid stepping on each other's work? Revision utilities are often built in to word processing software. For example, Figure 5-11 shows how Microsoft Word handles revisions. Text that has been added is underlined in blue, while deleted text is highlighted in blue. You can often configure revision utilities to mark edits by different authors in different colors so that everyone knows who worked on what.

5

Revision
marks in a
document
Figure 5-11.

Monitoring Workflow You can also use workflow programs to
synchronize the efforts of the team. For example, you might have a
document that needs to be looked at first by Holly, then by Andy, and
finally by Yun. Using a workflow program, you can configure the document
to be sent to each person in a specified order. When that person is done, the
document might be automatically e-mailed to the next person on the list, or
a notice may be mailed to the next person indicating where the document is
and how much time the person has to review it.

Access at the Corporate Level

What type of information do you want your entire company to be able to
access? In any company, communication is part of the key to success; too
often, mistakes happen because one department forgets or misunderstands
what another was doing.

Creating a Central Location When you are designing your access chart, be
sure you create a central location for information that is vital to the
company. For example, suppose the Marketing department has just
developed their latest specification sheets for your new product. What if no
one else in the company can get to these sheets ? There might be mistakes in
the specification sheets caused by miscommunications. What if Marketing
e-mailed everyone in the company and told them that the new specification
sheets were on the Intranet's Web server? True, not everyone would
immediately run for their browser to check out the specs, but at least they
would have the opportunity to do so.

TIP: Try to think of other situations where the whole company should be able to see documents. When you have come up with a few different situations, you can begin to decide how to handle them. Probably the best method is to create a centralized location for certain pieces of information.

Using a Public Directory   In the previous situation, there might be a subfolder of the Marketing folder to which everyone in the company has read access. You might also create a public directory on the file server where such information can be stored. Public directories are also good for information that is requested often from a department. Perhaps the MIS department gets continually bombarded with requests from people to install the latest version of Microsoft Office on their computers. If the files were on the file server, people could run the installation themselves, without having to bother MIS for so much as an installation CD.

Maintaining a Central Location   There is one possible drawback to creating central locations—people don't always use them properly. If you give people a spot to drop all of their specifications sheets, for example, after a little time you may discover that all the specs sheets from 1940 on have found their way into a public location. No one needs the information, but there it sits, taking up valuable space. The Webmaster or some other designated person might want to address this issue by periodically scanning folders or directories, checking for large numbers of old files; then he or she can contact those responsible for the folder or directory to see if it is necessary to keep the information. If that doesn't work, you can always back up the information, if you have the means, and delete what appears to be outdated. You'd be amazed at how few people notice the information is gone! If anyone does complain, you can always restore the information from the backup. This, perhaps, is not the most politically correct move and one that definitely should not be done unless you can make a reliable backup of the information, but it does get rid of the files!

5

CAUTION: Beware of junk files cluttering up your servers. Sometimes when people are given a place to store files, they fill up the space until someone draws the line!

Getting User Input   If you have problems coming up with situations where a central location would be beneficial, maybe you should sit down with the workgroup leaders. Ask them what situations require access to areas other than their own. Even if you think you've come up with situations, you might still want to have such a meeting; employees can often easily describe situations where they wish they had been better informed! Study these situations to find out how storing the information differently might have averted the problem.

Access at the World Wide Web Level

Are you going to be connected to the Internet? If so, you need to decide whether or not you are going to allow people outside of your company to access your Intranet. If you are willing to set up and maintain a fresh Web site for your customers to see, you might be ready to open it up to the rest of the world as well. If, on the other hand, you are just starting to get up to speed on the World Wide Web, you might want to first experiment internally. See what works and what doesn't. You can also begin to estimate the amount of work it will take your company to maintain a Web site that is to be accessed by customers.

If you are not going to allow external access to your Intranet, you have now finished setting up your access structure. Now you need to set up access restrictions to prevent the outside world from getting in. Ways of setting these restrictions are discussed in detail in Chapter 9. However, if you are going to allow outside people to visit you through the wires, you need to decide what information these people should have access to.

Working with Your Web Server   Most of the time, outside people access information on your Intranet via your Web server or your FTP server. If your company cannot afford two separate Web servers, your Web server might contain information for both your Intranet and the Internet. If this is the case, you need to be especially careful about how you design your folder and access structure on your Web server. For example, you don't want your customers (or competitors) to access information explaining the weaknesses in your product! Setting up your folder structure and access rights carefully on your Web server can prevent such mistakes.

T **IP:**   Think before you copy files to the Web server. Maybe only one person should have the ability to copy files in the folder you want customers to access, so that someone else in the company can't accidentally copy files to it. (This scenario assumes, of course, that you are using Web-server software that supports having multiple Webmasters.)

One effective technique, shown in Figure 5-12, is to have two main folders—one for external, and one for internal, use. Then, any folders that need to be created for either area can be subfolders under the main external or internal folder. Such a folder structure makes a clear distinction between internal and external information.

FTP Server Issues   Setting access to an FTP server involves a thought process similar to that of setting up the Web server's access structure. Be sure that you are not allowing those outside your company access to restricted information. You can protect a portion of your FTP site by requiring a username and password and not allowing people to log in as "anonymous" (the standard guest login name). You can also compress files and put a password on them. That way, if a person does manage to access a restricted area of your FTP site, he or she won't be able to uncompress the file because they won't have the password.

A Special Case: Remote Users   One special case to consider when you are assigning access rights is that of the remote user. If you have people connecting to your Intranet outside of your network, you might need to set

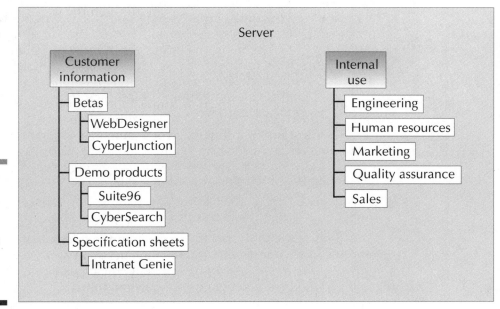

The potential
information
structure for
server
accessed both
internally and
externally
Figure 5-12.

5

standards for sending and receiving information. This is not setting access in a traditional sense, but it does involve determining who will be able to see the information. For example, suppose you want to e-mail confidential information, such as your detailed plan for the next product, to certain employees. If you are just e-mailing the information inside your network, there is probably no need to encrypt it. You might, however, also be e-mailing the information to employees located in other cities. What if a competitor happens to intercept the message and it hasn't been encrypted? That competitor will then have all of your product plans in its hands. Encrypting confidential information might, therefore, be a standard you demand when people in your Intranet are sending information to remote employees.

T **IP:**   For information about available security options, see Chapter 9.

Putting It All Together

If you have thought out your management and administration before implementing your Intranet, you are on the path to success. The issues that arise if you haven't planned ahead can become tangled messes that take months to unravel. Therefore, taking a little extra time to think now can save you a lot of headaches in the future. An Intranet is a strategy and an arsenal for improving competitiveness, reducing costs, and gaining productivity. Without effective management and administration, however, your Intranet can become a nightmare of lost files, improperly configured software, and confused employees.

Some of the most important management activities in your Intranet that need to be addressed include

♦   Setting up the proper Intranet tools for the users.

♦   Giving people the correct access to the tools. Don't make the security so impenetrable that the users can't find the tools they need.

♦   Distributing the tools effectively and providing sufficient maintenance of tools (such as upgrading them when necessary).

♦   Anticipating the growth of the Intranet. How will the information evolve? What workflows will you be attempting to automate? What other hardware and computer platforms might you migrate to?

♦   Maintaining open, yet secure, paths to information.

- ◆ Emphasizing the need for currency of information.
- ◆ Checking the integrity of the dynamic linking found in the Web pages on your Web server.

Your Intranet is a unique opportunity to create and display information using the latest technological breakthroughs. Don't let such a chance pass you by because you haven't taken the time to plan the management and administration of it. Start with strong organization. The roles that people will play need to be defined, and you should have some idea about who will be playing those roles. Avoid last-minute realizations that you have an incomplete staff. If you think you might need to contact outside resources, start researching them now so that you are not forced to choose a company under deadline pressure.

Next, determine where you are going to place the information your role players will be needing. Don't limit yourself to one location, such as a file server or Web server. Some pieces of information might be easier for people to find and use on a news server, for example. Be sure that you have carefully considered all possible locations for the information and that you choose the best possible place. A wrong decision here might make valuable information useless to the majority of people, because if they can't find and use the information easily, they won't use it at all. As an administrator, you should be setting an effective example of information structure for all in your Intranet to follow.

Finally, decide who should have access to what, not only internally, but if you are connected to the Internet, externally. Keep in mind that you are better off giving people too little access than too much. It's a lot easier to allow someone access to an area than to recover from the damage of someone being where they shouldn't. Also be sure to set standards for sending information outside of your company. What type of information must people encrypt? Should certain information never be sent to others?

5

Though you may encounter a few bumps on the road to the perfect Intranet, don't be alarmed. Simply make small adjustments to your administrative and management plans as you go. Don't be afraid to make such adjustments. Sometimes being afraid to veer from a plan causes more problems than making a minor, rational change to it. It is also important to ask for help from others. Do you know someone at another company who has set up an Intranet? Be sure to find out what their experience was so that you don't repeat their mistakes. Finally, keep looking to the future. Deal with Intranet problems as they arise, but always look to your vision of your Intranet so that you never veer too far off course. Do all of this, and your Intranet is sure to be a success!

Frequently Asked Questions

♦ **What are the roles that need to be filled in an Intranet?**

To have a smoothly running Intranet, you need to have one or more central Webmasters managing it. Those who have less responsibility—but just as much impact on the Intranet—include workgroup leaders, content creators, artists, and programmers.

♦ **Do I need to hire extra people to fill these roles?**

Not necessarily. These people might already be a part of your company. However, if you do not have the expertise in-house, or you want extra help during the initial phases of your Intranet setup, consider hiring consultants or utilizing outside agencies.

♦ **Where should I store the information on my Intranet?**

You will probably store the information in a variety of places, such as on a file server, Web server, news server or FTP server. Considering who will be accessing the information, and what they need it for, can help you decide where information should be placed.

♦ **How do I define access levels to the Intranet's information structure?**

The easiest method is to divide the information structure as your company is divided. For example, set up directories on your file server that reflect your company's departmental structure.

♦ **What problems might I encounter in the management and administration of my Intranet?**

The main problems include people not understanding what their responsibilities relating to the Intranet are, resulting in confused, frustrated employees; people not placing Information in the proper places; and people being given improper access to the information. However, with a little planning, you can avoid these pitfalls!

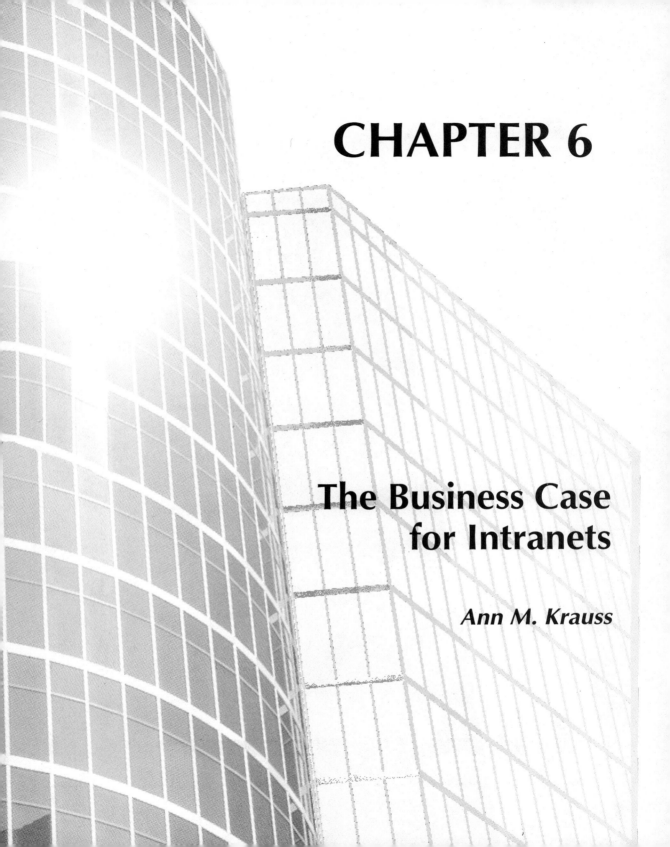

CHAPTER 6

The Business Case
for Intranets

Ann M. Krauss

Chapter Objectives

♦ Understand key business factors to consider for implementing a successful Intranet

♦ Learn how an Intranet can save money for your organization

♦ Discover how to save time and enhance productivity through Intranet implementation

♦ Learn strategies that will help to ensure acceptance and optimal use of the corporate Intranet within your organization

♦ Learn how to continue to maximize your Intranet investment and realize competitive advantages

♦ Find out through case studies how other companies are using an Intranet/Extranet to achieve business goals

There are many reasons to implement an Intranet, but as with any implementation of new technology, an organization should consider the tangible business benefits during the planning, installation, implementation, and ongoing maintenance phases of the Intranet process. It is highly recommended that you carefully consider the benefits to be gained through all phases of your corporate Intranet prior to the installation process. A regular reassessment of your Intranet will also provide insight into the ongoing value of the resource to your company. Periodic adjustments might be necessary to continue to maximize the effectiveness of your Intranet.

This chapter guides you through the steps toward achieving a better understanding of the business benefits that you can expect to realize by establishing an Intranet at your organization. Furthermore, you will learn how to maximize the benefits of an Intranet so that the technology will have an impact on your bottom line, improve your productivity, reduce your costs of doing business, and increase the speed and efficiency of communications with employees, vendors, customers, and others.

Evaluation of Key Business Factors for Achieving a Successful Intranet

Are Intranets just a trend that the trade and business publications enjoy writing about, or are they something that will really help your business? The answer is that it depends on several key business factors above and beyond the technical considerations. If you evaluate these key factors, you will begin to understand how an Intranet can save time and money for your organization. Start by asking yourself the following questions about costs, time, corporate culture, capabilities, and the advantages of an Intranet over alternative groupware solutions.

6

The following are cost considerations for implementing an Intranet:

♦   How much will it cost to purchase the software and hardware itself?

♦   How much will it cost to install the hardware and software?

♦   How much will it cost to plan and design a productive Intranet for my organization?

♦   How much will it cost to train employees to use the Intranet?

♦   How much will it cost to maintain the Intranet?

♦   What will it cost to convert from existing information management systems?

♦ What software will need to be developed to interface with existing systems?

♦ What is the cost of the staff to manage the Intranet?

♦ How much will it cost to develop or purchase necessary Intranet applications?

The following are time considerations for implementing an Intranet:

♦ How much time will it take to install and implement a productive Intranet?

♦ How much time will it take to update the Intranet on a regular basis?

♦ How much time will it take to distribute corporate information on the Intranet, and will it be faster than previous methods?

♦ How much time will it take to train employees to use the Intranet?

♦ How much time will it take to get legacy data translated and ported?

♦ How much time will it take to set up/configure users and systems?

♦ How can information transfer times be improved to avoid bandwidth saturation?

♦ How much time will it take to develop necessary Intranet applications?

The following are considerations regarding the impact of an Intranet on your organization's corporate culture:

♦ Is management ready to enforce paperless policies and to equip employees with online tools?

♦ Is your organization committed to making the Intranet successful in order to fully realize the benefits?

♦ Will your employees easily adapt to the new technology?

The following are capabilities considerations for implementing an Intranet:

♦ What Intranet applications are available in the organization at the moment?

♦ What are the tasks to be automated by using an Intranet?

♦ How much system performance is needed?

♦ Will multimedia play a big part of information delivery?

♦ Are interfaces to existing capabilities critical or can new capabilities be engineered?

The following are considerations of advantages of an Intranet over alternatives:

♦   What are the benefits of implementing an Intranet over a proprietary groupware solution?

♦   Why does your organization need an Intranet rather than just a plain LAN?

♦   What are the benefits of implementing an Intranet suite rather than a piecemeal solution?

Saving Money Through Intranet Implementation

Will an Intranet save money for your organization? Certainly a lot of other companies are considering this issue as Intranets are fast making their mark in the corporate world. According to Forrester Research in Cambridge, Massachusetts, 22 percent of Fortune 1,000 companies already use Web servers for internal applications, and another 40 percent are seriously considering them. The Business Research Group in Newton, Massachusetts, reports that 23 percent of the decision makers at 169 medium- and large-size companies already have implemented or have plans to implement Web technology internally. An additional 20 percent say they are studying the internal use of Web technology. An Intranet will save money for your organization, but how much and to what extent will depend on your strategic implementation decisions. You should be certain to identify optimal uses for Intranet technology and apply them at your organization. You can also learn from examples of how other companies are saving money. For example:

♦   Federal Express is saving $2 million a year on customer support [by using an Intranet].[1] FedEx has installed several parallel systems to handle different areas of customer support. One of them is a 128 node IBM SP with over a terabyte of storage that ties to another large SP that provides Web requests.

6

Intranet electronic documents and communications can save companies significant amounts of money because it is less expensive to create and store digitized information than physical copies of information. According to the American Paper Institute, U.S. businesses consume more than 22 million tons of paper each year. But the high consumption and cost of paper is insignificant in comparison to the expense and wasted effort expended to manage it. Businesses spend as much as $100 billion annually to manage paper, and middle managers spend nearly 45 percent of their time processing it.[2]

High storage costs are a critical factor to consider. With the going rate for office space averaging $40 per square foot, the typical company pays more than $360 a year to store a typical five-drawer file cabinet's worth of documents (about 17,500 pieces of paper).[3] Internet and Intranet technologies let you reduce storage. With Internet and Intranet communication transport and information management protocols such as HTML, HTTP, and TCP/IP, a company can view and work with documents and other information resources that may not even be physically stored on the company's own network or computing systems. Within a single company, these technologies enable open standards-based resource sharing, which stretches the company's existing resources to maximize return of investment on computing and network resources.

Intranets will likely be a good investment for your organization, even if you consider all costs associated with Intranet installation, implementation, training, management, and maintenance. Obviously, an Intranet solution that requires a high level of technical expertise to install, implement, train, manage, and maintain will be more expensive than one that has been designed to be easy to install, use, and upgrade.

An all-in-one Intranet software suite may reduce or eliminate the need for a high level of technical expertise for installation and support, as well as the need for extensive employee training, depending on the complexity of the Intranet required. An Intranet suite provides integration of the components necessary for a productive Intranet in a single package. It contains a full set of Web client and server software, including easy-to-use, built-in Web page creation tools, Intranet/Internet/LAN resource search and retrieval, electronic document distribution and management, organization of Intranet/Internet/LAN resources, network administration, conversion of legacy documents, and productivity applications such as threaded group discussions and secure e-mail. Multilevel security for optimal protection of Intranet and Internet transmissions, information, and transactions is another vital component of the all-in-one Intranet suite. Remote administration—the ability to manage access rights and the information hierarchy from any local or remote PC in addition to the Web server—paired with content creation, will empower multiple people within your company to manage Web pages and other network file source links. An Intranet suite also incorporates built-in wizards and templates, which will guide your company through the installation and implementation process.

An alternative to an Intranet suite would be the assembling of individual components from a variety of vendors to create an Intranet. The benefit to this "best of breed" approach is that your network could consist of the best possible applications offered in the industry. The inherent disadvantages to this approach are higher costs to purchase separate products, the inability to share common network administration utilities such as user preferences and secure certificates, and difficulties in implementing a multiple-user network if the standards are not designed to work together at the application programming interface (API) level. These are issues that may be very difficult to deal with without an experienced, Intranet-savvy support team.

Intranets are based on open standards, but sometimes standards do not mature as quickly as vendors release products to meet customer needs. Consensus on the specification for a particular standard may not yet be reached, and therefore, the ability to incorporate the standard uniformly into emerging products often does not keep pace with customer demands for new product capabilities or vendors' imaginations. This causes difficulties in implementing a solution that depends on numerous vendors' products. If the standards have not yet matured, certain vendors may be both shipping product *and* lobbying for their controversial solution to become commonly accepted by the industry. A piecemeal "best of breed" approach may thus cause interoperability issues even if it is purported to be based on open standards. Of course, in some situations it is necessary to take the risk and implement a great new product capability that can make your organization more competitive.

Whether your organization implements an Intranet suite or a piecemeal solution, you will need to consider whether the Intranet will be developed in-house or with outside assistance. With outside assistance, the level of initial and ongoing assistance will have an additional impact on total costs. Particularly with a piecemeal solution, using external support for your initial Intranet installation instead of paying the costs of training internal resources may offset the cost equation; but don't forget to factor in the costs of continuing support without internal expertise. Using an Intranet suite will help to reduce startup costs whether the Intranet is built in-house or out. An Intranet suite provides prepackaged network integration that would otherwise need to be custom integrated by someone—either in-house or outside of your organization. (Intranet suites versus piecemeal solutions are discussed further later in this chapter.)

6

Once the costs of an Intranet are assessed, you will want to explore some of the tangible money-saving benefits you can expect to realize through successful implementation. Most businesses with 20 or more employees cannot afford *not* to have an Intranet. An Intranet can achieve immediate cost savings of doing business in the following ways:

◆ Electronic distribution of documents is less costly than paper-based distribution.

- An Intranet is an inexpensive way to enable global accessibility to corporate resources and global communication, especially compared with remote dial-in.

- Duplication of efforts in publishing and accessing corporate-wide information is reduced or eliminated.

- Employee productivity is improved.

- The necessity for extensive training is reduced.

- Use of open networking technology saves money and protects your investment.

- Implementation of secure information channels keeps security costs within limits.

- Reliance on hardware (that is, hard drive space) is reduced.

- Synchronized delivery to remote users is efficient and economical.

- Fingertip access to information and company and worldwide knowledge gives you a competitive edge.

Your organization may wish to assess the hard dollars that will be saved by implementing an Intranet. In order to do this, someone in the organization must provide the amounts currently required to publish and disseminate paper-based documents, for instance. Other costs that may be reduced should be examined, for example:

- Current costs of enabling remote users to access corporate information and to communicate on a global basis.

- Current costs of creation and production of departmental and corporatewide information.

- Current costs of processing purchase orders, help desk requests, service orders, and so on, as relevant to your business.

- Current costs of updating phone lists, employee benefits information, sales reports, and so on.

- Current costs of communications with key customers, resellers, and vendors.

- Costs of not being able to deliver a capability to your customer with current technology. (Missed opportunity costs such as these may be difficult to assess, but are important to take into consideration nonetheless.) For instance, if you are unable to provide customers with online technical support, they may turn to your competition.

Once the current costs are reviewed and examined, a cost-savings estimate may be developed. A quarterly, semiannual, or annual review of actual cost savings will then help your company to realize the true value of your investment in Intranet technology. Use the checklist in Table 6-1 as a guide for analyzing costs.

T IP: If you take the time to review some of the actual cost savings before, during, and after installation, you will more fully realize and appreciate the benefits you are deriving from an Intranet. As you become more familiar with your Intranet, look for new ways that you might further maximize the technology to your organization's advantage. Ideally, this should be an ongoing process.

Saving Time and Enhancing Productivity Through Intranet Implementation

The old saying "two heads are better than one" provides a basis for understanding how Intranets will enhance productivity. Beyond the more obvious productivity benefit of faster, more efficient production and dissemination of corporate documents and information, Intranets can provide the means for more efficient communication and collaboration. For instance, project participants can access the Intranet from any location and may immediately gain access to information from their fellow participants. Threaded group discussions through an Intranet newsgroup could help

Cost-Saving Checkpoints	Notes
Find an Intranet software package (perhaps an Intranet suite) that is easy to install and use.	
Consider hardware costs (you may already have what you need).	
Consider the amount of technical expertise needed to install, implement, manage, and maintain the Intranet.	
Examine the costs associated with training employees to use the Intranet.	
Research current costs that will be reduced by an Intranet solution.	
Regularly review estimated versus actual cost savings of the Intranet.	

Intranet Money-Saving Checklist
Table 6-1.

6

participants to identify and act on common issues without the necessity for lengthy meetings or frustrating efforts to be certain that information has been shared with all participants. Automated notification and scheduling through e-mail can keep the activities of groups synchronized and on track.

Three main steps, as described here, will enhance the time-saving value of Intranet technology.

1. Designate departmental Intranet Webmasters in addition to, or instead of, an overall corporate Intranet Webmaster to reduce the reliance on one person or group. This will save time and improve efficiency of the Intranet, and avoid the bottleneck that occurs when everyone depends on a single point person or even a single department. By distributing the responsibility for creating, updating, and maintaining the Intranet's content throughout the organization, you will achieve more effective participation, more timely information, and a spirit of cooperation.

    It may be more appropriate for your organization's overall goals to designate a single Intranet Webmaster, which might serve to reduce training time and costs. This decision should be carefully weighed because despite the initial training time and costs associated with a more distributed approach to Intranet content management, in the long run you may find that these initial costs are minimal compared with the opportunity costs to your organization of restricting content administration to a single person or department. Of course, someone will need to be accountable for maintaining the Web server and other Intranet services, but you may wish to consider the distributed approach for Intranet content management. Consider these potentially detrimental effects of a nondistributed approach:

    ♦   Significant delays in updating corporate and department information

    ♦   Less useful or inappropriate departmental information

    ♦   Reduced sense of pride of ownership

    ♦   Reduced overall participation in Intranet utilization

    ♦   Missed opportunities in time saving and overall productivity benefits

    As another alternative, you can reduce some of the training time and costs associated with the distributed approach by combining the best of both worlds. Develop a chief Intranet Webmaster who could train the departmental Webmasters and serve as an information resource for them whenever necessary. This will also reduce bottleneck issues and will help shorten the Intranet learning curve for the overall organization. Decentralization also encourages a higher degree of participation in the corporate Intranet through pride of ownership, which helps focus attention on solving problems, and may best achieve the goal of a more productive and useful Intranet.

2. Allocate appropriate access and content creation rights to appropriate individuals, departments, and groups so that information is protected where necessary, but is also readily available to those who need it. For example, it may not be appropriate to have sales representatives accessing the engineering schedules before products are available. Again, the responsibility for access and content-creation rights may be assigned to department representatives and does not need to be the sole responsibility of the Information Services department. (Refer to Chapter 9 for more details.)

3. Demonstrate how the Intranet will benefit individual employees. Perhaps start with some examples that will be of interest to everyone, such as a new application that will enable employees to monitor their 401K benefits or sign up for the latest benefit plans.

Decentralization of Intranet content-creation and management responsibilities, and enhancing productivity through use of e-mail and Intranet newsgroups, will go a long way toward ensuring time savings and higher productivity. In order to realize lasting benefits of any and all time-saving or cost-saving measures, your company must consider the impact of the new Intranet on the organization. The development of corporate policies and internal strategies for Intranet implementation and utilization will be a critical element in long-term success.

 TIP: Decentralization of Intranet Webmasters will reduce bottleneck issues and will help to shorten the Intranet learning curve for everyone.

6

Corporate Policies and Internal Strategies for Successful Intranet Implementation

Once your Intranet is installed, some changes in corporate policies and strategies may serve to ensure a successful Intranet implementation. An overall commitment to the technology will show the best results for the organization, but the commitment may not be an automatic one throughout the organization. A new Intranet will be readily adopted by some and perhaps not so readily adopted by others. The organization's policies regarding use of the Intranet are no less important than decisions about which software and hardware to use. An Intranet will most certainly represent a cultural shift in the organization away from many old ways of doing things. A company that has committed to implementing an Intranet should be sure to take the time to introduce corresponding policies that will encourage effective utilization of the technology throughout the organization. "Lightweight" policies and creative ideas for encouragement of Intranet usage will inspire, rather than intimidate, users.

Examples of policies that might be implemented to help ensure a successful Intranet are

♦ Have department managers rotate responsibility for departmental Web page updates, so that more employees will understand and appreciate the ease of creating Web pages.

♦ Use threaded discussion groups rather than e-mail for project updates.

♦ Enable access to phone lists, internal job postings, company newsletters, and so on, via the Intranet.

♦ Using information conversion tools, convert existing product information to Web format and make this information available to all employees: place troubleshooting tips, product pricing and specifications, and human resources information online.

♦ Have a competition between departments for the best departmental Intranet Web page or, better still, a contest for the best application that can be placed on the Intranet. This can include back ends for database access, forms entry, automated routing/notification applications, resource schedulers, and so on.

♦ Require that all employees submit purchase orders or help desk requests on the Intranet. This will affect a large number of employees and encourage them to use the Intranet and, over time, to realize the time-saving benefits for themselves.

In a report about the implementation of Intranets for educational institutions, "Inventing an INTRAnet—A Metaphor for Building a Master Plan for Institutional Technology Growth," the importance of confidence and satisfaction with an Intranet is discussed. This example could also apply to employees within a corporate setting:

> Additional anecdotal evidence suggests that student confidence/satisfaction is high when students have predictable access to everyday technology needs without excessive delays, and some access to specialized technology they will use only occasionally. They also appear to derive satisfaction from knowing that their chosen school is up to date, even if they do not personally use many of its facilities.[4]

Just as students often seem to take the technology itself for granted, so might many of the employees within your organization. Many employees or students will expect the best technology to be there when they need it, and they will enjoy knowing that their company or educational institution is up to date. Some of those same employees or students will expect the best technology to be there even when they don't need it, but still enjoy the satisfaction of knowing that they belong to a progressive organization. The implementation of an Intranet will propel your organization to new levels of excellence in communications, while flattening your companies' organizational structure by enabling employees of various departments or students from different classes to work together.

For example, as a company launches a new product, employees from all departments may share ideas, documents, spreadsheets, market research, and presentation materials in real time. Using the threaded discussion groups, workflow, and Intranet resource management tools, the company is able to release the new product in less time with fewer mistakes and more innovative enhancements from marketing, engineering, technical support, and sales. Project participants may participate in conferencing and are able to simultaneously access documents from remote sites during online Web meetings. The power of collaboration and cooperation is realized in the resulting new product without a loss in efficiency or productivity.

"It really has a lot to do with whether companies have a proactive management mind-set," says Art Hutchinson, an analyst at Northeast Consulting Resources in Boston. "Early adopters are more likely to roll out publishing tools because they are accustomed to taking risks, introducing new technologies, empowering employees."[5]

TIP: Employees will more likely embrace the new Intranet if lightweight policies and creative ideas for encouragement of Intranet usage are implemented to inspire even the more timid users.

6

Competitive Advantage Through Intranet Adoption

The time to implement an Intranet is now! Companies considering Intranet implementation should immediately begin to leverage Intranet technology in order to gain significant competitive advantages. The sooner your company begins to use an Intranet, the better your chances of being several steps ahead of the competition. The more that your organization uses

Intranet technology, the more new ideas will spring forth for maximizing its effectiveness. Among the immediate competitive advantages your organization can expect to realize are

♦ Arming of sales and technical people with the most up-to-date information

♦ Fast, global distribution of product information (descriptions, pricing, delivery) to customers, with compelling, creative multimedia presentations

♦ Enabling of secure electronic commerce, including online ordering, financial transactions, and "cyber-catalogs" to display product lines

For more specifics about how companies are leveraging Intranet technology to their competitive advantage, see the "Case Study" sections at the end of this chapter.

Assessment of Alternatives to Intranets and Various Intranet Choices

Businesses typically examine various alternatives to meeting corporate needs. Once your organization has determined the basic issues that an Intranet may help to resolve, you will first want to verify that an Intranet will be the best alternative when compared with other possible solutions. Beyond the comparison of alternatives to an Intranet implementation, your company will want to make the best possible choice of an Intranet solution.

Intranets Versus Traditional Groupware

Much has been written about whether to use an Intranet or a traditional groupware solution. The major focus of the debate centers around the point that Intranets are based on open technology and that traditional groupware is proprietary. Another key issue that is often discussed is that traditional groupware products are more mature and offer more collaborative and workflow capabilities than Intranet products. More recently, some people have suggested that the whole debate is moot because the gaps between groupware and Intranets are closing. "Basically, the Internet camp is rushing to write application programming interfaces (APIs) so that developers can add groupware functionality to their products, while the groupware vendors are feverishly embracing and integrating Web technologies into their product lines," explains Ray Laracuenta, senior research analyst at the Gartner Group.[6] Intranets can let users "do a lot of what groupware does very easily and a lot cheaper," says Burt Knight, a Concord, New Hampshire, consultant working with an East Coast financial services company to design a large Intranet.[7]

Not only are Intranets cheaper, they are also based entirely on open technology. An Intranet applies the Internet paradigm to the internal corporate network. The Internet is based on open standards to achieve a network that not only operates easily with various computing resources but would continue to function even if a portion of it broke down. Intranets were designed from the ground up to be open, whereas groupware was designed to be proprietary. That is not to say that groupware cannot be enhanced to operate interdependently, but just as proprietary LANs were superseded by open TCP/IP networks, most traditional groupware will eventually be replaced by Intranet technology or groupware that is Web-enabled. "Intranet groupware" is a new classification for a hybrid that offers some or all of the collaborative benefits of traditional groupware paired with the open Intranet technology. This may well emerge as the optimal choice as these technologies merge in new products.

Ease of use of Intranets or Intranet groupware alternatives surpass most traditional groupware alternatives because Intranets utilize a familiar browser interface. The fact is that the browser interface makes for a single-point, common, distributable solution. The browser is highly integrated with back-end delivery. The back ends may grow and improve daily and can be made immediately available through the common browser interface. Intranets are less cumbersome and don't necessarily require a team of experts to install, implement, administer, and maintain. Of course, the level of technical expertise necessary for implementing Intranets will vary depending on the degrees of complexity of specific implementations. Because Intranets are scaleable, a company may begin with a basic Intranet with less technical support constraints and later move to implementing more complex capabilities that might demand a higher level of technical expertise and increased support needs.

6

The Intranet Choice: All-in-One Suites or Piecemeal Alternatives

As described earlier in the chapter, an Intranet suite is an all-inclusive Intranet software solution that provides integration of the components necessary for a productive Intranet in a single package. Piecemeal alternatives require a company to put together the various Intranet components themselves, either from a variety of vendor solutions or through a hodgepodge of freeware.

Intranet suites offer several advantages over piecemeal alternatives, not the least of which are cost considerations. Despite the fact that a piecemeal "best of breed" or freeware solution might seem appealing when considering only the up-front costs, further examination may reveal numerous hidden costs. Hidden costs of piecemeal alternatives include the cost of a high degree of technical expertise necessary to create, administer, and maintain the Intranet. Troubleshooting is a much more complex process when a piecemeal solution is implemented, as finger-pointing between vendors ensues in many cases. A single point of contact through an Intranet suite eases troubleshooting and saves time and effort. Freeware may not provide sufficient support and software maintenance, so technical difficulties in implementing a piecemeal solution can wind up costing a company more in the long run.

Boyd Waters, a Macintosh systems analyst with Chiron in Emeryville, California, helped a consulting firm develop an Intranet for Wells Fargo Bank in San Francisco with an old Sparcstation running SunOS4.1 and the Web server software available from the National Center for Super Computing Applications. "Unexpected problems would come up with different software versions, and of course there was no technical support, so it made it pretty challenging," Waters says. "If you're using these [piecemeal] tools, you need to have a really clean system, one very well maintained, and that necessitates a Unix system administrator."[8]

Ron Daggett, president of Tao Computer Services and an expert Intranet consultant, compared the costs of installing a Windows NT-based Intranet suite with a Unix server-based or piecemeal Intranet solution. Daggett was able to set up a basic Intranet using the Intranet suite in about two and a half hours. Within three days, the Intranet was completely set up and running, including the internal Web page design and the Back Office phone directory. Daggett estimates that the same project would have taken at least two to three weeks to accomplish with a piecemeal Intranet solution or a Unix server-based solution. As Daggett's billable rate is $125 per hour, this translates into an 80 percent cost savings to the company that hires Daggett to build an Intranet for them. You can find more about Ron Daggett's personal experience with setting up an Intranet for his own company in "Case Study #1" later in this chapter.

Beyond LANs: Convergence of Intranet, Internet, and LAN

The optimal Intranet will build on existing LAN technology, in addition to Intranet and Internet technologies. Global effectiveness of the Intranet will be realized through easier and more effective management of corporate resources, enhanced accessibility of information, and further empowerment of users within the organization. New levels of communication and information sharing may be achieved. Convergence of paths and types of communication, such as text, multimedia, video, and searchable data warehouses, is also made possible.

Through this collaboration of existing and new technologies, a more powerful network emerges. This new Intranet definition extends the Intranet beyond geographic boundaries to enable global support of customers, remote access to corporate resources, and "virtual companies." (*Virtual companies* are multiple companies working together on a project or product as though they were one company, or people in separate locations working together as if they were in the same place.)

The tools of the Intranet/Extranet allow vendors and suppliers to interact dynamically with common tools providing information sharing and low-cost connections. An *Extranet* is defined as extending an Intranet beyond a single organization to let companies provide key customers, suppliers, or other partners with information that is not available on their Web site. A company may make an Extranet available to strategic partners via secure access over the Internet.

Significant cost savings and competitive advantages are gained through converging LAN, Internet, and Intranet technologies. A recent study by U.S. Computer revealed that using the Internet significantly reduces the cost of corporate Intranets. The study reports savings over four years of as much as $11 million for large networks. The study compared the costs of dedicated leased-lines versus frame relay technologies, and Internet-based Secure Virtual Private Networks (SVPNs). SVPNs are made possible by a new method of encrypting network-layer security devices that enable secure data transmission over the Internet.

For the high-priority corporate backbone case, the study found that an Internet-based approach could reduce costs by nearly 50 percent and $1.3 million. This assumed that a redundant leased-line network and a separate Internet connection at each key corporate location could be replaced by a single Internet-based frame relay network with proper use of frame relay Committed Information Rate (CIR) to guarantee bandwidth between corporate locations. CIR is the minimum speed guaranteed via your connection to the Frame Relay cloud.

6

For the low-priority branch office case, the study found that an Internet-based approach could reduce costs by as much as 23 percent and $240,000. This compared a private leased-line network with an Internet-based leased-line network as competitors for a new network. In the worst case, a break-even point was reached within 12 months of investing in the new network architecture.[9]

Remote Access to Corporate Resources

The global nature of the Intranet allows employees and project team members to access corporate resources while on the road or from remote offices. Documents, spreadsheets, graphics, or word processor files may be shared by users in various physical locations. Intranet technology helps a company's employees communicate more effectively and collaborate with each other no matter where they are.

In the Space Systems division of Rockwell Aerospace, in Pico Rivera, California, engineers and designers use an Intranet for online access to schematics of components of the space shuttle, for which Rockwell was the principal contractor. "This eliminates the reliance on other, less efficient ways of viewing the drawings," says Paul Liles, Rockwell's director of IS planning and security.[10]

Intranet technologies not only remove physical boundaries, but also are more cost-effective than other possible methods of telecommuting or remote access. Remote users may access the corporate Intranet using a local phone number and an Internet service provider, saving long-distance charges, charges for overnight mail delivery, or other possible means of remote communication or collaboration.

Virtual Companies:
Breaking Through Traditional Boundaries

"The Intranet has broken down the walls within corporations," says Steven Jobs, CEO of NeXT Computer.[11]

Intranets are breaking through the traditional idea that a "company" is confined to a physical geographic boundary. The convergence of Intranet and Internet enables new dimensions in organizations both large and small. As stated earlier, a virtual corporation can either be separate companies working together as if they were one or people in separate locations working together as if they were in the same place.

General Electric, in Fairfield, Connecticut, uses its Intranet as a way to get more and better information to employees at their desktops and to give employees more convenient access to information, says corporate public relations spokesman, Ted Meyer. Plans call for eventually linking all 220,000 GE employees worldwide via the company Intranet.

GE's Intranet, called the GE Information Network, or GEIN, contains the company's annual report and other financial and business information that GE stock-owning employees can use to manage their investments. In addition, the company gives employees online access via GEIN to its travel center so they can help schedule their own business trips, Meyer says. "I see some potential for savings, from the simple fact that we can save a lot on postage, especially globally, and in a lot of phone messages and travel."[12]

Even a small company composed of partners from separate geographical locations can communicate and share information as if they were all located in the same building! The first case study we'll look at is an example of a small company using an Intranet to create a virtual corporation.

Case Study #1: Technical Computing Services Industry

Intranet Mission Accomplished:

⇒ **Enabled a virtual corporation with secure remote access and communications**

⇒ **Provided cost-saving and time-saving Intranet suite implementation**

⇒ **Provided a productive Intranet in much less time than alternative solutions**

⇒ **Saved on long-distance phone bills**

For a small Intranet and Internet consulting company with partners in remote locations, an Intranet offers a means to set up a virtual corporation providing secure remote access and enhancing communications without incurring expensive long-distance bills.

Ron Daggett, president of Tao Computer Services, implemented an Intranet software suite for his company for two reasons: he wanted to realize the benefits for his own company, and he and his partners wanted hands-on experience with creative and fast ways to implement productive Intranets for Tao's clients.

Tao Computer Services is based in Henryville, Indiana, with remote offices in other Indiana locations and in Phoenix, Arizona. Tao's network consists of one Microsoft Windows NT server, two Unix servers, one Windows NT client, and several Windows 95 clients.

Tao Computer Services wanted to establish a virtual corporation, consisting of an Intranet accessible via the Internet, so that all of the company's partners could enjoy cost-effective and timely communication between several physically separate locations. Ron wanted an Intranet that was easy to install and implement without requiring time-consuming and complicated Unix configuration.

By using an Intranet software suite, called Intranet Genie, that is designed for Microsoft Windows 3.1x, Windows 95, and Windows NT, Ron was able to set up his basic Intranet in about two and a half hours, and within three days, the company's Intranet was completely set up and running, including their internal Web page design and Back Office phone directory. All of Ron's partners are connected to the corporate Intranet via dial-up connections with Internet service providers. The partners dial local phone numbers to access the corporate Intranet.

Ron estimates that the same project would have taken at least two to three weeks had he selected a Unix server instead. As Ron's billable rate is $125 per hour, the implementation of Intranet Genie over a Unix server or piecemeal Intranet solution saved considerable time and money. Companies hiring Daggett to set up their corporate Intranets would also realize about an 80 percent savings if they chose an Intranet suite over a piecemeal or a Unix server solution.

Ron explains that many of his customers want to stay away from having to hire high-powered, high-priced Unix gurus, so an Intranet suite for the Windows environment is a desirable product for them. Ron helps his customers set up their Intranet using an Intranet suite and helps them build Web pages and special applications initially; but then he expects that the customers will be able to use, maintain, and modify Intranet Genie without much further assistance. For certain customers that request additional assistance, Ron can remotely administer their Intranets from his office.[13]

Case Study #2: Finance/Banking Industry

Intranet Mission Accomplished:

⇒ **Secured internal transactions and Internet e-mail**

⇒ **Connected remote bank branches with NetWare LANs to the Intranet**

⇒ **Streamlined help desk requests**

⇒ **Saved training time and eased file sharing among users**

For a midsize company in the banking industry, an Intranet offers the necessary security for protecting internal transactions and Internet e-mail. As most banks do have a number of remote locations, cost-effective connectivity is also imperative. An Intranet may save money on long-distance charges by enabling remote users to dial in to the corporate Intranet with a local phone number. Even a number of bank branches with remote NetWare LANs may connect to a corporate Intranet.

Leon Davis, network administrator at First Bank in St. Louis, Missouri, has implemented an Intranet software suite with a multilevel security architecture that protects internal communications within departments and within the company as well as protecting the Intranet from outside intrusion. The departmental Intranet Webmasters can define access rights to the Intranet server based on user, group, or IP address. Leon can also define access rights to the server for the company overall. In addition, users are able to send encrypted e-mail messages inside and outside of the company. In the future, Leon plans to implement client and server authentication capabilities

6

to further enhance Intranet and Internet security and to protect sensitive internal information.

First Bank has branches in several states. The company has 20 NetWare local area networks with two thirds of the LANs and three IBM AS/400 minicomputers linked via a wide area network (WAN). Recently two Microsoft Windows NT servers were added to the First Bank network; one of the servers was added as a Systems Network Architecture (SNA) gateway/application server and the other to handle Intranet tasks. SNA is a proprietary protocol that has allowed IBM's customers to create their own private networks. SNA enables connectivity between all IBM computer systems on the network.

Leon Davis selected an Intranet software suite with an IPX to IP gateway option. Leon set up his initial Intranet and connected his NetWare LANs in a single day. The product that Leon selected provided easy Web page building and remote administration capabilities. These two key features empower First Bank's various departments and remote offices to create and control their own internal Web sites, reducing their reliance on the Information Systems (IS) department.

First Bank has realized additional savings in time and costs by incorporating help desk request and group discussion capabilities into their Intranet. Handling internal help desk requests on the Intranet reduces long-distance phone charges in many cases and also reduces processing time. Threaded group discussions allow users who encounter similar problems to find solutions on the Intranet rather than calling the help desk.

First Bank's Intranet takes advantage of the power of open systems networking without extensive training. Because the company's users are mostly familiar with the graphical client or browser interface, they can share files easily and do not need to perform complicated file transfers based on network mapping schemes.

Departments within First Bank that are currently using and benefiting from the corporate Intranet include the IS, accounting, and public relations/advertising departments. Five hundred users are currently utilizing the Intranet software suite's Intranet clients to access the Intranet server via Windows 3.1x and Windows 95-based personal computers. Beyond meeting all of the initially desired goals, the departments enjoy having a central place to keep calendars and schedules, to set up meeting rooms, and to share various types of documents.

"The installation of an Intranet software suite is a breeze. The wizards are easy to work with and the Webmaster setup and Web document creation are intuitive. This is my first time setting up an Intranet, and the program pretty much did everything by itself. Believe it or not, it is definitely possible to set up, configure, and use an Intranet in a day or less," explained Leon.

"Of course Intranets are also scaleable, so when we're ready to go to the next stage, we will be able to easily add on additional components and build custom applications to meet our specialized needs."[14]

Case Study #3: Manufacturing Industry

Intranet Mission Accomplished:

⇒ **Improved expense and billing tracking**

⇒ **Ability to download software updates even from remote locations**

⇒ **Enhanced communication with key customers and suppliers, as well as between employees**

For a small manufacturing company, the key reasons for implementing an Intranet included the need to speed up communications, enhance productivity, and track billable hours. The company also wanted to enhance communications with key customers and suppliers, as well as between employees.

The Word Machinery Company, based in Cockeysville, Maryland, is a manufacturer of capital goods equipment for the corrugated finishing industry—a $100 million dollar business. Equipment is sold and serviced throughout the world.

Word Machinery selected a desktop Intranet software suite designed for Microsoft Windows 3.x, Windows 95, and Windows NT and set up their Intranet in a single day. The company's art department has been designated as the Intranet Webmasters responsible for creating all of the content for the corporate Intranet that supports all 35 of the company's employees and the Extranet, which supports their key customers and suppliers.

Word Machinery's employees are often sent to such remote locations as Asia and India, and prior to the implementation of an Intranet, it was difficult for employees to download programs or to communicate effectively with the main office from the remote locations. The tracking of billable hours and expenses had become a difficult, time-consuming task that needed to be more effectively automated.

Word Machinery is currently using the Intranet for taking care of mundane expenses so that technicians can process billing on a weekly basis. An expense-tracking Intranet application has been developed and built using

6

the source code for back-end services, and it is included in the Intranet software suite package. Field operatives are now able to use the Intranet to communicate with headquarters while on the road, and they can download programs and software updates.

Key customers and suppliers can communicate securely over the Internet with Word Machinery's Extranet, and they have access to information that is not made available to the general public. For example, they may access account information, including invoices. The customers may also place service requests via the Extranet and may check the status of those requests. Key suppliers receive automated purchase orders via the Extranet and may submit proposals to Word Machinery for needs that are regularly posted by the purchasing department.[15]

Case Study #4: Public Relations Industry

Intranet Mission Accomplished:

⇒ **Realized faster access to knowledge resources**

⇒ **Improved document publishing and distribution**

⇒ **Empowered team members and strengthened the community bond**

For a public relations agency, an Intranet offers fast access to knowledge resources, as well as speedy and efficient document publishing and distribution. The Intranet's improved efficiency of access to information enables a public relations company to more quickly take advantage of publicity opportunities on behalf of their clients, to access competitive information that may affect clients' strategic messages, and to keep up on emerging trends. Improved document management enables a public relations agency to process press releases more efficiently and to share critical client information among the various representatives assigned to specific accounts.

Interactive Public Relations, a firm based in San Francisco, California, recently implemented an Intranet to empower team members and to increase the value of their product. They have found that the Intranet helps to inform and to share data. Their favorite feature is the ability to publish multiple media quickly.

Interactive is realizing an immediate impact on the bottom line through a reduced need for training and a faster learning curve. Since the browser application is easy to teach and to learn, the company is able to rely on getting corporate information to people quickly without a lot of training.

"As we begin to upgrade document management and database integration into our Intranet, we will expect the browser model to show competitive, if not superior, solutions in dynamic information management," explained Ben Harrison, principal at Interactive Public Relations. "Just about all functions of our business have a place on the Intranet."

Interactive selected an Intranet software suite that offers support for Microsoft Windows NT on the server side and Microsoft Windows 95 on the client side. In addition to the Intranet software, Interactive's corporate network consists of clone Pentium workstations and servers, a Novell 4.0 server, a Microsoft Windows NT server, Microsoft Windows 95 desktops, 3Com Hubs, Ascend Router, Ascend Bridge, 10BaseT, and ISDN.

6

Interactive Public Relations became aware of the Intranet technology through one of their clients, who was building a market in the Intranet space. Ben quickly realized that the Intranet technology was something that made sense for Interactive Public Relations and that it would be fairly easy and straightforward to implement.

"In investigating the technology and how it might apply to our specific needs, we realized that the material costs to implement were minimal and that we already had the necessary personnel to handle the management of the project, " Ben said.

Interactive has also realized a cultural benefit of the new Intranet through a strengthened sense of community among employees. Team members appreciate being more informed as a group.

"Improving access to a common knowledge base builds unity of purpose," said Ben. "Anything that helps everyone pull together in one direction is a performance boost."

Interactive's management believes that the company has a significant competitive advantage over other public relations firms that are not using an Intranet. As most public relations firms are not typically vested heavily in large-scale custom data solutions that are available from high-end software specialists such as Sybase and Oracle, an Intranet may complement the lower-end databases typically used by PR firms for sharing information.

"Gathering knowledge, formulating strategies, and gaining mind share faster and smarter than other firms is an advantage to securing publicity," Ben explained.

For the future, Interactive Public Relations hopes to find products that address even more of the public relations industry's vertical market needs. The company will look for strong querying and list-building capabilities for management of publicity opportunities. Also on the horizon, they expect to be able to utilize warehousing controls for many forms of information content, to include input, cataloging, search, and retrieval.[16]

Case Study #5: Financial/Investment Advisory Industry

Intranet Mission Accomplished:

⇒ **Realized faster and more efficient data access**

⇒ **Increased productivity and efficiency**

⇒ **Improved communications**

⇒ **Boosted employee morale and sentiment by reducing frustration in locating necessary information**

For an investment advisory firm, fast and efficient data access is not only desirable, it is required by the Investment Advisory Act of 1940. A vast amount of information must be available on demand, and the information must be well organized. The investment advisory business demands a tremendous amount of document handling and intensive document management.

Wisconsin Asset Management (WAM) is an investment advisory firm based in Milwaukee, Wisconsin. They selected an Intranet software suite that they found to have significant advantages over other possible Intranet solutions because of the rich set of services offered, including threaded group discussion application, secure e-mail, built-in Web page creation tools, a built-in Web browser and Web server, and a powerful Intranet search engine. Figure 6-1 illustrates how WAM's Intranet fits into its service plan.

In addition to the Intranet software suite, Wisconsin Asset Management's Intranet network consists of a LAN file server PC and nine client PCs. The server is a Pentium 166 with a 4GB hard drive, 8x CD, 64MB memory, running Windows NT 3.51. The network uses 10BaseT cabling with a midrange quality hub. All of the client computers are Pentiums operating Windows 95 and running at speeds from 100 to 150Mhz. All client computers have at least 32MB memory and 1GB disk space (with the exception of one 486). Most client computers have 17-inch monitors. The desktop publishing computer has an internal Zip drive and a Hewlett-Packard ScanJet 4c color scanner.

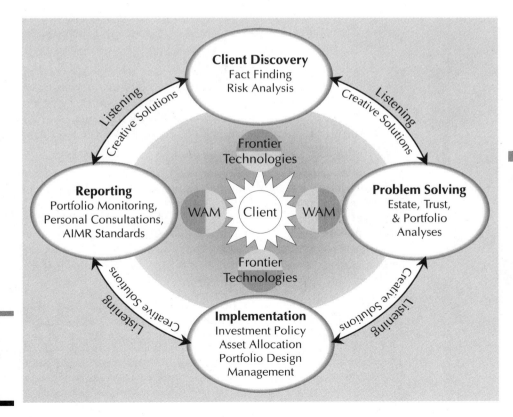

WAM's
Intranet is
integral to its
service plan
Figure 6-1.

6

With their new Intranet, employees at Wisconsin Asset Management can access client and other important information quickly. This is accomplished by using the Intranet suite's built-in Web page creation tools to create home page links to necessary documents so that they may be accessed from a single point, despite the fact that the documents may be physically stored in many different places. Employees may also conduct queries to search for documents or files through a single interface. Word processing files, spreadsheets, presentations, and HTML documents are among the types of information that may be searched. Automatic monitoring of these documents and files notifies users of any updated information that becomes available.

"We are so heavily regulated that we almost need procedures for procedures," explained Mark Crawford," senior portfolio manager for Wisconsin Asset Management. "Being able to index and link various disconnected information, and being able to customize it the way we want it, should allow us to adhere to our compliance requirements."

Wisconsin Asset Management's Intranet has also enhanced interoffice communications through use of e-mail and threaded group discussions. The company can now conduct ongoing staff meetings essentially whenever it is convenient. Employees may post messages to each other using the threaded group discussions application and can view and respond to those messages in an organized and topical manner.

"We really appreciate the threaded group discussions because they are a great way to keep written records of conversations that we have with each other and with clients, as we are required to do by the SEC," said Paul Feider, operations/technology manager and Intranet Webmaster for Wisconsin Asset Management.

For quite some time, Lori Crawford, president and portfolio manager for Wisconsin Asset Management, had voiced the need to better organize and access necessary documents and information in an expeditious manner. She was also concerned over the frustrations expressed by employees with the difficulties in retrieving and locating necessary information in a timely manner, as well as the conflicts that sometime arose when written records of conversations were not available. Lori has been quite pleased with the results she has seen with the new Intranet.

"With our Intranet, we are now able to access client and other important information so much faster than before, and we have enhanced our interoffice communications, allowing us to provide better service to our clients," said Lori Crawford. "Information is power, and the more power we have, the better we can serve our clients and conduct our business."[17]

Putting It All Together

Although an Intranet offers many practical business benefits, an organization should take the time to carefully evaluate individual factors, both obvious and hidden, that will provide the maximum benefits to the particular company. Hidden costs of implementing piecemeal Intranets or groupware solutions should be taken into account when determining the overall cost-effectiveness of an Intranet alternative. Internal corporate policies and strategies can be as important to a successful and profitable Intranet implementation as the selection of the best Intranet product. An Intranet can provide a powerful competitive advantage if implemented for maximum effectiveness with consideration of ongoing protection of investment and evaluation of creative and strategic utilization.

Endnotes

1. "Advanced Business Applications on the World Wide Web—Intranets," *Digital Lagoon,* http://www.lagoon.com/Hot/IntranetTalk/Intranets.html.

2. Bill Eager, "Online and the Bottom Line: E-mail Is Money," *Data Communications* (March 21, 1996), http://www.data.com/Business_Case/Online_Bottom_Line.html.

3. Ibid.

4. R. W. Cavenagh, "Inventing an INTRAnet—A Metaphor for Building a Master Plan for Institutional Technology Growth," http://media.dickinson.edu/Inventing_an_INTRAnet.html.

5. Teri Robinson, "Who's Running This Intranet Anyway?" *LAN Times* (June 17, 1996), http://www.lantimes.com/96jun/606s017a.html.

6. Lee Bruno, "Groupware vs. Webware," *Data Communications* (March 1996), http://www.data.com/Tutorials/Groupware_vs_Webware.html.

7. Jim Carr, "Intranets Deliver Internet Technology Can Offer Cheap, Multiplatform Access to Corporate Data on Private Networks," *InfoWorld* 18, no. 8 (February 19, 1996), http://www.infoworld.com/cgi-bin/displayArchives.pl?dt_IWE08-96_65.htm.

8. Ibid.

9. "Intranet Based SVPNs: The Cost of Ownership Executive Summary," *U.S. Computer* (March 12, 1996), http://www.incog.com/execsumm.html.

10. See note 8 above.

11. See note 2 above.

12. See note 8 above.

6

13. Frontier Technologies, "Frontier Technologies Case Study/User Profile—Frontier Technologies Intranet Genie—Profile of Tao Computer Services" (October 1, 1996).

14. Frontier Technologies, "Frontier Technologies Case Study/User Profile—Frontier Technologies Intranet Genie—Profile of First Bank" (October 3, 1996).

15. Frontier Technologies, "Frontier Technologies Case Study/User Profile—Frontier Technologies Intranet Genie—Profile Word Machinery Company" (October 3, 1996).

16. Frontier Technologies interview with Ben Harrison, principal of Interactive Public Relations (October 25, 1996).

17. "Frontier Technologies Case Study/User Profile—Frontier Technologies Intranet Genie—Profile of Wisconsin Asset Management" (October 23, 1996).

Frequently Asked Questions

♦ **What are the key business factors to consider for a successful Intranet?**

Key business factors to consider for a successful Intranet are cost, time, corporate cultural impact, capabilities, and Intranet advantages over alternative solutions.

♦ **How can an Intranet save money for my organization?**

An Intranet will save money for your organization, but how much and to what extent will depend on your strategic implementation decisions. You should be certain to employ optimal uses for Intranet technology and apply them to your organization. You can also learn from the ways other companies are saving money with their Intranets.

♦ **How can I save time and enhance productivity through Intranet implementation?**

Beyond the more obvious productivity benefits of faster, more efficient production and dissemination of corporate documents and information, Intranets are capable of providing the means for more efficient communication and collaboration. Designate departmental Intranet Webmasters in addition to, or instead of, an overall corporate Intranet Webmaster to reduce reliance on one central person or group. Allocate appropriate access and content-creation rights to appropriate individuals, departments, or groups so that information is protected where necessary, but is also readily available to those who need it.

♦ **What strategies can I employ to help ensure acceptance and optimal use of my organization's Intranet?**

Lightweight policies and creative ideas for encouragement of Intranet usage will inspire, rather than intimidate, users. For instance, have a competition between departments for the best departmental Web page.

6

♦ **How can my organization continue to maximize its Intranet investment and realize competitive advantages?**

The sooner your company begins to utilize an Intranet, the better your chances of being several steps ahead of the competition. The more that your organization uses Intranet technology, the more new ideas will spring forth for maximizing its effectiveness. You can learn from what other companies have done, as well as through hands-on experience with your own Intranet.

♦ **How are other companies strategically implementing Intranets/Extranets, and how are they using them to achieve business goals?**

Other companies are

- ♦ Creating virtual corporations
- ♦ Saving on long distance bills
- ♦ Using Intranet suites to establish productive Intranets sooner
- ♦ Securing internal transactions and Internet e-mail
- ♦ Connecting remote branches with NetWare LANs to the Intranet
- ♦ Streamlining help desk requests
- ♦ Saving training time and easing file sharing among users
- ♦ Realizing faster access to knowledge resources
- ♦ Improving document publishing and distribution
- ♦ Empowering team members and strengthening bonds among co-workers
- ♦ Increasing productivity and efficiency
- ♦ Improving communications
- ♦ Realizing faster and more efficient data access

CHAPTER 7

Planning, Installing, and Configuring an Intranet

Susan Archer
with *Michael Beirne, Michael K. Bosch*
John F. Moehrke, John C. Weise

Chapter Objectives

♦ Find out what a systems administrator needs to know to set up an Intranet

♦ Grasp concepts that users on an Intranet need to know

♦ Understand how to share information on an Intranet

♦ Understand how to integrate existing documents and databases with an Intranet

♦ Learn what hardware is needed to set up an Intranet

♦ Learn what software is needed to set up an Intranet

♦ Learn how to connect an Intranet to the Internet

Installing an Intranet involves choosing the best tools for your organization. The local area network (LAN) connectivity, hardware, and software you choose provide new capabilities that help your organization become more productive. This chapter explains the trade-offs that are necessary when you make choices about the configuration of your Intranet. The process of installing your Intranet includes

♦ Selecting the best hardware and software to use with your *existing* hardware and software.

♦ Installing and configuring your Intranet.

♦ Setting up an Internet connection if you decide you want one.

As with any project, it's important in your planning process to decide who is going to do what work and who is going to have certain levels of security access. See Chapter 5 for a thorough discussion of management and administration issues.

After you install an Intranet, the work processes of the people in your organization will change. This chapter highlights some of these changes and gives you an opportunity to be proactive in dealing with potential issues.

When you install and configure an Intranet, you are going to need some new hardware and software. This chapter explains what you will need and provides comprehensive information about how to connect to the Internet.

This chapter also walks you through several major configuration decisions that affect the tools you use and then tells you how to start planning and installing your own Intranet.

Your Existing Computer Hardware

Your hardware platform has a major effect on what software you use for your Intranet. Many organizations already have a large investment in existing computers, and it's important to make the best use of this investment. On the other hand, as you're getting ready to install your Intranet, this is a good time to take a hard look at your existing technologies and make some decisions about what hardware you want to use in the future.

7

The Increasing Use of PCs

One general trend in computer usage is toward increased use of PCs and smaller computers with less emphasis on large mainframes. Many companies are using more PCs for tasks that used to be done by mainframes.

A major reason for this trend is the Windows NT operating system. This robust operating system offers features that used to be associated only with mainframe operating systems. For example, Windows NT Server has true 32-bit, preemptive multitasking that provides independent simultaneous processing by different applications. If one application on the server crashes, other running processes are usually not affected. In addition, Windows NT provides security for users and groups to prevent unauthorized access. The features of Windows NT make it possible to run mission-critical applications on a relatively inexpensive PC platform. Other forces driving the trend toward greater use of PCs include the increasing power of PCs, the increasing number of people using computers, and the high cost of paying technical mainframe experts what they are worth. Put another way, PCs are generally easier to use than mainframe systems, so people with limited technical expertise can run them.

Mainframe Alternatives

Although many mainframe systems now support Intranet applications, you need to consider whether Intranet applications are the most cost-effective use of your mainframe computing power. There is a trade-off between putting your Intranet on your mainframe and putting it on a PC-based LAN. For example, nightly settlement of electronic credit card purchases and research that involves complex equations are the kinds of tasks that mainframes traditionally do best. The sheer size and quantity of data that a mainframe can handle make it the system of choice for applications like these.

On the other hand, for things like distributing this week's sales figures to the sales force or maintaining a company phone list, a mainframe is probably too much machine for the task. Many organizations are thinking about ways to take the load off of their mainframes. At the same time, these organizations are trying to save money by automating processes like depositing checks, ordering literature, and distributing drawings to the shop floor.

The Well-Balanced Option

Organizations are in a tight squeeze. They have a diverse group of employees and clients with various computer skills. Their employees range from people who have never used a mouse to technical experts. In addition, organizations need to have the highest quality security for their data. So how do organizations reconcile the need to implement new technologies to automate tasks with the need to keep training simple and data security tight?

One part of the answer is to provide the easiest, most secure system to use, and this is where a PC-based Intranet becomes an attractive option. The rest of this chapter provides detailed information about setting up a PC-based Intranet in your organization.

Your Existing LAN

All LANs are made up of three building blocks: LAN hardware, communication software used to transport information across the LAN, and various applications that use the network. Figure 7-1 illustrates these building blocks using a screen capture of the Windows 95 Network Configuration dialog box for a PC on a LAN.

The Physical Hardware

All networks have physical hardware that makes up the network. Regardless of whether the hardware is a satellite dish or a coaxial cable, all networks have some kind of physical equipment that is the basis for interconnecting the computers within the network. Each computer on the Intranet needs to have access to the network. When a PC is part of a LAN, a network adapter card is the hardware used to connect the PC to the LAN. An Intranet can run on any LAN topology including Ethernet, FDDI, Token Ring, and others.

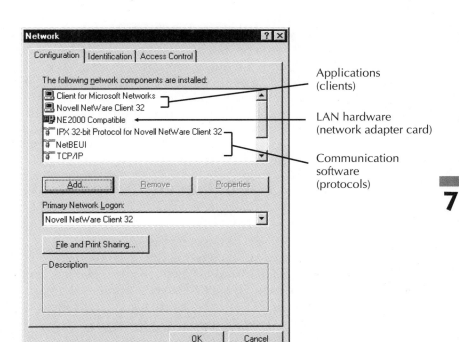

Building blocks of a LAN

Figure 7-1.

7

NOTE: In Figure 7-1, the third item, NE2000 Compatible, identifies the network adapter card in the PC for which the network is being configured.

The Communications Protocol

The communications protocol used on a network transports messages across the network. Protocols are like a language that computers use to talk to one another. For example, if someone speaks German to you and you don't know German, you can't understand what the person is saying. The same thing is true for computer protocols. If one computer is using one protocol and another computer is using a different protocol, the two computers can't communicate with each other.

NOTE: In Figure 7-1, the PC has three protocols installed: IPX 32-bit Protocol for Novell NetWare Client 32, NetBEUI, and TCP/IP. Each protocol is a different language used to transport information through the adapter card and onto the LAN.

The Applications

The applications on a LAN can be network applications or applications like e-mail, word processors, and browsers. In Figure 7-1, two network client applications are illustrated: Client for Microsoft Networks and Novell NetWare Client 32. In this configuration, the Client for Microsoft Networks uses the NetBEUI protocol to send and receive information across the LAN. The Novell NetWare Client 32 on this PC uses the IPX 32-bit Protocol for Novell NetWare Client 32. The applications that use the TCP/IP protocol are Intranet applications that aren't configured in this part of Windows 95. Shown in Figure 7-1 is one possible configuration in which the client applications are providing a middle layer between the communications protocol and the operating system of the PC. Clients used in this way can make more than one communications protocol available to the operating system. Other combinations of clients and protocols are also possible.

NOTE: As you read this chapter, you will find the term "client" used in many different ways. There are network client applications such as those illustrated in Figure 7-1, as well as other client applications like e-mail and browsers. The latter type provide different kinds of services than do the network client applications, explained here, which provide the network middle-layer function.

Intranet Software

Intranet software communicates over your existing LAN, but you may need additional LAN connections for TCP/IP servers. In addition, you are going to need to install the *Transmission Control Protocol/Internet Protocol (TCP/IP)*, the communications protocol used on the Internet. The software that transmits messages using the TCP/IP protocol is called a TCP/IP *stack*, and every machine you want on your TCP/IP-based Intranet must have one.

T IP: Intranet applications help your users share information more effectively within your organization. Most organizations include e-mail clients and e-mail server applications. Web-based client software includes browsers, search applications with advanced query techniques, and content creation tools. Web servers distribute Intranet e-mail information and can connect to existing databases on PCs and mainframes. Newsreaders are somewhat less well-known applications that can be powerful information distribution tools on an Intranet. Depending on how you want to configure your Intranet, you may want additional applications that perform file transfers and provide terminal emulation for your mainframes.

This section discusses different ways to set up a TCP/IP network on your LAN and explains different features you may want to look for as you're making decisions about Intranet software purchases.

The TCP/IP Protocol

TCP/IP is the communications protocol used on the Internet, and it provides the basis for installing an Intranet on your LAN. The TCP/IP protocol is actually many protocols working together to transport electronic packets and provide connections across a network. A *packet* is a single unit of data sent from one computer to another across a network. Packets usually contain a *header,* which includes identity and address information; and *data,* an e-mail message, a file, or other information. A *connection* provides access to another computer, makes it possible to reliably send packets, and ensures that all packets have been correctly received and sequenced. TCP/IP also makes it possible for multiple applications on users' desktops to have connections with multiple hosts.

7

TCP/IP is like a phone call. For example, a person can call your home from any phone in the world. The person dials your phone number, the telephone network connects to your phone, and your phone rings. The caller's words and your words are transmitted in the right order, so you can understand each other. When the conversation is complete, you and the caller hang up the phone. In a similar way, the TCP/IP protocol uses a number, the *IP address,* to make a connection to a specific computer. The connection lasts until all packets are sent and received.

What Routers Do

Routers on the Internet receive packets and forward them to the next destination based on the packet's IP address. An IP address is 4 bytes, and looks like this: 192.104.32.1. Like a telephone number, an IP address is unique. Routers on a TCP/IP network forward packets to other routers based on the IP address of the computer.

The TCP/IP Stack

Within each computer on the Internet, there is a TCP/IP stack that acts like an electronic mail carrier. The TCP/IP stack transmits outgoing packets to the correct destination and delivers incoming packets to the Intranet applications on your computer. The TCP/IP stack communicates between the TCP/IP protocol and your computer's operating system. Unix, Macintosh, and PC operating systems all work differently and, therefore, their TCP/IP stacks use different processes to transmit messages between the operating system and the TCP/IP protocol. Nevertheless, the TCP/IP stacks for these operating systems all can interact.

Using the Windows Sockets Standard

For the Windows operating system, the most common way to set up a TCP/IP-based Intranet is to install a TCP/IP stack on each PC on your LAN. A stack is a TCP/IP application program interface (API) that conforms to the Windows Sockets standard, released in 1992. Before the release of the Windows Sockets standard, software developers had created many different, incompatible TCP/IP APIs. TCP/IP application developers had to support different TCP/IP implementations, and this was very costly. Berkeley Sockets, created by Berkeley Software Distribution (BSD) of the University of California, was the basis for the Windows Sockets standard.

NOTE: Today, TCP/IP stacks are usually Winsock compliant, meaning that they usually conform to the Windows Sockets standard. In other words, any Internet software you buy that is Winsock compliant works with any other Winsock-compliant software.

A Typical TCP/IP Configuration

In a typical TCP/IP configuration, each computer has its own TCP/IP stack, which sends and receives messages using the existing software and hardware on your LAN. To use TCP/IP in conjunction with your existing LAN, each computer, or host, on the network needs to have its own, unique IP address that provides the TCP/IP protocol with the address information it needs. A *host* is one of the computers on a TCP/IP network and can be a PC, a workstation, a mainframe, a Unix system, or any other computer.

Each host has an IP address and a hostname. For example, a network PC might have the IP address "192.104.32.1" and the hostname "gateway.frontiertech.com." The hostname is usually easier to remember than the IP address, and this is why most users tend to use a hostname when they are connecting to a computer on a TCP/IP network.

The Domain Name System

The *Domain Name System (DNS)* is like a worldwide phone directory. Instead of phone numbers, the DNS provides a way to keep track of IP addresses, hostnames, and aliases. An *alias* is another name for the host. The Internet is subdivided into *domains,* which are names of various groups of computers. A domain can be all of the computers in a particular country, geographic area, or organization. For example, all of the computers in the United Kingdom are in the uk domain. All of the computers owned by Frontier Technologies Corporation are in the frontiertech.com domain. Figure 7-2 illustrates a network PC and a Domain Name System server.

In the U.S., the domain type is a suffix on the domain name that identifies the kind of organization to which you're connecting. For example, *.com* indicates commercial, *.edu* indicates an educational institution, *.net* indicates network operations, *.mil* indicates military, *.gov* indicates government, and *.org* indicates organization.

7

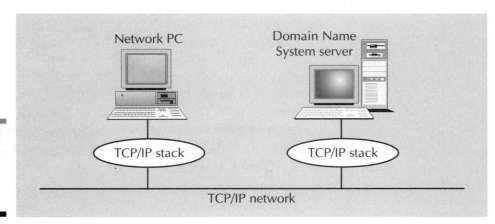

A Network PC and a Domain Name System server

Figure 7-2.

T IP: The important thing to realize is that for any relatively large TCP/IP-based network, you need a DNS server to keep track of all the IP addresses and hostnames for your computers. If you have a relatively small network, about ten PCs or less, you can use host tables on each PC to resolve IP addresses and hostnames.

Host Table

A *host table* is a listing of all IP addresses, hostnames, and aliases that a particular computer might need to reach. Each computer on the network needs its own host table. If new computers are added or information in the host table changes, the host table in every computer needs to be updated. This kind of manual maintenance becomes overly laborious after you get more than about ten PCs on your network.

The Benefits of a DNS Server

The benefit of a DNS server is that you enter each IP address and hostname change once, as shown in Table 7-1. All of the other PCs on your network connect to the DNS server for *IP address resolution,* the process of translating a hostname or alias to an IP address. If you install a DNS server on your LAN, you enter the IP address name of the DNS server in the stack configuration of every PC on your network, but once this is done, you never have to do it again as long as your DNS server keeps the same IP address.

Using TCP/IP Applications with an IPX Network

If you have an IPX-based LAN, such as Novell NetWare, you might want to use TCP/IP-based Intranet applications rather than install TCP/IP on every desktop and the additional servers you would need to run TCP/IP. This configuration makes it possible to continue using your IPX-based LAN. You could install a special stack so that the TCP/IP-based applications on each PC don't need a full TCP/IP stack. The special stack converts TCP/IP messages from the client applications on the PC into IPX messages. These IPX messages travel over the IPX network to a port on the NT gateway server. An NT service listens at the designated port and transmits messages through a

Example of a Domain Name System Server Table
Table 7-1.

Computer	Use	IP Address	Hostname
Network PC	User PC	192.104.32.1	gateway.frontiertech.com
DNS server	Domain Name System server	192.104.32.5	ns.frontiertech.com

TCP/IP stack on the PC that acts as the IPX gateway. The TCP/IP messages can go to Intranet server applications on the same PC as the IPX gateway or out to the Internet. Figure 7-3 illustrates this configuration.

Security Issues

From the standpoint of Internet security, the IPX gateway acts like a natural firewall. A *firewall* is a server that is the only access point between your network and the Internet and makes it more difficult for an intruder to hack into your network. For more on network security, see "Protecting Your Network from Intruders," later in this chapter. The IPX gateway is the only PC that connects to the Internet. If an intruder tries to get into your network, the only machine he or she can attack is the IPX gateway.

The Host Table Alternative

If you're using a TCP/IPX configuration, you don't necessarily need a DNS server. Only one PC connects to the Intranet server applications or to the Internet, so it is easy to maintain your configuration in a host table, such as the one in Table 7-2.

Working with E-mail

E-mail lets users send and receive information over your Intranet. When users have questions or need to provide information to particular individuals or groups of people, they can send e-mail messages. This speeds up the flow of communication and provides a way to get in touch with someone who is out of the office. Users can answer e-mail when they have time and aren't dealing with other distractions. To set up e-mail, you need an e-mail server.

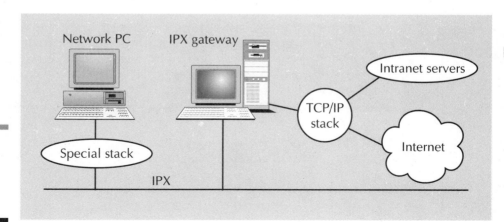

Using a special stack over an IPX network

Figure 7-3.

7

Computer	Use	IP Address	Hostname
IPX gateway	TCP/IP and IPX gateway	192.104.32.5	IPXGate.frontiertech.com
	Mail server	192.104.32.5	ns.frontiertech.com
	Web server	192.104.32.5	www.frontiertech.com
Network PC	User PC	Not needed	Not needed

Host Table
Entries for an
IPX Gateway
Table 7-2.

In addition, each user's desktop computer needs an e-mail application installed on it.

Mail Servers

Mail servers receive e-mail messages and transmit them to the correct user e-mail addresses. This section discusses different kinds of mail servers and why you would want to use them.

SMTP Mail Server   All e-mail applications that run over a TCP/IP stack use the Simple Mail Transport Protocol (SMTP) to transport e-mail messages. If you already have an e-mail application that doesn't support SMTP, you are facing a choice: you can keep your existing e-mail application and use it on your LAN or, if you plan to connect to the Internet and allow your users to send and receive Internet e-mail, you can upgrade to an application that supports SMTP. If you decide on the latter, you will also need a *relay host,* which routes outgoing mail and acts as an SMTP server.

NOTE: When e-mail delivery is based on SMTP, users need to have their PCs on and their e-mail available most of the time. This is because when you use SMTP by itself, e-mail messages are delivered directly to the user's PC. On your Intranet, your mail server would try to deliver the e-mail messages for a period of time, usually four to five days. If the user's e-mail application isn't available during that time, the e-mail message is never delivered, in which case the person who sent the message usually receives a copy and a warning that the e-mail was never delivered.

POP3 Mail Server   To prevent possible loss of e-mail messages, many organizations install a Post Office Protocol (POP3) server on their Intranet. If your Intranet is attached to the Internet, your users can dial in from time to time and get their e-mail without worrying about losing any e-mail messages. This isn't possible if you are only using SMTP. A POP3 server stores a user's e-mail messages until the user starts the e-mail application, which automatically connects to the POP3 server and asks for any new e-mail messages. At that point, the e-mail messages are downloaded to the user's PC and deleted from the POP3 server. E-mail message retrieval with POP3 is active (that is, initiated by your PC) rather than passive (initiated by another computer), as with SMTP. In other words, with POP3, you ask for your e-mail rather than wait for it to arrive.

NOTE: The major drawback to using a POP3 server is that you only get one chance to download your e-mail messages. If a busy executive gets POP3 e-mail messages at work but wants to read them at home, that person is out of luck, because the messages are on the PC at work. If the same executive is on the road and dials in for new messages using a company laptop, that laptop then has the new e-mail messages on it. If the laptop gets returned to the information systems department and the hard drive gets reformatted, the downloaded e-mail messages are gone.

IMAP4 Mail Server   Another e-mail protocol, Internet Message Access Protocol Version 4 (IMAP4) overcomes this drawback of POP3. With IMAP4, the e-mail messages remain on the IMAP4 mail server until the user chooses to delete them. In addition, users can add, rename, and delete mailboxes on the IMAP4 mail server and retrieve message attributes, text, or portions of the message.

E-mail Applications for Users' Desktops

This section discusses features to consider when you are deciding what e-mail applications to install on your users' desktops. These features enhance the usability of your e-mail application and ensure the security of your e-mail traffic.

MAPI   The Messaging Application Program Interface (MAPI) makes your e-mail application available from other programs. For example, in some browsers, clicking on a mail hypertext link automatically brings up your e-mail application with the e-mail address already in the correct entry field. An advanced use of the MAPI protocol is to enable Web-based workflow applications to do things like forward purchase orders to the correct managers within a company for authorization. These workflow applications use MAPI to send messages to users or for processes within the workflow applications. Many Windows-based applications that support MAPI can notify users when new e-mail messages are available. Even if you aren't planning on sophisticated uses of e-mail now, you should consider getting a

7

MAPI-enabled e-mail application, because things could change, and you might want to be prepared.

T **IP:** MAPI-enabled e-mail applications make e-mail available from browsers. Sophisticated workflow applications use MAPI-enabled e-mail to send messages from the workflow application.

MIME   The Multipurpose Internet Mail Extension (MIME) is another useful feature to have in your e-mail applications. MIME support gives you the ability to attach files to e-mail messages. For example, it allows you to attach spreadsheets, marketing presentations, documents, database files, audio and video files, and any other files to an e-mail message. The person receiving the message uses an existing application to run the file. You could use this feature to send proposals, budgets, or presentations out for review and comment, and then to receive the results and make changes accordingly.

S/MIME   Another variation of MIME, the Secure Multipurpose Internet Mail Extension (S/MIME) provides the means for e-mail to be encrypted from the time it leaves the sender's computer until the time it reaches the receiver's computer. This way, important information is transmitted across the Internet in a secure fashion. To use S/MIME, both the sender and the receiver of the e-mail message must have an e-mail application that supports it. Chapter 9 explains S/MIME in greater detail.

Central E-mail Address Book   A helpful feature that comes with many e-mail programs is the capability of setting up a central e-mail address book with the e-mail addresses of all users and groups in your organization. All of the users in your organization can access the central e-mail address book, which makes it easy to find e-mail addresses as people come and go.

Mail Filtering   Many e-mail applications also have some sort of filtering mechanism so that e-mail from certain users always goes to a particular e-mail directory. For example, if you have an office or business partner in France, you may want to put all of the e-mail from users in France in a French folder. Figure 7-4 shows an e-mail window used to define a rule that automatically stores all messages from PierreL in a French folder within the user's mailbox.

Mail Searching   Mail searching is another capability that is available with many e-mail applications. Search functions let you look for a search word or phrase in several e-mail messages or within a single message. Two kinds of

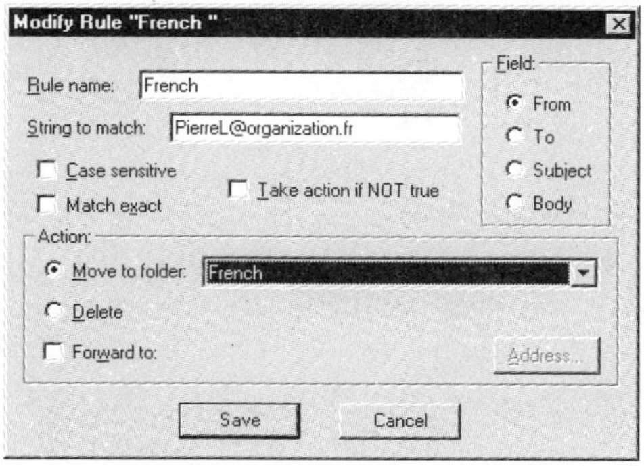

Filtering
e-mail
messages
based on the
user's e-mail
address
Figure 7-4.

search facilities are available. One lets you search several e-mail messages by looking for a search string in the messages within a mail folder. For example, Figure 7-5 shows a search for the word "e-mail" in the body of several e-mail messages.

Another type of search facility, which many e-mail applications have, lets you open an individual message and search for a phrase within the individual message. This is similar to the *find* capability you see in many word processing packages.

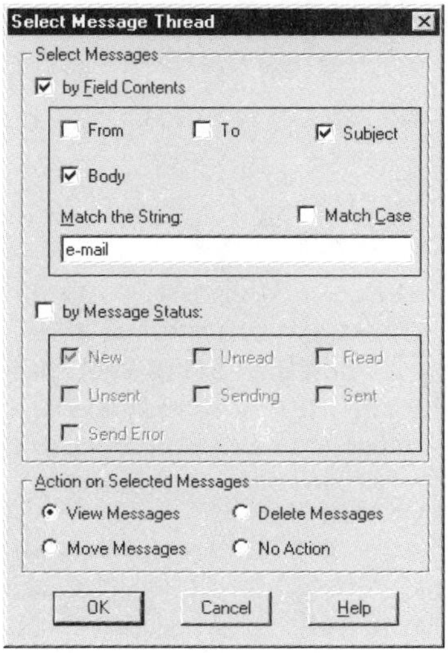

Mail search
for a word in
several e-mail
messages
Figure 7-5.

7

Summary of E-mail Features

The following features deserve consideration as you set up e-mail on
your Intranet:

◆ **Mail Servers**

  ◆ *SMTP mail servers* transmit e-mail messages directly to the end-user's
    computer. If the user's computer isn't available, the messages may
    time out.

  ◆ *POP3 mail servers* store a user's e-mail messages until the user's
    e-mail application requests new e-mail messages. Users can only
    download e-mail messages once.

  ◆ *IMAP4 mail servers* store a user's e-mail messages and notify the user
    when new e-mail messages come in. Multiple downloads of the
    same e-mail message are possible, but require more storage space.

◆ **E-mail Applications for Users' Desktops**

  ◆ *MAPI* provides e-mail support in browsers and other applications.

  ◆ *MIME* easily transmits documents, spreadsheets, presentations,
    video, and other kinds of files.

  ◆ *S/MIME* provides a way to ensure the security of e-mail
    transmissions.

  ◆ *Central e-mail address books* make it easy to keep track of users'
    e-mail addresses in your organization.

  ◆ *Mail filtering* makes it easy to organize and find e-mail messages.

  ◆ *Mail searching* helps you find a phrase in a specific e-mail message or
    in several messages.

Your Web Server

To create and use a Web site, you need a Web server. To access your Web site,
you need to install a browser on all of your users' desktops, and you need tools
for creating and maintaining Web pages. Search applications that let users
search your Web site or search file servers on your network enhance the
productivity gains your organization receives from implementing an Intranet.

Many people are familiar with what is possible with an Internet Web site.
Typically, an organization's marketing, public relations, or advertising
department is responsible for the content of an Internet site. A single
department usually creates and maintains the HTML pages. If you're using
back-end applications, one or more programmers in the management
information systems (MIS) department is responsible for creating and
maintaining the back-end applications. A *back-end application* is a program

that receives data from the Web server and does some kind or processing based on the data.

An Intranet is different from the Internet in that it gives Web capabilities to everyone in an organization. Everyone can create content and post it to your organization's Intranet Web server. For example, at Frontier Technologies, all departments maintain their own information on the company Intranet. Each department changes its information at will and moves the changed files to the Intranet Web server. Some Web servers don't allow this much flexibility, however.

T **IP:**   As you're planning your Web server, you need to keep ease of administration in mind. Imagine if you had a hundred or more people creating and changing Web content on a daily basis and the MIS group had to keep track of all the file changes! This could quickly become overwhelming.

Secure Web Server Connections

Providing a secure connection between your users and your Web server helps ensure the integrity of your Intranet. If your Intranet is connected to the Internet, it is potentially a bigger issue than if it isn't. In any case, most Web servers today support Secure Sockets Layer (SSL) version 2.0 or SSL version 3.0. These protocols are explained in greater detail in Chapter 9. For the purposes of this chapter, it's important for you to know that these protocols are available. Look for a Web server that supports the security protocols that are going to provide the desired level of security between your Web server and your users' browsers. Figure 7-6 shows a dialog box in a Web server used to configure SSL version 2.0.

7

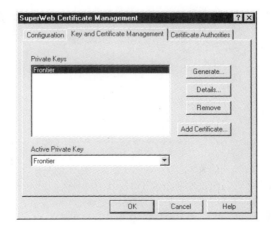

Tab dialog boxes used to configure SSL security

Figure 7-6.

If you decide to use SSL security, you're going to need to be able to obtain security certificates. You can obtain these by contacting a certificate authority or by obtaining software that generates and maintains security certificates. Figure 7-6 shows tab dialog boxes used to request a security certificate online from several certificate authorities listed under the Certificate Authorities tab.

Other kinds of online security that are available with many Web servers let you prohibit access by IP address or by domain name. If you implement this kind of security, you can specify what IP addresses and domains can access your Web server. All other IP addresses and domains are automatically locked out. For example, machines within your Intranet are able to connect to your Web server; but if anyone else on the Internet tries to connect, your Web server rejects the connection. Figure 7-7 illustrates address restriction in a Web server.

Secure Access to Web Server Content

Web servers distribute HTML pages created by the users in your organization. In addition, Web servers can connect to PC databases and mainframe databases on your organization's network. This section explains security issues relative to the information stored on your Web server.

Access Rights to Your Intranet Web Server   As discussed in Chapter 5, different people in your organization need several different kinds of access rights to your Intranet Web server. Access to some information, such as sales

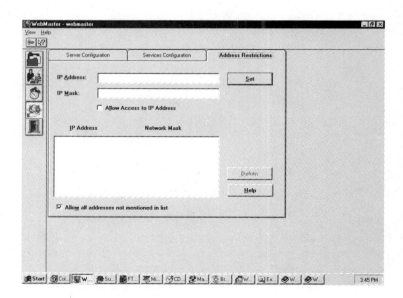

Address
restrictions in
a Web server
Figure 7-7.

figures, ought to be restricted. But access to other information, such as a Web-based phone book, ought to be universally available. In addition, more people will be creating content as your organization grows. As information changes, it needs to be able to be updated easily.

Establishing Different Kinds of User Access   So what do you look for? To begin with, you need a way to create different groups of users and define different levels of information access to those users. For example, suppose the sales department wanted to have access to daily sales reports that showed shipments to date and sales for the month and year. The accounting department would create reports and update them on a daily basis, so sales representatives could easily find out when products were being shipped to their customers. Figure 7-8 shows how you could set this up so that the systems specialist in accounting would be responsible for updating the Intranet sales information every day.

The systems administrator creates a folder and assigns the folder to the systems specialist in accounting. In addition, the systems administrator sets up a group and gives the systems specialist in accounting authorization to assign people to the group. The systems specialist assigns read privileges to everyone in accounting and sales. On a daily basis, the systems specialist updates the sales report. If employees in the engineering department try to read the sales report, they are locked out of the sales report page.

TIP: As you consider purchasing Web server software, an important feature to keep in mind is the ability to maintain multiple groups and provide information security based on those groups.

Secure Updating of Information   Delegating ownership of the Intranet content on your Web server prevents many problems inherent in updating the information, because those who care about the information have full control over and are fully responsible for it. In the sales example, the systems specialist in the accounting department is responsible for posting the daily sales report to the Intranet Web site. The systems specialist cares about providing the information because it simplifies distribution. For example, if the information isn't easily available, sales representatives would need to constantly hound the accounting department to double check sales figures and commissions. If daily figures are available, sales representatives can view the sales information, note any discrepancies, and escalate any problems. If a sales representative promises shipment of a product on a particular day and the shipment doesn't take place, the sales representative knows and can proactively handle the problem.

7

Multiple Layers of Access Look for administrative applications that provide multiple layers of access so that your Intranet Web site can grow and change as your organization grows and changes. In addition, the applications used to maintain the information need to be easy to use. As your Intranet grows, more of the people creating and using the content will be users rather than technicians. The tools you use need to be easy enough for those with little technical background to use.

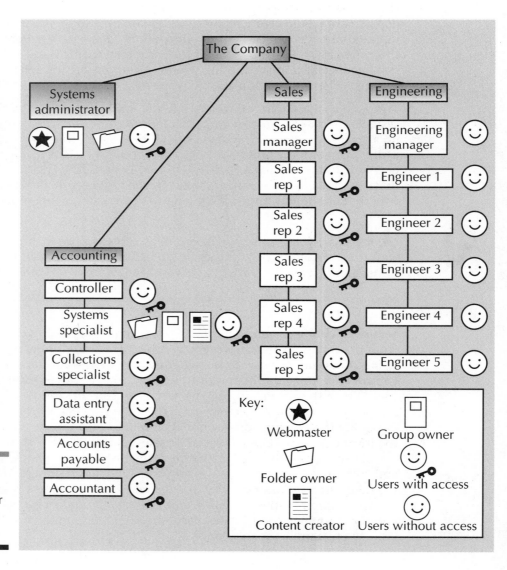

Providing a daily sales report on your Intranet
Figure 7-8.

The Web Server Configuration Interface Web server developers use different interfaces to configure their Web servers. Some choose to do maintenance through a browser. The strength of this approach is that the administration application is independent of the hardware platform. You can have users at PCs, Unix terminals, and Macintoshes all do configuration through their browsers. The drawback of this approach is that it can require considerable navigation to get to the more advanced features. The browser may also be somewhat slower than an interface on the computer itself. A browser is limited to the capabilities of HTML.

Remote Administration Applications Figure 7-9 shows a remote administration application on a user's desktop. It is called a *remote administration application* because it is not on the same PC as the Web server. If it were on the same PC as the Web server, it would be called a *local administration application*. All Windows operating systems support dragging and dropping files. Using the remote administrative application, any user with proper authorization can sit at their own PC and transfer files to the Web server. For example, the systems specialist discussed previously in the sales report example could drag and drop the sales report to the correct folder on the Web server.

The drawback of a graphical user interface (GUI) like the one in Figure 7-9 is that it is hardware dependent, but the strength of it is its power. With a GUI interface, you can do things like drag and drop files from a network drive to your Web server, so information is available on your Web site. This approach saves time for the systems administrator because updating becomes a

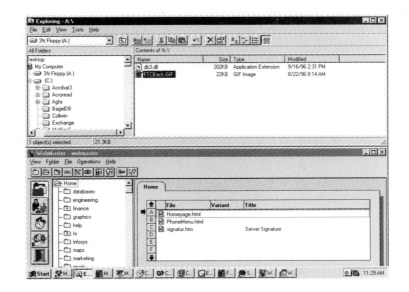

Updating Web server content from the user's desktop

Figure 7-9.

7

distributed process instead of another task the systems administrator has to perform. This kind of capability saves time and makes information available faster.

As you think about your Web server, be sure to look for remote administration applications that users can have on their desktops. Otherwise, someone needs to sit down at the computer where the Web server is running and do the file transfer to the Web server on their own. Being able to manage the information on your Web server only from the Web server itself is a potential bottleneck to getting the most out of your Intranet.

T **IP:** Look for remote administration tools like the one illustrated in Figure 7-9. This tool gives users the ability to update Intranet information from their desktops without involving the systems administrator.

Document Security Defined in Your Web Server   Many Web servers use the existing file structures on the C: drive of the PC running the Web server or on a network drive. In these servers, there is no access security for updating documents aside from the security defined for the particular drive. Another approach is to define document security within the Web server. The access security explained previously in Figures 7-8 and 7-9 is based on the ability to have document security defined within the Web server.

To provide this security while maintaining the integrity of the documents stored on the Web server, it's possible to link the file on the Web server to the network drive. This is called a *dynamic link* because it allows users to update the documents on the Web server to the most recent version automatically by clicking the refresh button in the Web server.

Full-Text Searching

Many Web sites give users the ability to enter a word or phrase in a search form and find all of the documents that contain the requested text. To implement full-text searching on your Web server, look for a Web server that has a document indexer and a search engine. The document indexer reads all the documents on the Web site and reads the information into an index. The search engine then makes use of the index to find files containing a word or phrase that a user entered through a browser.

Document Indexing   As you're looking at indexing software, consider whether all words or only "important" words are indexed. Some indexing programs let you choose not to make words such as "and," "the," and "a" searchable. In these programs, all words that you don't choose are considered important words and are therefore searchable.

NOTE: Another aspect of indexing software to consider is how easy it is to refresh the index in order to add new documents and delete old ones. Many indexing programs run at predefined times in which you might, for example, reindex your Web server at midnight every night. Another option is real-time reindexing where the indexer runs every time a document is changed.

Full-Text Search Engines   Several proprietary search engines are available based on their own proprietary search methodology. The Wide Area Information Server (WAIS) is a standard for nonproprietary, full-text search engines used by some servers on the Internet.

Storing Documents in Different Formats on Your Web Server

After users create HTML documents, the HTML documents need to be stored on your Intranet Web server. Once an HTML document is on your Web server, your users can access the HTML document using a browser. Web servers typically store HTML documents for Web pages, but you may want to consider storing other kinds of documents on your Web site as well. For example, you may want to create sales reports that can be viewed from your browser using an existing helper application on your users' PCs. A *helper application* is a program on a user's desktop that can be launched from within a browser. You can also put existing documents on your Web server for easy access from a browser.

TIP: If you would prefer to have only HTML documents on your Web server, another option is to store files on a file server and make them searchable. This approach saves space on the hard drive of your Web server and reduces redundancy by making it possible to have a single version of the file on your file server. An additional benefit is that if updates occur, there is less of a chance that someone will forget to post the correct file.

7

Multihoming

Another feature to look for is *multihoming*, which gives you the ability to have more than one IP address on your NT server. Many Web servers allow you to run more than one instance of the Web server application on the same machine. For example, you might have one Web server configured for sales and marketing and a different Web server for engineering. The benefit of multihoming is that if you have an expensive PC, you can get more out of your investment by putting more than one Web server on it. If you don't have multihoming, you need a separate machine for every Web server in your organization.

Logging Capabilities

Logging capabilities are the final feature to consider. Some Web servers can generate statistics you can use to measure performance to identify what browsers are accessing your Web server and to find out how many times your Web server is accessed. You can also use these logging capabilities to see what Web pages are being used most often. As you analyze your counts, look to see if a few users are accessing certain pages many times or if many users are accessing the same page. This sort of analysis can help you more fully tailor your Intranet to the needs of your organization. Other kinds of logging are also available. Figure 7-10 shows an example of a log file.

Back-End Applications on Your Web Server

Some of the most powerful applications for Web servers involve creating Web server–backed applications. These programs may perform some kind of processing based on information received from the Web server. For example, suppose you want to create a phone list application for your organization, like the one illustrated in Figure 7-11. The phone list application accesses a database to get the information in the phone list.

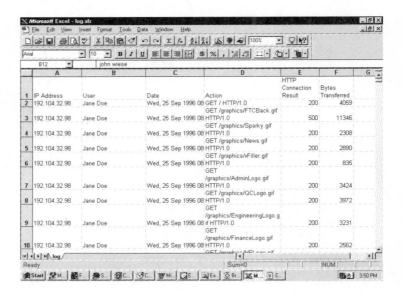

Example of a log file
Figure 7-10.

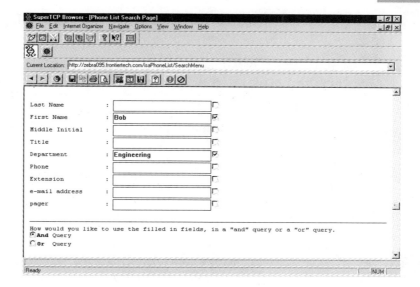

Example of a
phone list
back-end
application
Figure 7-11.

Writing a Back-End Application   Web server back-end applications are
written using the Common Gateway Interface (CGI), Windows CGI, Internet
Server Application Programming Interface (ISAPI), or Netscape Application
Programming Interface (NSAPI). Windows CGI back-end applications are
created using Visual Basic or any programming language that can create an
executable file. Some scripting packages, which use runtime libraries, are also
available for CGI. ISAPI, CGI, and NSAPI applications are created using C++
or another programming language that can create a dynamic link library
(DLL). For more information, see Chapter 8.

TIP: Because Visual Basic is easier to learn than C++, creating CGI and
Windows CGI back-end applications is easier than creating ISAPI or NSAPI
back-end applications. On the other hand, ISAPI and NSAPI back-end
applications are generally faster. If you're thinking about using back-end
applications, keep these trade-offs in mind.

7

Database Connections   Your back-end application could connect to a
database using a native database connection or using the Open Database
Connectivity (ODBC) interface. The advantage of using a native database
connection is that it's faster than ODBC. The advantage of using ODBC is
that many databases support it. If you change from one database vendor to
another and are using ODBC, you don't have to rewrite your back-end

application as long as your database has the same configuration. For more information about creating back-end applications, see Chapter 8.

Error Checking with JavaScript and VBScript   With JavaScript and VBScript you can embed a script in your HTML page that can do error checking of an HTML form, such as the phone list page discussed previously. For example, suppose you make a mistake in the phone list application and enter a phone number in the Department field on the HTML page, illustrated in Figure 7-11. Since the Web server back-end application does error checking, it returns an error telling you that you can't enter a number in the Department field. You then reenter the phone number and submit your request again. This error checking requires that messages go back and forth between your browser and the Web server, and this is relatively high overhead for something as simple as error checking.

T IP: With JavaScript and VBScript you can embed a script in your HTML page that can do the error checking before you send the contents of the form. After your entries are validated, the script allows the user to send the information to the Web server.

Java Applets and ActiveX Controls   A third approach to the phone list application is possible. You can use a true Java applet or an ActiveX control. Java applets can run on any platform, but ActiveX controls only run on certain platforms. When you use a Java applet or ActiveX control, many files are usually downloaded to your system, and this takes a while. It's possible to store Java files and ActiveX files on your PC. For more information, see Chapter 8.

T IP: If you're thinking about using your Web server in conjunction with one of your organization's databases, you need a Web server that supports the application program interface that is best for your organization. If you're planning to use JavaScript, VBScript, Java, or ActiveX, make sure your browser supports what you're using.

Workflow Applications   Other powerful applications that are becoming increasingly available for Intranets are workflow applications that automate internal processes. For example, Frontier Technologies has a purchase order system on the company Intranet. When it comes time to order PCs, vendor services, or some other item, users go to the internal Web page with their browser and make their requests. Requests are automatically routed to the right managers for their approvals. When a manager approves a purchase order, the user automatically receives an e-mail message saying the manager approved the purchase. This single, relatively simple workflow application has saved countless hours and has vastly simplified the purchase process.

Summary of Web Server Features

♦ Check to see if your Web server supports connection security, including SSL V2.0 or SSL V3.0. These protocols ensure the integrity of your connections and identify the host to which you are connected.

♦ Consider other kinds of online security such as permitting or denying access based on IP address or domain name.

♦ The ability to define security within the Web server enhances your ability to manage access to the contents on your Web server. Look for ways to create multiple security groups and users.

♦ Flexible access rights for updating Web server data is important for having an easy-to-manage Web site. Look for ways to create multiple security groups and users.

♦ The interface for configuring your Web server can be a multiplatform browser, a graphical user interface, or a file system.

♦ Consider making use of remote administration applications to update the contents of your Web server.

♦ A document indexer and full-text search engine on your Web server make the documents on your Web server searchable from the browsers on your users' desktops. Other applications for indexing file servers on your network are available as well.

♦ Multihoming gives you the ability to have more than one Web server running on the same Windows NT workstation or Windows NT server.

♦ Logging provides statistics used to measure performance and find out what Web pages are being used most often.

♦ If you want to use your Web server as a front end to a database application, check to see if your existing database uses ODBC or a native database interface. Also find out if your Web server supports CGI, Windows CGI, ISAPI, or NSAPI.

7

Browser Features to Consider

This section explains, from an installation and configuration standpoint, some browser features to consider. For information about other features to consider in a browser, see Chapter 3. Many organizations like the idea of having a single, easy-to-use Intranet interface for their users. This simplifies training and reduces the errors that users can make. Having all of your Intranet applications available from within your browser is a strategy you may want to consider.

Using Your Browser with Your Content Creation Software
Developers are continually adding all kinds of features to browsers. Some companies include Web content creation tools with their browsers, while others make it possible to view your complete Intranet in a directory structure from within your browser or in another graphical way. From within your browser, you can modify the contents of any page, add pages, or delete pages. Consider how you want your browser to integrate with Web content creation tools as you're deciding which browser is the best for your organization.

Using a Browser with Your Back-End Applications
The browser you choose needs to support the capabilities of your back-end applications. For example, if you're using forms, ActiveX controls, or Java applets, you need a browser that supports these capabilities. You may also want ActiveX controls and Java applets available from within your browser for the purpose of creating interactive, appealing Web pages.

Using a Browser with Your Search Application
You may want the search application you provide for your Intranet to be accessible from within your browser. Check the requirements of your search application and choose a browser that provides the support you want.

Using Your Browser with Other Applications
Many browsers support access to other applications. For example, some browsers let you post a file to an FTP site, send e-mail, start a terminal emulator, or start a newsreader from within them.

Browser Security
Many Web servers include SSL version 2 or SSL version 3 security to ensure the integrity of the connection between a Web browser and a Web server. If you decide to use one of these security protocols, your Web server and browser must both support it. Figure 7-12 shows a tab dialog box used in establishing SSL security in a Web browser.

Summary of Browser Features
When you're looking at browsers, check to see if they fully support the capabilities needed for using the following:

♦ Web content creation tools

♦ Back-end applications that use JavaScript, VBScript, Java, ActiveX, and other capabilities

♦ Search software for your Intranet

♦ Other applications including FTP, e-mail, newsreaders, and terminal emulators

♦ Connection security needed to access your Web server

Web Content Creation and Conversion

Creating content is an important part of having an Intranet. With a Web site that connects to the Internet, typically a single department or perhaps two or three departments are responsible for creating and maintaining the content. With an Intranet, every department in your organization potentially has the capability of creating and updating Intranet content on a daily basis. This section highlights planning, installation, and configuration issues relating to Web content creation tools and conversion tools.

Web Content Creation Tools

The first thing to consider with regard to Web content creation tools is ease of use, since relatively unsophisticated users will be working with them. Make sure that the tools you choose work in conjunction with your Web

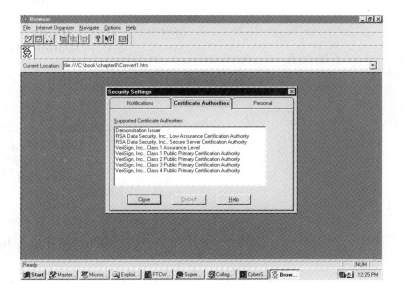

Tab dialog box used to define security in a browser

Figure 7-12.

7

server. Some Web servers include proprietary administration tools and may not allow you to use the Web content creation software you would like to use.

The Web content creation tools you want to use may integrate with a browser to give you a single user interface for your Intranet. Check that your browser supports the capabilities of your Web content creation tools. For example, If you choose a tool that supports Java, you also want a browser that supports Java.

Also keep in mind your back-end applications. Some developers provide front-end tools that require the use of their Web servers. Make sure that your browser supports the functions needed to access the back-end applications you want to use.

Web Conversion Software

This section discusses the planning, installation, and configuration issues related to Web conversion software. For more information about conversion strategies, see Chapter 10.

As you build your Web site, you're going to need to decide whether or not to convert existing documents, spreadsheets, presentations, and other files to HTML. There will be some files you will want to convert and others you will want to leave in their existing format. As you're considering Intranet software, think about document converters.

Document converters take existing files and turn them into HTML files. You might want to make a list of the different file formats already used within your organization and choose a document converter that handles as many of these formats as possible. Also think about whether you want to convert batches of documents, individual documents, or both.

 NOTE: Some document converters have easy-to-use tools for customizing your documents as you convert them. These applications can save a presentation style, which might include colors, the selected background, and fonts. That presentation style can then be applied to other documents. If you change the original document and need to convert it again, the existing presentation style can be used again with the same document.

Figure 7-13 is an HTML version of the text for the previous three paragraphs about document converters. It was created in about five minutes using a wizard to choose the HTML display options. A *wizard* is a simple program that takes you through a complex task one step at a time.

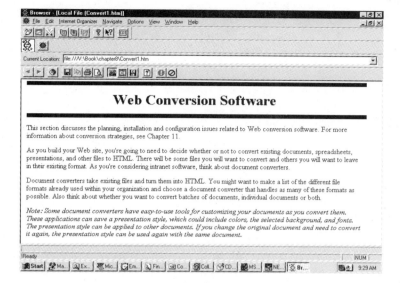

Example of
text turned
into HTML
using a
document
converter
Figure 7-13.

Searching

When users search for information on your Intranet, they can search your Web server or a file server. The information available depends on what indexed information you have available on your Intranet and whether or not it's indexed. Document indexers are available for indexing Web servers and file servers, as shown in Figure 7-14.

7

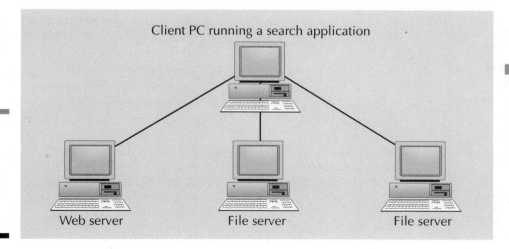

You can
search for
information
on your Web
server or on a
file server
Figure 7-14.

Online Searching

The Internet includes many search sites that index the World Wide Web. You can connect to these search sites, enter a word or phrase, and find resources on the Internet that can provide information. Some of these search sites are

> www.search.com
> www.lycos.com
> www.yahoo.com
> www.infoseek.com
> www.hotbot.com

Full-Text Searching

Many full-text query languages have what are called *Boolean operators* that add logic to your searches. For example, you might search for "Virtual" and "reality." In this type of query, you would get only documents containing the words "virtual" and "reality." If the document had only one of the words, it would not be returned in the search results. Some users are sophisticated enough to learn Boolean search syntax, but many don't have the time or inclination to become real experts.

 TIP: As you consider your options, look for search tools that are as close to standard speech as possible or that have wizards to help users do more complex queries.

Search Agents

Search agents are predefined searches that can be saved and used over and over again. After performing a search, the search agent returns URLs for the documents it finds. Typically, each search agent has its own storage area for the search results.

Searching by Filename and Description

File-level searching is also a powerful tool. The File Transfer Protocol (FTP) and Gopher are two file-related protocols that are supported in many browsers. When you view an FTP or Gopher site, what you typically see is a directory of files. *Archie* is a method of searching the directories and filenames on an FTP site. The only clue to the contents of the file Archie gives is the name of the file. *Veronica* is a method of searching Gopher files or directories. Like Archie, Veronica uses file-level information to search for files.

Working with Newsgroups

On the Internet, there are thousands of newsgroups containing information ranging from discussions of politics and economics to movie reviews and gardening. The information is in a question-and-answer format. One user posts a question, and anyone who knows the answer or part of the answer responds to the question. Answers are often cumulative. Each person who responds uses the last response and adds his or her comments. But what is the value of a newsreader on an Intranet?

Newsreaders on an Intranet

A newsreader is perfect for uses such as customer support and service. Frontier Technologies has a news server for the technical support department. When technicians can't answer questions posed by clients, they post questions to Frontiers' Intranet newsgroups. The members of the quality assurance and engineering departments read the news on a daily basis. The engineering department is spread over several locations, but all department members can read the same questions on the newsreader and respond to them. Most questions are resolved very quickly with this method. In addition, the news articles serve as a history so that people who join the organization can read past postings to the newsgroups and learn about the company's products.

Newsreader Features   The newsreaders for your users could also be relatively basic. Multithreading is a nice feature, because the original news article and the responses display in indented form under one another. If you don't have multithreaded newsgroups, questions and answers are separated from one another, and this can be confusing to readers. You also want a newsreader that provides good performance so it doesn't take long for users to download the news articles. Filtering of news articles is also helpful, in that once users have read articles, you want to be able to keep the articles from being displayed again. This way users don't waste time rereading news they've already seen.

7

Another feature to look for is keyword searching. If you're looking for a particular piece of information you aren't going to want to read several news articles to find the nugget of information you want. Keyword searching makes it possible to identify the news articles that have the greatest possibility of providing the information you want.

Using News Servers

To set up newsgroups, install at least one news server on your Intranet. Users need newsreaders on their desktops to post questions, view mail, and post responses. Some browsers also include newsreaders. Using your news server simply as an internal, Intranet news server is very different from using a news server to obtain news from the thousands of databases in the USENET system on the Internet. Internet news servers can retrieve news from more than 10,000 newsgroups around the world.

Maximizing Performance   Maximizing performance is critical, so Internet news servers have sophisticated methods of only retrieving news from the newsgroups that are actually being read by users and maximizing throughput from slow links. In addition, these news servers can block out access to some newsgroups and store thousands of news articles as efficiently as possible to save disk space.

Choosing the Right Features   If you're using a news server on your Intranet, these sophisticated features may not be as important, especially if you don't connect your Intranet to the Internet. You may decide to choose a news server with basic features, which could result in a lower cost for your news server software. To run a news server on your Intranet, you need to be able to set up newsgroups easily. A Windows-based graphical user interface (GUI) tends to support ease of use. From a security standpoint, you are probably going to want to restrict access by IP address or domain so that outsiders can't view your news, but people in different locations within your organization can read the newsgroups. In addition you need a way to age news articles and delete them so your news server doesn't use up too much disk space.

File Transfer

If you connect to the Internet and have users who need to transfer files, you may want to include File Transfer Protocol (FTP) applications. For example, the engineering and quality assurance departments at Frontier Technologies make extensive use of file transfers in transmitting files to customers. These files contain code, software documentation, fixes, and a variety of technical information. Users at our headquarters and remote offices have FTP applications on their desktops that they use to copy files to our main FTP server. Customers in Japan, Australia, Germany, France, and other countries around the world use FTP applications to pick up the files and send others.

To set up a file transfer on your Intranet, you need an FTP server and FTP applications on users' desktops. Many browsers automatically start up an FTP application when a user clicks on an FTP site. Security is important with FTP, because highly confidential information can be stored in files on an FTP site. Common security features with an FTP server include requiring the correct username and password to access a particular directory.

Terminal Emulators

If you have a mainframe on your Intranet, you may want to include terminal emulators on users' desktops for those applications that you haven't off-loaded to the Web-based part of your Intranet. Terminal emulators make use of the Telnet protocol, which can be used to access Unix, Tandem, IBM, and other mainframes through a host-specific terminal emulator. Many kinds of terminal emulators are available, including 3270, 5250, DG, WYSE, HP, and VT. As you consider terminal emulators, evaluate features including configuration options, keyboard mapping, graphics, and performance.

Integrated Solutions or Individual Applications

Many software vendors have created TCP/IP-based applications you can use on your Intranet. Some provide an integrated solution that includes all of the components you need to set up your Intranet, while other software vendors specialize in particular applications. You need to consider whether you want an all-in-one solution or whether you want to integrate different packages from different vendors.

 TIP: If you have limited technical expertise and a somewhat limited budget, taking an all-in-one solution is probably best. If you have strong technical expertise and a bigger budget, you can choose the best-of-breed applications from different vendors.

Planning an Effective Intranet

7

When you install and configure an Intranet, you are going to have various issues to handle. After your Intranet is up and running, you're going to want to evaluate the success of your installation. Installing an Intranet for your organization involves planning and preparation. In spite of your best plans, some things are going to go wrong. The following sections suggest some strategies for effective planning to help minimize problems.

Issues are not limited to technical considerations. Organizational dynamics, communication, and internal processes must be addressed to ensure success.

To protect your investment and maximize the potential productivity gains of your Intranet, consider the issues described in this section.

The Project Leader

Every project needs a leader, someone who is responsible for making the project happen and who also has the authority to accomplish the project goals. One person has to be responsible for setting up your Intranet. If you make a committee responsible, important details are certain to fall through the cracks and cause major problems. If the project leader doesn't have the authority to accomplish the goals, critical decisions aren't made in a timely manner. This prolongs the process, wastes time, and creates unnecessary problems.

 TIP: Choose your project leader when you begin the process of deciding what you want to accomplish with your Intranet. The project leader ought to be responsible for evaluating software and hardware, establishing a budget, and doing the installation.

To manage the project, the project leader needs to have clearly defined, reachable goals. Define the specific capabilities desired, the key issues, and risks to be managed, and develop a realistic picture of the associated costs and timing. Set a budget and schedule. Then establish at least a weekly review to monitor progress, to plan, and to address roadblocks that might occur.

Establishing a Schedule

It's important to establish a schedule for installing and configuring your Intranet. The following step-by-step checklist details the flow of events in setting up an Intranet:

1. Define the goals you want your Intranet installation to achieve, for example:

    ♦   To reduce the number of meetings in the organization by using e-mail and news to discuss issues and problems online.

    ♦   To reduce resources used to do routine tasks such as purchasing, tracking sales, and monitoring the progress of projects.

2. Evaluate the software and hardware needed to achieve your goals. Evaluating a small-scale implementation helps you determine if the hardware and software can achieve your goals.

3. Establish a budget and get approval.

4. Identify who is going to manage and administer your Intranet as explained in Chapter 5.

5. Order your software and hardware, and add cabling and LAN connections for new servers and any new user PCs.

6. Install and test your servers.

7. Train your users on the new technology they are going to be using.

8. Install and test your client applications with a small group of users.

9. Define a user maintenance and support plan.

10. Install your client applications throughout your organization.

It's always difficult to set up a schedule when you aren't sure exactly how long things are actually going to take. To establish a schedule, take the ten items above and use them as a starting point for your Intranet project. Establish your Intranet implementation team, and have weekly meetings to check progress on getting your Intranet running.

NOTE: Consistent leadership by the project leader is critical to the success of your implementation. A schedule keeps you focused, so that your Intranet installation goes smoothly.

Choosing a Consultant

Many people call themselves consultants and Internet experts, but how can you tell who is truly knowledgeable? The first thing to do is to check a consultant's references. If you're dealing with an individual, request a *curriculum vitae*, which provides information about the consultant's past jobs and educational background. Have the consultant sign a release, so that you can talk to previous employers and educational institutions. If you're dealing with a consulting firm, get corporate references and a curriculum vitae for each person who is going to participate in your project. Once again, get releases and talk to the references. You will find out many things and stand a much better chance of choosing an effective consultant who can truly help you.

7

T **IP:**   Before hiring the consultant, establish a schedule of deliverables and a project plan. Deliverables must be specific. To prevent problems, know up front what you're getting and help the consultant by removing any ambiguity from your expectations. Before the consultant begins helping you with your Intranet, it's a good idea to have the consultant sign a nondisclosure agreement, particularly if the consultant is working with internal corporate information.

Content Ownership

An Intranet is only as good as the information available on it. If content is out of date, inaccurate, or poorly prepared, your Intranet is not going to be effective. As you establish your Intranet, define who is responsible for the different content areas, and give these individuals the authority to update and otherwise manage the content under their control.

An Intranet Style Guide

You may want to think about creating a style guide for your Intranet. Done well, a style guide gives the information on your Intranet a common look and feel. One of the problems with a style guide is that if it's too complex, people aren't going to use it, and the effort spent creating the style guide is wasted. In addition, the different departments in your organization may want to express their creativity through their Intranet pages. If this is the case, you may want some general guidelines without being overly rigid. In general, it's a good idea to limit graphics to 256 colors.

Be aware that great content can be diminished by poor presentation. Training on a style guide gives your Intranet a consistent, coherent look and feel. Ensure that both the viewing and content creation applications readily support your organization's standards.

Ensuring Intranet Security

Intranet security has many dimensions. The content of your Intranet needs to be available to the people who need it, but protected from those who don't need to see it. Providing the appropriate levels of access and security on your Web server along with flexibility to grow and change with your organization is an important consideration.

Securing the connections for e-mail and browsing your Web site ensures that mail isn't intercepted and vital information doesn't get into the wrong hands. The various security protocols explained in detail in Chapter 9 provide security for e-mail and for information transmitted to and from a browser. Along with these considerations, connecting to the Internet potentially creates additional risks that can be addressed by using a firewall, proxy server, or IPX gateway. See "Protecting Your Network from Intruders" later in this chapter for more information.

In any event, you need to establish a trusted systems administrator to provide leadership in establishing and maintaining security. The systems administrator owns the password files and controls access to personal certificates, encryption keys, and other items related to security.

Maintaining Productivity

While this book is primarily concerned with Intranet implementation, Internet access may be important to your organization. Many managers worry that employee productivity will drop if employees have Internet access. In some ways, this is a valid concern. There are many games, images, and electronic malls on the Internet where employees can browse and waste time. On the other hand, there are many sites where employees can learn about and download new software, obtain competitive information, and do other kinds of online research that benefit your organization. Many companies today provide their latest product information on the Internet, and this may include your competitors.

 T IP: If you decide to connect to the Internet, your managers may want to consider establishing some policy guidelines for recreational use of the Internet by employees.

Measuring Your Intranet's Success

How you measure the success of your Intranet depends on what you were trying to accomplish in the first place. If your Intranet improves communication, simplifies a process that used to be a problem, leads to enhanced customer satisfaction, or is perceived as a benefit by employees in your organizations, then your Intranet is a success. A more quantitative evaluation may help to determine if an initial implementation should be expanded across your organization.

Installing and Configuring an Intranet

Installing and configuring an Intranet involves some changes to your LAN. In addition, you're going to need to purchase Intranet software and

7

potentially some high-powered machines for running your servers. If you decide to connect to the Internet, you're going to need to configure an Internet connection and set up an account with an Internet service provider.

Changes in Your Existing LAN

The overall architecture of your LAN stays the same when you install and configure an Intranet. But you may need to buy more PCs to run Intranet server applications such as a mail server, Web server, news server and Domain Name System server. The main consideration in deciding whether to buy new hardware is whether your existing computers have enough power. See "Intranet Servers" later in this section for more information. Adding these PCs would require additional LAN connections and adapter cards. Another potential change to your LAN is adding an Internet connection, which is discussed in "Connecting to the Internet" later in this chapter.

Required Software

Features of the software you need for installing an Intranet are explained in "Intranet Software" earlier in this chapter. Recall that Intranets are an example of a client-server architecture. Clients are typically applications that run on users' desktops, while servers are on high-powered machines that provide information used by the client applications. Table 7-3 provides a summary of the software you need to install an Intranet. Many browsers provide all of the functionality listed on the client side. Keep in mind that the listed software is needed whether or not you connect to the Internet.

Installing Server and Desktop Machines

To install an Intranet, you're probably going to need new machines for Intranet servers, and you may want to add or upgrade machines on users' desktops. For all of your new PCs, you're going to need network adapter cards and LAN connections. The performance needs for new servers can be estimated as functions of the number of users and the anticipated transaction volume. The software server packages typically define minimum system requirements for a successful installation.

Intranet Servers

Anyone who reads the ads in the Sunday paper knows that PCs are becoming increasingly high powered. The amount of memory, the speed, and the hard-drive capacity of PCs are growing daily. To determine what

If You Have This Client Software	You Need This Server Software
One of the following stacks: a TCP/IP stack or a Special IP/IPX stack for use with IPX networks like Novell NetWare or a TCP/IP stack.	If you're using a special stack, you need an IPX gateway server to provide access to the TCP/IP server applications and the Internet.
If you have a small network, you can use host tables on each machine to provide name resolution. Don't use a Domain Name System server if you're using host tables.	If you have a larger network or plan to connect to the Internet, you need a Domain Name System server. If you're connecting to the Internet, you may want your Internet service provider to do name resolution for your network. Don't use host tables if you're using a Domain Name System server.
E-mail client	Mail server
Browser	Web server. If database access applications are part of your implementation, possibly include database servers using ODBC and SQL that can connect to the Web server.
Document converter to HTML format	Web server that is easy to update and reindex
Newsreader	News server
FTP client application	FTP server application
Terminal emulators	Mainframes that require a specific terminal emulator

Software
Needed to
Install an
Intranet
Table 7-3.

7

kind of PC you need for different uses on your Intranet, look at the PC sale ads in your Sunday newspaper. Volume discounters advertise regularly. As you scan the ads, look for PCs that would fall into the general categories listed in Table 7-4. For all uses, it's a good idea to double the memory on any machine you buy. Table 7-4 gives you some guidelines for purchasing new server hardware.

Kind of Use	Number of Users	Number of Back-End Applications	What You See in Your Sunday Paper
Low power	1 to 50	0	standard PCs
Medium power	50 to 500	1 to 5	High-powered PCs
High power	500+	More than 5	These usually aren't advertised. Call corporate sales for information.

Server Hardware Needed Depending on Your Configuration
Table 7-4.

As far as existing hardware is concerned, use the following as general guidelines for the type of machine you need for the different kinds of uses:

♦ For a low-power server, you need a Pentium with 24MB of RAM and a 1-gigabyte hard drive.

♦ For a medium-power server, you need a Pentium Pro with 32 to 168MB of RAM and 2 to 6 gigabytes of storage on the hard drive.

♦ For a high-power server, you need a multiple-CPU or RISC machine with 64 to 256MB of RAM and 4 to 16 gigabytes or more of storage.

Client Machines for Users' Desktops

Using the descriptions in Table 7-4, a standard PC is probably enough machine for most users. For software developers and other high-end users, a more powerful machine is recommended. For existing client machines, you need a minimum of a 486 and enough hard drive space for your software. You need 8MB of RAM for Windows 3.x, 12 to 16MB of RAM for Windows 95, and 16MB of RAM for Windows NT. Larger memory stores are needed for high performance applications and for power users who run multiple applications all at the same time.

Configuring for a Non-Internet Connection

If you decide not to connect to the Internet and later change your mind, you are going to need to change your network configuration. Every host on a TCP/IP-based LAN must have an IP address. If you have a standalone Intranet that doesn't connect to the Internet, you can use any IP addresses you want. Good IP addresses to choose for a stand-alone Intranet are 1.0.0.0 through 1.255.255.255, because these are test IP addresses from an Internet perspective. If you ever connect to the Internet and one of your IP addresses wasn't changed properly, any traffic for the IP address would be discarded, instead of being routed to some other place on the Internet.

T IP: If you decide not to connect to the Internet, use IP addresses 1.0.0.0 through 1.255.255.255. If you ever connect to the Internet and the IP address isn't changed, the messages are discarded instead of sent to the wrong person.

Avoiding Later Connection Problems

The problem with using IP addresses you assign yourself is that if you decide to connect to the Internet, you're going to have to change the IP address on every computer that is attached to the Internet. To minimize hassles in the event you decide to connect to the Internet in the future, you could do one of the following:

♦ Use a firewall with or without a proxy server. The firewall is the only machine that connects to the Internet. Behind this single machine, your network could stay the way it is, and the conversion to an Internet connection would be relatively easy. The speed of the proxy server and firewall would need to be sufficient to give you the performance you want on your Internet link. See "Protecting Your Network from Intruders," later in this chapter.

♦ Use a special stack that runs over an IPX-based network like NetWare. The PCs on your network have the special stack installed on them that translates between the IP-based applications on the desktop and your IPX-based LAN. The messages from the desktop applications go to an IPX gateway that connects to the Internet. All of the Internet traffic could come and go through one machine.

Nonconnection Options

If you decide not to connect to the Internet, you have the following options available for setting up a TCP/IP-based Intranet:

7

♦ Use the TCP/IP protocol on your network and assign your own IP addresses to the machines on your network.

♦ Use an IPX-based LAN and install special stacks on the users' desktops and an IPX gateway on a machine on your LAN. The IPX gateway would provide access to your TCP/IP server applications.

Connecting to the Internet

As you have considered your Intranet, you may have decided to also have an Internet connection. For example, if you have offices in several locations or many people on the road, you may want to have an Internet connection. With this Internet connection, everyone in your organization, regardless of their physical location, can access the information on your Intranet. It is possible in such a configuration to set up your Web server to only accept connections for users within your organization and lock out all other connection attempts. If you're planning on connecting to the Internet, there are additional installation and configuration considerations. These considerations include setting up your Internet connections, assigning IP addresses, and protecting your network from Internet intruders.

Most LANs that access the Internet have a dedicated line. The following sections explain how to set up your Internet connection; assign IP addresses; and protect your network from intruders using a firewall, proxy server, or IPX gateway.

Setting Up a Leased-Line Connection

Most LANs connect to the Internet through a dedicated line that makes a connection available according to a schedule. Various options are available that provide access for 8 hours a day, 24 hours a day, or some other period of time. You're going to need a link, such as one of those listed in Table 7-5.

Choosing an Internet Service Provider   Only the large Internet service providers furnish dedicated lines. The following are examples of companies that make connecting to the Internet fast and easy:

♦   BBN Planet at 1-301-982-4600

♦   UUNet at 1-800-488-6384

♦   PSINet at 1-800-827-7482

Getting a Domain Name   When you call to set up your Internet connection, ask about getting a domain name. You need a unique domain name to identify your organization on the Internet. The domain name is part of the e-mail address for everyone in your organization and is also part of the hostname for every machine in your organization. Some Internet service providers can give you a domain name that they set up for the networks they service. Others want you to get in touch with InterNIC Registration Service Center. Their Web site is www.ds.internic.net.

The Domain Name System Server   You're going to need a Domain Name System server for your network to connect to the Internet. You can choose

What You Want to Do	Number of Users	Budget	Connection Speed
Have a Web server with simple Web pages that include text and a few simple images. Users can send e-mail and do very limited Web browsing. If users are doing heavy Web browsing, you need a faster connection.	1 to 5 with browsing; 25 without browsing	Small	Dial-up or leased line 28.8K modem
Have a Web server with relatively complex Web pages that include text and a moderate amount of images. Users can send e-mail and browse.	5 to 25 with browsing; 25 to 50 without browsing	Moderate	56K ISDN or leased line
Have a Web server with complex Web pages and many images. A mail server can download mail groups to a news server. Users can e-mail and browse at will.	50 to 1000	Large	T1
Organizations that require high-volume Internet access would need a connection that is this fast.	1000+	Large	T3

Connection Speeds for Different Uses
Table 7-5.

to have a Domain Name System server on your network or have your Internet service provider maintain your domain information for you. The drawback to the second option is that all of the messages your users send to each other go to your Internet service provider for domain resolution. The Domain Name System server then routes the message to the correct user on your network. The advantage to this configuration is that you don't have to maintain a Domain Name System server yourself.

7

IP Addresses   Also ask your Internet service provider about IP addresses for the computers on your Intranet. You can assign these IP addresses to the computers on your network in various ways, as explained later in this chapter in the section "Assigning IP Addresses."

Internet Connection Speeds   Another consideration as you're evaluating Internet service providers is the speed of their Internet connection. Your Internet service provider connects to the backbone of the Internet. Some organizations who have installed a really fast Internet connection to their network, such as a T1 or T3, find that their Internet service provider's link is slower. Ask your Internet service provider about this before you set up your link.

Assigning IP Addresses

Two general methods are available for assigning IP addresses to the PCs on your LAN: fixed and dynamic addressing.

Fixed IP Addresses   Fixed IP addresses are entered as part of the configuration of the individual stacks on each PC on your Intranet. Every organization that connects to the Internet has a fixed number of IP addresses.

Dynamic IP Addresses   In comparison to fixed IP addresses, dynamic IP addresses are never entered in the individual stacks on your Intranet. If your organization has more users than IP addresses, you could use a dynamic IP address server to share the limited number of IP addresses among your users. The following protocols make it possible to dynamically assign IP addresses using a server on your LAN:

♦ The Boot Protocol (BOOTP) provides startup information. When you use BOOTP, the PC gets information such as the IP address mask, its own IP address, and other information from a BOOTP server.

♦ The Reverse Address Resolution Protocol (RARP) is an Internet protocol used to obtain an IP address based on the address of the computer's adapter card. Typical uses of RARP are on an Ethernet or Token Ring LAN.

♦ The Dynamic Host Configuration Protocol (DHCP) is a protocol used to get startup information from a DHCP server. When you use DHCP, the PC gets information such as the IP address mask, an IP address, and other information from a DHCP sever. DHCP is an enhanced form of BOOTP, which includes the idea of an address lease time. This is the length of time the client is allowed to use the assigned IP address. Some systems on the Internet, including some routers, don't support DHCP.

 NOTE: If you use some form of dynamic assignment of IP addresses, the users on your network must truly have client machines and not be running server applications. This is because true servers have an IP address and hostname that always stays the same. In addition, all users would have to have a POP3 or IMAP4 account on a mail server in order to get their e-mail.

Protecting Your Network from Intruders

Different networks have varying needs for protection from intruders on the Internet. Each organization needs to consider the trade-offs between the costs and benefits of using a firewall, proxy server, or IPX gateway. This section provides configuration and installation information for these different kinds of security implementations.

NOTE: A router is a machine that connects one network segment to another and transmits packets between the two based on the IP addresses in the packets. Firewalls, proxy servers, and IPX gateways are all routers. If you aren't an expert at setting up routers, strongly consider having a knowledgeable consultant set up your router.

Using Firewalls

A firewall protects a network by only routing packets that meet certain requirements. Usually, a firewall filters packets based on the source, destination address, and ports used to make a connection. For example, a firewall might only route packets to or from a trusted machine, or disallow any incoming packets that are connection requests.

To understand how a firewall works, first consider an unprotected network. The client PCs connect directly to the Internet and access Internet servers. On a network like this, every machine that connects to the Internet is vulnerable to an intruder. If a firewall is installed on the same network, clients have to get permission from the firewall to be able to connect to a host on the Internet. Messages coming in from hosts on the Internet also have to get permission from the firewall to connect to a host on the network. A firewall is always dealing with two connections. The first connection is between the network PC, and the second connection is to the host on the Internet, as shown in Figure 7-15.

If someone tries to hack into the network, the only machine they can touch is the firewall. All network information is behind the firewall, so the network is safe from an intruder.

7

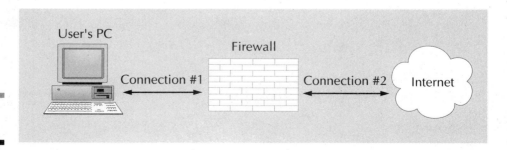

A firewall
Figure 7-15.

Using Proxy Servers

Most proxy servers service a particular type of protocol, for example, Gopher, HTML or FTP. Some proxy servers, such as a SOCKS server, can handle any protocol. Client PCs running TCP/IP applications connect to the proxy server that handles the application's protocol. The proxy server then connects to the firewall in order to connect to the Internet. The firewall is typically configured to only allow the proxy servers to get through the firewall and connect to the Internet. The firewall refuses to connect with any client PC that requests an Internet connection. The proxy server is on a trusted machine that the firewall allows to connect to the Internet, as shown in Figure 7-16.

Another configuration option is to have the proxy server on the same machine as the firewall software, which gives it access to the protected and unprotected sides of the firewall. The proxy server passes information back and forth so that the PC client and Internet server can act as if they are directly connected.

NOTE: Examples of proxy servers that only handle requests for a particular application protocol are HTTP proxy servers for Web connections and FTP proxy servers. This type of proxy looks like an actual server, and the way it determines the Internet destination is specific to that protocol. Others, like a SOCKS proxy server, handle all kinds of protocols.

Using IPX Gateways

As explained in "Using TCP/IP Applications with an IPX Network," earlier in chapter, you can use an IPX gateway PC if you have a network such as Novell NetWare. The IPX gateway PC acts as a natural firewall because it forwards all messages to the Internet from the network machines. The only machine that could be intruded upon from the Internet is the IPX gateway PC.

Setting Up a Dial-Up Connection

Another thing to think about as you're setting up your Internet access is the possibility of giving certain members of your organization dial-up access to

A proxy server
inside a
firewall
Figure 7-16.

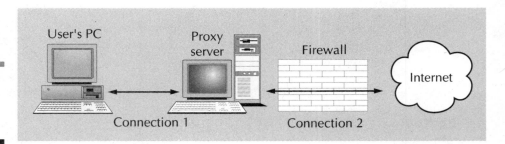

your Intranet through the Internet. Sales people, trainers, and others who are working off-site can benefit from dialing in through the Internet. They can send e-mail, obtain information from your Intranet, send in orders, and use your Intranet in other ways.

Internet Service Providers

Some large, security-conscious companies set up their own dial-up services. If this is beyond the resources of your company, then you need an Internet service provider that offers dial-up services. Most companies use an Internet service provider. For this reason, the remainder of this section focuses on how to set up a dial-up connection through an Internet service provider.

TIP: Whenever possible, you want employees to be able to use a local phone number when they are dialing in to the Internet. You're going to want a large Internet service provider that provides local numbers in many areas for employees who travel often. If you have an office in another location, you may want to provide Internet access through an Internet service provider in the same area. It doesn't have to be the same Internet service provider used in your home office. Depending on the configuration you want to use, you may want to set up accounts with more than one Internet service provider.

Modems and ISDN Lines

Modems and ISDN hardware are available for making dial-up connections through your Internet service provider. A modem can transfer data at different speeds. A good minimum modem speed for accessing the Internet is 28.8 Kbps (kilobits per second). If you use a modem, you can use a standard telephone line to connect to the Internet. ISDN hardware transfers data at speeds of 56 Kbps and higher. ISDN lines are digital, like a computer, instead of analog, like a phone line. For this reason, ISDN lines transfer data very rapidly. If you choose to use ISDN hardware:

♦ Your phone company must supply a special ISDN phone connection.

♦ Your Internet service provider must provide ISDN service.

7

Putting It All Together

This chapter has discussed features you may want to look for as you consider what software you need to implement your Intranet. In addition, this chapter has identified some of the issues that you need to address in order to successfully implement and evaluate your Intranet. Finally, this chapter has explained different installation and configuration options for your Intranet, depending on whether or not you connect to the Internet.

Frequently Asked Questions

♦ **What do I need to know if I'm a systems administrator and want to set up an Intranet?**

Systems administrators need to have a general understanding of networking in order to set up an Intranet. As you set up your Intranet, you are going to learn more about TCP/IP and the individual applications that make up your Intranet. You don't need to be a networking guru or a programmer.

♦ **What do I need to know if I'm a user on an Intranet?**

You need a general understanding of how to use a computer and a willingness to try new things. After Intranet applications are on your desktop, you can use the online Help to get you started with your new software.

♦ **How long does it take to install an Intranet?**

If you have the background information including your domain name, IP addresses, e-mail addresses, hostnames, and user groups defined, installing Intranet servers and desktop applications can take as little time as a single day.

♦ **How can I share information on my Intranet?**

On your Intranet, you can have HTML documents, as well as existing documents, spreadsheets, videos, or whatever else you already have on your network. Some Intranets include comprehensive search capabilities and easy-to-use document creation and conversion software. This is especially true if the client and server software are in an integrated package.

♦ **Can I use my existing documents, databases, and other information on an Intranet?**

You can use the information that is currently on your network. You can create Web server back-end applications to access your existing databases. You can choose to convert existing files to HTML or keep them as they are. The choice depends on your organization's goals.

♦ **What hardware do I need to set up an Intranet?**

At a minimum, you need an existing LAN, a server machine such as a PC running Windows NT, and one client PC running TCP/IP desktop applications.

♦ **What software do I need in order to set up an Intranet?**

You need to install a TCP/IP or TCP/IPX stack on each PC. On users' desktops, install the TCP/IP user applications. Also install the servers needed to run the user applications. Use host tables or a Domain Name System server to provide TCP/IP routing.

♦ **What is needed to connect an organization to the Internet?**

You need a dedicated line or a dial-up connection to connect to the Internet. You can go through an Internet service provider or set up your own connection to the Internet backbone. Depending on what you want to achieve with your Intranet, you don't necessarily have to connect to the Internet.

7

CHAPTER 8

Creating Content

John A. Luoma
with Susan Archer, Michael Beirne,
Michael Lee, Susan L. Moore,
John C. Weise

Chapter Objectives

♦ Explain how to create a back-end service for your Web server

♦ Outline some design guidelines for the pages on your Web site

♦ Discuss the structures available to create HTML page content

♦ Describe some of the multimedia options available to Webmasters

You have considered all the steps needed to install and configure your Intranet Web server. You still have one important step to accomplish, and that is to create content for your Web pages. Content is the most important element of your Web server. If the content is not useful to your users, there is not much point in having a Web site. There are many components that may comprise the content on the Web server, including text, graphics, sound, video, and back-end services and databases.

Each component presents the Webmaster with its own implementation challenges and rewards. Your job in creating content is to strike a balance between high tech and high function. This chapter will highlight some of the ways in which you, as a Webmaster, can build Web pages that are functional and fun at the same time.

Content for your Web site can be a simple text-only HTML page or as complicated as a back-end application that pulls information from a corporate database. This chapter will give you a little flavor of the more complicated elements you could incorporate into your site. Some of the material in this chapter may be at a skill level that is higher than the average user possesses.

Do not be frightened off by the programming examples; they are intended to give you a feel for what is possible in an interactive site. Hopefully, there is some information included here to stretch your imagination and push you to the next level of Web authoring.

Creating Back-End Services

A back-end service is a software application that processes information delivered from a Web server or obtained from an external source such as a database. The Web server receives information from a browser in an HTML (Hypertext Markup Language) form. The service may receive data from a Web server and store it in a database, or it may take data from a database and send it back to the Web server in the form of a report. Back-end services are the components that make your Intranet interactive. Without back-end services, Web servers are only publishing tools. You request a page, and the server delivers it to you as a formatted page. Through the use of a back-end service, you can take a request from a browser and manipulate the result in ways restricted only by your own imagination.

Programming Alternatives

You have many choices when you are creating back-end services. If you are an experienced software engineer who is familiar with languages such as C and C++ that allow you to create dynamic link libraries (DLLs), then you can

8

use Internet Service Application Programming Interface (ISAPI). If you are less experienced and prefer Visual Basic, then you can probably migrate more toward Common Gateway Interface (CGI) and Windows CGI (WinCGI) back-end applications.

 TIP: If you have no programming experience, creating a back-end application may prove to be a challenge for you. You may want to give the project to those experienced at writing back-end applications. Some software vendors include back-end applications with their software packages. You can use the wizards these applications provide for setup and customization, instead of using a programming utility.

The following sections cover some of the more prevalent programming interfaces used to write back-end applications and the most common language used to write each type of back-end application.

Standard CGI

A Standard CGI back-end application—WinCGI is discussed in a later section—can be created without using a Windows-based Web server, such as a Unix Web server. CGI takes the information passed by the Web server and stores it in environment variables. These variables are then used by the back-end service to perform any data manipulation or querying of outside sources, such as a database. If data needs to be returned to the Web user, it's done through standard output—meaning that the data is sent to the Web user's computer a line at a time.

 NOTE: For more information on CGI and the other factors that make up a Web-centric Internet, see Chapter 3.

The Perl Language

A language that is popular amongst CGI back-end creators is Perl. Larry Wall originally created Perl, or Practical Extension and Reporting Language, for Unix, though versions of Perl also exist for the Macintosh, OS/2, Windows 95, and Windows NT platforms. Perl probably feels most familiar to people who have an experience using Unix, Unix shell scripts, or DOS batch files.

The Perl Advantage

The real strength of Perl is that it can easily manipulate text files and strings. Since an HTML document is little more than a decorated text file, Perl is ideal for generating documents and reports from a Web server. Perl is also useful for more general system administration tools. For example, you can create a service that creates logging reports for Web servers that use the Common Logging Format (CLF). Instead of reading a long, unformatted text file, you can generate a custom report that gives you, for example, information on how many times a particular IP address has connected to your Web server, or how many educational institutions have.

 T<small>**IP:**</small> You can use a number of public-domain Perl utilities and samples as starting points for your personalized applications. There are sites on the Internet that provide samples for you to look at or download, such as http://www.perl.com.

How It Works

Perl is an interpreted scripting language, which means you do not compile a Perl script like you do a C or C++ program. When you start a Perl script, you are telling the Perl interpreter to interpret the Perl *script* or source code directly, which significantly speeds up back-end development time. Instead of having to recompile your code every time you make a change, you can enter the change and see immediately if it works, making Perl scripts easier to modify and debug.

For example, if you wanted to make a cosmetic change to the HTML page the Perl script generates, you could do so and just drop the modified script onto your Web server. If you had used C, you would have to first go to a computer with a C compiler on it, make the change, compile the code, and copy it back to your Web server. However, a Perl program may take a performance hit during execution of the script because the script always has to run the interpreter. Comparatively, code that is compiled before runtime immediately runs when it is called, because it doesn't need to be interpreted.

String and Text Manipulation   Built in to the Perl language are many string and text manipulation operations and functions that are more efficient and robust compared to ones that might exist in C or C++. Perl scripts can also return slightly different results depending on the browser being used, or a script could present different versions of the same document depending on whether the person is connecting to the site inside or outside of your Intranet.

8

C or Perl Array

1	A
2	B
3	C
4	B
5	D

Perl Array Only

1123	A
This	B
Hello	C
Wow	B
256	D

How C and
Perl define
arrays
Figure 8-1.

The Associative-Array Data Structure With Perl's associative-array data
structure, the language has immediate support for mapping functions that
map one set of strings on another set of strings or numbers. Figure 8-1 shows
how typical languages such as C and Perl define an array. The array is
indexed by numbers only. Perl can define an array in the same fashion.
However, Perl can also index an array with strings.

Let's say that you wanted to create a program that counted the number of
times each word in a document appeared. If you are using C, then you need
to manipulate the array so you can relate the numbers to the appropriate
words. You would also have to guess how many unique words are in the
document, so that you could define the correct array size. Using Perl, you
can create an array indexed with the words themselves. You also don't need
to define an array size in Perl, because the language knows that when a new
element (in this case, word count) needs to be added, it increases the array
size by one.

A Sample Program
The following is the Perl code used to create programs like the one described
in the previous section:

```
#!/usr/local/bin/perl
#
# The above line isn't useful on Win32 systems.
#
# count.pl
```

```
#
# This program counts the number of times the nth word of list of lines that
# are comma separated appears in that column.
#
# This should work as the basis for parsing some log files.
#
# For this example, we won't set the $entryToCount to come in from the
# command line, but set it to a fixed value $entryToCount = 1;
# Step through all of the lines in the program.
while (<STDIN>) {

# Set the array entries in fields to be the contents of the read in line,
# using commas to separate each entry.
   @fields = split(/,/);

   #Because Perl arrays are zero based like C, if we want to count the
   #$entryToCount entry, we need to subtract one from it (the first entry is
   #in slot zero, etc)
   #
   # Also, this line is where all of the magic occurs--we're adding one to
   #the entry in countArray that corresponds to the $entryToCount entry of
   #fields.
   $countArray{$fields[$entryToCount - 1 ]}++;
}


# Now, we'll step through all of the entries of countArray, and print out
# the number of times each word appeared.
while (($entry,$timesAppeared) = each(%countArray))
{
        print "$entry appeared $timesAppeared times\n";
}
```

Some Sample Input   So that you can see what a program such as the one shown in the previous example does, here is some sample input:

```
hello,there,how,are,you
this,is,a,test
hello,there
wow,what,is,this
1224,215,2356,236,23
hello,now,what
this,is,something
1223,23,sdfj,,dfg
this,too
1224,dfgdfg
```

8

The Input's Output   The previously shown input has the following output:

```
1223 appeared 1 times
this appeared 3 times
1224 appeared 2 times
hello appeared 3 times
wow appeared 1 times
```

Perl's New Features

The most recent version of Perl, Perl5, has the following great new features:

♦ More modularity

♦ More object-oriented features

♦ Written in a more readable and usable way for novice users

There is also an ISAPI dynamic library in development, so Windows NT Web servers can take advantage of Perl and the performance improvements of ISAPI without creating a CGI back end.

Finding Out More About Perl

There are many Perl resources available, both online and in bookstores. There are plenty of Web sites with Perl information, with http://www.perl.com, http://www.perl.hip.com, and http://www.bio.cam.ac.uk/cgi-lib/ being good starting points. There are also many libraries and applications specially designed for Web applications. These are freely available (and modifiable) as either examples or to put into production use. The book *Programming Perl*—written by the creator of Perl, Larry Wall, and co-authored by Randal Schwartz—is also a solid reference work for the language. Make sure you look for recent versions of the book that discuss Perl5, to understand the latest enhancements to the language. The Usenet newsgroups comp.lang.perl.announce and comp.lang.perl.misc are also good places to obtain up-to-the-minute information about the language.

CAUTION: Be sure you do *not* place the Perl interpreter (or any interpreter) in the same directory as the script. Many Web servers store CGI scripts in a \CGI-BIN\ directory. If you place your interpreter in this directory, outside people can access the interpreter and run almost anything on your computer. This problem can affect Web servers on any platform. For information on different storage methods and for the latest updates on this problem, please see http://www.perl.com/perl/news/latro-announce.html.

Downloading and Running Perl

If you don't already have it, you need to have the Perl interpreter to run a Perl script. Perl is becoming more and more a common feature on Unix systems, and might have already been installed by your Unix system administrator. If no one has installed Perl on your system, you need to download Perl from the Internet. This is another advantage of Perl—it's free! The sites listed in the previous sections should tell you where to get the latest revision of the Perl language for your particular platform.

 TIP: You also want to download many of the additional libraries and routines that are available all around the Internet. These libraries and source code perform many of the functions that any Web-based script needs to provide. Though you could create these on your own, why reinvent the wheel when you can legally obtain the already-written code.

Windows CGI

Designed for Windows-based Web servers, Windows CGI, or WinCGI, has a different method of handling variables than Standard CGI. Instead of placing data retrieved from a Web user and storing it in environment variables, WinCGI stores the data in the following separate files:

◆ *The profile file* This file contains data from, or pointers to, the HTML form.

◆ *The content file* This file contains the custom data from the specific server implementations according to the CGI standard. In addition, if the form data normally placed in the profile file exceeds 64K, it is placed in the content file.

These files are then sent to the back-end application, which manipulates the data in whatever fashion the program dictates. If data needs to be returned to the Web user, then it is copied into one file, which is sent to the Web user.

 TIP: For more information on WinCGI back-end applications, see Chapter 3.

8

The Visual Basic Language

The most common language used to create WinCGI programs is Visual Basic. Visual Basic is an object-based language that supports many of the same principles as true object-oriented programming (OOP) languages. This means that your programs are composed of objects such as controls, forms, other programs, and system objects like printers and file structures. Visual Basic combines the objects, making program design faster and more efficient. You can reuse objects created in your other programs or access a multitude of readily available, off-the-shelf objects.

T IP: Both Microsoft and third-party vendors sell, and distribute for free, pieces of code with a .VBX or .OCX extension. These objects perform specific functions that can be incorporated into your program, saving precious coding hours.

Visual Basic has become a popular WinCGI language due to its popularity as a corporate programming solution. If you have Visual Basic programmers in your IS department, they can quickly come up to speed on creating back-end Web applications.

Reading and Displaying HTML

The most obvious task that you will need to perform when interacting with a Web server and client browser is reading and displaying HTML code. To help you accomplish this, there is a file called *cgi32.bas* that can be obtained from various sites around the Internet, including O'Reilly & Associates, Inc. The file includes functions for reading and displaying HTML pages. These functions can help you build the HTML interface.

You are somewhat restricted by the HTML interface because your connection to the Web server is *stateless*, which means that every time you read or post information to the server, a connection is established, information is passed, and the connection is closed. You cannot rely on data you sent or received on your last connection to the server, because that connection has been closed, and the server no longer retains any references to the previous connections. Each connection with the server must be a self-contained transaction. If you want to maintain an ongoing conversation with the server, you must maintain some type of temp file to store the data.

Another way to maintain a conversation with the server is to embed data onto your page as hidden fields. After you obtain information from the server or user that may be necessary for some process that may takes place several pages from now, you can store the data in hidden fields. You pass the data back and forth between the server and the browser within the hidden fields until you reach the page that needs that information, at which point, you simply read it in from the hidden fields.

TIP: If you haven't used Visual Basic before, you might want to pick up a book such as Gurewich and Gurewich's *Teach Yourself Visual Basic 4 in 21 Days*. The more advanced programmer might want a book such as *Special Edition: Using Visual Basic 4* by Webb, McKelvy, Martinsen, Maxwell, and Regelski.

Running Visual Basic

You will need to obtain a copy of Microsoft's Visual Basic programming language. This package includes an integrated development environment, shown in Figure 8-2, encompassing most of the tools needed to create a back-end application. In addition, you will need a file to support your WinCGI application called *cgi.bas* (or *cgi32.bas* for 32-bit versions of Visual Basic). You can get this file from a number of locations around the Internet, including O'Reilly and Associates, Inc. (http://software.ora.com). It contains all the functions needed to interact in an HTML environment.

A Sample Program

The example included in the following sections, written in Visual Basic, shows how you can extract data from a form you create. This form can be placed on your Web site for visitors to fill in. The WinCGI back end then takes the information people enter on the form and saves it to a file or e-mails it to a particular person.

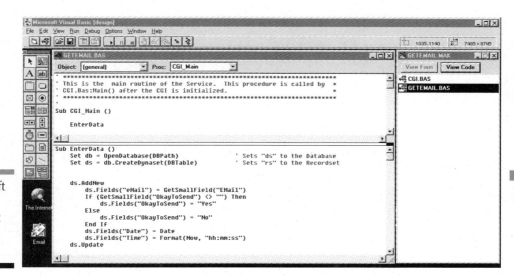

The Microsoft Visual Basic development environment
Figure 8-2.

8

Creating a Form   Earlier in the chapter, we discussed forms. You can use a form you have already created, or you can create a new one before beginning this section. You can place any type of form control on the form—including edit boxes, list boxes, radio buttons, and check boxes. The back-end service can read the data from all of these form controls.

Adding Hidden Fields   In order for your form to work with the back-end service we are going to create, you need to first add a few hidden fields to it. These fields actually provide the data collection methods. Here's how to add the fields:

1. Open your form in your HTML editor.

NOTE: If you are using WebDesigner, the HTML editor included with the CD, be sure when you create the form to place */FORMHELP* in the Action field of the Form Attributes. This is the name referenced in the next section by the back-end service.

2. Move your cursor to a location somewhere under the <FORM> tag. Be sure you are not in the middle of any tags.

3. The first field you need to add tells the back end if you want to save the data a user enters in a file. Enter the following if you want to save the user's information in a file:

```
<INPUT TYPE=HIDDEN NAME="Save_To_File" VALUE="Yes">
```

and then go to Step 4. You can also enter the following if you do *not* want the information stored in a file:

```
<INPUT TYPE=HIDDEN NAME="Save_To_File" VALUE="No">
```

and skip to Step 5.

4. Because you want the information saved in a file, you must tell the service to create the file and write the text to it. Enter the following:

```
<INPUT TYPE=HIDDEN NAME="Data_File" VALUE="C:\MyDir\FormX.csv">
```

NOTE: You should put your own path and filename in the VALUE section of the information. You could, for example, create a directory on the Web server called "FormData." You could then copy the file to this directory. If you use the name FormData, the hidden field would look like this:

```
<INPUT TYPE=HIDDEN NAME="Data_File" VALUE="C:\FormData\FormX.csv">
```

If you chose to perform the action described in the previous step, move on to step 7.

5. If you want to send the information on the form to one or more people with e-mail, you need to add the following entry:

```
<INPUT TYPE=HIDDEN NAME="Mail_Information" VALUE="Yes">
```

and then go to Step 6. If you don't want to e-mail the information, enter the following:

```
<INPUT TYPE=HIDDEN NAME="Mail_Information" VALUE="No">
```

and go to Step 7.

6. Because you have decided to mail the information, you need to add fields so that the mail can be processed. These fields are REQUIRED, if you have decided to use Mail_Information!

NOTE: Mailing the information only works with an SMTP mail server.

Enter the following:

```
<INPUT TYPE=HIDDEN NAME="Mail_Server_Name"
VALUE="Mailserver.YourCompany.Com">
```

This field should contain the name or IP address of your SMTP mail server in the VALUE section. For example, you could enter **"ns.frontiertech.com"** or **192.104.32.3**. Next, enter

```
<INPUT TYPE=HIDDEN NAME="Mail_To_Address"
VALUE="JoeSmith@YourCompany.Com">
```

The VALUE section of this field should contain the address to which you want information mailed. (If you want to, you can instead make this field visible. You could create a visible list box containing people's names or product names. The value of each item could then be an e-mail address.) Now, enter the following:

```
<INPUT TYPE=HIDDEN NAME="Mail_Server_Login" VALUE="JoeSmith">
```

This field should contain the username of someone on your mail server (probably the Webmaster or a system administrator). The mail that is sent looks like it came from this person.

7. Whether you write the form's information to a file or you e-mail it, you MUST enter the following field:

8

```
<INPUT TYPE=HIDDEN NAME="Field_Names"
VALUE="FirstName~LastName~Address~City~State~Zip">
```

This field tells the service what fields are on your form. If you do not list a field here, it is not read in and processed. You need to insert all of the field names separated by a ~ into the VALUE section. If you are not sure what the field names are, you can find out by switching back to the HTML Edit mode of WebDesigner and right-clicking on a field. (Remember: If you used radio buttons, for example, on your form, you need to enter the Group Name of the buttons, not the value of each button.)

8. The rest of the tags that you can add are not required, but can make your response page more unique. Here are some examples:

   ♦ You could enter a field that tells the service what text to put in the title bar on the response page. For example:

   ```
   <INPUT TYPE=HIDDEN NAME="Response_Title" VALUE="Thank You Page">
   ```

   ♦ You could also enter the following field that tells the service what text to display on the response page:

   ```
   <INPUT TYPE=HIDDEN NAME="Response_Text" VALUE="Thank you
   for filling out our form.">
   ```

   ♦ You could include a field, like the following one, that tells the service what link to put on the response page.

   ```
   <INPUT TYPE=HIDDEN NAME="Response_Link"
   VALUE="http://www.YourServer.com">
   ```

   ♦ Finally, you could add a field that tells the service what text to insert for the Response_Link. For example:

   ```
   <INPUT TYPE=HIDDEN NAME="Response_Link_Text"
   VALUE="Go back to our Home page.">
   ```

9. When you have finished adding fields, be sure to save the form to your Web server. Next, try to access the form through a browser to see how it works (for example, enter **http://yourserver.com/formpage.htm**).

The Completed Form   Here's what a sample form might look like, if you included all of the required fields:

```
<HTML>
<HEAD>
<TITLE>
This is a sample
</TITLE>
</HEAD>
<BODY>
```

```
<H1>
Please enter your information below
</H1>
<HR SIZE=5>
<FORM METHOD=POST ACTION="/FORMHELP">

<!--          This is the section of hidden fields          -->

<INPUT TYPE=HIDDEN NAME="Save_To_File" VALUE="Yes">
<INPUT TYPE=HIDDEN NAME="Data_File" VALUE="C:\FormData\Sample.csv">
<INPUT TYPE=HIDDEN NAME="Mail_Information" VALUE="No">
<INPUT TYPE=HIDDEN NAME="Response_Title" VALUE="Sample Form">
<INPUT TYPE=HIDDEN NAME="Response_Text" VALUE="Thank you for your use of this sample form.">
<INPUT TYPE=HIDDEN NAME="Response_Link" VALUE="http://www.YourServer.com/Homepage.htm">
<INPUT TYPE=HIDDEN NAME="Response_Link_Text" VALUE="Back to our home page.">
<INPUT TYPE=HIDDEN NAME="Field_Names" VALUE="FirstName~LastName~Address~City~State~Zip~Phone~E-mail">
<!--          End of the hidden fields          -->

<PRE>
First Name:<INPUT TYPE=INPUT NAME="FirstName"><BR>
Last Name: <INPUT TYPE=INPUT NAME="LastName"><BR>
Address:   <INPUT TYPE=INPUT NAME="Address"><BR>
City:      <INPUT TYPE=INPUT NAME="City"><BR>
State:     <INPUT TYPE=INPUT NAME="State"><BR>
Zip:       <INPUT TYPE=INPUT NAME="Zip"><BR>
Phone #:   <INPUT TYPE=INPUT NAME="Phone"><BR>
E-mail:    <INPUT TYPE=INPUT NAME="E-mail"><BR>
</PRE>
<HR SIZE=5>
<INPUT TYPE=SUBMIT VALUE="Enter Information">
</FORM>
</BODY>
</HTML>
```

Creating Some Sample Code

To help you on your way to creating WinCGI back-end services in Visual Basic, we have included a code sample for you to look at. This sample is a *form helper*, which takes data users have entered in a form and e-mails it to one or more people, saves it to a file, or both. You can customize it to work with any form. (The places to customize are noted in the code.) To create the sample code described, follow these steps:

1. Begin by opening up your Visual Basic environment. Be sure to include CGI.BAS in your project, as you need it throughout the code.

2. First we must declare the necessary variable to accomplish the task of processing the form that is being submitted. The Option Explicit

8

command tells Visual Basic to make sure all variables have been declared in the order to be used.

```
' ****************************************************************
' Global Variable Declarations Section                          '
' ****************************************************************
Option Explicit

' ****************************************************************
' Local (Module) Variable Declaration Section                   '
' ****************************************************************
Const IsTRUE = 1
Const IsFalse = 0

' Used to store the names of the fields on the form.
Dim aFieldNames(500, 2) As String

' The following variables store information from the form.
Dim SaveToFile As Integer
Dim SaveFileName As String
Dim SendMail As Integer
Dim MailServer As String
Dim MailLogin As String
Dim MailToAddress As String
Dim FieldNames As String

Dim LastForm As form
Dim HTMLFileName As String

' ****************************************************************
' Constant Variable Declaration Section                         '
' ****************************************************************
' These are variables which are used on the error pages.
Const ServiceName = "Help Desk"
Const AuthorsE-mail = YourName@YourCompany.Com
Const AuthorsName = "Your Name"

' This is used when we need to output information for debugging.
' You can make this any filename you want to--however, the path
' must already exist.
Const DebugFile = "C:\Genie\HelpDesk.Dat"
```

3. Now that the necessary variables are in place, we can begin our program. You are required to have a CGI_Main() and an Inter_Main() procedure in your code. The CGI_Main() is responsible for taking control from the CGI.BAS module once it is finished initializing the environment variables. This is where your

program actually begins. The `Inter_Main()` is responsible for responding to an interactive execution—in other words, when a user runs the program from a command prompt or from a file manager such as Windows Explorer.

```
' *********************************************************************
' This is the main routine of the Service. This procedure is called by *
' CGI.Bas:Main() after the CGI is initialized.                         *
' *********************************************************************
Sub CGI_Main ()

    If RequestMethod = "POST" Then
        EnterData                     ' Process the user's form
    Else
        ReturnForm                    ' Return the Form for input.
    End If
End Sub                               ' End of CGI_Main()


' *********************************************************************
' This is the routine that runs when the user executes the program '
' from the Web server itself, interactively.                        '
' *********************************************************************
Sub Inter_Main ()
    MsgBox "This program only runs through the Web server."
End Sub
```

4. If the user has accessed the service as a GET, then we must return an error page telling them that this is not possible. The following subroutine performs this action.

NOTE: GETs and POSTs are the methods used to call a back-end service. A GET sends a name=value pair in the universal resource locator (URL) itself. A name=value pair is generated by a control via HTML. The POST method also sends name=value pairs. The POST method places the pairs in the body of the message, not in the URL. Upon receiving these pairs, the Web server places them in a separate file. This file is where the CGI code obtains the information. Most back-end services today are called with POSTs.

```
' *********************************************************************
' This subroutine is used to return a form to the user for input. Once *
' the form is complete, the service runs again, calling EnterData().   *
' *********************************************************************
Sub ReturnForm ()
    On Error GoTo ReturnFormError
```

8

```
    send ("Content-type: text/HTML")
    send ("")
    send ("<HTML>")
    send ("<Font Size=+3>")
    send ("This Service does not allow a 'GET' to be performed on it.")
    send ("You may only perform a 'POST' on this service.")
    send ("</Font>")
    send ("</HTML>")
    Exit Sub

ReturnFormError:
    send ("Content-type: text/HTML")
    send ("")
    send ("<HTML><TITLE>VB Error!!</TITLE>")
    send ("<H1>A Visual Basic error has occurred!</H2><HR>")
    send ("<I>Please note the following, and e-mail the author.</I>")
    send ("")
    send ("Service's Name:        " + ServiceName)
    send ("Subroutine :          ReturnForm()")
    send ("E-mail Service Author: <A HREF=""mailto:" + AuthorsE-mail + """>")
    send (AuthorsName + "</A></HTML>")
End Sub                                    ' End of ReturnForm()
```

5. If the user has correctly accessed the service through a form, then you can begin to process the form's information. The following is the subroutine that accomplishes this task.

```
'
'*****************************************************************************
' This subroutine is used to retrieve the data from the form and process   *
' it.                                                                       *
'
'*****************************************************************************
Sub EnterData ()
    On Error GoTo EnterDataError
    Dim sFieldNamesTemp As String
    Dim sSendMail As String
    Dim sSaveDatabase As String
    Dim sDatabaseFile As String
    Dim iFileNum As Integer
    Dim sOutput As Variant
    Dim sTempString As String
    Dim i As Integer
    Dim j As Integer
    Dim NumFields As Integer

    ' First, let's get the information from the hidden fields on the form.
```

```
sFieldNamesTemp = GetSmallField("Field_Names")
sSendMail = GetSmallField("Mail_Information")
sSaveDatabase = GetSmallField("Save_To_File")

' Retrieve the names of the fields from the hidden form fields.
i = 1
j = 1
Do
    While (Mid(sFieldNamesTemp, i, 1) <> "~") And _
                (i <= Len(sFieldNamesTemp))
        sTempString = sTempString & Mid(sFieldNamesTemp, i, 1)
        i = i + 1
    Wend
    i = i + 1
    aFieldNames(j, 1) = sTempString
    sTempString = ""
    j = j + 1
Loop Until i >= Len(sFieldNamesTemp) + 1
NumFields = j - 1

' Now retrieve the data from those fields on the form.
For i = 1 To (j - 1)
    aFieldNames(i, 2) = GetSmallField(aFieldNames(i, 1))
Next I

' If the user is going to send the information using e-mail, you first
' create the mail file. Then you send the mail using the hidden
' information on the form.
If UCase(sSendMail) = "YES" Then
    Create_Mail_File (NumFields)
    Send_Mail
End If

' If the user page is going to be stored into a database, you must output
' the information to a comma delimited text file.
If UCase(sSaveDatabase) = "YES" Then
    sDatabaseFile = GetSmallField("Data_File")
    sOutput = ""
    iFileNum = FreeFile
    Open sDatabaseFile For Append Access Write As #iFileNum
    For i = 1 To (j - 2)
    sOutput = sOutput & """" & aFieldNames(i, 2) & ""","
    Next I
    sOutput = sOutput & """" & aFieldNames(j - 1, 2) & """"
    Print #iFileNum, sOutput
    Close #iFileNum
End If
```

8

```
    ' Send those who submitted a form a response telling them that their
    ' information was processed successfully.
    SuccessFrm
Exit Sub
EnterDataError:
    send ("Content-type: text/HTML")
    send ("")
    send ("<HTML><TITLE>VB Error!!</TITLE>")
    send ("<H1>A Visual Basic error has occurred!</H2><HR>")
    send ("<I>Please note the following, and e-mail the author.</I><BR>")
    send ("<BR>")
    send ("Service's Name:           " + ServiceName + "<BR>")
    send ("Subroutine :              EnterData()" + "<BR>")
    send ("E-mail Service Author: <A HREF=""mailto:" + AuthorsE-mail + """>")
    send (AuthorsName + "</A></HTML>")
    End
End Sub
```

6. In this subroutine, you create the file you want to e-mail to the address stored in the hidden field on the form. This file contains each of the fields on the form, the data they contain, and the date and time the form was submitted.

```
Sub Create_Mail_File (NumFields As Integer)
    On Error GoTo Create_Mail_FileError
    Dim iFileNum As Integer                   ' Stores next available File#
    Dim i As Integer
    iFileNum = FreeFile                       ' Get the next FileNumber
    Open ("C:\Genie\helpdesk.txt") For Output Access Write As iFileNum
```

NOTE: You can change the name of the text file to which you are writing by editing the path and filename given in the previous example. You just need to be sure that the path exists.

```
    Print #iFileNum, "The following information was sent by a _
                    user from the Web site..."
    Print #iFileNum, " "
    Print #iFileNum, "Date: " & Date
    Print #iFileNum, "Time: " & Format(Now, "hh:mm:ss")
    Print #iFileNum, " "
    For i = 1 To NumFields
    Print #iFileNum, aFieldNames(i, 1) & " = " & aFieldNames(i, 2)
    Next I
    Close iFileNum
```

```
    Exit Sub              ' Exit Create_Mail_File()


Create_Mail_FileError:
    send ("Content-type: text/HTML")
    send ("")
    send ("<HTML><TITLE>VB Error!!</TITLE>")
    send ("<H1>A Visual Basic error has occurred!</H2><HR>")
    send ("<I>Please note the following, and e-mail the author.</I><BR>")
    send ("")
    send ("Service's Name:        " + ServiceName + "<BR>")
    send ("Subroutine :           Create_Mail_File()<BR>")
    send ("E-mail Service Author: <A HREF=""mailto:" + AuthorsE-mail _
        + """>" AuthorsName + "</A></HTML>")
    End
End Sub                                  ' End of Create_Mail_File()
```

7. In the following subroutine, you are sending the mail file that was just created to the address retrieved from the form. To do this, we use a public domain mail program called Blat mail. You might be able to get Blat from http://nt.info.nl/applications/mail.htm. Otherwise, you can use an e-mail client application that supports command line parameters.

```
' ***********************************************************************
' This is used to send out the mail message to the approvers.           *
' ***********************************************************************
Sub Send_Mail ()
    On Error Resume Next
    Dim intHandle As Integer
    Dim sMessage As String
    Dim sMailServer As String
    Dim sMailTo As String
    Dim sMailLogin As String

    sMailServer = GetSmallField("Mail_Server_Name")
    sMailTo = GetSmallField("Mail_To_Address")
    sMailLogin = GetSmallField("Mail_Server_Login")
    intHandle = Shell("c:\Supertcp\blat.exe -install " & _
```

 NOTE: Enter the correct path to the e-mail client application that you are using.

8

```
            sMailServer & " " & sMailLogin)
    If Err = False Then
        Do While True
```

```
          AppActivate "Blat"
          If Err Then
               Err = False
               Exit Do
          End If
     Loop
   End If
   sMessage = "c:\blat\blat.exe C:\genie\helpdesk.txt -t " & sMailTo
   intHandle = Shell(sMessage)
   Exit Sub              ' Exit Send_Mail()
Send_MailError:
   send ("Content-type: text/HTML")
   send ("")
   send ("<HTML><TITLE>VB Error!!</TITLE>")
   send ("<H1>A Visual Basic error has occurred!</H2><HR>")
   send ("<I>Please note the following, and e-mail the author.</I><BR>")
   send ("")
   send ("Service's Name:         " + ServiceName + "<BR>")
   send ("Subroutine :            Send_Mail()<BR>")
   send ("E-mail Service Author: <A HREF=""mailto:" + AuthorsE-mail _
        + """>" + AuthorsName + "</A></HTML>")
End Sub              ' End of Send_Mail()
```

8. The following code is used to output information passed through the string `Info` into a text file for debugging purposes.

```
' ****************************************************************************
' This subroutine is used to print out information while debugging the *
' service. All of the information is stored in "C:\debug.txt"          *
' ****************************************************************************
Sub debugout (Info As String)
    Dim iFileNum As Integer          ' Stores next available File#
    iFileNum = FreeFile              ' Get the next FileNumber
    Open DebugFile For Append Access Write As iFileNum
    Print #iFileNum, Info
    Close iFileNum
End Sub                              ' End of Debugout()
```

9. The following subroutine is used to send the form submitters a response telling them their form has been processed and thanking them for their time. Again, you use information stored in hidden fields on the form so you can customize the title and response text. You also insert a custom link to move the users to another location.

```
' **********************************************************************
' This subroutine is used to return a success page to the user when the   *
' input is complete, valid, and has been entered into the database.        *
' **********************************************************************
Sub SuccessFrm ()
    Dim sTitle As String
    Dim sText As String
    Dim sLink As String
    Dim sLinkText As String

    sText = GetSmallField("Response_Text")
    sTitle = GetSmallField("Response_Title")
    sLink = GetSmallField("Response_Link")
    sLinkText = GetSmallField("Response_Link_Text")
    send ("content-type: text/html")
    send ("")
    send ("<HTML>")
    If sTitle = "" Then
    send ("<TITLE>No Title</TITLE>")
    Else
    send ("<TITLE>" & sTitle & "</TITLE>")
    End If
    send ("<BODY BGCOLOR=#ffffff>")
    send ("<H1>Thank You!</H1>")
    send ("<HR SIZE=5>")
    send ("<FONTSIZE=+3><I>")
    If sText = "" Then
        send ("Thank you for your information.")
    Else
        send (sText)
    End If
    If sLink <> "" And sLinkText <> "" Then
        send ("<BR><A HREF=""" & sLink & """>" & sLinkText & "</A>")
    End If
    send ("</FONT>")
    send ("</BODY>")
    send ("</HTML>")
End Sub                                    ' End of SuccessFrm()
```

Now you have some ideas about writing a Visual Basic, WinCGI back-end service. You can either copy the code directly or use it as a reference to give you ideas about what you can do with your own back-end applications.

8

Working with ISAPI Back Ends

ISAPI, or Internet Service Application Programming Interface, was created to be faster than CGI or WinCGI back-end applications. Instead of being executable files, such as CGI and WinCGI back ends, ISAPI back ends are actually dynamic link libraries (DLLs). DLLs contain compiled functions that are ready to run. They are not a part of the source code, but rather a group of functions that can be called by source code. The first time the DLL is called it loads into memory. Some servers allow you an option to automatically load the DLL into memory at startup making the service run even faster.

NOTE: For more information on the Internet Service Application Programming Interface (ISAPI), see Chapter 3.

The C++ Language

C and C++ were developed at Bell Labs. C was created in the early 1970s while Dennis Ritchie was working on a project to develop the Unix operating system. Ritchie needed a language that was geared toward problem solving. Most assembly languages of the day were focused on the manipulation of specific hardware components. With C, programmers could use a more structured approach to programming because of its well-developed looping structures.

An Extension of C

C++ is an extension of the C language developed at Bell Labs by Bjarne Stroustrup. Even the name, C++, is derived from the increment operator in C, which is ++, alluding to the fact that C++ is an incremented version of C. C++ also includes some of the data typing and object-oriented features of Simula67—a simulation language from Norway.

TIP: Because C++ is a superset of the original C language, most valid C programs are also valid C++ programs. Your investment in C programs can be leveraged into code that should run with your new C++ programs.

How C++ Works

C++ incorporates many of the low-level programming functionality of languages such as assembly. This makes C++ very flexible but also a very complex language. Many of the functions that are handled by higher-level language services, such as memory management, must be explicitly managed by your program. The result is a program that can be maximized for speed.

A Compiled Language   C++ is a compiled language, in contrast to Perl or Visual Basic, which are interpreted languages. The result of compiled C++ source code is an executable file with low-level machine instructions that can be understood by the operating system. Figure 8-3 shows the steps

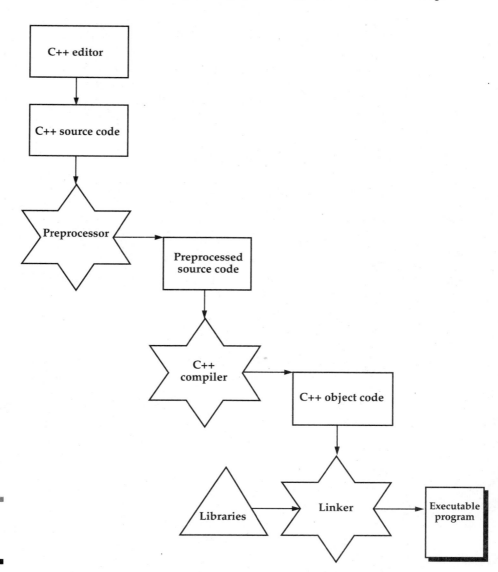

Creating a
C++ program
Figure 8-3.

8

needed to create a C++ program. The interpreted languages also result in an executable file as part of the "make" process. When you run a Visual Basic program, however, there is a DLL that loads to interpret the Visual Basic constructs into machine instructions while you are running the program. This translation takes time, making interpreted languages slower than compiled languages.

The Level of Skill Required   The skill set needed to program in C++ is more advanced than in some other languages like Visual Basic. Most Information Systems departments have programmers, but you are more likely to find Visual Basic programmers rather than C++ programmers. If you do not employ C++ programmers, you may find help from a local value-added reseller or systems integrator. A reseller that specializes in Web applications can help you design and implement a back-end service for a specific project. Contracting services outside your company is a good idea if your projects are fairly well defined and static in nature. If you have a particularly dynamic project to implement or if your need for Web-application creation is ongoing, it may be more economical for you to hire or train a C++ programmer.

TIP: There are many good books written about C++, including Stroustrup's *The C++ Programming Language* and Overland's *C++ in Plain English.*

ISAPI-Compliant Web Servers

Many Web applications for the Windows NT platform are written to the ISAPI standard. This specification, published by Microsoft and Purveyor, ties in with many Web servers and existing program languages like Visual Basic and, especially, Visual C++. One other Web server that is ISAPI compliant is Frontier's SuperWeb server, included on the accompanying CD. By using the ISAPI function calls, you can interact with a Web server to create specialized applications, such as connections to legacy databases. Netscape publishes a similar API called NSAPI that can be used if you are running Netscape's Web servers.

The C++ Compiler

In order to create C++ programs, you need a C++ compiler such as Microsoft's Visual C++. Visual C++ includes an entire development environment called Developer Studio, shown in Figure 8-4, that organizes the elements needed to create C++ programs.

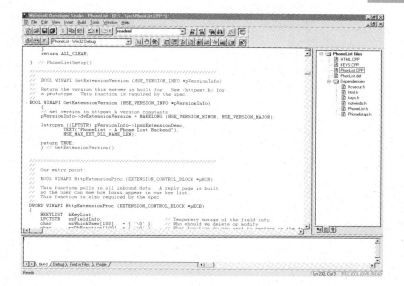

The
Microsoft C++
Developer
Studio
Figure 8-4.

The Text Editor   Most compiler programs also include a text editor that has special functions related to structured coding, but any text editor, such as Notepad, works as well.

TIP: Testing your Web application on a live server can cause your Web server to crash. Many Web server packages include a less functional version of their server that may be run on a standard desktop to make debugging Web applications more convenient. (Frontier's SuperWeb Server comes with a "debug server" that runs on a Windows 95 or NT desktop.) You can then do all your testing in a closed environment and only put your code on a live server after most of the bugs have been worked out.

A C++ Example

Now you're ready for an example. The ISAPI back end that follows is written in C++. The point of the program is to read in data created with a form and return it to the user. You might use this back end as a verification for users so that they can check information they have entered before they submit it. You might also use sections of the program as starting points to build on. You can get a feel for how you retrieve data from a form by reading over the code. You can then take the data and manipulate it in a way that is helpful to you. If you used the same form as is shown in the next section, you might store the data in a customer database to create a future mailing

8

list. You could also create different fields on the form; you could ask the visitors for their software feature preferences, and then use the data as search criteria. You could then search your product database and return a list of products that best match the visitor in the form of an HTML page.

Creating a Form   Earlier in this chapter, you learned how to create a form. In Figure 8-5, you see the form created for the ISAPI back end sample in a later section. If you want to use the same form, you can enter the HTML code in your HTML editor. If you are using a WYSIWYG editor, then create the appropriate form controls—or edit boxes and radio buttons—looking at the HTML code to see what you should name the controls.

 NOTE: The form shown in our example is a basic one. It's designed to show you how an ISAPI back end works, as opposed to being aesthetically pleasing.

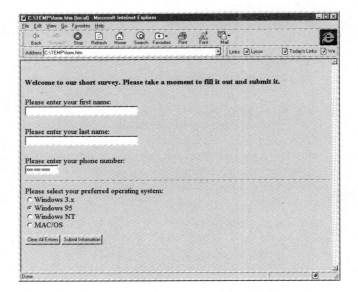

A WYSIWYG view of a sample form

Figure 8-5.

The HTML Code Now take a look at the HTML code that created the form. You can either enter the code exactly or use it as a basis for creating your own form.

```
<HTML>
<HEAD>
</HEAD>
<FORM ACTION = "Register" METHOD = "Post" >
<BR>
<BR>
<B>Welcome to our short survey. Please take a moment to fill it out and submit it.</B><BR>
<BR>
<BR>
Please enter your first name:<BR>
<INPUT TYPE = TEXT NAME = "First Name" SIZE = 50 MAXLENGTH = 50><BR>
<BR>
<BR>
Please enter your last name:<BR>
<INPUT TYPE = TEXT NAME = "Last Name" SIZE = 50 MAXLENGTH = 50><BR>
<BR>
<BR>
Please enter your phone number: <BR>
<INPUT TYPE = TEXT NAME = "Phone Number" SIZE = 12 MAXLENGTH = 12 VALUE = "xxx-xxx-xxxx"><BR>

<HR>Please select your preferred operating system:<BR>
<INPUT TYPE = RADIO NAME = "Operating System" VALUE = "Windows 3.x">Windows 3.x<BR>

<INPUT TYPE = RADIO NAME = "Operating System" CHECKED VALUE = "Windows 95">Windows 95<BR>

<INPUT TYPE = RADIO NAME = "Operating System" VALUE = "Windows NT">Windows NT<BR>

<INPUT TYPE = RADIO NAME = "Operating System" VALUE = "MAC/OS">MAC/OS<BR>
<BR>

<INPUT TYPE = "RESET"VALUE = "Clear All Entries">
<INPUT TYPE = "SUBMIT"VALUE = "Submit Information"><BR>
<BR>

</FORM>
</HTML>
```

Creating the Code   Now that you've created the form, you can begin to create your ISAPI back end, so you can actually use your form on your Web server. To create an ISAPI extension in C++, you need to get a special file that Microsoft has written for you: HTML.H. If you have Microsoft Visual C++ (MSVC) 4.2, then you already have this file. The file defines the data structures ISAPI uses. There are some additional files included with MSVC 4.2 you might want to use, such as HTML.CPP, KEYS.H, KEYS.CPP, and HTTPEXT.H. These files make creating your ISAPI back ends easier. (See Chapter 3 for more details.)

NOTE: The following steps assume you already have C++ installed on your computer. If you do not have C++ installed, then you cannot use the example!

Once you have the correct files available on your computer, you can begin writing your ISAPI back-end application, which we will call "Register." Follow these steps:

1. Open up your C++ environment.
2. Create a new project.

TIP: Don't forget you are creating a DLL and not an EXE, and if you are using Microsoft C++, or a similar product that requires you to include files in your project, then you should include the KEYS.CPP and the HTML.CPP files.

3. First we must define all of the files included in the project and any variables that should be constant.

```
#define WIN32_LEAN_AND_MEAN     // the bare essential Win32 API
#include <windows.h>
#include <stdlib.h>
#include <ctype.h>              // for isprint()
#include <httpext.h>
#include <string.h>
#include <time.h>
#include "keys.h"
#include "html.h"
#define MAX_STMT_LEN 100
```

The HTTPEXT.H, KEYS.H, and HTML.H are files you use in many ISAPI services that you write. They enable your program to interact with the Web server. The HTML.H file contains many procedures that you can execute to send commands to the browser, while KEYS.H is used to find out about the fields on a form and the information they contain.

4. Next, prototype all of the functions to use in our "Register" ISAPI back end.

```
// prototype
void GetFieldInfo (EXTENSION_CONTROL_BLOCK *pECB,HANDLE
hContent, DWORD dwOffset, DWORD dwLength, char &szFieldInfo);
```

GetFieldInfo is used to get the information that is stored in a field when a form is posted by the user. In other words, when you fill in the form and then click a Submit button, the function `GetFieldInfo` retrieves the information stored in the field specified by the handle `hContent`.

```
void SendErrorPage( EXTENSION_CONTROL_BLOCK *pECB, LPCSTR szMsg );
void SendMainPage( EXTENSION_CONTROL_BLOCK *pECB );
void SendSuccessPage( EXTENSION_CONTROL_BLOCK *pECB );
```

5. Each of these functions does just what its name sounds like. SendErrorPage notifies the user of an error, should one occur. SendMainPage sends back the main page when the service is originally called or when a GET is performed on the service. SendSuccessPage sends the users a page with the information they have entered into the form.

NOTE: GETs and POSTs are the methods used to call a back-end service. A GET sends a name=value pair in the universal resource locator (URL) itself .

```
http://www.host.com/servicename?fieldname1=value1&fieldname2=
value2a+value2b
```

A name=value pair is generated by a control via HTML. The POST method also sends name=value pairs. The POST method places the pairs in the body of the message, not in the URL. Upon receiving these pairs, the Web server places them in a separate file. This file is where the CGI code obtains the information. Most back-end services today are called with POSTs.

TIP: Keep in mind that this is purely an example that could be modified to do more useful functions at a later date.

8

The first main section of code is the entry point into our DLL. When you are creating a DLL, you must have at least one entry point into it. Entry points are used by other programs or DLLs to run functions in your DLL. In this case, we have called our entry point DllEntryPoint. Entry points must also be specified in a .DEF file, which is included in your project and is discussed later in this section.

```
// DllEntryPoint allows us to initialize our state variables. You might keep
// state information, as the DLL often remains loaded for several client
// requests. The server may choose to unload this DLL, and you should save
// your state to disk, and reload it here. DllEntryPoint is called for both
// loading and unloading. See the Win32 SDK (Software Development Kit) from
// Microsoft for more info on how DLLs load and unload.
//
BOOL WINAPI DllEntryPoint (HINSTANCE hinstDLL, DWORD dwReason, LPVOID lpv)
{
   // Nothing to do here
   return (TRUE);
}
```

6. Our next function is also an entry point into our DLL and is required by the Web server in order to work as an ISAPI service.

```
// BOOL WINAPI GetExtensionVersion (HSE_VERSION_INFO *pVersionInfo)
//
// Return the version this server is built for. See <httpext.h> for a
// prototype. This function is required by the spec.
//
BOOL WINAPI GetExtensionVersion (HSE_VERSION_INFO *pVersionInfo)
{
   // set version to httpext.h version constants
   pVersionInfo->dwExtensionVersion = MAKELONG (HSE_VERSION_MINOR,
HSE_VERSION_MAJOR);
   lstrcpyn ( (LPTSTR) pVersionInfo->lpszExtensionDesc,
```

7. On the following line, note that the only change that needs to be made to this function is when you start a new service. You must change the TEXT(...) to reflect the name you want to register with the Web server when the DLL is started.

```
TEXT("REGISTER-An ISAPI Example"),
HSE_MAX_EXT_DLL_NAME_LEN );
   return TRUE;
} // GetExtensionVersion()
```

8. The next function in the code is the main part of the DLL. This is where most of the work is done, and it is also an entry point into the DLL.

```
// Our entry point:
// BOOL WINAPI HttpExtensionProc (EXTENSION_CONTROL_BLOCK *pECB)
//
// This function pulls in all inbound data. A reply page is built so the
// user can see how forms appear in our key list. This function is also
// required by the spec.
//
DWORD WINAPI HttpExtensionProc (EXTENSION_CONTROL_BLOCK *pECB)
{
```

9. hKeyList is used to store the list of the keys, or fields on the POSTed form. The four sz variables are used to store the information returned by the form.

```
HKEYLIST hKeyList;
HANDLE hContent;
char szFieldInfo[256]       = {\0 };
char szFirstName[256]       = { '\0' };
char szLastName[256]        = { '\0' };
char szPhoneNumber[256]     = { '\0' };
char szOperatingSystem[256] = { '\0' };
// Get the keys sent by the client.
hKeyList = GetKeyList (pECB);
LPVOID hSession = NULL;
#if 1
// Send the HTTP Headers first.
pECB->ServerSupportFunction( pECB->ConnID,
    HSE_REQ_SEND_RESPONSE_HEADER,NULL, NULL, NULL );
hSession = GetWebmSessionHandle( pECB );
#endif
```

10. First, we check to see if the service was called as a GET or a POST. If it was a GET, then we return the main page. In this case, the main page is really an error page, because this service does not support a GET call, but it is easily modified to support GETs.

```
// Check to see if the user is requesting the Main Page or is submitting
// their change.
if ( strcmp ( pECB->lpszMethod, "GET" ) == 0 )
{
SendMainPage( pECB );
}
```

11. If it was a POST, then we go on to retrieve the information from the page and process it. First, we make sure that there were fields on the form that was POSTed by doing the if(hKeyList).

8

```
else  // They are submitting their Information.
{
if (hKeyList)
{
// Open the content file.
hContent = CreateFile (GetContentPath (hKeyList),
GENERIC_READ,
0,              // No sharing mode
NULL,           // Default security attribs
OPEN_EXISTING,
FILE_ATTRIBUTE_NORMAL,  // In this sample, we seq. access this too.
NULL            // No template file
);
// Report errors as necessary.
if (hContent == INVALID_HANDLE_VALUE)
{
SendErrorPage( pECB, "Invalid Handle Value" );
FreeKeyList (hKeyList);
hKeyList = NULL;
}
}
```

12. Once again, check for an hKeyList.

```
// Report errors
if (!hKeyList)
{
SendErrorPage( pECB, "No keys sent or error decoding keys" );
CloseHandle (hContent);
}
else
{
HKEYLIST hKey;
```

13. Now we need to start using the hKeyList to obtain the information for all of the fields in the form, one by one.

```
// Loop through all of the keys.
hKey = hKeyList;
while (hKey)
{
// Details about the key.
LPCTSTR lpszKeyName;
DWORD dwOffset;
DWORD dwLength;
BOOL bHasCtrlChars;
int nInstance;
// We get info, and hKey points to next key in list.
hKey = GetKeyInfo (hKey,
&lpszKeyName,
```

```
                         &dwOffset,
                         &dwLength,
                         &bHasCtrlChars,
                         &nInstance);
```

14. This next check is to make sure that there was something in the field. If so, GetFieldInfo is used to obtain that information.

```
if (dwLength)
{
GetFieldInfo (pECB,
hContent,
dwOffset,
dwLength,
*szFieldInfo );
szFieldInfo[dwLength] = '\0';
```

15. Here, we put the information into the appropriate field variables.

```
// Copy the information into the corresponding fields.
if ( strcmp( lpszKeyName, "Last Name" ) == 0 )
{
strcpy( szLastName, szFieldInfo );
}
else
if ( strcmp( lpszKeyName, "First Name" ) == 0 )
{
strcpy( szFirstName, szFieldInfo );
}
else
if ( strcmp( lpszKeyName, "Phone Number" ) == 0 )
{
strcpy( szPhoneNumber, szFieldInfo );
}
else
if (strcmp( lpszKeyName, "Operating System") == 0 )
{
strcpy( szOperatingSystem, szFieldInfo );
}
}
}
SendSuccessPage( pECB, szLastName, szFirstName, szPhoneNumber, szOperatingSystem );
}
// Clean up.
CloseHandle (hContent);
FreeKeyList (hKeyList);
}
return HSE_STATUS_SUCCESS;
}
```

8

16. This is where we get the information for the current field being pointed to in our while loop.

```
//
// Retrieve all of the data for the current field.
//
void GetFieldInfo (EXTENSION_CONTROL_BLOCK *pECB, HANDLE hContent, DWORD
dwOffset, DWORD dwLength, char &szFieldInfo)
{
DWORD dwRead;
DWORD dwSize;
DWORD dwPos = 0;
//
// We move to the offset, but this sample sequentially accesses the keys
// anyway. Because the key data is saved in the same order as the key list,
// we could omit this as long as we only read dwLength bytes. However, it
// is necessary for random access.
//
SetFilePointer (hContent, dwOffset, NULL, FILE_BEGIN);
while (dwLength)
{
// Take min of 16 or dwLength.
dwSize = min(256, dwLength);
// Get data from content file.
if (ReadFile (hContent, &szFieldInfo, dwSize, &dwRead, NULL))
{
break;
}
else
{
// Write error to Web.
szFieldInfo = '\0';
break;
}
}
return;
}
```

17. This function should never actually be run in this example, but it is useful to show how to use the header files to output an error page to the user when an error does occur.

```
//
// Returns an error page to the user.
//
void SendErrorPage ( EXTENSION_CONTROL_BLOCK *pECB, LPCSTR szMsg )
{
```

```
char szMsg1[100];
wsprintf( szMsg1, "<HTML><TITLE>Register Error Page</TITLE>" );
WriteString( pECB, szMsg1 );
wsprintf( szMsg1, "<BODY BGCOLOR=#ffffff>" );
WriteString( pECB, szMsg1 );
wsprintf( szMsg1, "<H1>Error in Register Service</H1><HR><B>" );
WriteString( pECB, szMsg1 );
WriteString( pECB, szMsg );
wsprintf( szMsg1, "</B></BODY></HTML>" );
WriteString( pECB, szMsg1 );
return;
}
```

18. This next section is used to return a page showing the information entered on the form. You may want to modify this at a later date to have the information saved to a file or a database.

```
// Returns a success page to users with their information on it.
//
void SendSuccessPage( EXTENSION_CONTROL_BLOCK *pECB, char szLastName[],
char szFirstName[], char szPhoneNumber[], char szOperatingSystem[] )
{
char szMsg[100];
```

19. HtmlCreatePage is used to start an HTML page, and HtmlEndPage is used to end the page. Each of the commands in between is used to send lines to the HTML page, which is being sent to the browser. wsprintf copies into the first variable, the second variable, or the string, while WriteString writes out to the page the second variable or string and can be found in the HTML.H file.

```
HtmlCreatePage( pECB, TEXT("Register Success Page") );
wsprintf( szMsg, "<BODY BGCOLOR=#ffffff>" );
WriteString( pECB, szMsg );
HtmlHeading( pECB, 1, TEXT("Your Page was filled in as follows: ") );
HtmlHorizontalRule( pECB );
wsprintf( szMsg, "Last Name: %s <BR>", szLastName );
WriteString( pECB, szMsg );
wsprintf( szMsg, "First Name: %s <BR>", szFirstName );
WriteString( pECB, szMsg );
wsprintf( szMsg, "Phone Number: %s <BR>", szPhoneNumber );
WriteString( pECB, szMsg );
wsprintf( szMsg, "Operating System: %s <BR>", szOperatingSystem );
WriteString( pECB, szMsg );
HtmlEndPage( pECB );
return;
}
```

8

20. Finally, there is the function to return when the service is accessed using a GET, which we do not allow in this example.

```
// Returns a form to the user to fill in.
//
void SendMainPage( EXTENSION_CONTROL_BLOCK *pECB )
{
char szMsg[100];
HtmlCreatePage( pECB, "Register Example" );
wsprintf( szMsg, "<BODY BGCOLOR=#ffffff>" );
WriteString( pECB, szMsg );
wsprintf( szMsg, "<CENTER>" );
WriteString( pECB, szMsg );
HtmlHeading( pECB, 1, "Register Example " );
wsprintf( szMsg, "<CENTER>" );
WriteString( pECB, szMsg );
HtmlHorizontalRule( pECB );
wsprintf( szMsg, "You cannot perform a GET on this service. Please try a POST
from the provided HTML page/form." );
WriteString( pECB, szMsg );
HtmlEndPage( pECB );
return;
}
```

21. Now that you have entered all of the data, you should compile your program and find any typing mistakes and syntax problems.

22. Fix the errors!

23. At this point in the process, we recommend that, if your compiler supports it, you compile a debug version of your project. By creating a debug version, you are able to step through the code as it runs and get a feel for what is actually happening. You might then better be able to identify any problems in your logic.

24. If you are ready to place the file on your Web server, then you need to read the documentation that accompanies your Web server. You may need to register the file with the Web server or copy the file to a particular location.

Design Considerations

HTML has incredible power and flexibility. You can use it to create virtually any kind of information you want. The downside of all this flexibility is that if you don't follow a few guiding principles, you can easily create discordant pages that don't communicate effectively. This following sections cover some basic Web page design principles.

Overall Appearance

The overall appearance of your site is very important in holding the user's interest and reflecting a positive corporate image. You want the site to have a tasteful mixture of elements. You must choose the elements to include and those that are not necessary.

Functionality: The Prime Objective

The purpose of your site is to relay information to your audience. The fact that you *can* write a Java script to make characters cartwheel across the screen does not mean you should. Functionality is the primary objective of your Intranet, and cool graphics are appropriate in many cases. Another objective of your site is to let the user know that they are at your site no matter which page they are on. You want a consistent look and feel throughout your site.

Establishing an Order of Importance

When you are laying out the information on your Web pages, you want the most important information to be where people look for it first. The position of the most important information depends on the language in which you are writing your information. For example, Figure 8-6 shows the most important parts of an HTML page in order of importance, if your language reads from left to right like English, French, German, Kanji, and Simple Chinese. Figure 8-7 shows the most important parts of an HTML page in order of importance, if your language reads from right to left like Hebrew and Arabic.

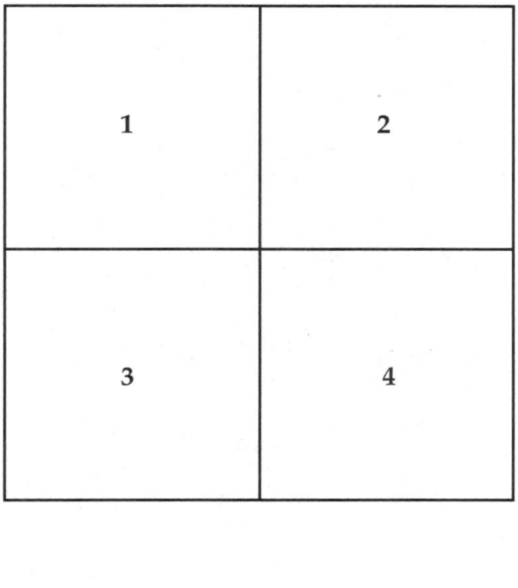

A left-to-right
flow of
information
Figure 8-6.

8

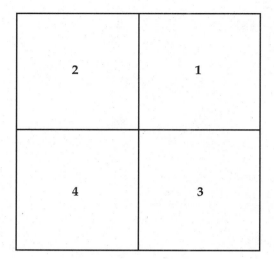

A right-to-left
flow of
information
Figure 8-7.

Using the Right Fonts

The fonts you use in the text can make a surprising difference in the overall
look and feel of your Web pages. Figure 8-8 shows two different fonts. The
font on the top line of the figure has *serifs*, which are extra beginning and
ending marks on many of the letters. The purpose of the serifs is to help
guide your eye across a line of text. The serif font shown is Century
Schoolbook. The font on the bottom line of the figure doesn't have serifs,
which makes it a *sans* serif font. The name of this sans serif font is Arial.

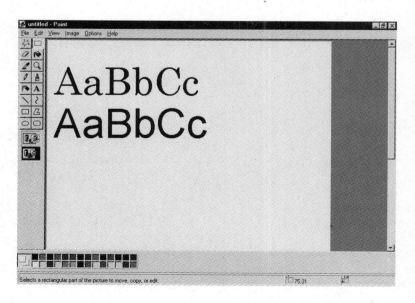

A serif and a
sans serif font
Figure 8-8.

So what does all of this have to do with creating Web pages? Consider Figure 8-9 and Figure 8-10 and decide which one looks better to you. The font used in Figure 8-9 is the sans serif font, Arial, and the font used in Figure 8-10 is the serif font, Century Schoolbook. Decide which one you like, and design your Web pages using the type of font that suits your Web site. Font selection can set the mood of a particular page. Serif fonts are generally considered to be more formal, while the Arial font adds a more technical feel to the page.

Working with White Space

Understanding some basic rules of thumb for using white space can make your Web pages much more visually appealing. Take a look at Figure 8-11 and compare it to Figure 8-9. The only difference between the two is the use of white space. Figure 8-11 incorporates white space in the left and right margins to focus attention on the graphics. You can see how effective use of white space can highlight aspects of your Web page.

To Increase Readability

Research has shown that people read a shorter line of text faster than they can a longer line. Design the text in your Web pages to have a maximum line length of about 70 characters. This is the longest line length that most people can read without hurting readability. White space can also direct your attention to a particular element of the page. When you surround a line of text with white space, it naturally draws your eye to that element.

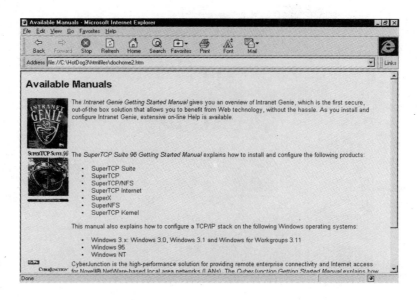

A Web
page in sans
serif font
Figure 8-9.

8

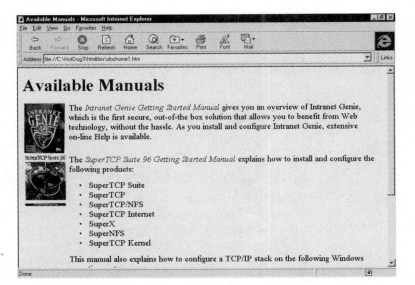

A Web page
in a serif font
Figure 8-10.

Designing White Space

You probably won't realize it when you look at Figure 8-12, but the Available Manuals page is built on an underlying grid of three columns. The first column takes up 20 percent of the Web page, the second column takes up 60 percent, and the third column takes up 20 percent. Here we use white space to visually organize the page into different sections. The first column

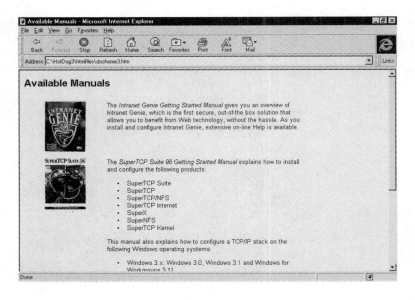

An effective
use of
white space
Figure 8-11.

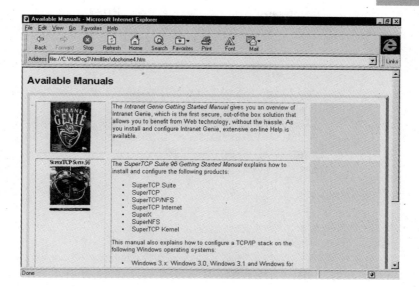

An underlying
three-column
grid
Figure 8-12.

contains a good deal of white space, and the third column is composed
solely of white space, focusing your attention on the graphics in column one
and the text in column two.

A three-column grid, like the one shown in Figure 8-12, gives you many
versatile ways to set up your Web page. When you design your Web page,
you can use fewer columns or more columns, depending on the design you
want. Whatever you decide, use two or three page templates for all of the
Web pages you create. This gives your site a consistent look and feel.

Using Tables

The Web page shown in Figure 8-12 was created using an HTML table. Each
image is in a single cell, and the text that accompanies each image is in the
same row. One pointer with creating tables is that you have the option of
defining a fixed width for your columns or choosing a percentage. The
percentage is a better idea, because the window adjusts to the size of the
browser window on a user's machine. If you have a fixed width, your Web
page could get cut off if the browser window is too small.

To Organize Your Page
Tables also organize your images and text in a grid-like manner. When you
have a large amount of data, tables are an excellent way of displaying that
information. You can insert any valid HTML code into your table cells,
including text, images, hyperlinks, and more. There are also options

8

available for formatting and presentation. Figure 8-13 shows how you can organize textual information in an HTML table format.

Constructing a Table

The basic elements of table construction are the beginning <TABLE> and ending </TABLE> tags, the row definition tags <TR> </TR>, and the two types of cell definition: header cells <TH> </TH> and normal cells <TD> </TD>. You can combine this handful of tags into simple grids or a complex matrix of tabular information. Here is an example of a basic table layout and the resulting Web page:

```
<TABLE BORDER=1 >
<TR>
    <TH></TH>
    <TH>Cell 2</TH>
    <TH>Cell 3</TH>
    <TH>Cell 4</TH>
    <TH>Cell 5</TH>
</TR>
<TR>
    <TH>Cell 6</TH>
    <TD>Cell 7</TD>
    <TD>Cell 8</TD>
    <TD>Cell 9</TD>
    <TD>Cell 10</TH>
</TR>
<TR>
    <TH>Cell 11</TH>
    <TD>Cell 12</TD>
    <TD>Cell 13</TD>
    <TD>Cell 14</TD>
    <TD>Cell 15</TH>
</TR>
</TABLE>
```

You can add additional tags to tables that affect the overall layout. Width can be specified by pixels <TABLE WIDTH=350> or by percent of the window's width <TABLE WIDTH=75%>. Width can be specified for table cells or the entire table.

```
<TH WIDTH=75%>

<TD WIDTH=75%>

<TABLE WIDTH=75%>
```

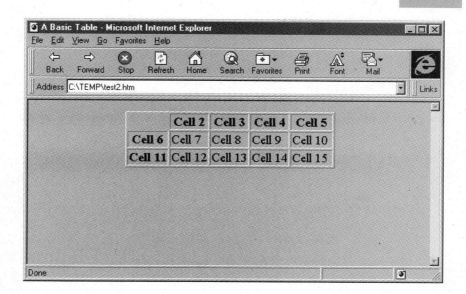

A basic table
Figure 8-13.

You can change the background color with the BGCOLOR command. You can specify a background color for specific cells, rows, or the entire table.

```
<TH BGCOLOR=TEAL>
```

```
<TD BGCOLOR=TEAL>
```

```
<TR BGCOLOR=TEAL>
```

```
<TABLE BGCOLOR=TEAL>
```

Cells can be stretched to span multiple columns or rows.

```
<TH COLSPAN=2>
```

```
<TD COLSPAN=2>
```

```
<TH ROWSPAN=3>
```

```
<TD ROWSPAN=3>
```

There are additional tags to adjust cell alignment and cell spacing.

8

TIP: The best way to learn how to effectively use tables is to browse sites on the Internet and view the source for pages that incorporate interesting tables. You can cut and paste portions of these tables and insert the framework into your own pages. You can then insert your own data into that framework.

Creating Columns with Frames

Another way to create different columns of text is to use frames. Figure 8-14 shows an example. The columns of text may be in columns down the page, or they may be in rows across the page. As you can see, each column has a scroll bar that can be adjusted independently of the other columns. If you want to make a column smaller, you can adjust the width with your mouse. The Web page illustrated in Figure 8-12 was created using an HTML table. Each image is in a single cell, and the text that accompanies each image is in the same row.

How to Use Color

When you are thinking about the colors of the various elements on your Web pages, think about including the colors in your organization's logo. You want your Web pages to reflect your organization's image, and choosing the same colors as your organization helps to maintain a consistent image. If you do not want to include your corporate colors, you could choose a theme

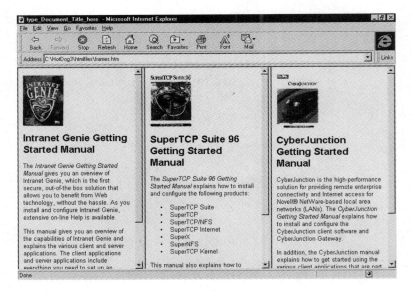

Creating columns with frames
Figure 8-14.

that is complimentary to your logo or choose colors that are fashionable, such as lighter colors for spring and darker colors for fall.

Including Images

The images you use on your Web pages ought to reflect your organization's image. You can include your organization's logo, or use images that reflect your organization's products or reflect other aspects of your organization that make it unique. Here again, it is important that your graphics conform to a style. If you have a consistent style, visitors are more likely to associate the site with your company.

Where to Get Design Ideas

Browse the following Web sites for more information on designing HTML pages:

- ◆ Beginners Guide to HTML at
  http://www.ncsa.uiuc.edu/general/internet/www/htmlprimer.html
- ◆ Netscape: Creating Net Sites at
  http://home.netscape.com/home/how-to-create-web-services.html
- ◆ The HTML Writer's Guild Web site at http://www.hwg.org
- ◆ The Web Developer's Virtual Library at http://www.stars.com
- ◆ JASC Web Developer's Forum at http://www.jasc.com/webdev.html
- ◆ The WebGuru's Own Dark Secrets at
  http://www.sausage.com.au/secrets.htm
- ◆ Creating a killer Web site at www.killersites.com
- ◆ An interesting "Meta - Tag" information
  http://www.nmsu.edu/~czimmerm/html/meta-tags.html

Technical Restrictions

The previous section outlined some of the design considerations that affect the way you construct your Intranet site. There are also technical considerations that influence the way you build your pages. The ability to create high tech Web pages has outpaced the ability to deliver these pages on slower connections. You can create a page full of spectacular graphics, ActiveX applications, or Java scripts that delivers a high amount of functionality; but if it takes 5 minutes to download, you have probably lost your audience. You have a little more control with an Intranet because you know who your users are; you know what type of link they have to connect

8

to your Intranet; and you have a good idea what browsers are used to access the server. Knowing most of the restrictive parameters, you can build an Intranet Web site that is functional and exciting for your users.

HTML Options

One advantage of the "browser wars" is that the HTML programmer has many page-design options. The World Wide Web is full of inventive ways to combine standard and extended tags to create exciting Web pages. When you find an interesting page on the World Wide Web, such as the one shown in Figure 8-15, most browsers allow you to view its source HTML code. (This option is usually available on the menu bar.) You can then cut and paste the HTML to your own document, modify the code, and include your own information and graphics, as shown in Figure 8-16.

Bandwidth Conservation

There is a lot of discussion surrounding the subject of conserving Internet bandwidth. These discussions may also apply to your Intranet. It should be a goal of everyone creating content for your Intranet to minimize the bandwidth they are consuming—not only from the standpoint of conservation, but to realize that smaller files and pages mean a faster Intranet! Table 8-1 shows the transmission speeds for some of the more common connections.

Notice in Table 8-1 how the standard Ethernet connection on a local LAN is 434 times faster than a 28.8Kbps dial-up connection. You may have

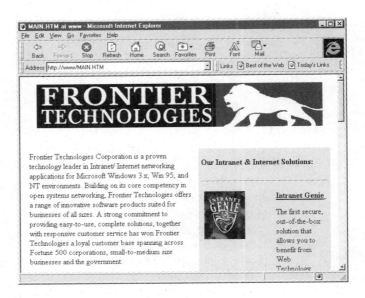

An original HTML page format
Figure 8-15.

An original
format with
your content
inserted
Figure 8-16.

remote users connected to your LAN through a dial-up connection like the topology shown in Figure 8-17. If you have remote users dialing into your Intranet, you must be sure that your site is designed to accommodate those slower connections.

TIP: If all your users are local, you have a little more flexibility in using higher bandwidth components. The graphics you use may be a little larger than those used in a dial-up connection, and video or telephony may be a more viable solution.

Carrier Service	Bandwidth	Comparison to Dial-Up 28.8Kbps Speed
Dial-up 14.4Kbps modem	14.4Kbps	0.50X
Dial-up 28.8Kbps modem	28.8Kbps	1.00X
Leased line	56Kbps	2.4X
ISDN line	128Kbps	5.55X
T-1 line	1.544Kbps	67X
Ethernet LAN	10,000Kbps	434X
T-3 line	44,736Kbps	1942X

Some
Common
Transmission
Speeds
Table 8-1.

8

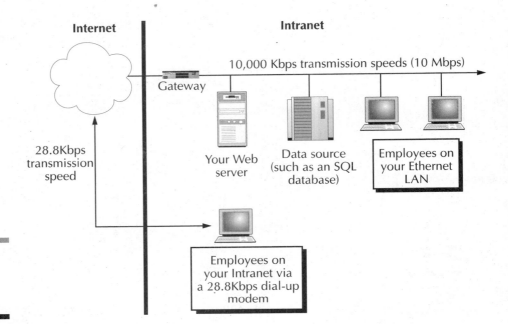

A typical
connection
topology
Figure 8-17.

Graphics and Intranet Performance

Graphics are instrumental in conveying ideas and are a major component of the content you create. Graphics can also strongly impact the performance of you Intranet. The trick is to strike a balance between the size of graphics and the quality of the image.

TIP: The Bandwidth Conservation Society has an excellent site at http://www.infohiway.com/way/faster/index.html that describes ways to make your graphics smaller. Although the site is aimed at conserving Internet bandwidth, the same concepts apply to your Intranet.

Graphics Syntax
The syntax to include an image into your page is

```
<IMG SCR="/homepage.gif" ALT ="Brushwood Enterprises Homepage">
```

Between the first set of quote marks, put the URL of the image file. If the image file is a GIF file, the filename must end with .gif. If it is a JPEG, the file must end in .jpg. After the ALT, you can put any text you would like to appear, in case the browser doesn't support graphics. If you don't include the ALT, the word IMAGE appears on the screen of the Web user whose browser doesn't support graphics.

Using clickable images or image maps involves adding the following map filename you want to associate with the image:

```
<A HREF="/homepage.map">
<IMG SRC="/homepage.gif" ALT="Brushwood Enterprises Homepage" ISMAP>
</A>
```

The <A HREF tag lets you identify the map file to associate with the image. In this case, the map filename is *homepage.map*. Next, identify the image using the <IMG SCR tag as you would when inserting a nonclickable image. Placing ISMAP after the image filename indicates that the image is an image map or has a map file associated with it.

Graphics Formats

Although there are other choices for Web-graphic formats, GIF and JPEG are the most widely used. GIF files are used when you want your image to layer on top of the background color or background image. If you save your image in GIF89a format you can identify areas of the image that show up as transparent to the background color or backup graphic, as shown in Figure 8-18. GIF89a format also supports animation. You can use tools like the GIF Construction Set (http://www.mindworkshop.com/alchemy/alchemy.html) to create animated GIFs to add excitement and motion to your pages.

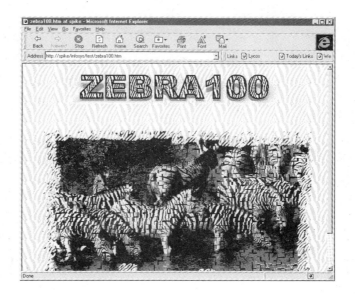

Some
transparent
GIFs
Figure 8-18.

8

Adjusting the Color

Adjusting the color palette used to represent a graphic can alter the size considerably. Most Web graphics use an 8-bit palette representing 256 colors. Rarely do you use all 256 colors in your graphic. By reducing the color palette to a smaller number of colors you can also reduce the size of the overall image. You must strike a balance between a smaller number of colors and the quality of your image. As you reduce the number of colors in the palette, you may also reduce the overall image quality, especially photographic images. You can save your image several different ways, changing the color parameters each time and comparing the resulting image.

When the dimensions of your graphics are small, you can reduce the color palette easily without sacrificing quality. Figure 8-19 shows how you can change from one color palette to another by selecting the Mode option from the Adobe Photoshop menu bar. Table 8-2 illustrates the number of available colors.

Hardware Considerations

Hardware considerations also affect Intranet performance. If your users are running slower 386 or 486 machines, you may get unacceptable performance when downloading large graphics or running video. If everyone has 200Mhz Pentium machines, performance definitely increases. This doesn't mean 386 owners are left out in the cold. It's also a good idea to provide multiple ways of connecting to the same link. You may have a spectacular image-mapped graphic that takes the user to any department in

Changing the color palette in Adobe Photoshop
Figure 8-19.

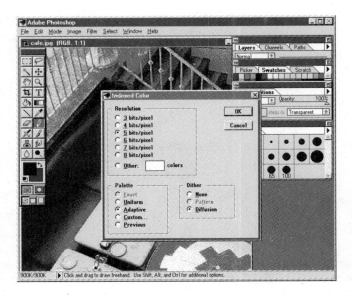

Number of Bits	Number of Colors
1	2
2	4
3	8
4	16
5	32
6	64
7	128
8	256
16	65,536
24	16,777,216

The Number
of Colors in a
Color Palette
Table 8-2.

the company, but if that browser has graphics turned off, you will need to provide an alternative way to navigate to the same pages.

T IP: It is a good practice to provide high-bandwidth and low-bandwidth alternatives to important sections of your Intranet to accommodate a wider range of users. People with slower workstations should still have access to the most crucial parts of your Intranet. Low-bandwidth paths are essential if some users are using text-only browsers.

Multimedia and the Intranet

Multimedia is one of the fastest-growing segments of Web and Intranet content development. Web pages are rapidly moving from a flat-page environment to a world of sight, sound, and motion. Advances in multimedia software and hardware functionality and usability make content development easier than ever. An Intranet can be an ideal place to develop and disseminate multimedia. The following sections discuss strategies and requirements for developing Intranet multimedia, as well as tools for authoring and deploying multimedia content.

Bandwidth and Hardware Requirements

One of the first issues to consider is whether multimedia content is viable on your Intranet. Unfortunately, one of the downsides to using multimedia

8

content is the amount of bandwidth it requires. Bandwidth is the size of the data pipe through which multimedia content is delivered. Sending text-based files takes very little bandwidth when compared with the amount required to send graphics and sound files. Multimedia applications generally require at least a 28.8Kbps modem connection. Ideally, if you wish to implement multimedia over your Intranet, your users should be connected at LAN speeds. Because many corporate networks operate at Ethernet speeds or better, an Intranet can be ideal for implementing multimedia.

In addition to a large data pipe, your users also need appropriate hardware to access multimedia content. Minimally, your users' PCs need 8MB of RAM, SuperVGA support, and a sound card. Ideally, the Intranet workstations that utilize multimedia over the network should have a Pentium or PowerPC processor, 16 to 32MB of RAM, as well as one of the more robust operating systems, such as Windows 95, MacOS 7.5.3, or Windows NT 4.0.

The Multimedia Browser

The software your workstations require greatly depend on the types of media you are using over the Intranet. The Web browser is the most important tool required to access multimedia content. While most Web browsers have at least some multimedia support, some are definitely better than others. Some browsers may not be able to access certain media types. Microsoft's Internet Explorer and Netscape's Navigator are the two premier Web browsers on the market today. They support most multimedia technologies either natively or with the help of a plug-in application.

T **IP:**   A *plug-in* is a helper application that works in conjunction with your Web browser. It may allow your browser to do such things as display video or play audio. Much of the client software we reference later in this chapter is distributed as Web browser plug-ins.

Multimedia Overkill

Your ultimate goal for using multimedia on your Intranet should be better communication and interaction with your end users. If you look around on the World Wide Web, you occasionally find Web pages with a lot of flash but not a lot of content. There might be all sorts of animations and sound but no useful information. Multimedia can be expensive to create and disseminate, so it should do something more than just look good. The benefits derived from your multimedia application should obviously outweigh the costs involved with implementing it. Before you decide to implement multimedia on your Intranet, think about the following:

- Who is my audience?
- What is the information that I need to convey?
- What is the best medium to convey this information?

TIP: You may discover that a simple text page can get a point across simpler and more efficiently than a full audio/video Web page extravaganza, not to mention cheaper.

Microsoft has many excellent examples of pages that integrate multimedia. Microsoft's Mungo Park site (http://mungopark.msn.com/contents/splash.asp), shown in Figure 8-20, includes video and sound files, as well as a good use of graphics.

Creating Multimedia Content

Multimedia combines various elements into a single, stand-alone creation or an interactive presentation. The elements that make up a multimedia presentation might include various combinations of graphics, text, audio, and video. These elements are typically created with the help of specialized

Microsoft's use of multimedia components

Figure 8-20.

software that creates and edits in a specific medium. Most multimedia content is created with the help of the following tools:

- Paint programs (digital artwork, photos)
- Illustration programs for still images (modeled and rendered objects)
- Video digitizing/editing/effects programs
- Audio sampling/editing programs
- Word processors
- Database programs
- Animation programs

Specific content-creation software packages are discussed in the following sections.

Software Packages

There are several software packages on the market that can help you create multimedia content. Some of this software is very specific in what it can do for you. For example, you may use one program to do image rendering, a second to do audio sampling and editing, and a third to combine these elements. There are also all-in-one multimedia authoring suites that come with almost everything you need to create and present multimedia over your Intranet. The following sections cover some of the more well-known multimedia authoring software titles.

Macromedia Director Multimedia Studio   Director Multimedia Studio provides an integrated suite of applications that can help you build and combine all of the multimedia elements that we have previously mentioned. Director includes an object-based scripting/programming language called Lingo, as well as a program called Shockwave that can be used to create animations for Web browser playback. Additionally, there is a free Shockwave plug-in for Netscape and Internet Explorer that lets you view Shockwave animations from within the browser.

 NOTE: Director is a complex program. Users of Director and Lingo should at least be familiar with basic programming principles. You can find more information on Director and other Macromedia multimedia software at http://www.macromedia.com.

Asymetrix ToolBook   ToolBook multimedia applications are built upon the book metaphor. The application is the "book" and the media elements are the "pages." ToolBook's real strength lies in its powerful scripting/programming language called OpenScript. Because of its complexity, users of ToolBook should be familiar with the rudiments of programming. ToolBook is ideal for multimedia developers who wish to disseminate Web-based training materials across the Intranet. Asymetrix also supplies a free, runtime Netscape and Internet Explorer plug-in called Neuron. Neuron lets you view ToolBook-created multimedia from within your browser.

T IP: You can find more information on ToolBook as well as other Asymetrix multimedia software at http://www.asymetrix.com.

AimTech IconAuthor Of the authoring tools we've discussed thus far, IconAuthor is arguably the easiest to use. IconAuthor uses a graphical flow-chart metaphor to help you design your applications. If you can write a flow chart you can create multimedia applications in IconAuthor. AimTech also provides a free runtime player called Present that lets you view IconAuthor applications from within Netscape or Internet Explorer.

T IP: For more information on IconAuthor and other AimTech multimedia software go to http://www.aimtech.com.

Adobe Photoshop Considered by many as the best image-processing tool, Adobe Photoshop is used by multimedia authors to edit computer-generated images, scanned images, and digital photographs.

Adobe Premiere Premiere is a video editing program. It includes tools that allow multimedia developers to capture, edit, and compress movies for playback over an Intranet.

T IP: For more information about Adobe's authoring tools, go to http://www.adobe.com on the World Wide Web.

Deploying Audio

8

Audio is arguably the most widely used form of multimedia on Intranets today. Companies are integrating sound into their Intranet Web pages for such things as employee training and time-sensitive information delivery.

Intranet users can click on a Web hyperlink for real-time audio on demand. It's no longer necessary to download an entire audio clip before being able to listen to it's contents.

With recent advances in compression and streaming technologies, the first part of an audio clip is stored in the workstation's RAM. While that part of the audio file is being played through the browser or audio application, the next part of the file is being downloaded and stored. This process continues until the full clip has been played. In essence, the Web browser or audio application plays the audio as it's being received.

T IP: This technology allows companies to broadcast important corporate events and meetings live over the Intranet for those who cannot personally attend. Furthermore, the event can be archived on the Intranet for easy retrieval.

Audio Streaming Solutions   If you are serious about putting audio content on your Intranet, you need appropriate client- and/or server-based software. There are several products on the market that facilitate the storage and delivery of audio-based multimedia across an Intranet. The most well-known audio solution is a product from Progressive Networks called Real Audio. Real Audio provides client and server software that allows for the storage and retrieval of audio multimedia. The server streams standard audio files, such as WAV or AU files, over the Intranet via the TCP or UDP transport layer. The client interprets and plays the audio file in real time. Xing Technologies' Streamworks and Macromedia's Shockwave software also provide similar audio solutions. In addition to audio support, Steamworks and Shockwave also have video-streaming capabilities, which we discuss later in this chapter.

N OTE: Be aware that these software packages have various hardware/software requirements and may not be compatible with each other. Ask your software vendor about these issues before making any implementation decisions.

Audio on the Cheap   If your multimedia budget is limited, you can still do audio in an inexpensive, if not limited, fashion. You don't necessarily have to purchase expensive client and server software to jazz up your Intranet with audio. There is a wealth of audio clips on the Internet that you can download and link on your Intranet's Web pages. If you wish, you can even record your own audio clips. You need to plug a microphone or some other audio source, such as a tape recorder, into your sound card. Use the software that came with your sound card or software, such as Windows Sound Recorder, to record and save the sound file in one of the common sound-file formats.

NOTE: There are laws governing the reproduction or reuse of sound clips. Be sure to get written permission from the original owner of any sound clip before incorporating it into your Intranet.

WAV and AU Files   The most common audio file formats used on the Internet and Intranets today are WAV and AU files. You could place these files on your Intranet server and hyperlink them on your Web pages. Users who wish to listen to them would click on the link, download the file, and listen to it through their audio software. Keep in mind that even short audio clips that are saved in this fashion can be huge. A 20-second sound clip could be a megabyte or more in size.

Deploying Video and Animation

There are several tools and technologies that can help you add motion to your Intranet's Web pages. Some are quite complex and require varying degrees of programming skill, while others are very simple to learn and use. Video content can range from near-TV quality, full-motion video clips to choppy cartoon-like animations. The three most common video formats used on Intranets today are AVI, MOV, and MPEG files.

Bandwidth Restrictions   One of the biggest drawbacks to using video is the bandwidth it requires. Video files can be rather large and take a significant amount of time to download. For example, a 30-second clip in 24-bit color displayed in quarter-screen size at 15 frames a second takes up approximately 25MB of disk space. A 28.8Kbps modem might take as long as three hours to download a clip this size. An Intranet environment can be ideal for deploying video, because nodes are typically connected at Ethernet speeds (10Mbps) or faster.

Video Streaming Solutions   Like the audio streaming solutions previously mentioned, there are video streaming solutions. In days gone by, if you wanted to view a video, you had to download the clip in its entirety before you could play it back. If the video file was large, it might take hours before you could view it. Streaming is a technology that facilitates fast downloads. It is no longer necessary to download the entire video file before you can view it. A streamed audio feed plays as you are receiving it. There are two

8

types of streaming-video solutions: player-only programs and proprietary, player/server systems. The player-only programs typically stream video without the need for a complementing video server or special video formats. Digigami provides a Netscape plug-in called CineWeb that can view AVI, MOV, and MPEG files on demand. In addition to player-only programs, there are more complex server/player-based streaming solutions. In these solutions, the server piece stores the video and works in unison with the player piece. The player can only view video that is sent to it from the server, and it views it in real time. Once the player interprets and presents the data it receives from the server, it discards it. The video is not saved on the player machine. This is somewhat analogous to a television broadcast. One of the more well-known streaming player/server solutions on the market is a product called VDOLive from the VDONet Corporation. The VDOLive server streams converted AVI files to a VDOLive Web browser player/plug-in. Xing Technologies has a similar player/server solution called Streamworks.

Emerging Technologies

There are several emerging technologies in multimedia of which you should be aware. Some of these technologies may not be fully developed or robust enough for your Intranet, but do warrant mention.

VRML and Three-Dimensional Web Pages

VRML stands for Virtual Reality Modeling Language. VRML allows you to create Web pages in three dimensions just as HTML allows you to create them in two. VRML has the potential of being a very useful tool in creating Web-based multimedia. Imagine an Intranet site created in VRML where you could walk through virtual doors to go from point to point instead of using text-based hyperlinks. Walking through a door would be equivalent to clicking on a hyperlink in a standard Web browser. A virtual filing cabinet might represent a database that you could browse through much as you would browse through any normal filing cabinet.

The idea here is ease of use. Users of VRML-created worlds do not have to know anything about URLs or database queries. The only requirement would be the ability to navigate in a three-dimensional environment, which we all do everyday anyway. Microsoft Internet Explorer and Netscape both have plug-in support for VRML. There are several 3-D authoring tools, including QuickDraw 3D Xtra from Macromedia and TrueSpace from Caligari. You can create 3-D worlds with these tools and convert them into VRML.

T **IP:** The http://www.caligari.com/lvltwo/vrmlprim.html World Wide Web address gives a nice overview of VRML.

The JAVA Programming Language

JAVA is an object-oriented programming language developed by Sun Microsystems. Just as you can write multimedia applications in programming languages such as C++, you can write multimedia in JAVA. JAVA applications, or applets, run through your Web browser. Browsers such as Microsoft's Internet Explorer and Netscape have the ability to interpret and execute applications written in JAVA. It does not matter what operating system you are running, as long as the Web browser you are using can interpret JAVA.

T **IP:** JAVA is a complex programming language and can be difficult to learn and implement. Fortunately, there is a lot of documentation on the Internet and in bookstores on JAVA programming. Many authoring tools, including Macromedia Director, include support for JAVA. The http://www.javasoft.com/doc/index.html World Wide Web address gives some information on JAVA and its capabilities.

ActiveX Controls

ActiveX is Microsoft's version of OLE for the Internet and Intranets. ActiveX controls allow you to use non-HTML content from within a Web browser. If for example you wish to create a Web page that was able to access and display Microsoft Word and Excel documents, you could do so by embedding an ActiveX control into the Web page. Any browser with support for ActiveX could then view the Word and Excel documents from within the Web browser.

Likewise you could create a multimedia application with the help of some authoring tool. You could then provide an ActiveX control with a Web page that would allow anyone with an ActiveX-enabled browser to view your multimedia application. This ActiveX control could facilitate the playback of such things as audio or video, or both, from within the browser. ActiveX controls are typically written in one of the more well-known programming languages, such as C++, or Visual Basic.

8

T IP: The http://www.microsoft.com/activex/gallery/ World Wide Web address gives some good examples and samples of ActiveX controls you could use in Web page development.

GIF89a Animations

The last emerging technology isn't all that new. It's been around since 1989. Furthermore, unlike the technologies we've previously discussed, you don't have to know how to program to create and display GIF89a files. You may have noticed GIF89a files on the Internet and not even realized it. GIF89a files are simple looped animations. They are made up of a series of frames. A typical file has approximately 10 frames. Once the frames are downloaded, they are loaded and reloaded from your browser's cache. A Gif89a animation may be a button that flashes or a hand that waves. Gif89a files don't really do much but are a great way to jazz up a Web page. Gif89a support is built into Microsoft Internet Explorer and Netscape. You can build Gif89a files with a shareware application called Gif Construction Set.

T IP: You can find out more about this program and Gif89a technology at http://www.mindworkshop.com/alchemy/gcsdemo.html.

Putting It All Together

This chapter described some of the ways to create back-end services for your Web site. We looked at some of the more common languages used, as well as some of the more common design problems faced by the HTML program and how to avoid them. Finally, we took a look at some of the ways you can incorporate multimedia into your Web pages.

Reference and Further Reading

Wall, Larry and Randal L. Schwartz. *Programming Perl*. Sebastopol, CA: O'Reilly & Associates, Inc., 1991.

Frequently Asked Questions

♦ **What are some of the programming options available to create back-end services?**

The complexity of the project you are trying to accomplish will be the key factor in determining which tool you use to create your back-end service. A simple form that stores information in a database can easily be accomplished through the use of a Perl script or a small Visual Basic application. A more sophisticated project like an online catalog may warrant the use of a higher-level language, such as C++, that can respond quickly to the user's requests.

♦ **What design principles do I follow to create Web pages?**

Web publishing is very similar to desktop publishing. Many of the principles that guide the desktop publishing industry can be applied to the Web. One of the key elements is to know your audience. You have a pretty good idea of who will be stopping at your site, so choose a style that fits your users. If you are maintaining a site meant for your company's employees, a more casual site may be a nice break from a hectic corporate environment. Consider using more stylistic graphics and some casual fonts. You may also incorporate an entertainment factor by including a few links to your favorite comic strip's sites.

♦ **What version of HTML tags should I use in my Web pages?**

The list of tags available to the HTML programmer is changing rapidly. Lists, bullets, tables, and frames are probably some of the most common structures used in Web pages, but you are limited only by your audience. If you know that all your users will be using a specific browser, by all means take advantage of all the latest tags supported by that browser. On the other hand, if you are not sure who your users might be, it is best to offer several paths to important data. This will ensure that even the oldest browser will have access to your site.

♦ **Should I use multimedia in my Web pages?**

The most commonly used forms of multimedia are sound, animated graphics, and video. Of the three, sound and animated graphics are within the reach of most of the hardware and software available to users on the Web today. Even with the latest streaming technology, video is still reserved for Intranets with high bandwidth capabilities. You won't make any friends if users have to download a 2MB video clip over a 28.8Kbps dial-up connection every time they load your page. Wise use of multimedia elements will make your pages more exciting and possibly more effective. Once again, be sure to consider all your Intranet users when incorporating multimedia.

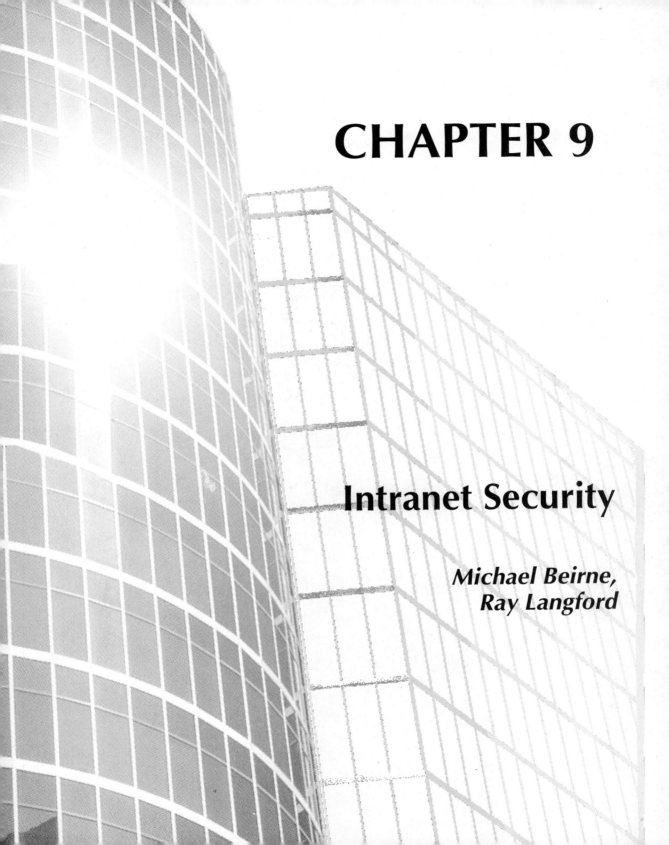

CHAPTER 9

Intranet Security

Michael Beirne,
Ray Langford

Chapter Objectives

◆ Learn the basics of network security

◆ Identify the threats to your Intranet

◆ Uncover the vulnerabilities of your Intranet

◆ Implement strategies for an Intranet security policy

◆ Explore the rudiments of perimeter and firewall security, and Intranet application security requirements

◆ Learn about encryption/digital signatures, authentication schemes, and security management techniques

◆ Become familiar with the emerging security protocol standards

S top for a second and think about the importance of security to your Intranet. What if your Intranet is infiltrated by electronic intruders or hackers who snoop around for such things as passwords or account information; sensitive, confidential, or valuable corporate information is compromised; hackers damage your network and the systems connected to it; employees use the Intranet for inappropriate or illegal activity, exposing the company to liability; individuals impersonate representatives of the company via e-mail or Web communication; or virus strains work their way on to your Intranet and the systems connected to it?

Preparing for the Unexpected

It's not that things *will* happen if you don't implement appropriate security measures across your Intranet, but rather that they *can* happen. Some of the suggestions and strategies mentioned in this chapter may seem excessive or even paranoid. Some of the ideas we present may not even be appropriate for your Intranet. We don't wish to frighten or alarm, but rather to inform. Our aim is to discuss the risks, highlight emerging security solutions, and provide strategies for deploying a complete security program across your Intranet.

TIP: Security can be expensive, difficult to implement, high maintenance, and cause intense prolonged headaches. The costs of having your entire information hierarchy wiped out, however, provides compelling reasons for appropriate security measures.

There are really only two steps in securing an Intranet:

◆ Identifying potential threats and vulnerabilities

◆ Implementing appropriate countermeasures

The Primary Issues

The primary issues in a complete security program are the protection of an Intranet's data, its applications, and its hardware. This includes ensuring that users can only perform tasks they are authorized for and only obtain the information they are authorized to have. The word "security" connotes protection against attack by some nefarious hacker, but remember that it should also control the effects of errors and equipment failures. The idea here is to build a complete security program. The more pervasive your security program is, the safer your Intranet is from unforeseen pitfalls.

Some Basic Security Concepts

Before we discuss the specific tools you can use to secure your Intranet, it helps to understand the basic concepts that are essential to any security system.

Know Your Enemy

It is a good idea to think about who might try to infiltrate your Intranet and what might motivate this individual to do this. It could be some cyberpunk with too much time on his hands or an employee in your sales department who is wondering how his paycheck compares to his co-worker's. You are never totally secure on your Intranet, but you can make sure the network security measures you implement are beyond either the ability or motivation of would-be attackers.

Know the Risk and Cost

Analyze the risk of a specific security breach versus the cost of preventing such a breach. Security measures can be expensive and cause work delays. A firewall is a security measure that many Intranets implement to protect the network perimeter from outsiders. Additionally it can prevent insiders from knowingly or unknowingly sending sensitive data outside the network. Purchasing firewall software and hardware for an Intranet with 50 nodes can easily cost you $10,000 or more. The costs involved with administering a firewall can also be significant.

TIP: Ask yourself if the risks of compromise are great enough to warrant the cost of a specific security measure. We'll discuss risk and cost in more detail, later in this chapter.

Additionally, remember that security costs aren't always quantifiable. For example, a firewall might slow the average connection speed to the Internet for your users. This may only mean a few kilobytes per second in most situations, but if you multiply the extra time required for all your Intranet nodes over a year's time, it could be significant. Time that would normally be spent completing daily mission critical tasks is instead spent waiting for data to download.

Examine Your Assumptions

It is easy to assume things about the construction of your Intranet and the security measures implemented over it. For example, don't assume that just because you have a firewall that there aren't other entry points to your network. A thief doesn't always enter through the front door. If you assume that your firewall is the only entry point to your Intranet, you may be ignoring such things as physical security. Be aware that your assumptions can breed security holes. Take regular inventory of the security measures implemented across your Intranet and identify any assumptions you may have about them.

Remember That People Are People

If you implement security measures that are difficult for users to understand or use, you are asking for trouble. Unless users understand why they need to follow certain security procedures, they can resist and perhaps circumvent those measures, and in turn open up security holes on the Intranet. For example, if the software and procedures used to encrypt e-mail on your Intranet are difficult to use or time consuming, don't be surprised if the software is used incorrectly, or worse, your users choose not to use encryption at all.

 TIP: Even the strongest encryption algorithm is useless if it's not being used. Although it is not always possible, the ideal security measure should not require any input or follow-through from the end user. It should be transparent.

Identify Access Points

Make sure to limit exposure of your systems to attack. This is best accomplished by identifying all access points to the Intranet. You can have an expensive, top-of-the-line firewall to keep outsiders off your network, but all it takes is a $50 modem connected to one of the PCs on the Intranet to make the firewall worthless in a security sense. Why install a secure front door if you're going to leave the windows wide open? Always remember that your Intranet is only as secure as its weakest security point.

Remember Physical Security

Forget about networks or firewalls for a second. If attackers have physical access to your Intranet server or one of the clients, those intruders can pretty much do whatever they want. By "physical security", we are referring to measures of the lock and key variety. Physically secure the Intranet server and all Intranet nodes.

Be Aware of the Effects of Change

As your Intranet and the services it provides grow and change, be aware of the effects these changes could have on your security program. Try to anticipate the growth and change that your Intranet might go through. It may be easier and more cost-effective to implement a security countermeasure now even if this countermeasure is not necessary right away. If, for example, you know that your company is considering electronic commerce options on your Web site for the future, it may be a good idea to purchase appropriate hardware/software now as opposed to later. The costs involved with implementation later may be significantly higher if you wait.

Some of these costs may be related to such things as

♦ Purchase and reinstallation of updated security software

♦ Change in security procedures

♦ Retraining of the user base

 NOTE: The Computer Emergency Response Team (CERT) is an organization that provides various security services for the Internet community. These services include a hot line for reporting security incidents, as well as a collection of security documentation and information. You can find more information on CERT and the services they provide at the following Internet address: http://www.cert.org/cert.faqintro.html

Security Threats to Your Intranet

An Intranet, and any data that passes through it, is vulnerable to attack. There is no such thing as a totally secure Intranet. Depending on how your Intranet is configured, some threats may or may not pertain to your particular topology. For example, if you are setting up a small Intranet that is not connected to the Internet, many of the issues we discuss in the following sections become less threatening or even irrelevant. However, as we stated earlier, your Intranet and the services that it provides may grow or change. This growth and change can breed unexpected threats and give rise to unforeseen vulnerabilities. The following sections highlight many of the threats you need to be aware of.

Types of Threats

Threats can come from inside the Intranet or from any connected, external networks, including the Internet. Various studies have indicated that the majority of threats (80 to 95 percent) come from within the internal network. Although your focus should be on identifying threats that come from inside the firewall, do not forget the threats that come from outside the firewall. Threats come in all shapes and sizes. Some are more common than others. Table 9-1 illustrates the types of security threats to your Intranet.

NOTE: Understanding the threat environment will help you decide which countermeasures to implement on your Intranet. The following sections highlight specific examples of threats. Later in the chapter, we discuss potential countermeasures.

Malicious Code

Malicious code refers to uninvited software that can do any number of things to your Intranet and the systems connected to it. Malicious code can attack personal computers as well as more sophisticated systems, including your Intranet servers. The best defense against malicious code is to keep it off your Intranet entirely. Unfortunately this is not an easy task.

Vulnerability	Threat
Corporate network	The connectivity an Intranet provides and the protocols it uses may expose your corporate network to attack. Any network systems, including mainframes, databases, and file systems, that are directly or indirectly connected to your Intranet are potentially vulnerable.
Intranet servers	Servers directly connected to your Intranet are subject to intrusion, and, therefore, all of the information stored on these servers can be viewed and altered.
Data transmission	Information that is transmitted over your Intranet is subject to attack. The confidentiality and integrity of this information can be compromised by unauthorized individuals.
Service availability	An attack by nefarious individuals can disable the systems on your network or the entire network.
Repudiation	Electronic communication can be repudiated. One or more participants in an electronic dialogue can later deny participation in that dialogue.

Types of
Security
Threats to
Your Intranet
Table 9-1.

9

T IP: Educate your users on the dangers of malicious software and implement guidelines for installing and using untrusted software on the Intranet. Furthermore, make sure that you have the appropriate tools to detect and clean malicious software. There is a variety of software packages, including e-mail viewers and Web browsers, that have the ability to invoke virus detection and eradication software when Internet downloads and/or connections are initiated.

Malicious-code software includes

♦ *Virus* A code segment that replicates by attaching itself to another program in computer memory or on a disk. The virus may do any number of things once it has been run or specific conditions have been met. It may just flash a message on a specific date or it may destroy your hard drive. There are many different types of viruses, including overwriting, polymorphic, resident, stealth, and variants. Most viruses infect systems via software and files that are installed on a PC. For example, a user could download a document from the Internet that is infected with a virus. If the user views the document on one of the Intranet PCs and subsequently shares the document with others via e-mail, the virus could potentially spread across the Intranet and cause damage.

♦ *Trojan horse* A program that purports to be something that it is not. It may include malicious code that can do unexpected (and undesirable) things once it's been installed on a system. A prime example of a Trojan horse is a program called PKZ300.ZIP. It was placed on various Internet sites for anyone to download. It identified itself as an upgrade to a popular compression utility. Anyone who downloaded the file to their computer soon realized that it didn't quite do what it was advertised to do. When users attempted to expand or install the file, it erased each and every file on their hard drive.

♦ *Worm* A program that breaks into a network and then reproduces itself. Unlike a virus, a worm is self-contained and does not require a host program. While a virus piggybacks on files to get from one computer system to another, a worm is able to get around by itself via network connections. Probably the most well-known worm was unleashed on the Internet on November 2, 1988, by Robert Tappan Morris, a 23-year-old grad student at Cornell University. Mr. Morris' Internet Worm eventually broke into over 6,000 computer systems across the country. All of the systems that the Internet Worm infiltrated were Unix based. The worm was written to exploit security holes it found in Unix programs such as Sendmail and Fingerd. After gaining access to a system, the worm disabled the system by reproducing itself and running all the copies of itself simultaneously. This process would use up all the system resources on the computer systems, rendering them unusable. In a short period of time, Mr. Morris' worm crashed a large segment of the Internet. Ironically, the code for the Internet Worm was only 91 lines in length.

Physical and Infrastructure Threats

Power outages or natural disasters such as floods and lightning strikes are examples of physical or infrastructure threats. Physical tampering or hardware destruction also falls into this category. System backups are a simple way to prevent loss of your Intranet data to such unpredictable threats. Don't forget to take these threats into consideration when forging and implementing your security program.

The Threat of Hackers

Hackers can break into your Intranet for various reasons. Some just want to snoop around, while others may wish to steal information or damage your network and its systems. Unfortunately, there is no way to identify the motivations of a hacker. Above all, do not underestimate the damage they can do to your Intranet. Although hackers and their exploits are somewhat overhyped, they are still a threat that needs to be taken seriously.

Corporate Espionage

As companies move their proprietary secrets from their filing cabinets to their Intranets, electronic espionage can increase. Be aware of the value of the information you put up on your Intranet. Be aware that competitors and enemies of your company could greatly benefit from any secrets they may find on your Intranet.

Disgruntled Employees

Disgruntled employees can create both mischief and sabotage on a computer system. Employees are the group most familiar with their employer's computers and applications, including knowing what actions might cause the most damage. If an employee is leaving the company, invalidate his or her passwords and delete all system accounts in a timely manner.

Fraud and Theft

Most companies utilize some sort of computer-based accounting system. Additionally, many companies are starting to buy and sell goods and services over the Internet. The threat of computer fraud and theft increases as accounting and commerce systems move into the electronic age. Furthermore, electronic fund transfers are becoming the standard. Authentication software is a key countermeasure against fraud and theft. We discuss emerging authentication-security measures later in this chapter.

Security Vulnerabilities

There are security vulnerabilities that you need to be aware of as you build your Intranet and implement a security program over it. In the next section we discuss some of the more well-known vulnerabilities to Intranet/Internet-based networks, including password systems and TCP/IP, message authenticity, and weak security policies.

The Password System

Passwords systems are, by far, the most exploited vulnerability on networks. Password attacks involve compromising a password on a system. It has been estimated that insecure passwords cause 80 percent of all network security problems. There is readily available software that enters a dictionary of password guesses until it eventually matches a password. If a user's password can be found in the dictionary it can most likely be cracked by such software. Even though password attacks are simple in concept, they are surprisingly successful given the fact that it is a relatively simple attack to prevent. Make sure that passwords on your Intranet are changed often and secure from compromise. User's passwords should be selected with the following criteria in mind:

♦ Minimum of eight characters in length

♦ Mix of letters, numbers, and symbols

♦ Both upper- and lowercase

♦ Shouldn't be found in the dictionary

The Language of TCP/IP

TCP/IP, the language of Intranets and the public Internet, is not inherently secure. Furthermore, applications that use TCP/IP as their transport can be vulnerable to attack. TCP/IP was created with the idea of interconnecting various military, research, and university sites. The idea was not to limit access, but to expand it. When TCP/IP and many of its related protocols were defined, security was not a concern. Many Intranet/Internet protocols have only recently been enhanced to support native security functionality.

NOTE: One of TCP/IP's biggest shortcomings is its inability to authenticate the identity of a host. Furthermore, it is relatively easy to imitate other IP hosts and difficult to provide a secure and private communication channel between hosts. Be aware that in certain Intranet environments, these vulnerabilities can be easily exploited by individuals with a little knowledge and the right tools.

Network snooping and IP spoofing (explained in the following sections) are perhaps the most common attacks that exploit weaknesses in the TCP/IP protocol.

Sniffer/Snoop Attacks   Intruders can easily gain access to files and passwords by using sniffer or snoop software and hardware. Sniffer software and hardware monitors and captures TCP/IP packets as they pass from computer to computer across a network. These packets can contain password information as well as sensitive data. One of the more publicized cases of an intruder hacking into a TCP/IP network occurred on March 24, 1994, at Rome Laboratories. The intruder used sniffer software to capture network-user passwords and from there accessed confidential internal information. Fortunately, the intruder was detected and eventually arrested. Most strategies to stop sniffer attacks are time consuming or impractical for the typical IS department. The use of strong cryptography on your Intranet is probably the best defense against sniffer software or hardware.

NOTE: Later in this chapter, we discuss such technologies as S/MIME and Secure Sockets Layer, which are encryption-based technologies. These technologies may hopefully render sniffer software and hardware attacks obsolete.

IP Spoofing   IP spoofing is a practice where an attacking computer assumes the identity of a trusted computer on a network to gain access to a third computer and any services or information that it provides. To illustrate IP spoofing, let's assume there are three computers called Alpha, Beta, and Zed. Alpha and Beta are located on your Intranet. Alpha is an internal Web server that normally only grants access to trusted computers located on the Intranet, including Beta. Zed is located off of the Intranet. Because Zed is not located on the Intranet and is unknown to Alpha, it normally has no access rights to Alpha. To access Alpha, Zed will *spoof* Alpha into thinking that it is actually Beta. Zed negotiates an IP connection with Alpha by using Beta's IP address, as well as specific information about IP sequencing numbers that Alpha normally uses. Once Zed negotiates a session with Alpha, it must also disable Beta's ability to receive packets from Alpha. After all, if Beta received packets from Alpha indicating that they were communicating, when in fact they were not, it would reply to Alpha and the spoofing attack would be over. Zed does this by sending an overflow of packets to Beta while simultaneously communicating with Alpha. Beta's capacity would be overrun by these packets—in effect, disabling its ability to send or receive any IP packets. Alpha would meanwhile assume that it is talking to Beta when in fact it is talking Zed. Zed would have all the access rights to Alpha that Beta normally has. Figure 9-1 illustrates a spoofing attack.

TIP: The best way to defend against spoofing attacks is to set up a firewall and configure it to reject or drop any incoming packets that claim to originate from inside the Intranet. We will discuss firewalls in more detail later in this chapter.

Message Authenticity

Authenticating who you are communicating with can also become a security issue on your Intranet and the Internet. If someone with an e-mail address of president@whitehouse.gov sent you an e-mail, how could you verify that the sender is indeed the person he or she says they are? By the same token, when you connect to http://www.whitehouse.gov, how can you verify that you are connecting to the site that URL purports it to be? TCP/IP and HTTP alone make it relatively simple to impersonate a host, person, or

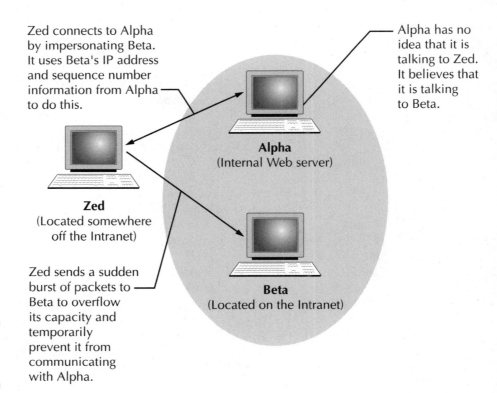

Zed connects to Alpha by impersonating Beta. It uses Beta's IP address and sequence number information from Alpha to do this.

Alpha has no idea that it is talking to Zed. It believes that it is talking to Beta.

Alpha
(Internal Web server)

Zed
(Located somewhere off the Intranet)

Zed sends a sudden burst of packets to Beta to overflow its capacity and temporarily prevent it from communicating with Alpha.

Beta
(Located on the Intranet)

A spoofing attack
Figure 9-1.

organization. Digital certificates uniquely identify individuals and organizations and are a relatively new solution to these questions of user and system authentication. The specifics of digital signatures are discussed later in the chapter.

Weak Security Policies

A weak or poorly implemented security policy can open security holes leaving your Intranet vulnerable. Companies should provide a security policy for all users of its networks and systems. This can be one of the easier and most inexpensive ways to close security holes on your Intranet. It does require some time and perhaps vigilance, but it can save your Intranet and network from attack. In the next section, we discuss security policy development and implementation.

Implementing a Security Policy

You and your company will need to take strong and specific measures to disseminate a complete security program across your Intranet. A complete security program uses a solid and comprehensive security policy as its basis. In the following sections, we discuss strategies for creating an effective security policy for your Intranet.

Setting Goals

The first step to devising an Intranet security policy is to set the goals you want to achieve with it. Start by asking yourself the following:

♦ What am I protecting?
♦ What threatens these things I wish to protect?

Additionally, it is a good idea to consult with other persons who are using and administering the Intranet. Ask what they feel should be the corporate security priorities. If, for example, your primary goal is to protect your legacy database systems against attack from outsiders, a firewall and its administration might be a big priority in your security program and any security policies you implement. Determine your goals, and from your goals determine your priorities.

Costs Versus Risk

Before assigning security goals and priorities, take inventory of the potential threats and vulnerabilities we discussed earlier and compare the cost of a specific security breach to the cost of implementing and administering a security countermeasure against that breach. If the countermeasure costs more than the eventual cost of the security breach, then maybe the countermeasure is not worth implementing. After all, only a fool would buy a $500 automobile and then buy a $1,000 car alarm to protect it, right?

Unfortunately, it's not always a clear-cut decision. It is sometimes difficult to put a price tag on an Intranet asset and its ultimate worth to a company. Say, for example, that all of your Intranet users from the bottom of the corporate hierarchy to the top use e-mail across the network and Internet. The overwhelming majority of the e-mail sent back and forth would be meaningless and useless to anyone other than the original sender and the intended recipient of the message. Think, however, of the value of certain information sent across your Intranet via e-mail. What if a manager in your quality assurance department sent an e-mail to the manager of your production department and innocently referred to a defect in one of your products. This information might seem harmless enough, until you think about the damage this information might do to your company and its reputation if it fell into the hands of a competitor or enemy. Always consider the ultimate cost of a security breach.

Writing It Down

After determining the security goals and priorities for your company, put it down in writing. Ideally, the document you create is analogous to a standard employee handbook. It should include guidelines that clearly state what's expected from each and every Intranet user and administrator. This might include such things as

♦ Users' rights and responsibilities

♦ Acceptable use of the Intranet and its resources

♦ Virus and malicious code procedures

♦ Account maintenance procedures

♦ Password guidelines

♦ Procedures for securing and using Intranet applications

♦ Procedures for identifying and reporting security problems and breaches

TIP: Most of the protocols and policies used on the Internet are defined in a collection of documents called RFCs (Request For Comments). RFC1244 is a document entitled "Site Security Handbook." It is a great reference for information on setting up a security policy on an Intranet. You can find this document on the Internet at the following address: http://ds.internic.net/ds/dspg1intdoc.html

Your Intranet Security Policy would be a good document to use to inaugurate your Intranet server. Put it up on the Intranet server for all to see and use.

Working with Firewalls

A firewall's job is to define and defend a perimeter of a network. They are generally placed in between an internal, trusted network and an external, untrusted network. Firewalls are the network equivalent of a doorman for an Intranet and the subnetworks found therein. In a simple sense, a firewall determines who is authorized to enter or leave a protected network or subnetwork. A firewall can protect your private Intranet from the public Internet, but it can also protect different subnetworks on your Intranet. For example, your finance department may have a Web server that you wish to secure from the rest of the Intranet. This could be accomplished by using a firewall between your finance department subnetwork and the rest of the Intranet. The following sections discuss the different firewall implementations.

Packet-Filtering Firewalls

Many Intranets that are connected to the Internet connect through a single router. This router, more often than not, is where the firewall/filtering software runs. Many routers have built-in packet-filtering capabilities. The biggest advantages of packet filters are their speed and transparency to users. Neither the source nor destination needs to be aware of a packet-filtering firewall between them. Your router/firewall vendor should have further information on its configuration and filtering capabilities.

How Packets Work

To understand how a packet-filtering router works, you need to know what a packet is. All information that is sent out over your Intranet or the Internet is sent in discrete chunks of data called *packets*. If, for example, you are using your browser to view a Web page on your Intranet, the initial query to the HTTP server might be made up of several packets of information. Each packet has a header that includes such information as your Internet Protocol (IP) address, the IP address of the HTTP server, and the port on the server you wish to access. The HTTP server returns the Web page you requested in the form of several packets of information that are reassembled into a format your Web browser can interpret. A packet-filtering firewall regulates the transport of this data between network nodes by reading and reacting to the information found in each packet that tries to traverse it.

An Internet/Intranet Example

Let's say, for example, that your Intranet is connected to the Internet. We'll also assume that you wish to restrict access to an HTTP server on your Intranet so that only those network nodes located inside the firewall can get to it. A way to do this would be to set up a rule on your firewall to reject or drop any incoming packets requesting connection to your HTTP server's port. The firewall would search for this port number in the header of all incoming packets. Any incoming packet headers that include a port query that matches the port on your HTTP server, and therefore the port number in your firewall rule, are either discarded or rejected. All other traffic coming into your Intranet should be unaffected. Figure 9-2 illustrates this example.

Proxy Servers

A proxy server can be used as a stand-alone firewall or in conjunction with other firewall hardware and/or software. For example, a company may wish to set up a packet-filtering firewall for perimeter security and use it in conjunction with a proxy server. The proxy server would provide a

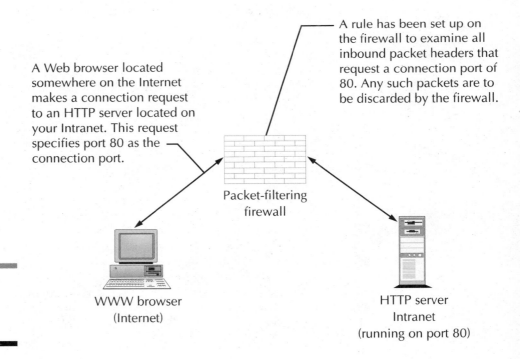

A rule has been set up on the firewall to examine all inbound packet headers that request a connection port of 80. Any such packets are to be discarded by the firewall.

A Web browser located somewhere on the Internet makes a connection request to an HTTP server located on your Intranet. This request specifies port 80 as the connection port.

Packet-filtering firewall

WWW browser
(Internet)

HTTP server
Intranet
(running on port 80)

A packet-filtering firewall

Figure 9-2.

controllable doorway through the firewall and out to the unprotected external network. Proxy servers pass packets back and forth between source and destination computers just as packet-filtering firewalls do. The difference between the two is described as follows:

♦ A packet-filtering firewall works on a packet-by-packet basis. It merely monitors the packet traffic and reacts to it based on rules you provide to it. A packet-filtering firewall is unaware of the content of the packets.

♦ A proxy server simultaneously connects to both the source and destination nodes. It receives a connection request from the source computer, establishes a connection, and then terminates that same connection. At the same time, the proxy server establishes a connection to the destination computer and, likewise, terminates this same connection. This provides superior security because the source and destination computers are never actually connected to each other.

For example, if you are connecting to an Internet site from a Web browser on your Intranet, your browser would first establish a connection to the proxy server. The proxy server would look and act just like a Web server to your Web browser. The proxy server would then make a second connection to the destination WWW server. The proxy server would look and act just like a Web browser to the destination Web browser. These connections would run concurrently and would be transparent to both the source and destination computers. Figure 9-3 illustrates a proxy server. The different types of proxy servers are described in the following sections.

An Application-Specific Proxy Server

An application-specific proxy only handles connections for a specific application protocol. For example, you may decide to install an FTP proxy server on your Intranet. It would listen for FTP connection requests. After receiving a connection request and user ID information from some FTP client on your Intranet, the FTP proxy server would then determine, based on the criteria you provide, if there are any restrictions on the connection. If the connection is allowed, the FTP proxy would establish a second connection to the destination FTP server, and then shuttle information between the two simultaneously running connections.

The trick is that the FTP proxy server knows how to act like both an FTP server and an FTP client. Remember that this server will *only* handle FTP traffic. If you have users who wish to use their browsers to connect to World Wide Web sites, they could not use the FTP proxy server to get out to the Internet. You would need to install an HTTP proxy server to service any Web browsers on your Intranet.

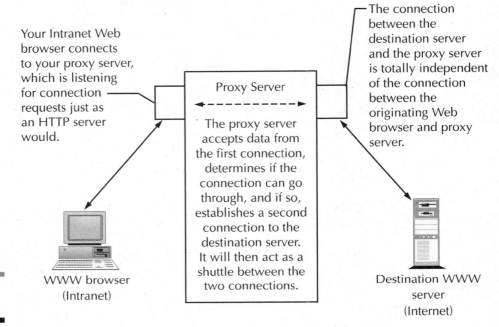

Your Intranet Web browser connects to your proxy server, which is listening for connection requests just as an HTTP server would.

The connection between the destination server and the proxy server is totally independent of the connection between the originating Web browser and proxy server.

Proxy Server

The proxy server accepts data from the first connection, determines if the connection can go through, and if so, establishes a second connection to the destination server. It will then act as a shuttle between the two connections.

WWW browser
(Intranet)

Destination WWW
server
(Internet)

A proxy server
Figure 9-3.

NOTE: Application-specific proxy servers are not always transparent to the end user. It can be complicated to use an application proxy server with certain Intranet software.

A SOCKS (Circuit) Proxy Server

A SOCKS proxy server works pretty much the same way as other proxy servers. The main difference is that the server is unaware of the protocols that are passing through it. SOCKS is a protocol in itself. Because of this fact, any applications that wish to use a SOCKS proxy server must have a way to communicate with the SOCKS server. Either the TCP/IP software or the application itself needs to support the SOCKS protocol. The advantage of a SOCKS server is that a single proxy server can handle network traffic from a variety of applications. You don't have to administer a proxy server for each application (for example, FTP, HTTP, and Gopher) that is used on your Intranet.

NOTE: Once the appropriate SOCKS-aware TCP/IP or applications software is installed and configured on the Intranet's clients, the SOCKS server should be totally transparent to any client that needs to use it. A user would connect to an external Web site in exactly the same fashion as an internal Web site.

Securing Your Intranet Applications

There are a number of different aspects of securing your Intranet applications, including such things as security policies, secure access and control for applications, and implementation of secure protocols. Your Intranet may utilize both client/server and store-and-forward types of applications that require different methods of security. For interactive client/server applications (Web, search, directories, etc.) protocols like Secure Sockets Layer (SSL) or Private Communications Technology (PCT) are more appropriate, whereas for store-and-forward applications (e-mail, discussion, etc.) protocols like Secure MIME (S/MIME) are more applicable. We discuss the specifics behind these protocols later in this chapter.

Encryption, Decryption, and Digital Signatures

For individuals to communicate, collaborate, and access sensitive information in both an Internet and Intranet environment, there are a number of requirements that must be met to ensure that your network resources are protected. Confidentiality, access control, integrity, authentication, and nonrepudiation are the key criteria and necessary parts of any complete Internet and Intranet security program. Cryptography has emerged as a potential solution to all of these security requirements. Encryption, decryption, and digital signatures are all subsets of the science of cryptography.

Encryption/Decryption

Encryption addresses confidentiality and access control requirements by making data unavailable to unauthorized individuals. Encryption changes readable format data into an unreadable format. Decryption, by contrast, changes this unreadable format back into readable, plain text. This encryption and decryption is carried out with the help of a key or keys. Only authorized individuals would have the information (key) required to encrypt and subsequently decrypt messages. The specifics of key cryptography are as follows:

♦ *Confidentiality*   Ensures that data in either a client/server connection (Web client/server) or end-to-end communication (e-mail) is not disclosed to unauthorized persons.

♦ *Access control*   Ensures that only those who are authorized to view or modify data on a corporate server can access that data.

Digital Signatures

Digital signatures address integrity, authentication, and nonrepudiation requirements. A digital signature is analogous to a handwritten signature, in that a digital signature can be used to assure a reader of the (nonrepudiable) source of the information. A digital signature travels with the data or attached to the data/text file. In addition, a digital signature can ensure that any unauthorized changes to the data are detected (integrity). The specifics of digital signatures are as follows:

♦ *Integrity*   Ensures that the data has not been altered since it was originally created. There are a number of situations in which integrity of data is critical; for example, in e-mail communications where it is important to be sure the content of a message has not been altered.

♦ *Authentication*   Provides proof of the source of data in that one can verify the authenticity and identity of the originator of the connection (Web client/server) or message (e-mail).

♦ *Nonrepudiation*   When someone repudiates involvement in a situation under dispute, they deny having any involvement in the problematic situation. Nonrepudiation in the context of Internet or Intranet security refers to ensuring that someone cannot deny involvement in an electronic transaction; for example, if someone were to send an e-mail message stating opinions or a position, the sender could not later deny that the message was sent.

Key Cryptography

There are two basic methods of key cryptography, which function as follows:

♦ *Symmetric or private key cryptography*   This method has been around as long as the science of cryptography itself. A message is scrambled using a secret key and unscrambled using the same secret key. This method does not work well in situations where you are exchanging encrypted data with more than a few people. The biggest problem is finding a secure way to exchange secret keys with all parties that you will be communicating with. Furthermore, you also have to remember which key decrypts which data. This type of cryptography system is not practical for a typical Intranet.

♦ *Asymmetric or public key cryptography* This method solves many of the problems of private key cryptography. Public key cryptography uses a pair of keys that are related mathematically. One of the keys is available to the public and the other is kept private. Messages that are encrypted with the public key can only be decrypted with the private key, and, likewise, messages that are encrypted with the private key can only be decrypted by the public key.

Sending an Encrypted Message   Let's assume that you wish to send an encrypted message to an Intranet user called Harry, and that both you and Harry have a public/private key set. You would encrypt the message by using Harry's public key. Harry could make his public key available to you via a certificate server or e-mail. It doesn't matter who has access to Harry's public key because you would need access to Harry's private key to decrypt a message encrypted with his public key. In fact, anyone who has access to Harry's public key can encrypt messages with it, and since only Harry has access to his private key, only he can decrypt these messages.

Digitally Signing a Message   Public-key cryptography also gives you the ability to digitally sign a message. A digital signature electronically verifies the identity of a data sender and the integrity of the data itself. For example, if Harry wanted to send you a signed message, he would encrypt the message with his private key. Once you receive the message, you would use Harry's public key to decrypt it. Again, you would get Harry's public key from a certificate server via e-mail or from within the message itself. If you are able to use Harry's public key to decrypt the message, the data must have been signed by the private key known only by Harry.

CAUTION: Encryption/Decryption and Digital Signatures are only effective if the appropriate encryption keys are used and they are kept private. All encrypted information can potentially be cracked, but exposure of the encryption keys unlocks all data. For this reason, operations using key encryption must be handled carefully, because much of the security is built upon the trust of the parties involved. Furthermore, the loss of an encryption key can make data inaccessible.

Certificates and Certificate Authorities

One of the problems with asymmetric key cryptography is the issue of trust. If someone wants to impersonate another person, all she needs to do is generate a public/private key set and publish the public key under someone else's name. For example, Harry could create a public/private key set and make the public key available under your name. Any documents signed with the bogus private key that Harry created could be verified with the bogus public key he's published in your name. Harry could, in essence, sign his messages with your name. People could be fooled into thinking that his messages are actually yours. The problem is verifying that the public key is indeed from the person it says it is. You could physically hand your public key to everyone that you are communicating with, but this becomes impractical with more than a few people. The best solution to this problem is the use of certificates and certificate authorities:

♦ *A public key certificate*   This is a digital document that attaches the identity of an individual or server to a public/private key set. Unfortunately, this document could be forged as well, which makes the concept of a certificate authority necessary.

♦ *A certificate authority (CA)*   This is a trusted authority that vouches for the identities of individuals or servers to whom it issues certificates. It is essential that the CA's public key is distributed from a trusted server.

Some software vendors are distributing well-known CA's public keys with their security-aware applications. The CA's identity might be vouched for with a certificate signed by another CA. There could conceivably be a hierarchy structure where verification of identity is distributed among several CAs. A CA from above would verify that a CA below it can be trusted, and so forth. There might be different requirements, depending on the CA, to prove one's identity.

NOTE: This process of ascertaining identity is called the *proofing process*. Some CAs might only require your word that you are who you say you are, while others might require you to appear in person with proper identification in hand. Keep in mind that a CA is only useful if it is trusted.

Client Authentication

Client authentication is a process whereby a server identifies and authenticates a client/user. This process would require that your Intranet server supports the ability to authenticate client applications that establish a secure channel session with either passwords or with public-key certificates, both of which would need to be integrated into your Intranet server architecture. Additionally, your Intranet e-mail clients may require the ability to identify and authenticate other e-mail users using secure end-to-end communication.

NOTE: This can be accomplished with public-key certificates that would need to be integrated into your e-mail application. An application that uses public-key certificates can electronically establish its identity with another network host.

Certificate-Based Authentication

Access to information stored on an Intranet server can be controlled by mapping a user's certificates to groups or user accounts and assigning access control permissions to the group or user account using the standard access control list (ACL) mechanisms that would be a part of your Intranet servers. An ACL permits or limits access to an Intranet resource based on such things as usernames, passwords, and groups.

Secure Channel/Certificate Authentication
Client authentication using a secure channel and certificates requires the following:

♦ The secure channel protocol must be able to authenticate bidirectionally, which means both the client and server must handle certificates.

♦ The client must be able to verify server certificates, request and store personal certificates, and present a personal certificate to the server when requested by the server.

♦ The server must be able to request a server certificate, verify client certificates, and map client certificates received from the client to the standard, access control list used on the server.

An emerging standard for secure channel protocol used by many Intranet clients and servers is Secure Sockets Layer version 3 (SSL3). The SSL3 protocol supports all the requirements for certificate-based client authentication.

NOTE: Typical Intranet applications that support a secure channel are the Web (HTTP) client and server, the discussion (NNTP) client and server, and the directory (LDAP) client and server.

Secure End-to-End Communication
The requirements for secure, end-to-end communication are similar to that for a secure channel.

♦ The secure end-to-end communication protocol must be able to provide bidirectional message signature and enveloping (encryption) operations.

♦ The end application (used in end-to-end communication) must be able to verify received certificates, request and store personal certificates, and use the user's private key to sign messages. The end application must also be able to envelope messages by acquiring and using the certificate for users at the other end of the secure end-to-end communication.

An emerging standard for secure end-to-end communication protocol used by many Intranet applications is S/MIME. The S/MIME protocol supports all the requirements for certificate-based client authentication.

NOTE: Typical Intranet applications that support secure end-to-end communication are the e-mail (SMTP/POP) application and the discussion (NNTP) client.

The Advantages of Certificate-Based Authentication

Client authentication based on certificates has the following advantages over other types of client authentication based on passwords, IP addresses, DNS names, or e-mail addresses:

♦ *No passwords flowing from client to server*   Since certificates are public information, users are authenticated without sending sensitive information like passwords over a network.

♦ *Better means of identifying the user*   Certificates contain verifiable information about the user's identity, rather than authentication based on a user's IP address, domain name, or e-mail address. Also, IP addresses can be dynamic—based on the network configuration, since domain names and e-mail address can be easily spoofed.

♦ *Improved user experience through single logon*   As users connect to many different Intranet servers, they no longer have to log into each one. They simply log on once to the client application and their certificate is presented to the server providing their identity information.

♦ *Stronger authentication*   Since certificates are based on public-key technology, strong authentication is provided by the public part the user has and usually freely distributes to others—the certificate, which contains the user's identity and public key, and the private part the user knows, which is the private key and password that protects it.

♦ *Simpler administration* When using client authentication based on certificates, administration can be simplified and costs can be lowered. This comes from the ability to configure servers to grant access to users that present a certificate issued by an approved list of certificate authorities. When configured in this way, servers do not need to maintain an access control list (ACL). Other configurations provide mechanisms for the administrator to configure per-user-certificate associations. When configured this way, the administrator has more flexibility in providing access control, while still avoiding the problems of distributing individual passwords.

NOTE: An Intranet Web server may support multiple methods of certificate-based authentication for granting access to the information managed by the Web server. There is support for general access based on the certificate issuer, support for departmental access based on the certificate issuer or issuer list, and the ability for the administrator to associate a certificate to a particular user in the access control list either manually or automatically via a user, one-time password-based logon.

Password-Based Authentication

Even with public-key security growing more popular, there is still a need to provide a means of client authentication, using distributed, password-based authentication for secure connections to Intranet servers. This is especially true in cases where the overhead for managing users' certificates becomes greater than managing distributed passwords. When a server-authenticated secure channel (no certificate-based client authentication) is used between the client and server, password-based authentication may be sufficient in cases where it is acceptable to manage distributed passwords. The server-authenticated secure channel provides the ability for the client to verify the identity of the server and to use an encrypted channel between the client and server, so the password does not flow onto the network in the clear.

TIP: Intranet administrators can control access to information by mapping passwords and/or certificates to user accounts and groups on Intranet servers. Access-control permissions can then be assigned using the usual methods provided by your Intranet servers.

Private-Key Management

In an Intranet environment, administrators may choose different methods for managing the private keys held by the company's employees. Each individual company decides what method to use based on company policies for managing information. Currently, the following methods are used for handling private keys for signing and encryption operations:

♦ *The single-key system* With this method, the same key is used for both signing and encrypting.

♦ *The dual-key system* This method uses separate keys for signing and encrypting.

The Common Method   The most common method of private-key management involves a single key and requires users to create and manage their own private keys independently. This gives the individual users the most privacy. It can become, however, quite troublesome for network administrators, as users encrypt company data with private keys known only to them. Problems can arise if an employee's private key were to be compromised in some way (lost, stolen, or by simply forgetting the password).

The Dual-Key Advantage   The best solution is to use a dual-key system (two private keys)—one for signing operations and one for encryption. The signing key can be created by, managed by, and known only to the individual user, whereas the encryption key is created by the administrator and stored, and a copy of the private key is supplied to the individual users. This allows the users to maintain privacy for signing operations while still allowing the company to protect and recover any corporate data that may have been encrypted.

 NOTE: Today, most applications cannot share private-key information, and users are often required to create and manage private keys on a per-application basis. As more standards develop, all applications can share personal information like private keys and certificates.

Hardware-Based Security Devices

In most applications, public-key signing operations and the bulk of data encryption take place in software. The user's private key is stored in the local file system and encrypted using a password-based encryption key. Both personal certificates and the trusted root certificates used to verify signatures on certificates are stored in the local file system in a certificate store. The certificates are generally stored in the clear, since most certificates contain only public information. When signing operations occur, the user's private key must be decrypted into the computer's memory to allow the cryptographic processing to occur, leaving a potential for the private key to be compromised. Currently, there is no simple way to move personal information (private keys, certificates, etc.) from, say, a user's work computer to their home computer or to allow a user to work securely from a shared computer.

The Hardware Solution

Software can be simple and inexpensive, since it requires no additional hardware. However, as has been pointed out, there are some potential drawbacks. A hardware-based device can solve the problem of private-key generation and storage, personal certificate storage, and trusted root certificate storage, using the private key in signing operations. Also, some hardware devices (for example, the Atalla WebSafe device) offer hardware-based, high-speed signing and encryption operations. Hardware devices may come in the following forms:

♦ *Smart cards*   Credit card devices that can generate and store private keys and certificates.

♦ *SmartDisks*   Devices the size of floppy disks that can store private keys and certificates as well as perform cryptographic operations like signing and bulk encryption.

♦ *Smart tokens*   PCMCIA devices that can store private keys and certificates as well as perform cryptographic operations like signing and bulk encryption. The U.S. government's Fortezza program is an example of a system that utilizes smart tokens.

Hardware-Based Benefits

Hardware-based security devices have the following benefits:

♦ *Increased security*   Since key pairs are generated on the device and never leave the device, the private key is impervious to some of the attacks that may be directed against private keys that are stored and processed in a computer's file system and system memory. Also, a hardware device typically has a better random number generator (which is used in key creation) than a software-based, pseudo-random number generator.

♦ *Portability of personal information*   In today's enterprise-wide deployment of secure access, users will need to use secure applications from many locations—at home, while traveling, or via shared computers within the organization. Any computers equipped with either smart card readers or floppy drives (in the case of the SmartDisk device) can authenticate users to securely access sensitive data.

NOTE: Software-based solutions would require users to migrate their personal information (private keys and certificates) among computers via floppy disks or the network, neither of which is a suitable solution.

♦ *Standard interfaces*   Most hardware devices support standard interfaces like the PKCS#11 Cryptoki standard for access to cryptographic hardware devices. This allows users to plug in different devices that support this standard without requiring changes in the applications.

♦ *Improved performance*   Some hardware devices, specifically those designed for server use, support high-speed cryptographic operations for digital signatures.

The Certificate Issuer and Server

A certificate issuer and server provides the means to issue, revoke, renew, and manage certificates. It should make certificate-management tasks as simple as possible. A certificate issuer and server must adhere to standards where possible. Today, the standard format for accepting certificate requests is the Public Key Cryptography Standard PKCS#10. The standard certificate format is X.509 (version 1 or 3).

The certificate issuer and server should maintain a database of information such as a certificate revocation list (CRL), auditing information about issued certificates, copies of the certificates, policy information about issuing certificates, and information about the issuers that can sign certificates. The issuing system must also allow easy creation of a hierarchical-based issuer list. The root-level issuers and any issuers that are created that can sign under the authority of the root issuer must be easily managed. The certificate-issuing policy must also be clearly defined for each issuer.

TIP: An internal Intranet certificate-issuing system should provide a standards-based, public-key cryptography key management solution that ensures management of key updates are automatic, transparent to users, and have no additional cost attached. This ensures that, as network security is deployed on the Intranet, network administration costs are minimized, yet critical centralized controls are maintained.

Private-Key Management

The most vulnerable point of a certificate-issuing system is the protection of the issuer's private keys. If an issuer's private keys are compromised, any certificates signed by that issuer can be suspect, and must be reissued. Therefore, a strong mechanism must be employed to protect the issuer's private keys. An Intranet certificate-issuing system should support strong encryption of each issuer's private key based on a password supplied by the issuing system administrator.

Policy Management

Certificates are issued according to a policy that is specific to each issuer that grants or signs certificates. This policy defines what criteria must be met in order to issue a certificate. The criteria can include things like proofing requirements that state the level of identification a certificate requester must present before being issued a certificate. The level of proofing (the trust that users place in a certificate) can range from strong in-person identification to weak e-mail requests.

Requesting Mechanisms

There are a number of ways for requesting certificates for different applications' clients and servers. Client certificates are generally requested either via the Web browser or via the e-mail application. Server-certificates requests are generally done through some type of manual process. In implementations where the applications allow sharing of private key and certificate information, usually only one method is employed. The industry trend is moving toward Web-based certificate requests due to the ease and flexibility they provide in presentation and certificate-policy enforcement.

Certificate Management

Managing issued certificates is very important. It allows application clients and servers to look up certificate information and to determine the validity of a certificate they would receive. The validation may occur offline via distributed certificate revocation lists (CRLs), or it may occur online via a connection to a certificate server to retrieve a certificate's status. In addition to determining a certificate's revocation status, an application (like e-mail) may need to look up and retrieve a user's certificate to encrypt messages for secure end-to-end communication. The different certificate services required to perform the operations described may not be provided by just a certificate server. The certificate server may employ a directory server for storage and distribution of issued certificates. Table 9-2 summarizes the situations that would require access to either a certificate server or directory server.

Public Versus Private Issuing

When building a certificate-issuing infrastructure in an organization and establishing a certificate authority (CA), there is generally a Public CA or a Private CA. Which type an organization chooses depends on how they expect the issued certificates to be used.

With Internet Access

If an organization is setting up a server with Internet access, a public CA would most likely be chosen to issue certificates for that server. This allows a commonly known and trusted public third-party entity to issue and manage certificates for the corporation's Internet servers. This also ensures that any Internet client is able to verify the authenticity of the company's Internet servers. The trusted, third-party CA needs to perform due diligence in

Certificate Information Needed	Server to Request
Need to look up a user's certificate to send him or her encrypted e-mail.	Directory
Need to update a CRL that is stored locally and used to check the revocation status of received certificates offline. The user realizes that the CRL may not always contain the most up-to-date information about the certificate-revocation status.	Directory
A client application (Web browser, CyberSearch, e-mail, etc.) needs to check the revocation status of a certificate in real time.	Certificate

Server Certificate Queries
Table 9-2.

determining the identity (proofing) of those parties it issues certificates to in order to maintain a valuable and trusted service. In addition to server certificates, client certificates can also be issued by a public CA. This may be the case if an organization is providing some Internet services where subscribers, customers, or partners need to access the company's Internet servers in some authenticated way.

With Restricted Internal Access

If an organization is establishing an Intranet with restricted access to corporate resources on internal servers, then establishing a private CA might be the best choice. The organization's client and server applications would be configured with the organization's private CA trusted-root keys to allow them to verify the certificates issued by the private CA. The organization issues private certificates to its internal servers to allow only the client applications configured with the private CA trusted-root keys to gain access to and verify the authenticity of the company's Intranet servers. Each employee in the company is also issued one or more certificates for use in the client applications and e-mail. When connecting to a company's Intranet servers, only connections that use certificates issued by the private CA would be granted access to the Intranet servers. The Private CA allows the organization to easily manage strong access controls over distributed servers.

Table 9-3 demonstrates the issues outlined in the previous section.

Action	Advantages	Disadvantages
Use a private CA	Company can tightly control its certificate management policies Allows a company to easily experiment with certificate policies and certificate content	Internal overhead to perform certificate management
Use a public CA	Knowledgeable and experienced professional services Can use Public CA's technical, legal, and business expertise to solve problems associated with certificate usage	Less flexibility in certificate management Usually a per-certificate cost for clients and servers

Public Versus
Private CA
Uses
Table 9-3.

Single-User Logon

The benefits of providing a single-user logon are immediately apparent when using public-key certificates issued from a corporate certificate-issuing system. When corporate users connect to servers or send e-mail, they log on once to the desktop application, and then are able to send e-mail and browse from server to server without having to reauthenticate each time. The client applications perform the authentication automatically each time with the servers using client authentication. Not only do the users see benefit, but the administrators also see simplified administration of corporate resources.

For example, when a new employee joins a company, he or she may receive one or more corporate personal certificates issued by the company's certificate-issuing system. The corporate servers across the enterprise may also be issued corporate server certificates by the same certificate-issuing system. These server certificates recognize and accept corporate-issued personal certificates as a form of authentication to allow the employee to access corporate data. The employee may have different certificates issued to grant varied access rights to different servers, possibly based on department. Depending on the server the employee is connecting to, he or she may be prompted to use a particular certificate. The employee would log on once at the client machine to access his or her personal key and certificates. From that point on, depending on the server the employee is connecting to, the employee would be using a personal certificate to authenticate to that server. Each server would then grant access based on the permissions for that particular certificate.

Protocols for Secure Communications

There are standard protocols available today that make secure communication possible. These protocols generally fall into classifications that are covered in the following sections.

Secure Channels

A secure channel is created in a client/server relationship when one of the parties (usually the server) authenticates the other. As a result of the authentication process, an encrypted connection is usually established. This authenticated, encrypted connection is commonly referred to as a *secure channel*. There are many protocols available that can be used to implement a secure channel. The most common protocols are as follows:

♦ *Secure Sockets Layer (SSL)*   The SSL protocol has two versions that have been widely implemented: version 2 and version 3. The first widely available implementation of the SSL protocol was SSL version 2, and it first showed up in Netscape Communications Corporation's (www.netscape.com) Web client and server products. The SSL version 2 dealt mostly with authenticating the server and providing a secure (encrypted) channel between the client and server. Version 3 of SSL fixed some security problems in version 2 and primarily added robust client authentication. The SSL protocol concerns itself with providing a signed and encrypted channel between the client and server. The SSL protocol is the most popular and most widely implemented secure channel protocol. When one refers to a secure Web connection, they are most likely referring to an SSL secured connection.

♦ *Private Communications Technology (PCT)*   The PCT protocol is similar to SSL but adds additional functionality to the SSL protocol, particularly in authentication and protocol efficiency. The PCT protocol first showed up in the Microsoft Web client and server products. Implementations of PCT are compatible with SSL.

♦ *Transport Layer Security (TLS)*   The TLS protocol is an attempt to combine the two most-used secure channel protocols (SSL and PCT) into a single protocol. At present, the TLS standardization process is moving toward completion. The availability of a single protocol like TLS makes it easier for application developers and users to create and use secure applications.

♦ *Secure HTTP (SHTTP)*   The SHTTP protocol was the first published protocol that attempted to solve the problem of both channel-level and message-level security. The SHTTP protocol signs and encrypts at the document level, while using the client-to-server relationship to negotiate security parameters. The SHTTP protocol provides similar functionality to other secure channel solutions. However, protocols like SSL and PCT are more efficient. Because of this fact, SHTTP is currently not as popular as SSL and PCT.

Secure Messaging and Documents

A secure end-to-end communication is created in a store-and-forward environment where the end parties use message- or document-based security to send data back and forth. The messages and documents can be signed using digital signatures and/or encrypted using digital envelopes. The most common types of secure end-to-end communication are as follows:

♦ *Secure MIME (S/MIME)* The S/MIME protocol is the most recent and currently the most popular protocol used in commercial implementations. The S/MIME protocol is based on the Multipurpose Internet Mail Extensions (MIME) standard used in most Internet mail programs today and the Public Key Cryptography Standards (PKCS) for creating digital envelopes and digital signatures. The S/MIME protocol is relatively simple compared to other standards like MOSS (MOSS is discussed later in this list). The S/MIME protocol uses a hierarchical-based, certificate-trust system. With a hierarchical model, there is a common trusted certificate authority or CA that everyone trusts. This type of certificate management allows S/MIME to fit into corporate businesses and Intranets very nicely.

♦ *Pretty Good Privacy (PGP)* The PGP protocol has applications available on the Internet and is quite popular in Internet communities for exchanging secure e-mail. The PGP protocol uses public-key cryptography similarly to S/MIME. However, it differs mostly in its certificate-management methods. PGP uses an associative-trust model where each individual determines whom they trust and groups of trust are created as each individual signs others' certificates. (If Alice trusts Bob, and Bob trusts Eve, then Alice is likely to trust Eve, too). This type of certificate management works well for a small group of friends. Its limitations, however, are quickly realized in a business and Intranet environment.

♦ *MIME Object Security Services (MOSS)* The MOSS protocol is a combination of the (now defunct) Privacy Enhanced Mail (PEM) and MIME standards, which sought to bring the older PEM security standards and the MIME standard together to provide a new and up-to-date protocol. The MOSS protocol provides many options for supporting different types and modes of message security. The MOSS protocol predates others like S/MIME. MOSS shares many of the same cryptographic techniques and certificate-management structure with S/MIME. However, it has not gained the popularity of S/MIME due to its complexity.

♦ *Message Security Protocol (MSP)* The MSP protocol is a part of the U.S. Government's Defense Messaging System (DMS). This protocol is based on the X.400 mail standards and has been adapted for Internet type e-mail. The cryptography for the MSP protocol is primarily implemented on the Fortezza hardware token device using federal cryptography standards.

Secure Electronic Commerce

Secure electronic commerce is used by consumers or businesses who need to perform financial transactions electronically. The Secure Electronic Transactions (SET) protocol is an emerging standard that solves the problem of payment processing on the Internet. Payment processing on the Internet deals with transactions from the original card holder, through the merchant, to the card-issuer's banks.

Secure Channel Versus Secure Messaging

SSL, SHTTP, and S/MIME are the most common secure-messaging protocols being used today. Each of the different secure protocols was developed to solve different types of problems where digital signatures are used. The SSL and SHTTP protocols are both channel-oriented, client/server protocols, while the S/MIME protocol is end to end. The signing operations in SSL take place on the communications channel, while the SHTTP, and S/MIME protocols provide document-level signing. Another important distinction is the level of signing each protocol provides. With SSL and SHTTP the server is the signer of the channel or document. In S/MIME, the user is always the signer. In addition, an attractive part of document-level signing is that it allows you to archive the document data and associated signature information. Table 9-4 depicts some of the different signing services the protocols offer.

The S/MIME Protocol

The S/MIME protocol was designed to provide for document-level signing operations primarily in the context of store-and-forward applications like e-mail. S/MIME, however, could be used in any protocols (store-and-forward

Service	SSL	SHTTP	S/MIME
Client/server	x	x	
End to end			x
Secure channel	x		
Secure documents		x	x
Client/user signs using user's personal key	x	x	x
Server signs using server key	x	x	

A Comparison of Security Protocols
Table 9-4.

9

or client/server), where the MIME standard is present (like the Web). In S/MIME, the user signs a document, which is the MIME e-mail message to be sent. The receiver, upon receiving this message intact, can archive the message and the signature. Figure 9-4 depicts this relationship between the signature operation and the user.

The SHTTP Protocol

The SHTTP protocol was designed to allow document-level signing operations where the cryptographic parameters used can be negotiated interactively between the client and server. The SHTTP services are somewhere between what S/MIME offers with document-level signing and what SSL offers in interactive client/server. Figure 9-5 depicts the relationship between the signature operation and the client and server.

The SSL Protocol

The SSL protocol was designed to support a bidirectionally authenticated and encrypted channel. The client- and server-side signing operations on the channel data during the channel setup provide the authentication. Since the signature is performed on part of the channel setup data using the server's key, there is nothing to archive for later recovery. Figure 9-6 depicts the relationship between the signature operation and the client and server.

Payment Protocols

Payment protocols are needed so that consumers can confidently purchase goods electronically and merchants are able to automatically collect and

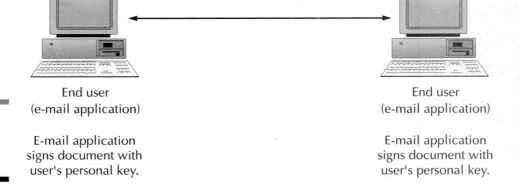

The S/MIME protocol in action
Figure 9-4.

End user
(e-mail application)

E-mail application signs document with user's personal key.

End user
(e-mail application)

E-mail application signs document with user's personal key.

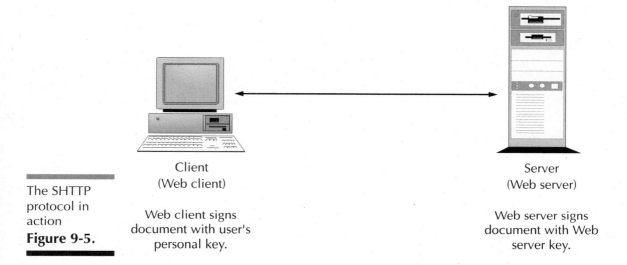

The SHTTP
protocol in
action
Figure 9-5.

Client
(Web client)

Server
(Web server)

Web client signs
document with user's
personal key.

Web server signs
document with Web
server key.

process payment information over the Internet. There are a number of
groups developing standards to facilitate electronic payments. The emerging
standard seems to be the Secure Electronic Transactions (SET) protocol.
Without protocols like SET, electronic transactions are only secure between
the consumer and merchant. Figure 9-7 depicts the current state of
electronic transactions.

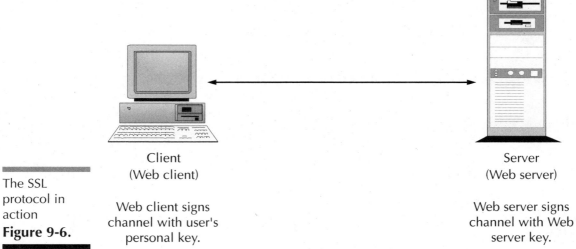

The SSL
protocol in
action
Figure 9-6.

Client
(Web client)

Server
(Web server)

Web client signs
channel with user's
personal key.

Web server signs
channel with Web
server key.

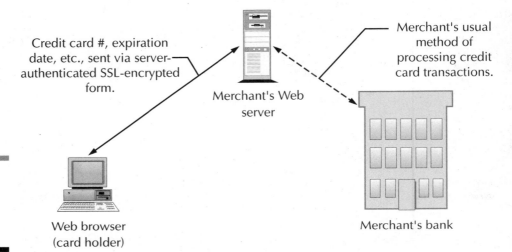

Credit card #, expiration date, etc., is decrypted
and processed using the merchant's normal
(possibly insecure) methods.

Credit card #, expiration
date, etc., sent via server-
authenticated SSL-encrypted
form.

Merchant's usual
method of
processing credit
card transactions.

Merchant's Web
server

The current
state of
electronic
transactions
Figure 9-7.

Web browser
(card holder)

Merchant's bank

By contrast, the SET protocol provides authentication for all parties in a
transaction, this includes the cardholder, merchant, and the banks involved.
The SET protocol preserves the confidentiality of the payment data by
encryption and leaves information like order description unencrypted. SET
uses standard Defense Messaging System (DMS) encryption as well as digital
signatures to authenticate all parties involved in the transaction.
Additionally, SET uses multiparty messages that allow the cardholder to
encrypt the payment data so that only the bank that needs it can decrypt it.
Eventually, SET can be integrated into the entire credit card processing
system. Figure 9-8 depicts how a SET-type system works by illustrating the
progression of credit card information from the transaction originator (the
cardholder), to the merchant, and from there into the banking system.

Putting It All Together

Securing your Intranet begins with understanding the risk environment and
identifying the vulnerabilities on your network. This information can be
used to create a security policy to guide your security program. A security
policy might include

♦   Users' rights and responsibilities

♦ Acceptable use of the Intranet and its resources

♦ Procedures for securing and using Intranet applications

♦ Procedures for identifying and reporting security problems and breaches

You also need to decide which security countermeasures need to be implemented on the Intranet. Do you need a firewall, and which, if any, cryptography technologies need to be used? You might find yourself wondering if the countermeasures are too much or not enough.

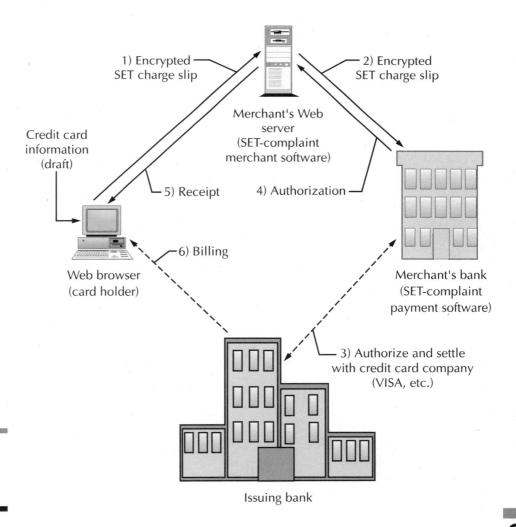

The SET protocol in action
Figure 9-8.

Unfortunately, implementing security is sort of like buying insurance for your Intranet. You can choose minimal coverage and hope that the pitfalls you don't have coverage for never occur, or you can pay extra for full coverage. Minimal coverage may be fine if your driving a rusty Yugo, but hardly sufficient if you're driving a brand new Cadillac. Whatever you do, don't underestimate the value of your Intranet and the data stored there. If it's worth having, it's worth protecting.

Frequently Asked Questions

♦ **Why do I need to secure my Intranet?**

Because there are inherent risks and vulnerabilities on any network. By leaving your Intranet insecure you are not only permitting attack, you are inviting it. You wouldn't leave your car unlocked in a busy mall parking lot, would you?

♦ **Where can I expect the majority of attacks on the Intranet to come from?**

Various studies have estimated that 80 to 95 percent of all network attacks come from within the internal network—in other words, inside the firewall.

♦ **Where do the majority of network security problems come from?**

It has been estimated that insecure passwords cause 80 percent of all network security problems.

♦ **What is malicious code?**

Malicious code refers to uninvited software that can do any number of things to your Intranet and the systems connected to it. A computer virus is an example of malicious code.

♦ **What is a sniffer?**

Sniffer software and hardware monitors and captures TCP/IP packets as they pass from computer to computer across a network. Sniffers can be used to gather passwords and other sensitive data as it passes over your Intranet.

♦ **What is an Intranet security policy?**

An Intranet security policy is a guideline that explains exactly what is expected from each and every Intranet user and administrator. It includes such things as users' rights and responsibilities, acceptable use of the Intranet and its resources, procedures for securing and using Intranet applications, and procedures for identifying and reporting security problems and breaches.

♦ **What is a firewall?**

A firewall defines and protects a perimeter on a network. Any data that enters or leaves a network would do so through the firewall and only if the firewall allows it.

♦ **What is a digital signature?**

A digital signature can be used to assure a reader of the (nonrepudiable) source of the information. In addition, a digital signature can ensure that any unauthorized changes to the data are detected (integrity).

♦ **What is a SmartDisk?**

A SmartDisk is a device the size of a floppy disk that can store private keys and certificates as well as perform cryptographic operations like signing and bulk encryption.

♦ **What is Secure Sockets Layer (SSL)?**

SSL is a cryptography protocol. It is an emerging standard for providing a signed and encrypted channel between a client and server. Many Web browsers and servers have SSL support built in.

♦ **What is Secure MIME (S/MIME)?**

S/MIME is a cryptography protocol that allows encryption and digital signatures to be used in conjunction with Multipurpose Internet Mail Extensions (MIME). Put simply, it is a protocol used to encrypt and digitally sign e-mail messages.

♦ **What is the Secure Electronic Transactions (SET) protocol?**

SET is an emerging standard that is used to facilitate electronic payments. SET secures electronic transactions between all parties involved in that transaction. These parties might include the cardholder, merchant, and the banks involved.

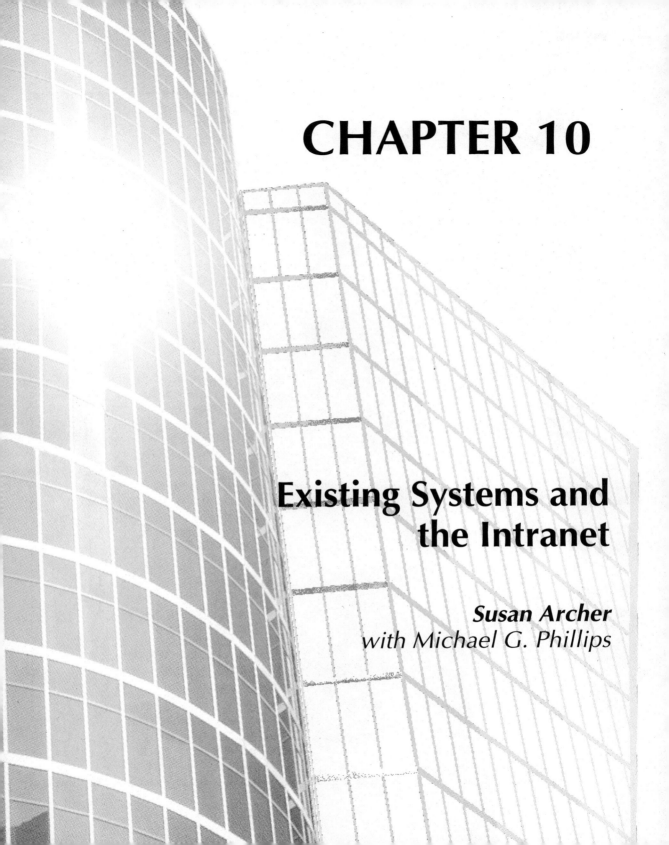

CHAPTER 10

Existing Systems and the Intranet

Susan Archer
with Michael G. Phillips

Chapter Objectives

◆ Define existing systems

◆ Understand the differences between relational databases and flat files

◆ Learn what applications work best on proprietary networks or on Web-based Intranets

◆ Explore different approaches to converting existing text

◆ Find out how to implement Web-based Intranets with existing systems

Existing systems are applications that someone built for your organization a while ago. Your existing system may be a strategic system that you plan to keep on its current hardware platform for many years to come. It may also be a legacy system that you're planning to re-engineer in the not-too-distant future. In either case, your existing system contains the combined wisdom and business rules of your organization. Many people have contributed over the years to its creation and maintenance. Regardless of any shortcomings it may have, your existing system performs mission-critical processing for your organization.

Integrating the Old with the New

If you're like most people who have an existing system, you're interested in implementing new capabilities while continuing to use what you have. This chapter explains approaches, like the ones that follow, for using an Intranet as a user interface to your existing system.

♦   Users can have a browser running on their computers, so that you can provide a series of Hypertext Markup Language (HTML) menus and HTML forms to provide information for data entry. The useful thing about this is that you can have the same user interface on any hardware platform as long as you can run a Web browser on it.

♦   Another use for an Intranet is reporting. You can create reports off your existing system, format them into HTML and display them on any platform that can run a browser.

NOTE: For the purposes of this chapter, it's important to make a distinction between an organization's proprietary network and the kind of Intranet discussed in this book. A *proprietary network* is a wide area network that is owned and operated by an organization, and does not include Web-based components. The term *Web-based Intranet* refers to an Intranet that could include browsers on the users' PCs, a Web server, and links to one or more existing databases.

This chapter begins with a discussion of what a database is and how the relational databases in current use are different from those in many existing systems. It's relatively easy to make relational databases accessible to your Web server using Open Database Connectivity (ODBC) and Structured Query Language (SQL). Older database structures require different tools to link them to a Web server. We continue with examples of a proprietary network and a Web-based Intranet, explain the components of each, and discuss their strengths and weaknesses.

Many organizations have considerable amounts of text in their existing systems. We'll be looking at some guidelines for converting this text to HTML or keeping the text in its original format. This chapter also includes some uniform resource locators (URLs) you can use to start finding the right tools for your organization.

TIP: Different hardware and software vendors, as well as trade magazines, have information about software and hardware you can use to create your Intranet solution.

Working with Existing Databases

The databases in existing systems are often made up of flat files or other data structures that are quite different from the relational databases commonly in use today. The following sections briefly describe the differences between relational databases and databases containing flat files.

What Is a Database?

A database is like an online filing cabinet. As shown in Figure 10-1, the filing cabinet has two drawers. In the top drawer are individual folders for the customer contacts of the fictitious retail wholesaler, the Cascade Bagel Shoppe. Each person who is contacted by the Bagel Shoppe's sales representatives has a file folder in the Contacts drawer. The second drawer in the filing cabinet has a record of the calls to each contact. Each folder in the calls drawer contains many call reports for a single customer contact.

The corresponding database in Figure 10-1 has two files in it. The first is the Contacts file. Within that file is a record for each customer. The Calls file has a record of the calls made to each customer contact. One record in the Contacts file can link to several records in the Calls file.

NOTE: All databases are made up of files and records. The records contain information like names, addresses, phone numbers, and so on. Databases can also contain other information such as text, images, sound, and video.

An Overview of Relational Databases

A relational database is a perfect database structure for creating a Customer
Contact database for the contact information shown in Figure 10-1. This is
because in a relational database you can associate many Calls records with a
single Contacts record. The user interface of the relational database provides
for quick retrieval of call information. For example, Figure 10-2 shows a
Contacts record. If you click the Calls button, you see the window shown in
Figure 10-3. The Contact ID field from the Contacts record works behind the
scenes to identify all of the Calls records for a particular contact. Because of
this key relationship, you can have one Contacts record but associate five or
more Calls records with it.

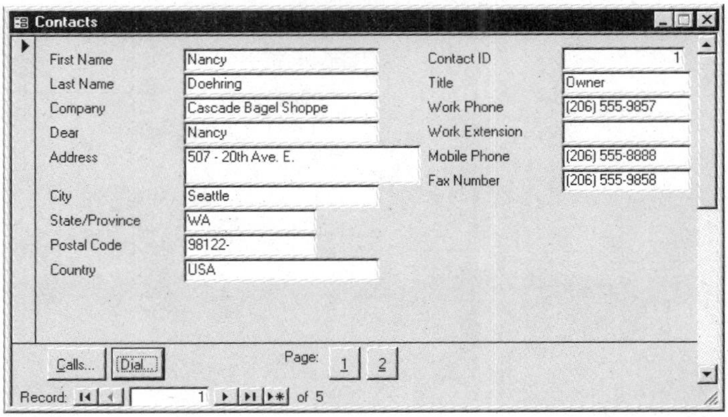

One record of
information
for a contact
in a relational
database
Figure 10-2.

How Reports Are Created

Figure 10-4 shows a report created from the records in the Customer Contact database. The Weekly Call Summary includes data from both the Contacts file and the Calls file as follows:

Summary Report Heading	File	Field
Date	Calls	Call Date
Time	Calls	Call Time
Contact Name	Contacts	Last Name, First Name
Subject	Calls	Subject
Work Phone	Contacts	Work Phone

Joining File Data Records

The technical term for pulling out information from two different files in a relational database is called *joining*. Joining appends data records in one file to data records in another file based on a common data field called a record key. If you look at Figure 10-5, you can see that the Contact ID field provides the key relationship between the Contacts record and the associated Calls record.

 NOTE: The Contact ID field appears in the window of the Contacts record (see Figure 10-2) but is a hidden field on the Calls record (see Figure 10-3).

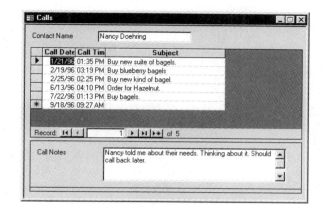

Five Call
records for
one contact in
a relational
database
Figure 10-3.

The Structured Query Language (SQL)

SQL provides a way of asking a relational database to provide information. Selection of the records depends on the search criteria defined using SQL statements. For example, Figure 10-5 shows a user interface for entering a query on the Customer Contact database. This query asks for the call

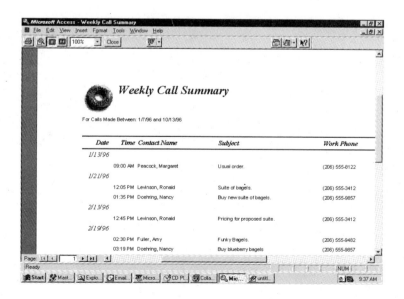

A Weekly Call
Summary
based on both
the Contact
and Call
records
Figure 10-4.

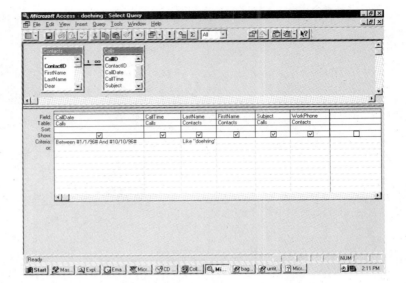

A user
interface for
entering an
SQL query
Figure 10-5.

information for Nancy Doehring from January 1, 1996, to October 10, 1996.
The two parts of the query are

♦ In the Calls column, the statement *Between #1/1/96# And #10/10/96#*
  asks for all records between January 1, 1996, and October 10, 1996.

♦ In the Contacts column, the statement *Like "doehring'* asks for records
  that match the name, Doehring. The statement is not case sensitive.

  The native SQL query for this request looks like this:

```
SELECT DISTINCTROW Calls.CallDate, Calls.CallTime, Contacts.LastName,
Contacts.FirstName, Calls.Subject, Contacts.WorkPhone
FROM Contacts INNER JOIN Calls ON Contacts.ContactID = Calls.ContactID
WHERE (((Calls.CallDate) Between #1/1/96# And #10/10/96#) AND
((Contacts.LastName) Like "doehring"));
```

TIP: Obviously, it's much easier to use an interface like the one in Figure
10-5 to enter an SQL query than to try and figure out the native SQL syntax.
If you want your users to be able to create their own customized queries with
very little training, a user-friendly interface, like the one in Figure 10-5, is
something to consider.

Figure 10-6 shows the results of the query in Figure 10-5.

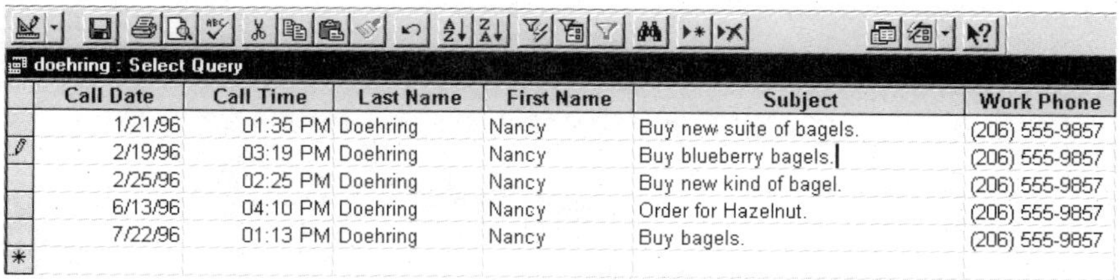

Call Date	Call Time	Last Name	First Name	Subject	Work Phone
1/21/96	01:35 PM	Doehring	Nancy	Buy new suite of bagels.	(206) 555-9857
2/19/96	03:19 PM	Doehring	Nancy	Buy blueberry bagels.	(206) 555-9857
2/25/96	02:25 PM	Doehring	Nancy	Buy new kind of bagel.	(206) 555-9857
6/13/96	04:10 PM	Doehring	Nancy	Order for Hazelnut.	(206) 555-9857
7/22/96	01:13 PM	Doehring	Nancy	Buy bagels.	(206) 555-9857

Figure 10-6. Results of the query entered in Figure 10-5

Open Database Connectivity (ODBC)

ODBC is an interface to relational databases that was first developed by Microsoft and has become a de facto standard. For the purposes of connecting between a Web server and a database, ODBC is a wonderful thing. This is because many database vendors support ODBC in addition to native database drivers for their databases. Using ODBC greatly simplifies integrating Web-based technology with an existing database. Windows NT and Windows 95 both let you easily set up an ODBC driver. To connect a Web server to a database that supports ODBC is simply a matter of mapping a network drive to the database and defining the mapped drive as an ODBC source. See Chapter 3 for an example. Using a browser, a user can access the database through a Web server.

An Overview of Flat Files

Many organizations have existing systems that contain flat files. For example, if you had a flat file containing the contact and call information for the Cascade Bagel Shoppe, all of the information would be in a single file, as shown in Figure 10-7.

To add the information for a call, do the following:

1. Copy an existing record.
2. Update the information in the following fields: Call Date, Call Time, Subject, Call Notes.

If your database is made up of flat files, as many existing systems are, connecting your Web server to your mainframe becomes a much more difficult task. For these databases, it's difficult if not impossible to use standard interfaces like SQL and ODBC. The example of a Web-based Intranet later in this chapter explores your connection options in much greater detail.

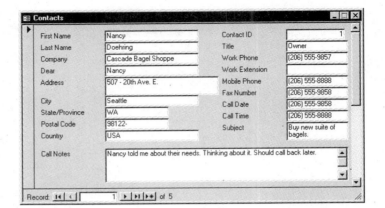

An example of
a flat file
Figure 10-7.

Working with Proprietary and Web-Based Intranets

If you aren't familiar with what a Web-based Intranet can do, it's hard to envision the benefits of using one with your existing system. This section describes a hypothetical bank, the ABC Bank, and how it uses an existing mainframe database to issue credit cards and handle credit card problems. The first part describes what happens when ABC Bank is using its proprietary network, which includes a centralized database application and a proprietary WAN. The second part describes what happens when the ABC Bank is using its database application with a Web-based Intranet as a user interface. The examples are fictitious, but if you have an existing system, you are probably dealing with issues similar to the ones highlighted here.

NOTE: The following examples are based on an IBM System Network Architecture (SNA) solution; but in many ways, these examples could apply to other mainframe systems. Digital Equipment Corporation; Sybase, Inc.; Tandem Computers Incorporated; and Unisys all provide some type of mainframe or minicomputer systems.

An Example of a Proprietary Network

A proprietary network usually includes the following components:

♦   Proprietary applications that run on a terminal or terminal emulator on users' desktops. These applications are usually text based and don't include any hypertext, multimedia, or images.

- ◆ A secure wide area network running over a protocol such as SNA or X.25.
- ◆ A database application on a mainframe or minicomputer that processes information entered by the users.

The example that follows explains how the ABC Bank might have implemented a proprietary network for its customers and branches throughout the Midwestern U.S. Figure 10-8 shows the architecture of the bank's proprietary network.

Software Issues

One of the services the bank provides is credit cards for its branches and customers. The credit cardholders use their credit cards at stores and automated teller machines (ATMs), but sometimes the cardholders have problems. An ATM doesn't give them the right amount of money, a merchant charges them twice, or some other problem occurs. The bank's branches and customers use a proprietary credit card application to handle problems and to add, update, or delete information for various cardholders.

Each service the Bank offers has a different proprietary application that runs on the same PC as the proprietary credit card software application. The PC has a dial-up or leased line to connect with the Bank's mainframe. At the Bank's data center, the operations staff maintains modems and communications software to handle the load of customers accessing the

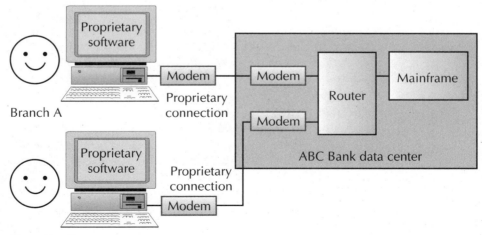

A proprietary network
Figure 10-8.

credit card and other applications on the mainframe. If the branches or customers have problems accessing the mainframe, the operations staff helps with troubleshooting.

From time to time, the programmers in the Bank's Software Development department change the program that the branches and customers use to access the Bank's mainframe. When changes are made, the Bank has to deliver the new software to each location. Sometimes, the branch or customer doesn't install the new software right away, or the upgraded software is lost. Other times, an inexperienced person does the upgrade and makes a mistake that makes it impossible to use any of the proprietary applications. Because the software is used on a daily basis, things like this cause major problems. The operations staff winds up troubleshooting problems with the software upgrades and sometimes has to go to the locations to straighten things out.

Security Issues
The wide area network used by the ABC Bank is an SNA network. Staff at ABC Bank's headquarters connect directly to the mainframe. Software developers have dumb terminals on their desks that they use to access the mainframe and write code. Less technical users, such as the sales and other support staff, access the mainframe from terminal emulators running on their desktops.

Customers and branch-bank staff can either have a leased line connection to the mainframe or a dial-up connection. The staff at the bank's data center maintain routers and massive banks of modems and communications hardware to keep everything working properly.

The network is secure because all access to any part of the network is controlled by the Bank. Before someone can dial in, they need to have a phone number and logon rights, which are controlled by the Bank. Time has shown that proprietary networks, like the one described here, are secure and reliable.

Database Issues
The credit card application uses a database containing flat files. The mainframe, where the credit card application resides, is on an SNA network. Additional applications that the Bank's customers and branches use are also on the mainframe. The branches and customers update the records in the database through their dial-up or leased-line connections to the mainframe.

Every night at midnight, the staff at the data center creates reports of the changes users have made to the records for their organization. These reports are made available to users online through another mainframe proprietary application.

The Benefits of a Proprietary Network

Perhaps the biggest benefit of a proprietary network is the strong network management capabilities that are available. Many organizations have service-level agreements (SLAs). For example, suppose the ABC Bank runs ATMs for its branches and customers. The staff at the Bank's data center monitors the ATMs to make sure they are available for use. Statistics generated at the Bank's data center record how long it takes to complete cash withdrawals from the ATMs and if the ATMs were available. If the statistics don't reflect the contractual level of service, the Bank can be responsible for very expensive fines for nonconformance to the SLAs in the contracts with its customers.

TIP: A proprietary network is probably the best kind of system for transaction-based applications such as credit card withdrawals from an ATM. The mainframe is able to poll the terminals, monitor their availability, and provide statistics for service-level agreements.

Many system managers would also say that another benefit is the tight security that can be enforced on a proprietary network. As explained in Chapter 9 and later in this chapter, strong security procedures can also be implemented for users that access an Intranet through a connection to the Internet.

The Disadvantages of a Proprietary Network

From the viewpoint of an average user, a proprietary network is difficult to learn and difficult to use. Training is a major issue. In general, mainframe applications are not intuitive. With high employee turnover in the positions that use the mainframe applications, training in correct usage of the system is a significant issue. Organizations that operate their own proprietary networks invest many resources in maintaining these networks.

NOTE: To some extent, an Internet connection can reduce the need to maintain large, proprietary networks. For reasons explained in the next section, an Intranet doesn't necessarily eliminate the need to maintain a TCP/IP-based network, but applications such as home banking, online purchases, reporting, and the like can be implemented on a Web-based Intranet and provide significant benefits to an organization.

An Example of a Web-Based Intranet

The Bank decided to implement a Web-based Intranet in order to simplify software maintenance. Using the Web-based Intranet, the Bank can modify the database application for the credit card application, and make changes to the HTML menus on the Web server. This saves time and money, compared to creating new software and distributing it to each customer and branch.

The components of the Bank's Web-based Intranet are shown in Figure 10-9 and described as follows:

♦ The browsers on user's desktops are client applications that connect to the Web server.

♦ Customers and branches can access the Bank's network either over the Internet or by dialing in to the Bank's Point-to-Point Protocol (PPP) server.

♦ Strong security that includes Secure Sockets Layer (SSL) version 2.0 or SSL version 3.0 provides a secure connection between the client and the server.

♦ A Web server with a back-end application maintains session information and translates data from the Web server into a format that the existing database can use.

♦ A database application that can receive information from the back-end application initiates processing and returns a response to the back-end application.

A Browser on Every Users' Desktop

If the Bank decides to use a Web-based Intranet to provide access to their mainframe applications, the branches and customers install a Web browser to replace their proprietary software applications. The common HTML interface in the browser lets the Bank share the same information with users running different hardware platforms. The Bank doesn't mandate what browsers the different locations use. However, the Bank does provide the following guidelines for the browsers:

♦ The browser needs to support SSL version 3, which includes SSL version 2 to provide a secure, authenticated link between the browser and the Bank's Web server.

♦ Users need to be able to enter a username and password, so they can connect to the Web server.

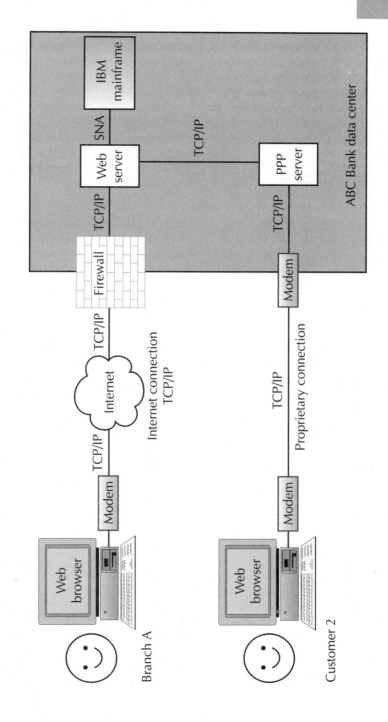

Using a
Web-based
Intranet
Figure 10-9.

NOTE: At this point, the Bank's applications do not require the use of Java, JavaScript, ActiveX, or similar controls. The Bank is not requiring users to get browsers that support these features.

Making a Connection

Two kinds of connections to the Web server are possible. Users can dial in through an Internet Service Provider or can dial in to the PPP server within the Intranet as follows:

♦ *The Internet connection* An Internet Service Provider provides Internet access that allows a connection to a Web server at the Bank's data center. The data center staff has configured the firewall to only allow access to the Web server. The firewall listens for connection attempts on the default port for Web connections, which is port 80. The firewall routes the packets directly to the Web server running under Windows NT.

♦ *The PPP server connection* The ABC Bank has some users who are nervous about using the Internet. For these users, the data center staff maintains modems and a PPP server for direct dial-up access. Users dial in to the PPP server over a standard telephone line without going over the Internet.

Security Issues

Application-level security on the Web server requires users to enter a username and password to obtain access. In addition, the Web server supports SSL version 3 security, which includes SSL version 2. SSL version 2 security requires the Web server to identify itself to the user's browser. SSL version 3 security has the capability to identify the user to the Web server.

Web Servers and Back-End Applications

A shown in Figure 10-9, the Web server is on a separate machine from the mainframe. The first reason for this is that converting between TCP/IP and SNA would be a significant drain on the performance of the mainframe. In addition, development of the back-end application can proceed on the NT-based Web server instead of on the productive mainframe or a duplicate database on a test mainframe. The back-end application interacts with the user by sending and receiving information on an HTML page.

The Web Server Installation The development staff installed a Web server and an SNA gateway on the high-powered PC running Windows NT Server. Many users at the Bank access the mainframe through SNA applications, so the Bank's technical staff decided to keep SNA as the protocol for the network that accesses the IBM mainframe directly.

How the Back End Works When the user first logs in, the back-end application on the Web server checks its database of valid users to make sure the user is authorized to access the mainframe application. After authenticating the user, the back-end application checks its user database to find out what applications the user may access. The back-end program dynamically creates an HTML page that shows a menu of the applications and embeds a "cookie" in the HTML page. Information in the cookie identifies the user, includes a time stamp, and includes other session information. The back-end program returns the HTML page it created to the Web server, and the Web server sends the Web page to the user. For example, if the user is adding a credit card, the user chooses the Add option and receives a Web form to complete. The user fills out the fields in the Web form and returns it to the Web server.

The back-end application can connect to the mainframe in the following ways:

♦ *Using a 3270 data stream* In this example, the back-end application reformats the data and uses a TCP/IP-based tn3270 application to transmit the data to the SNA gateway. The SNA gateway transmits the information to the application program interface on the mainframe for the credit card application.

T IP: Connecting to the mainframe in this way is just one strategy you can use when your mainframe application uses a database containing flat files. Other types of hardware-dependent solutions are also possible. As long as there is an application program interface (API) exposed on the mainframe, it's technically possible to access it.

♦ *Using ODBC and SQL* If your existing database supports ODBC and SQL, connecting your back-end application to your Web server is much simpler. As explained earlier in this chapter, once you make your ODBC connection using your existing LAN you can start running SQL queries to your mainframe application through HTML pages residing on your Web browser.

Database Issues

The credit card application adds the record for the user's credit card and returns a response across the SNA gateway, through the tn3270 application, to the back-end application on the Web server. The back-end application reformats the response into an HTML page and returns the HTML page to the Web server. After receiving the HTML page, the Web server sends the response to the user.

The Benefits of a Web-Based Intranet

The advantages of a Web-based Intranet approach are many. The Bank doesn't have to deal with distributing and installing software. Many of the branches and customers get their own browsers and set up their own access through an Internet service provider (ISP). Software maintenance occurs on the Web server within the Intranet. If the Bank changes its existing system, it changes the HTML pages on the Web server instead of sending new software to the customer and branch locations.

At the Bank's data center, the operations staff still maintains modems and communications software, but the load is potentially getting smaller as more branches and customers convert to Internet access. Incentives—such as faster, cheaper access over the Internet—give the branches and customers good reasons to migrate.

Training also becomes less of an issue. Browsers are typically much easier to learn than proprietary applications. The personnel at customer and branch locations can learn to use the browsers and navigate through the menus more easily than learning the proprietary software.

The Disadvantages of a Web-Based Intranet

The biggest weakness of a Web-based solution is in the area of network management. Another potential issue is scalability of the Web server. In addition, there are some start-up costs associated with developing your Intranet. However, over time, you're migrating to a less resource-intensive architecture, which becomes more cost-effective over the long term.

Network Management If the Bank were going to attach its automated teller machine (ATM) network to the Internet, there could be some problems with monitoring each individual ATM. SNA was built to do things like poll ATMs and monitor their status on a regular basis. TCP/IP was never built for polling and doesn't have built-in structures for maintaining session information, such as that needed to monitor ATMs. In addition, monitoring response times for the purposes of compliance with a service-level agreement gets much tougher if your ATM traffic is being routed across the Internet.

NOTE: As of the writing of this book, there are signs that vendors of various network monitoring solutions are starting to think about doing things like monitoring ATMs using TCP/IP. Within the TCP/IP suite of protocols is the Simple Network Management Protocol (SNMP), which is a starting point for creating more robust network monitoring tools than those that are currently available.

Scalability of Web Servers   Many organizations are thinking about using the Windows NT Server operating system from Microsoft for their Web servers, and hardware vendors have addressed the issue of scalability by building faster computers. What happens, however, if you have your Web server running on the fastest available PC running under the fastest available operating system and your performance is still too slow? The following options provide some viable solutions:

♦ Windows NT supports having multiple CPUs in the same machine. In addition, RISC chips are also supported by Windows NT. Taking advantage of these capabilities is one answer to scalability issues.

♦ Other options are available depending on how you route the traffic to your Web servers. One approach is putting different content on your available Web servers. When a user clicks on a hyperlink, the next HTML page could be on a different Web server than the Web server that provides your organization's home page.

♦ You could also use a router that provides a round-robin approach. In this configuration, a router sends a connection request to the next Web server on its list. This approach assumes that all of the machines have equal power and are handling the same number of concurrent requests.

NOTE: These assumptions are not the final word, as the machines running the Web servers may be different speeds and they may be handling different numbers of requests.

♦ Some vendors are providing a way to help route the incoming traffic to the Web server that can best handle the request. These routers provide ways to define thresholds based on the percent of the traffic sent to each

Web server. For example, suppose you have three Web servers, one on a 486, another on a Pentium 90, and a third on a Pentium 200. With these three machines, you might assign 20% of the traffic to the 486, 35% to the Pentium 90, and 45% to the Pentium 200. If you have 100 concurrent requests, 20 would go to the first PC, 35 would go to the second, and 45 would go to the third. If you had 200 concurrent requests, 40 would go to the first PC, 70 would go to the second, and 90 would go to the third.

♦   Other types of routing configurations are possible. An organization could have four mirrored Web servers—three for Internet traffic and one for internal use. In this configuration, when Internet traffic is high, internal people can still view the Web site without performance problems. Having mirrored Web servers also helps if a Web server crashes or needs maintenance.

TIP: These routers make a System Administrator's life easier, because if a Web server crashes in the middle of the night, the routing software can handle the situation; and if one of your mirrored Web servers needs maintenance, the others can handle the traffic until your first machine is working again.

Applications Issues

At the present time, user-oriented applications are the best solution for Web-based Intranets. Systems where users enter information—such as internal data-entry systems, home banking, online purchases, customer information, and technical support—easily lend themselves to Web-based implementations. In addition, reporting applications also make sense. Financial reports, regulatory information, sales reports, online documentation, and online training are good examples.

NOTE: Transaction-based, real-time functions—such as credit card withdrawals from ATMs—are more difficult from a network management viewpoint. In the coming years, as technology becomes available to monitor remote terminals from a Web-based Intranet, we are probably going to see ATMs using Web browsers as the user interface.

Working with Text

In addition to databases of associated files, legacy systems also include text. Sometimes it makes sense to keep this text in its original format and maintain it on the mainframe. Other times it's more cost-effective to take this text off the mainframe, store it on a PC-based Web server, and convert it to HTML. Some guidelines for text conversion follow.

Text on an Existing System

Sometimes text is associated with the data in a legacy database. If this text is an integrated part of the existing system, it may be a good idea to leave the text on the mainframe. For example, if your programmers or technical support staff are using some kind of mainframe editor to enter their text, then it makes sense to leave the text on the mainframe. On the other hand, if everyone involved in the process has PC-based tools on their desktops, then it might make sense to store the text on the Web server.

The ABC Bank has a technical support application that lists complaints with the credit card system. Customers and branches can access their complaints and find out what progress is being made on their particular issues. The information is in a text format and resides on the mainframe system. The inquiry feature of the credit card system lets users see a text file that documents the progress on their issues. When a request comes into the Web server for this text, the back-end program dynamically formats the text into HTML. It makes sense to keep this textual information on the mainframe because many technical people still have dumb terminals and use the mainframe text editor. As the technical staff migrate away from the dumb terminals, the time will come when putting the text on your Web server is a better option.

Online Policies and Procedures

Many organizations are trying to reduce costs by putting internal policies and procedures online. This approach makes information more accessible while reducing the costs of printing and distributing the internal policies and procedures. For example, the ABC Bank decided to convert their personnel procedures to HTML and make them available in a secured fashion on the company Intranet. The documents were downloaded from the mainframe and converted to HTML documents that reside in a PC-based Web server. The number of times the employee handbook is accessed is relatively low, so a smaller system could handle the traffic. In addition, using a PC-based HTML editor is faster than using the text-processing system on the mainframe.

HTML Conversion

You have the choice of converting existing information to HTML or keeping the information in its existing form. Different vendors have created HTML conversion tools for documents and other kinds of files. Some of these tools create HTML pages that have an attractive, sophisticated look and feel. After the conversion is complete, you may still need to do some reformatting to make your HTML pages look just the way you want them.

Information Maintenance Issues

As you consider your approach to converting legacy information, a key factor is ongoing maintenance. After you've converted something, you have the choice of either continuing to update the HTML version or continuing to update the original version. The decision you make depends on what you're going to do with the information. If you need to do things like print and distribute a document as a manual, you're probably going to want to continue updating the information in its original form. You can keep information only meant for electronic distribution in its original format as long as your users have a viewer or helper application that can display the files.

For example, suppose you have a Word document and all of the users in your organization have Word on their desktops. In this situation, you can put Word documents directly onto your Web server without converting them to HTML. To view a document, your users can open their browser, download the document, and launch Word as a helper application from within their browser. This same approach also works for spreadsheets, presentations, video, multimedia, sound, and other sorts of information.

Using Hyperlinks

Suppose the ABC Bank provides dental insurance to its employees and from time to time, employees have questions about what is and isn't covered. The Human Resources home page has a hypertext link to the home page of the company that provides the dental insurance. Employees can go to the Human Resources home page, click the hyperlink, and easily find information about their insurance plan.

Searching for Information

The Human Resources home page also includes a search form. Employees like the Web server's search capability, which allows them to enter a search word or phrase and find information quickly. For example, if an employee wants to know about the policy for taking a leave of absence, the employee enters "leave of absence" in the search form and is able to immediately view the information. State-of-the-art search engines have the ability to index many kinds of files. With one query, users could search HTML documents, word processing documents, news articles, and existing databases.

Tools for Implementing a Web-Based Intranet

The hardware vendors for the various mainframe platforms are working on tools to help you with implementing your Web-based Intranet. Check out these vendors' Web sites for more information:

♦ Cisco Systems at www.cisco.com

♦ Digital Equipment Corporations at www.digital.com

♦ Frontier Technologies Corporation at www.frontiertech.com

♦ Hewlett-Packard at www.hp.com

♦ HydraWEB Technologies at www.hydraweb.com

♦ IBM Corporation at www.ibm.com

♦ Microsoft Corporation at www.microsoft.com

♦ Oracle at www.oracle.com

♦ Sun Microsystems at www.sun.com

♦ Sybase, Inc. at www.sybase.com

♦ Tandem Computers Incorporated at www.tandem.com

♦ Unisys at www.unisys.com

If you can't find the tool you want on one of these Web sites, try searching on the following Internet search sites:

www.search.com
www.lycos.com
www.yahoo.com
www.innfoseek.com
www.hotbot.com

Also check the trade magazines and journals for your hardware vendor's products.

Putting It All Together

Your Web-based Intranet can extend the life of your existing systems by taking some of the mainframe processing load. The capabilities of relational databases, SQL, and ODBC aren't available with many existing database applications.

Proprietary networks are based on proprietary hardware platforms and communication protocols. The strengths of these systems are tight network management and, in the eyes of some system managers, tight security. The weaknesses of proprietary networks are that they are difficult to learn from a user's perspective, and the cost of distributing proprietary software and maintaining a proprietary network are high.

A Web-based Intranet can be implemented on many hardware platforms and is based on the TCP/IP protocol. The strengths of Web-based Intranets are that they reduce the costs of maintaining internal software, reduce the size of the proprietary network, and require less training. The drawbacks are that solutions in the areas of network management and load balancing are still in the process of being developed.

Both traditional and Web-based Intranets are valuable for different kinds of applications. A proprietary network is still the favored solution for real-time, transaction-intensive applications, like monitoring automated teller machines. A Web-based Intranet is preferred for user-intensive applications, such as data entry, home banking, online purchases, and reporting systems.

In addition to database applications, organizations also have existing text that may continue to reside on the mainframe or may be converted to HTML. Electronic delivery of information saves printing and distribution costs and also provides more up-to-date information.

10

Frequently Asked Questions

◆ **What is an existing system?**

An existing system is an older system that is usually on a mainframe or minicomputer. Often the information in an existing system is in flat files that can't be accessed using today's technology.

◆ **What are some important differences between relational databases and the flat files in many existing databases?**

A relational database makes it possible to relate several records in one file to a single record in another file. This structure reduces the amount of information needed to do data entry. In addition, many relational databases provide support for SQL and ODBC. Flat files do not allow relating several records in one file to a single record in another file. In addition, flat files don't allow you to use capabilities such as SQL and ODBC.

◆ **What kinds of applications work best on a proprietary network and what kinds of applications can be more cost-effective on a Web-based Intranet?**

A proprietary network is still the favored solution for real-time, transaction-intensive applications, like monitoring automated teller machines. A Web-based Intranet is preferred for user-intensive applications, such as data entry, home banking, online purchases, and reporting systems.

◆ **What are some different approaches to converting existing text?**

If text is an integral part of an existing system, keeping the text within the existing system probably works best. If documents are not part of an existing system, it often makes sense to convert them to HTML and make them available online.

◆ **Where can I find more information on tools I can use to implement a Web-based Intranet with my existing system?**

Look on the Web sites of your hardware vendor and of software vendors you know who provide software for your platform. Also look in trade magazines and try the Internet search sites listed in this chapter.

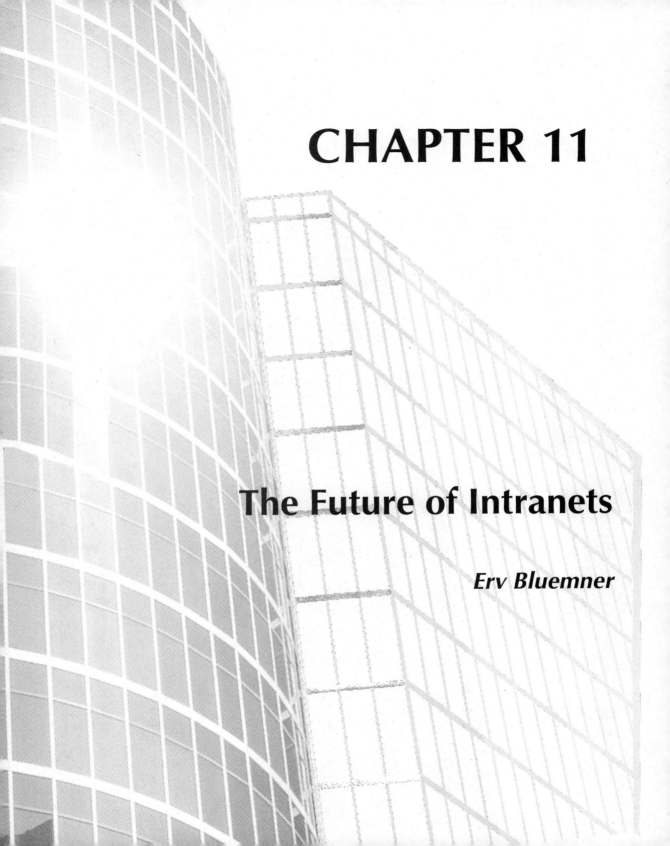

CHAPTER 11

The Future of Intranets

Erv Bluemner

Chapter Objectives

♦ Examine some of the technology trends emerging in the Intranet paradigm

♦ Understand how establishing the right Intranet technology will also promote Extranet introduction

♦ Explore how emerging Intranet technologies will open new business opportunities

While many companies will be able to harness the wealth of tools available today to construct Intranet capabilities that will improve productivity, the tools of tomorrow will take companies to a new level of competitive capability. Intranets already are providing a next generation model for automating the front office and field. Many Intranet platforms and solutions are being delivered today to address issues of information sharing and to promote the integrated collaboration of corporate teams. In many cases, companies are counting on Intranets to facilitate access to corporate databases and information stores. This new paradigm provides a common interface via the browser to dynamically link Web-centric information from both new and traditional sources and to deliver downloadable applications. It is our belief that Intranets will also provide the ultimate base platform technology for the next stage of corporate automation: reaching the customer. It will become increasingly important to select the right tools today that can be leveraged in both your Intranet and Extranet of tomorrow.

This chapter will suggest some evolutionary possibilities for the technologies upon which Intranets will be built. In retrospect, Microsoft was initially caught by surprise by the intensity and suddeness of the emergence of the Internet as a corporate tool. However, the reactive Microsoft blitzkrieg on the Internet and Intranets has already produced major new innovations (both from Microsoft and the competition hoping to keep pace) in browser technology; the operating system platform; and especially the evolution of ActiveX (a response to Sun's Java) and Java for downloadable object-oriented applications, scripting languages, and integrated transport/network communication. Many companies have attempted to conquer the bandwidth issues associated with transmission of multimedia (sound and graphics) and to make videoconferencing and the Internet Phone a reality. Three-dimensional worlds facilitated by the continued growth of the VRML programming standard bring a futuristic feel to our computer interaction and provide new ways to present data and analysis results, as well as navigate information sources. Content-creation tools require decreasing levels of software programming skills while offering increasing levels of features and professional presentation. These trends will not only continue but accelerate because of efforts by vendors to share in the predicted $12 billion worldwide revenue in Internet/Intranet software products between 1996 and 2000. The winners in this race will be those vendors who have a firm grasp on what problems they are trying to solve and bring creative, intuitive solutions to bear. In the following pages, we'll look at the emerging face of Intranet innovation.

It Won't Happen Without the Hardware

While much of the attention surrounding the Intranet is focused on the emergence of software tools and technology, some key technological innovations in hardware will be required if the vision of multimedia-rich information exchange is to be achieved. Multimedia transmission places very high requirements on network bandwidth and subsequent handling by client computers. Graphics and the 3-D VRML worlds will not be truly interactive without continued growth and delivery of specialized chips for processing the graphics primitives and accelerating such operations as surface texturing, shading, and light source effects. Real-time motion in these 3-D worlds creates even higher demands for dynamic display processing. Finally, the higher the resolution desired, the more demand on the processing for interpolation and geometric accuracy. The good news is that the performance level of the Unix workstation is migrating rapidly to the PC at new levels of economy.

New applications continue to drive the need for wireless capabilities. Roving physicians will consult their hospital's Web server to get patient information and results of lab tests from personal digital assistants (PDAs) hanging from their belts. Issues of signal fidelity and roving address connection must be handled. Web servers will need to handle increasing numbers of users, especially for database access. This will require specialized database engines for high-speed retrieval. The volume of online, Intranet server-based information may grow exponentially, which will put pressure on vendors to deliver low-cost, high-capacity disks. Backup devices and media will need to grow in size and speed as well to accommodate the volume.

The implementation of a corporate Intranet connection has a major advantage over an Internet connection. That advantage is simply the bandwidth of a LAN/WAN connection as opposed to the typical modem speed of the Internet connection. However, with the requirement to include remote corporate users, Intranet access may continue to be constrained to a 14Kbps or 28.8Kbps transfer rate. There is some good news with recent availability of V34.4 modems and work by U.S. Robotics, Rockwell, and others to bring POTS (Plain Old Telephone Service) technology up to the 56Kb level. With the emergence of downloadable applications, this will continue to be a major bottleneck over the next several years. Neither ISDN nor cable modems have shown any substantial growth when compared with usage. With reductions in the cost and improved availability of these capabilities, inroads should be made in the next several years.

Another key component in reducing line-bandwidth bottlenecks is the emergence of compression chips, which can be harnessed for both video and audio stream transmission. Perhaps the biggest impact on video playback on the desktop is the emergence of MPEG video compression that provides the

11

capability to play full-screen, 30 frames-per-second video from a hard disk or CD-ROM. Delivering video over the network is somewhat more complicated. Two approaches include (1) delivering video in data files containing either MPEG or Audio Video Interleaved (AVI) data and playing it back, or (2) streaming video, in which the client software decodes and plays the incoming sound or video streams on the fly. Streaming is intuitively more appealing to users who do not want to wait minutes for playback, but it's very difficult to make happen.

There are some inherent technical difficulties in streaming video. Video requires a continuous feed of frames (typically at 30 frames per second). Lost packets can result in lost video frames. To deal with the network bandwidth issue, vendors have developed ways to compress data while deliberately dropping frames and retaining video continuity but at reduced quality. Output speeds are typically reduced to less than 10 frames per second (this will improve) causing a somewhat jerky appearance. However, emerging techniques do deliver a good-quality audio stream with the reduced rate video. As the carriers look to newer technologies, advances in Optical such as the SONET (Synchronous Optical NETwork) will bring new performance levels with the ability to handle multiple bandwidth streams. The inherent bandwidth (155.5MBps) of this new technology should meet the need of video requirements. A critical issue remaining is the inherent capability of the workstation, which must have sufficient horsepower to handle buffering issues associated with the video stream capture and playback. This requires multimedia-specific onboard horsepower. Fortunately, PC manufacturers recognize this, and the next several years will see the inclusion of special graphic/video chips along with onboard compression.

While not immediately applicable to corporate Intranets at this time, some very interesting developments are taking place in the merging of television and Internet access. This convergence may become increasingly important as corporations find ways to deliver their products to customers. In the form of "Information Appliances," interactivity is rapidly coming to the television set top. In the Japanese marketplace, Wink Communications is on track to roll out 2 million interactive set top extenders to basic broadcast programming in 1997. There are up to 14 million Tokyo-based broadcasting outlet television viewers. These interactive extenders will allow push-button access to trivia questions, stock quotes, weather forecasts, and professional sports information. In the U.S., WebTV Networks Corporation is working with Microsoft, Citicorp, VeriFone, and others to provide television-based Internet service. One key aspect is a smart card slot on the set top box. The card can hold user identification or other configuration or preference data. Sony Electronics and Philips Electronics have also just begun shipping TV-based input terminal boxes. Mitsubishi intends to begin selling its

Internet-enabled DiamondWeb sets in the U.S. by early 1997. Along with the receiving hardware, the service delivery businesses will quickly evolve. London-based ViewCall Europe will shortly provide television-based Internet access. OnTV is a subscription-based service that allows television sets equipped with the proper browser hardware to connect to the Internet.

Networking Technology Continues to Evolve

As of this writing, the underlying transport protocols of the Internet, and hence the Intranet, are still evolving. The popularity of the Internet has created an interesting dilemma with respect to the number of available IP addresses. Current projections show that the Internet will run out of network addresses sometime between 2005 and 2011. The phenomenal growth of the Internet has also fueled several other problems. A big concern with TCP/IP designers is the incredibly large size of routing tables utilized in correctly forwarding TCP/IP packets on the Net. As the number of addresses grows, the routing table sizes begin to overwhelm the limits of many systems.

Beginning in 1990, the IETF began to examine these problems and has worked to promote a new TCP/IP standard known as IPv6, which was published in 1995. To meet the need, not only did the IP standard have to be changed, but changes had to be made to some 58 TCP/IP standards to accommodate IPv6. Migration to this standard will not and has not occurred instantly. Many millions of systems today are using IPv4. Because of the efforts made by the IPv6 team to make migration a reasonable activity and support backward compatibility, many of these systems will not migrate to the new standard. New machines will be able to execute essentially a dual stack supporting both IPv6 connections and IPv4. Interestingly enough, the new IPv6 also has been defined to include migration strategies for two popular network architectures and protocol suites. The IPv6 architecture specifically defines a migration path for both the connectionless services of the International Standards Organization (ISO) and Novell's NetWare.

Other improvements in TCP/IP have also been made. With the push to audio and video online conferencing, enhancements have been made to TCP/IP to support higher speed real-time performance. Hence, the Real Time Protocol (RTP) and Real Time Control Protocol (RTCP) have emerged. Network improvements are also striving to keep pace. We are beginning to see such emerging improvements as Fast Ethernet and ATM (Asynchronous Transfer Mode). To support real-time performance, especially for applications with tight time restraints and those that are unable to deal with unreliable network delivery, the new IPv6 standard provides for "reserving" or guaranteeing the availability of a desired level of bandwidth to meet the real-time requirement. For example, the RSVP Protocol (a resource reservation Protocol) is capable of reserving a significant portion of the available bandwidth in an ATM link to ensure the timely flow of a streaming video.

IPv6 has defined several extensions for security. A significant requirement on all IPv6 hosts is the ability to support authentication. In addition, IPv6 has a well-defined framework for exchanging confidential messages. Work continues on the IPSec (IP Secure) protocol specification to support further enhancements in secure packet exchange. The standard should be ratified in 1997, though several vendors have already begun to advertise IPSec capability.

11

Recently, systems have begun to utilize the Dynamic Host Configuration Protocol (DHCP) to obtain configuration information for operating on the network. DHCP focuses on providing network addresses to hosts. DHCP supports several modes of address assignment, including Manual Allocation (administrator-assigned fixed address), Automatic Allocation (combining a link address with an address prefix to create an address), and Dynamic Allocation (hosts sharing from a pool of network addresses). DHCP will eventually be able to define other configuration information, such as to tell a host its printers, domain name servers available, and file servers.

Network capability requirements will also continue to grow. There is a need to provide wireless capability to the traveling professional, and there is a strong need to get the same performance that can be utilized in the office into the home. Security will grow up to include not only confidentiality through encryption technology, but also notification of breech to users wherever in the world they may happen to be. Support for cash transactions over the wire will drive development of protective measures to inspire confidence in their use. It is clear that computers throughout the world must share a common basis. TCP/IP will likely evolve to meet that challenge.

The Network Computer (NC) Arrives

During 1996, the concept of the Network Computer was reborn. Led by the Oracle Corporation, one of the leaders in the database field, concepts for a reduced computer architecture system were defined. Oracle outlined a specification for a new, low-cost computing station that would have little or no onboard hard disk for application storing. It would offer a very simplified, but highly task-focused interface. Applications would largely be downloaded by servers on the network for immediate execution. The primary interface concept would evolve around a browser-like interface in order both to have a common user interface for application execution and to take advantage of the substantial power of the Web-centric information-linking capability of Web page documents. The target cost for such a device is about $500. The hope is that this device will eliminate much of the clutter of today's PC desktop, providing only the applications that are critical for the information professional to get his or her work accomplished. By simplifying the desktop environment, system administration and support costs should also be reduced. Oracle's NC division and partners hope to introduce this machine in the first half of 1997. Other players are entering the fray.

The goals of the Network Computer should fit well with many corporate information management strategies. Users will be automatically provided with the most current application. In fact, they are completely dependent on a network download to execute any software because their workstation will likely not have any local disk storage. The cost advantages are quite clear. Some users won't have the full range of capabilities that they require with this paradigm, however, and many will stay with the full-featured PC desktop. For others, for whom the computer is an alien device, the limited functionality may well simplify their interaction and promote higher productivity and confidence. It remains to be seen how much this introduction will affect the total volume of PC sales in the late 1990s.

From the perspective of Intranet software developers, the arrival of the Network Computer will place a tremendous burden on them to once again worry about the size of their applications. After all, if the primary utility of the NC is to run downloadable applications, then the time it takes to download the application will be a critical element in the perceived performance of the system. Design of the user interface must be clean and lightweight. Object design techniques and the use of distributed objects such as ActiveX and Java applets will be essential for effective application delivery.

Growth in the Software Foundation

The key to much of the growth of corporate Intranet and Internet capability has been the frenzy of software component development. Thousands of new software development companies have been founded on the opportunity presented by the Web paradigm, both inside and outside of corporate boundaries. New tools will continue to be produced at this frenetic pace. There will, however, be significant falloff in the ranks. Indeed, Internet software titles constitute less than 8 percent of the retail marketplace at this time. Many of these Internet developers will either cease to exist or will move quickly into Intranet development in an attempt to sell solutions to corporations. This will result in a proliferation of back ends that bring database access, analysis, and information retrieval to more usable levels via a Web-centric paradigm. Most development companies will pursue strategies that do not take them directly into competition with the Microsoft OS-level

11

desktop components. The browser discussion seems to be pretty well reduced to a handful of surviving players in what is really a struggle between two companies: Netscape and Microsoft. Major database players are moving quickly to enable access to their database servers via the Intranet paradigm of a browser GUI with Web server back ends—in this case tied to an ODBC/SQL-compliant interface. Opportunities will exist for additional niche back ends. Security support will be essential, especially in applications that are targeted toward electronic commerce. The information-rich content of an Intranet Web server will continue to promote the development of ever-more-effective search tools and capabilities.

Platform Technology: Objects Everywhere

In the last couple of years, the emergence of Web and Intranet solutions has been centered on Netscape Navigator and SuiteSpot Server Set and on the emergence of Sun's Java programming language and environment. Microsoft moved quickly to counter with the announcement of a complete ActiveX platform strategy. Much of this was hype in a concerted effort to buy time as only Microsoft can. But now that the pieces have fallen into place, they will play an important role as companies move to establish their Intranet platforms. ActiveX brings forth a heritage of OLE and COM windows development standards, with a major difference being that ActiveX controls bear the additional responsibility of having to be downloadable from the Web. Also, an ActiveX control is ideally designed to downscale gracefully in the event that the container application into which the control is placed doesn't support all the features the control might use. At loading time, with proper construction, the ActiveX control checks its environment and may scale itself to a mode of simpler operation based on the available feature set of the container software. It is reasonable to assume that the ActiveX paradigm, and downloadable Java applets as well, in the face of limited network bandwidth, will likely drive renewed interest in efficient code sizing, memory use, and program size in applications. Web-centric applications may appear to run very slowly if the downloadable applications are oversized and take many seconds to be transferred.

VBScript will continue to be a primary language tool for bringing ActiveX objects to Web pages. VBScript is, in fact, the native scripting language of Microsoft Internet Explorer. Because ActiveX is built on OLE, there is a huge set of OLE controls commercially available for bringing increased usability and feature sets to your Intranet users. A drawback is that Netscape is publicly stating that they will not support the ActiveX control paradigm. This is a difficult situation, as Netscape at the writing of this book has the largest installed base of Web browsers. However, Microsoft has closed the feature gap and, with the availability of ActiveX controls and Java support, begins to look like the likely long-term winner in the "browser wars" of the 1990s. Indeed, Microsoft plans to implement VBScript on HP, IBM, Sun, and Digital workstations. Macintosh incarnations are already available. In the foreseeable future, we will see a number of other browser vendors moving rapidly to support the ActiveX paradigm. To address the hole left by Netscape not natively offering support of ActiveX controls, at least one other vendor, NCompass Labs, is offering an ActiveX Netscape plug-in. As Microsoft continues to grow its Distributed Component Object Model (DCOM), starting with NT version 4.0, it is likely that ActiveX controls will be able to communicate and interact directly with other ActiveX controls on remote systems.

An additional concern of downloadable applications is the issue of malicious code. Microsoft is addressing this issue by providing mechanisms in the ActiveX development kit to let the user verify the signature of an application before permitting a control to be downloaded. It is hoped that this capability will instill confidence in users to download components without fear of virus or other booby traps.

Browsers Get Real (Time)

While the number of competitors in the browser market will continue to thin, there is still room for further innovative activity. The key is that plug-in architectures will evolve further, with Netscape Navigator leading the way. Many vendors will use both the ActiveX and Java VM capabilities to extend the capabilities of the major browsers and create niche markets for their products. Netscape and Microsoft will themselves work to provide a more dynamic presentation of multimedia content. For instance, to gain a more real-time experience, Netscape is integrating technology to view Adobe Acrobat's Portable Document Format (PDF)-based documents one page at a time during document downloading instead of requiring a complete document to download before being able to display it. Similar capabilities will also be applied to Shockwave by Macromedia for running Director movies over the Web. Real-time audio and video playback with RealAudio and VDOnet's VDOlive will achieve dynamic play through data streaming technology. New approaches will shift the concept of how real-time graphics sequences are played out. Unlike Shockwave, which transmits traditional rasterized graphics, new real-time Web graphics players—such as WebXpresso from DataView Corporation—send object-oriented, parametric models of the data to the browser, resulting in more nearly instantaneous feedback for the user's actions. Essentially, WebXpresso updates components or parameters of the displayed graphics model on the fly as opposed to retransmitting the entire individual animation frames that have changed—an approach that is quite bandwidth heavy.

With fewer, but more capable browsers becoming the standard, it becomes possible to relax so-called "good conduct rules," which ensured that the lowest common denominator browser could handle the display of the HTML page supplied by the Web server. Key limitations have included color reduction to 256, graphic file sizes to less than 20K, and the use of "ALT" tags for text-only browsers. The bar should quickly raise on these items with the ability to transmit at higher bandwidth and with higher resolution and more colors standard in monitors.

Navigation tools for Web browsing will continue to improve. Several recent products perform Web mapping to help users understand the hierarchy of information available, both from their Intranet Web server and from the Internet. Other products maintain a history of where you've browsed to help you get there again (Toshiba Zoowerks or HindSite by ISYS/Odyssey Development). These programs index the cache of traversed pages within your browser, so the next time you'd like to return to a site you've failed to bookmark, you simply enter a keyword or Boolean expression and the index returns the location with the date of your previous visit.

Further extensions to Web browsing may turn the Web PC into a more passive experience, like the PointCast experience in which Web content, including graphics, multimedia, audio, or text, might be fed to the user automatically. Both Netscape and Microsoft have this capability in the works.

Content Creation Becomes Automatic (or at Least Automated)

Significant progress will be made in the next several years in the area of Web page construction. "Building block" Web content-creation tools will emerge. These tools will allow users to snap together predefined, possibly parameterized, content components like building blocks to deliver a consistent look and feel. Increasingly, it has become important that Web sites don't look like an eclectic collection of ill-mated content elements. End users and companies desiring professional appearance will not accept patchwork solutions. To ensure consistency, new and emerging Web construction kits will use preconfigured content templates that can be modified with user preferences. It becomes a simple thing to have the company logo consistently sized, colored, and placed in all external marketing on the Web, for example.

Automation of editing functions will simplify the construction of graphical elements. Advanced edit tools will integrate HTML pages more automatically with back ends (Java or ActiveX applets) that perform such functions as database access. Wizards and drop-in objects will allow the insertion of a link to a database interface component so that Web users of the HTML page can access an Oracle or Sybase corporate database without any lower level knowledge of programming the Web server CGI or ISAPI interface layer. Even further automation advances will eventually result in the ability of the creation tool to "learn" patterns of construction from users, so that preferential use of presentation styles (colors, text sizing, font, background, headers, and so on) are automatically applied if desired. This could be based on the type of the document. Automations will also come in cases like online product catalogs or troubleshooting tips, where the structure of the presentation is repeated consistently, but specific content is different from item to item. One such new tool might be a "catalog" designer that allows the inherent variations from page to page to be automatically provided by a database source. This would save significant time versus a process of manually re-creating each catalog item from the last.

A key point as we move forward is the distinction between the "blank page" approach (FrontPage, WebPad, or Frontier's WebDesigner, which is contained on the CD included with this book) and the "lead the user with a step-by-step assist" approach (WebPublisher is a great example of a recent product of this ilk). In the blank page approach, a powerful, full set of options allows the user to create any range of graphics or content desired, from simple text, to stylized graphics, to frames and tables, starting essentially with a blank screen. An experienced user can quickly select the elements that are important and, using the tool, be completely free to go in any content-creation direction he or she desires. The step-by-step approach offers sample templates onto which users add the specifics of their needed content. In the WebPublisher model, the extent of options is somewhat reduced, but users get to something that's highly functional in much less time. Of course, by using a "cooky cutter" approach, you may not get the rich professional look needed to present your company's image on the corporate home page for external customers. But for that quick and easy human resources announcement, this approach may be just the ticket for getting the content out in just a few minutes.

The distinction between sophisticated drawing and graphics creation packages and Web content-creation tools will also gradually disappear. In fact, many of the graphics/"paintkit" creation companies have already entered the Web content-creation marketplace. As a final thought, Web site management could become part of the designer tool, such as document/folder placement, or search/storage for clip art-type entities. This seems to be the path of Microsoft's Frontpage product.

Search—A Fast Walk Through the Corporate Information Stores

Perhaps, the most compelling aspect of the Intranet paradigm is the information management capability. But, beyond new formats for information creation and presentation (HTML, multimedia, and downloadable Java and ActiveX apps) and the efficiencies offered by Web servers for storing information, there is the ubiquitous need to provide tools and algorithms for efficiently finding critical pieces of information across an almost unlimited multinetwork-network, multicomputer-computer "search" domain. The delivery of a next generation of search technologies may well prove to be the crowning technological achievement of the Internet, Intranet, Extranet era.

The Web-centric search paradigm begins with the ability to index files that are managed by a Web server or are part of the native computer file system. Typical access is provided through keyword, or keyword combined with Boolean operators for more complex information retrieval. Leadership products like the Frontier Technology Cybersearch 3.0 product allow users to index their own desktops, access remote Web-servers, integrate the search results of multiple Web-search sites (AltaVista, Lycos, Yahoo!, Excite, and others), and access remote indexing of corporate file servers, all in one integrated search retrieval. In a typical search query, the keyword is entered through a common search interface; the search request is formatted and communicated to the search server (possibly via HTTP at the Web Server); the search engine makes an access to the index engine, which returns the documents that match the query input; information is ordered as to relevancy versus the query string; and document addresses are returned in an ordered list as a Web page for browser display. More sophisticated options are rapidly emerging.

Search technologies are rapidly evolving in several ways. New search tools attempt to make the user more effective at constructing search queries in a variety of ways. As an example, some new products gather user preferences to direct search retrieval or learn from past query patterns. Next-generation systems may be able to infer from the pattern of previous searches, subparameters for search that will more accurately refine the set of relevant matches to the specific query. Others are actually using the cached retrievals of previous queries (whether or not they've been bookmarked). In this way, users do not have to remember the location they found three months ago; it's automatically part of the local index that can be searched. Category search processing can be used as a way to limit or group search inquiries. Other tools are starting to exploit more context-sensitive search algorithms. Very quickly we are beginning to see the first wave of natural language queries. Natural language carries the difficulties of resolving ambiguities in the search sentences and requires the ability to associate concepts and deal with syntactic or semantic ambiguities. Significant research has occurred in this area over the last 25 years.

A great deal of interest has been generated in the area of intelligent search agents. These software agents work on behalf of a user. The user specifies information that is of importance for him or her and the agent watches for the appearance of relevant content. For instance, the user indicates that information appearing on "wireless communication" should be returned. When an AT&T home page appears with a reference to the development of this technology, the information is automatically forwarded to the user. Agent technology will continue to rapidly improve in both performance and capability over the next several years. The challenge of covering the breadth of both internal and external information sources will provide significant opportunity for growth in the information search retrieval sector.

As stated, information management is one of the key capabilities of Web-centric systems. It seems likely, for the foreseeable future, that the independent search companies will be able to provide capabilities beyond the standard offerings of desktop operating system providers such as Microsoft. The breadth and complexity of the search problem space will require a continuous stream of innovative solutions not likely available from a single source. Very little has been accomplished in the way of information search standards or common architectural components to allow products to play together well—the exception being the availability of document filtering technology, such as that provided by Mastersoft or Inso, that defines the document structures to enable a wide variety of document types to be indexed.

VRML/3-D Worlds Bring a New Dimension to Information Access and Applications

In the beginning, there was VRML 1.0. A downloaded VRML 1.0 file from an HTTP server enables you to navigate with 6 degrees of freedom and link to other URLs. VRML is defined to construct an interactive hyperspace in which you can move along any of the three directions and rotate along three orientations. At the core of the 3-D model is a hierarchical map of all nodes representing the various aspects of a 3-D scene. The classical elements include textures, lighting, shading, geometry, and relational orientations, including nesting. As we move toward the latest specification, VRML 2.0, ratified in August, 1996, things get literally more dynamic. Based on SGI's Moving Worlds proposal, VRML 2.0 provides extensive facilities for defining motion and world dynamics. Virtual switches allow the animation of scene elements, such as initiating movement for an in-scene elevator or conveyor belt. Sound can be a dynamic element of a scene, for instance, increasing the level of a warning siren as you move closer to it. The ability to tie textures and even map video onto arbitrary objects increases the sense of realism in scenes constructed with VRML. A wealth of controls allows dynamics of background conditions, especially lighting effects and shading. Controls initiated by collision detection allow for responsive actions to take place, increasing the opportunity for programmable interactivity. For clarity of message presentation, text can be defined so it always faces the user.

In emerging products, the VRML editing tools work with other graphics creation tools to define the detailed graphics of individual components of a scene. Silicon Graphics' Open GL, supported by Microsoft and others, is an important graphics construction language and, in fact, a precursor to VRML evolution. Individual entities within a scene may be defined by Open GL code, then placed within the VRML program defining the scene.

Like HTML, a VRML scene can be constructed completely in text mode, including the specification of Java applets. Over the next year, ActiveX extensions will also appear. New VRML editors will provide the ability to work entirely in object-level space, without text programming of the associated VRML constructs. This will allow nonprogrammer designers (marketing, advertising, copy personnel) to produce professional levels of 3-D interactive scenes, such as 3-D shopping malls, online catalogs, or a 3-D corridor of products and associated technical tips. Preconfigured objects with built-in capabilities will be provided. For instance, in building an office, it will be possible to select placement of a door that has been preconfigured to open and close.

A key component in the delivery of a 3-D VRML production capability is the viewer or browser. It is critical for an acceptable and pleasing experience that the browser provide excellent navigation capability. It is important that the controls are intuitive and responsive. Proper rendering and speed are, of course, critical elements. The best of the emerging browsers take advantage of hardware acceleration using 3-D accelerator boards. Over the next several years, much of the necessary graphics/rendering capabilities will become integrated in the PC. For those with Unix workstations, several products that are already available provide the inherent graphics acceleration, rendering engines, and the necessary internal bus bandwidth to effectively move large 3-D geometries.

The market will fill with Open GL and VRML renderers. Hardware accelerators like the GLINT chip for fast Open GL will be mass-produced for inclusion in PC packages. Because of the time between major software releases, as long as 18 months, and reflecting the awareness of a need for standards, many of the popular VRML and 3-D packages provide plug-in APIs. So if a new texture routine becomes available for rendering the surface of a peach more accurately, it can work in the context of an existing 3-D rendering package by plugging in.

VRML and 3-D interactive technologies are much different than classical multimedia graphics or video displays. In 3-D interactive, the shapes and objects are produced and rendered in real time as opposed to a prerecorded video sequence that is simply played back. This opens great opportunities for fully interactive sessions, which can be fully navigated by control of the user.

Of course, this capability cannot be achieved without some serious complexity in programming, and to be interactive, the data bandwidth and rendering capability of the client machine become paramount issues.

The applications supported by VRML and 3-D are wide and varied. For example, and somewhat unexpectedly, VR interfaces and 3-D software are changing the way financial traders perceive the market. Traders can immerse themselves in an animated 3-D scene where they chart market movements by interacting with 3-D audio and visual cues. The market data appears as 3-D objects. By moving through the 3-D trading world, users walk around real-time graphs, bar charts, and floating text. A leader in this field is Dive Laboratories, a virtual reality company. Data for these systems is picked up from live data broadcasts provided by financial news services. Software maps individual stocks as well as groups of related stocks. Comparisons of growth and related financial metrics can be graphically assessed. It's possible to set monitor points, such as flashing green or red points, as stock values hit predesignated buy or sell points.

Web Servers Grow Up

Web servers provide the server components of the Intranet client/server model. Much of the growth in capability of Intranets will depend on the continuing evolution of Web server performance and features. Major efforts are under way by both Netscape and Microsoft, as well as a host of others, to compete in this arena. The winners will be defined by the most innovative combination of user-oriented capabilities and high-speed delivery. Many companies first see their Intranet Web servers as delivering the information content for Web pages. End users want Web pages that extract information from corporate databases, derive user-configurable reports, and launch downloadable applications to perform a variety of analytical and information-processing functions. At the next tier, users are demanding that the information hierarchy of the corporation be made available to search queries by retrieving the location of critical information from Web server information indexes. Others, seeking improvements in productivity, are demanding extensions to collaborative capabilities, including improved messaging; workflow-based task scheduling; integrated calendaring; and online conferencing technologies, including video, whiteboarding, and audio. Finally, everyone is interested in ensuring that interactions among users and between corporations can be conducted over private, secure, and authenticated communication channels. Security is the key to playing in the Web server game from here on. There is a lot of work to be done, but the competition to bring out new capabilities will produce rapid innovation and a host of new products to get these jobs accomplished before the turn of the century.

11

Improvements in the management of the Web server will accompany improvements in the speed at which Web servers are able to respond to HTTP requests to upload Web pages. Most emerging systems will need to provide remote administration capabilities for setting group and individual access rights to Web content. It is becoming increasingly clear that without distributed management of the Web server, the Webmaster becomes a bottleneck for effective utilization. He or she is simply unable to support the large community of users that can be handled by modern Web servers. Facilities will be needed to more effectively map logical URLs to physical directories. Advances in search indexing will require integration with the access rights control on protected information sources. Users should not be allowed to reach or even know of the existence of documents that are under access restriction. Better tools will emerge to ensure the integrity of information links between Web documents. Hyperlink management requires simple but comprehensive graphical interfaces that promote rapid repair of dangling links to documents that no longer exist. The integrity of the information Web must be maintained to preserve user confidence.

Web security improvements will start with the ability to authenticate both the Web server and client. The strongest emerging protocol to support this is the SSLv3 standard promoted by Netscape. Today, these systems use certificates that are provided by an external source such as Verisign (for which they charge a fee for each client and server certificate). This level of confidence is probably not needed in many Intranet situations, and it is likely that new server products will include certificate-issuing capabilities. This is a planned feature in a near release of the Frontier Intranet Genie product, for instance. Message integrity checking is also key. To address authority-related issues, standards will emerge to apply digital certificates to the signing of digital documents. It will be important to be able to verify that indeed the company's CFO signed off on the new computer system. Other security features will include various levels of access control filters. Users will be able to restrict access by domain, IP range, and individual page.

An extremely important area of growth for Web servers will be in the tools that become available for linking to corporate databases. Nearly all of the major database manufacturers (Oracle, Sybase, Informix) are rushing to provide CGI, ISAPI, or NSAPI server interface APIs to support back-end server application interfaces to their ODBC/SQL-compliant database engines. Rushing in from the other spectrum, new Intranet-oriented companies familiar with server side back ends and Web forms are building programmer-less database interface construction capability. These packages allow users to specify data sources, designated record/table fields, and a format for presenting the retrieved database content, all from a browser-initiated sequence of Web forms. Equally important for some companies will be the availability of high-performance gateways to legacy systems, including CICS and DB2.

Web servers will also need to grow additional services. Considerable development effort is being expended to automate extensions to emerging directory service protocols such as DNS and LDAP (Lightweight Directory Access Protocol). E-mail server capability will continue to grow. Most emerging e-mail servers will be based on the IMAP4 specification, which more effectively supports replicated access to the client's message store. This protocol provides excellent support for the roving e-mail user or user with both home and office access. Another feature that exists on some servers today and will become prevalent on most forthcoming servers, is proxy server capability. Proxy servers can cache commonly requested Web pages for faster access.

Specialty servers will also emerge for such functions as the development of Web catalogs or to support electronic stores. Capabilities may include order forms, search engines, purchase tracking, billing support, and so on. Support for electronic commerce from specialized back-end services that can be accessed via Web pages will be a strong niche play for some Web servers, but look for extensions that support advertising initiatives to grow faster in the next three or four years. Web servers will be equipped with facilities to process the demographics of users and feed advertising content to them based on specified preferences, their past Web page access patterns, and other demographic details.

Intranet/Extranet Applications Emerge and Grow

The appearance of some of the technologies defined so far will open new opportunities for companies wishing to apply their Intranet capability in an end-user commercial interaction—that is, an Extranet. Some interesting possibilities just beginning are described here.

Electronic Funds Transfer

A recent newspaper byline proclaimed: "Banking services—not banks—needed in the next century." Online transactions and digital wallets will be important components in an e-commerce world. Work is under way to deliver stored value cards and other electronic payment systems. Online ordering of merchandise will provide consumers with an effective, convenient capability for many common shopping activities. Corporations will see their potential customer bases grow to include many additional global regions. However, the pace of electronic commerce will be affected by the development of adequate security measures to ensure noninterference and no piracy, as well as the acceptance by the general public that safeguards can really be trusted. However, these are not the only issues. In October 1996, the first FDIC public examination of smart cards and telepayment processes came amid the agency's review of whether stored value cards should qualify for federal deposit insurance. Card fraud and counterfeiting emerged as important concerns in the initial reports of this investigation.

In a related area, products are being quickly introduced to support home banking. Microsoft in late 1996 was pushing its Open Financial Connectivity (OFC) specification used in its MONEY software package. This constituted a direct challenge to the Intuit Quicken (9 million user base) product. The emerging Microsoft capability promises brokerage services and other features, such as 15 minutes delayed stock quotes, through its Investor Portfolio software. OFC also defines a secure standardized method for interacting with account information or bill payment requests. In 1997, Elvis will arrive. Elvis is a set of ActiveX controls that are designed to handle a series of home banking and bill payment functions with a Web browser. Elvis should be able to look up a statement, transfer funds, and check a balance. We see continued growth of these financial online applications in the home banking sector. Competition is heated between the banking industry and the major platform and application vendors. Because of this competition, it may likely be several years before the standards that will be required to ensure interoperability between providers will be resolved.

Online Shopping

Online shopping services have been appearing on the Net over the last couple of years. So while not quite a new trend, there is likely to be incredible interest and energy put into furthering online shopping services in the next several years and into the next century. Online shopping carries some of the same consumer confidence baggage as electronic funds transfer and home banking. However, there are some interesting technologies that differ in this realm. Successful merchandisers will need to take advantage of all the latest multimedia and 3-D presentation capabilities to win over consumers. Online, any company, regardless of size, can paint a dazzling cyber-image. Artificial intelligence techniques can be applied at Web servers to effectively match customer preferences with the right set of product advertisements and product specifications to best capture the customer's attention. In one recent approach, refurbished computers are offered to a subscribing user group in an "auction" format. The bidding starts at $0, and a closing time for the last bid, usually 24 to 48 hours, is established. Online, users see the latest competitive bid and can place bids at any time. Action on this approach has been described as a "feeding frenzy," often resulting in final bids in excess of retail value. It simply becomes too difficult to let the little old lady from Pasadena get the product.

Some companies entering the online shopping area will work as intermediaries for a number of vendors. The Ziff-Davis publishing company is promoting its online *NetBuyer*. Its popular *Computer Shopper* consumer magazine has 188 vendors participating. There are 16 categories of products, plus editorial content, comparisons, and tech tips. Ziff-Davis sells banners that promote their vendors' products at $1,850–$10,800 a month.

Advertising

As reported in the November 1996 *PC Magazine*, "Web based advertising revenue increased 83 percent within the second quarter and is well on its way to reaching $312 million by the end of the year and $5 billion a year by the year 2000, according to a study by Jupiter Communications, a New York City-based market-research firm." The leader of the pack in the first half of the year was Netscape with over $9 million in ad revenue, followed by four of the most popular search sites—InfoSeek, Yahoo!, Lycos, and Excite, with revenues ranging from $3.6 million to $5.7 million. The real question, which has been difficult to answer, is how much real business in transactions has resulted from the advertising. It's not likely that this question will be fully answered in the next year or so.

Web/Intranet/Extranet customer interactions do have some interesting characteristics and differentiators from classical media advertising (newspaper and magazine ads, and TV commercials). With online access comes the opportunity to interactively screen the customer and put the appropriate advertising, based on the customer's profile and some demographic reasoning, in front of the customer. It's possible for popular search sites, for instance, to track the pattern of Web locations an individual visits and form best-guess reasoning on the sort of advertising and, presumably, products that will most appeal to this specific customer.

Interactive Services (Business Opportunities Begin to Explode)

For many years, the hotel industry has been one of the driving forces for interactive television. We can now look forward to the emergence of a number of related interactive services, ranging from Internet/Intranet access, to online shopping, to vacation-planning services, to time-shifted entertainment delivery. Business travelers will readily pay for high-speed links back to the home office database when connecting their own laptop computers. Others will need a complete access interface, including the terminal that might well be the television. Hilton is just now making available a "smart desk" concept consisting of a standard computer with high-speed link, office software, Internet access tools, and software to send and receive faxes. With picture-in-picture capability, the TV may, in fact, serve both functions at one time. Online, interactive gaming within 3-D VRML worlds will eventually take over from the direct in-hotel-room computer gaming (Sega and Nintendo) just emerging in some leading hotel chains. More standard services will include e-mail, Yellow Pages service, travel scheduling and booking, local attraction viewing, meal arrangements, and catalog browsing.

Management of information distribution requires a well-coordinated approach and the appropriate tools. The folks at PointCast in Cupertino, California, have developed a widely viewed information network today that will expand to include more regionalized information, such as local weather reports, as well as grow content to include regional and national newspapers. The PointCast model is highly visual, using such motifs as a scrolling ticker tape to deliver stock prices and trading transactions, as well as extensive investment details in the form of charts and plots. The PointCast presentation will run in both a selected front-screen mode or as a screen saver. In the future, this sort of delivery capability will become a standard component of the corporate Intranet. In fact, PointCast will likely lead the way with the future delivery of its "Iserver," which will allow the continuous broadcast of corporate information on the local Intranet.

11

Soon, it will be possible to order tickets to many events online. Major players such as Ticketmaster, IBM, and Walt Disney Company have begun to create online ticketing capabilities for theme parks, musical events, repertory theater, and sporting events. It will be possible to go online, view the prospective seating options available at that time, select the seats, and initiate payment. Payment may work in one of several ways. One option is to be billed, a second is to immediately use your credit card, a third may be the use of a digital wallet or e-cash, and fourth may be the use of a subscription service in which the credit card number has been previously provided and verified with the provider.

Multimedia-Based Applications

Digital photography, while already appearing, is poised to revolutionize the picture-taking world. But first, the prices of digital cameras need to come down. A new approach, beginning to be offered by the Kodak Digital Processing team, invites you to send in a roll of film and receive a free Kodak picture disk, a floppy containing up to 28 digitized images. With Microsoft's Picture It Software you can edit the photos and share them over your business Intranet. As an added service, Kodak will soon offer an extended Web catalog of finishing options that you can use to upload to Kodak your digitally stored photographs for creation of posters, advertising material, or even to place on promotional items such as coffee mugs and sweatshirts. And, since these are digital images, a huge variety of postprocessing options are available. The lighting can be changed, images can be superimposed, color schemas altered, and the size adjusted.

Putting It All Together

The Intranet and emerging Extranet paradigms will likely prove to be the information platforms of the next decade or so. Companies that clearly understand their own internal bottlenecks and bring the right innovative Intranet technologies to bear will be able to take advantage of all the emerging opportunities. Opportunities for direct customer and global interaction will further fuel the onset of the Extranet paradigm, leveraging directly the tools and technologies introduced for constructing the corporate Intranet. The competitive opportunities afforded by a change in the structure of computing platforms doesn't come along very often and is quite visibly producing a torrent of new products. At best, for the next couple of years, it will be difficult for the standards needed to ensure interoperability at the desktop to keep pace. Successful companies will need to carefully consider which products to apply as solutions to their problems, but the competition and the new capabilities provided by the emerging Intranet technologies will outpace companies that do not choose to participate or wait too long to enter the fray.

APPENDIX A

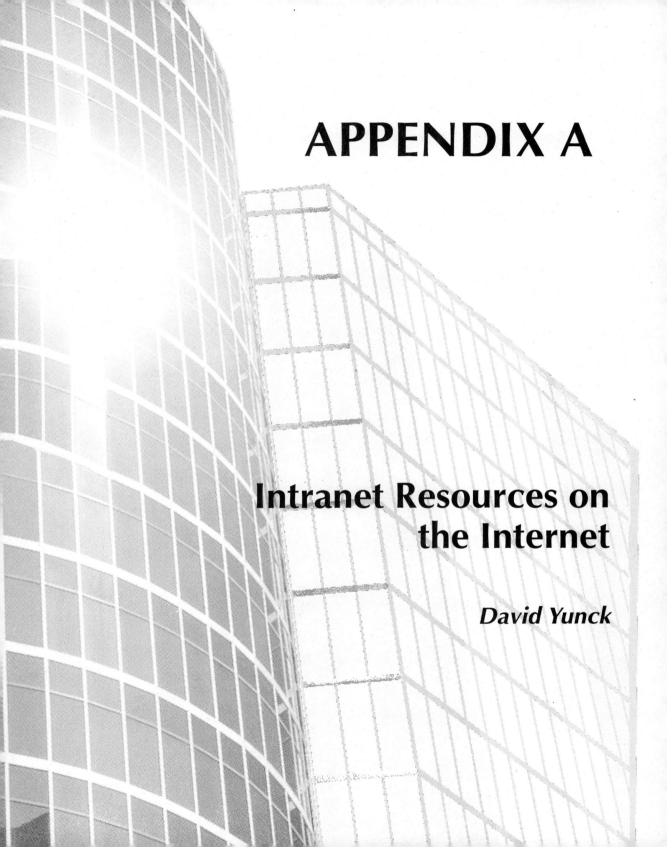

Intranet Resources on the Internet

David Yunck

Information is power! To further assist you in setting up an effective and efficient corporate Intranet, we provide you with a list of valuable resources that complement the content of this book. This appendix is a collection of Internet-based Intranet information ranging from Web sites to Internet mail lists to Usenet newsgroups.

World Wide Web Intranet Resources

Here are a number of Web sites that provide Intranet-related information to users. In the future, we will definitely see more sites that build on this list.

A

Building a Corporate Intranet: How to use Internet Tools to Bring the Information Superhighway In-House
http://webcom.com/wordmark/

The Complete Intranet Resource
http://www.intrack.wm/intranet.htm

David Strom's Web Informant
http://www.strom.com

Inetra Home for Intranet Planners
http://www.kensho.com/hip/

Institute for Academic Technology: Intranet Readings and Resources
http://www.iat.unc.edu/guides/irg-34.html#www

Intranet Design
http://www.innergy.com/

Intranet Journal
http://www.brill.com/intranet

Intranet Resource Centre
http://www.infoweb.com.au/intralnk.htm

Intranets: How the Web is Used Within Enterprises
http://www.cio.com/WebMaster/sem3_intro.html

Intranut
http://www.intranut.com//index.htm

Server Watch
http://www.serverwatch.iworld.com

WebCompare
http://webcompare.iworld.com/

Intranet Resources on Usenet Newsgroups

Newsgroups provide a forum for discussion of topics that pertain to specific areas of interest. Participants access information on a newsgroup server using a newsreader client software package. At the moment, no newsgroups relate specifically to Intranets. However, the following list will point you toward newsgroups that discuss concepts and tools that help make up an intranet:

    comp.groupware
    comp.infosystems
    comp.infosystems.www.authoring.cgi
    comp.infosystems.www.servers.misc
    comp.os.ms-windows.networking.tcp-ip
    comp.os.authoring.html
    comp.os.authoring.misc
    comp.os.browsers.misc

Intranet Resources Mailing List

Mailing lists are similar to newsgroups except that subscribers receive specific information from other subscribers and, in turn, can respond to individuals or to the entire list of subscribers via their e-mail.

The dsdelft.nl mailing list is such a resource. To subscribe, send an e-mail to majordomo@dsdelft.nl with the text **subscribe intranet-lijst** in the body of the message. To unsubscribe, send an e-mail to majordomo@dsdelft.nl with the text **unsubscribe intranet-lijst *<your mail address>*** in the body of the message.

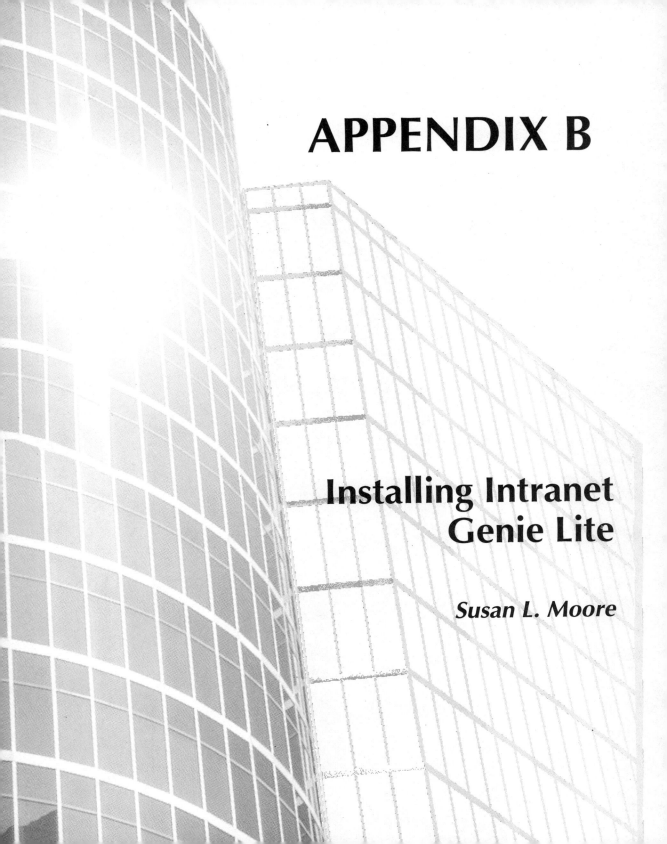

APPENDIX B

Installing Intranet Genie Lite

Susan L. Moore

In the back of your book, you should have a CD-ROM. Included on the CD-ROM is a Lite version of Frontier Technologies' Intranet Genie™—software that allows you to benefit from Web technology, without the hassle. By now, you know why you need an Intranet: Electronic distribution of information makes your organization more efficient, thereby reducing costs and increasing productivity. Secure, versatile, scaleable, and affordable, Intranet Genie is especially useful for small- to medium-sized businesses, or corporate departments that want to take advantage of an NT-based server solution. With all the necessary ingredients in a single box, Intranet Genie simplifies the entire process of establishing and managing an Intranet.

What's in Intranet Genie Lite?

The product you have on your CD-ROM is a scaled-down, three-user version of Intranet Genie. Once you have installed Intranet Genie Lite, you can begin to utilize the many applications that make an Intranet valuable to your company. Here are the pieces included with Intranet Genie Lite:

B

♦ *SuperWeb Server* SuperWeb™ Server is a multipurpose vehicle for sharing information internally and publishing information externally. Both internal and external audiences will find it uncomplicated, yet it does more than an ordinary Web server. Its modular design allows users to easily integrate their Web information with third-party or in-house applications, such as inventory systems or electronic data interchange (EDI) systems.

♦ *WebMaster* Using WebMaster, you can set up and maintain your Web site quickly and easily. It has intuitive interfaces for setting up your groups, users, files, and folders. Check how often the files on your Web site have been accessed by checking their logs. The SuperWeb Master, a role normally played by the system administrator, can even configure the server using WebMaster, making all maintenance in one easy-to-find location. To maintain your Web site, you can access the WebDesigner, ImageMaster, and HyperCheck applications right from WebMaster.

♦ *WebDesigner* WebDesigner can act as a stand-alone HTML editor or can be used to create and modify documents registered with SuperWeb Server. You can use WebDesigner to open and edit documents registered with SuperWeb Server. You can then edit and save documents on your SuperWeb Server. WebDesigner supports many standard HTML features, such as tables, frames, forms, and lists.

♦ *HyperCheck* Who wants to put pages on their Web site without knowing whether or not the hyperlinks contain valid URLs? Use SuperWeb's HyperCheck to check the hyperlinks of one file, a group of files, or even your entire Web site. Not only can you check the links to other pages on your site, but you can also check any links you have created to external Web pages.

♦ *ImageMaster* You can use ImageMaster to create maps on images (such as .GIF files) so that clicking on different regions of the image sends Web users to different pages. In today's fast-paced world, you need to grab people's attention quickly. Exciting graphics can help you do so, and increase the chance of Web users returning to your Web site to check out your latest graphics. Making these graphics functional makes your page even more practical, yet fun to use. For example, if the state of Wisconsin decided to create a home page for tourism, what better way to make the page shine than to provide Web users with a state map to click on. If they click on Milwaukee, for example, they get the tourist information for the Milwaukee area.

♦ *Tapestry Browser* The high-performance browser in Intranet Genie Lite lets you view World Wide Web, Gopher, Archie, Veronica, and CSO Phone Book sites. It displays Web, Gopher, and other Internet sites by categories in the Internet Organizer. To open a connection, all you do is double-click on it. This version of Tapestry Browser currently supports SSLv2 for secure transfer of information.

♦ *Serial Number Server* The Serial Number Server assigns serial numbers to the three PCs on your network that are running the Intranet Genie Lite client applications. The Serial Server Manager lets you see which clients are assigned which serial numbers, and allows you to edit any error messages the client computers might see.

♦ *SuperWeb Debug Server* The debug version has the appearance of the regular SuperWeb Server, but it is only to be used for testing back-end services (or even a Web page) before putting it on your real SuperWeb Server for everyone to use. The Debug Server must be installed on a different Windows NT computer than the one you run your live SuperWeb Server on. To install the SuperWeb Debug Server, see the section "Installing Additional Components of Intranet Genie Lite."

What's in the Full Version of Intranet Genie?

If you decide to purchase the full version of Intranet Genie (which includes Windows 3.1x support), you could also get applications such as:

- E-mail
- Newsreader
- Indexing tool
- HTML conversion tool
- Database access utility
- Metasearch of premier Internet search sites

Also included with the full Intranet Genie are servers such as:

- POP3 Mail Server
- DNS Server
- News Server

The full version of Intranet Genie includes CyberSearch, a personal information manager and time saver. Just type in a keyword, and a list of possible resources appears, ranked by relevancy—simply double-click on the reference to access it. You can also use CyberSearch to search the indexes created by your indexing utility.

For more information about the full version of Intranet Genie, contact Frontier Technologies at 1 (800) 929-3054, or visit our Web site at http://www.frontiertech.com.

B

Other Information on Your CD-ROM

Besides Intranet Genie Lite, your CD-ROM also includes the following pieces:

- Internet Explorer, Microsoft's Internet browser. Installation of Internet Explorer is covered later in this appendix.
- Product overviews, which explain some of the features and functionality of products from Frontier Technologies. Included are overviews of CyberJunction, CyberSearch, and the SuperTCP Suite family. The first time you view one of the demonstrations, you will be directed through a brief installation of DemoShield.
- A README.WRI file is contained in the root of your CD-ROM (such as d:\, where d: is your CD-ROM drive). If you have any questions about Intranet Genie Lite, first consult this file before contacting Frontier Technologies' technical support.

Installing Intranet Genie Lite on Windows NT

On Windows NT, you can choose to install the client applications, the server applications, or both. Client applications include Tapestry Browser, WebMaster, WebDesigner, HyperCheck, and ImageMaster. The servers include SuperWeb Server and Serial Number Server. See the earlier section "What's in Intranet Genie Lite?" for a description of the applications.

CAUTION: You need to install the server applications on one Windows NT computer so that your client computers have something to connect to. You can install the client applications up to three times. You can place one, two, or all three of the client sets on a Windows NT computer.

System Requirements

Before you install Intranet Genie Lite, be sure your computer meets the following criteria.

Client Installation

◆ Windows NT 3.51 or 4.0 (server or workstation) installed and running properly

◆ 486/66 or higher processor

◆ 16MB of memory (RAM)

◆ 35MB of hard drive space

◆ TCP/IP stack installed and running (consult your Windows NT documentation if you are not sure if you have a TCP/IP stack)

◆ CD-ROM drive

Server Installation

◆ Windows NT 3.51 (workstation or server) or 4.0 (server) installed and running properly

◆ 486/66 or higher processor; Pentium 90 recommended

◆ 16MB of memory (RAM); 32MB or more recommended

◆ 50MB of hard drive space for Intranet Genie Lite; additional space is needed for users' files

◆ TCP/IP stack installed and running (consult your Windows NT documentation if you are not sure if you have a TCP/IP stack)

◆ CD-ROM drive

Installing Intranet Genie Lite for the First Time

CAUTION: Before you install the servers, you *must* be logged on to the Windows NT computer with an account that has **administrator privileges** and the user rights **"Log on as a Service"** and **"Log on Locally."** To do this, open User Manager (under the Administrative Tools group) and consult the online Help. If you need more instructions, see Microsoft's Help, and see the Help file on your CD-ROM (d:\server\cddisk\info4ms.hlp, where d:\ is your CD-ROM drive). If you use the Help file on the CD-ROM, note that you do not need to configure a Postmaster account, because you are not installing a mail server.

TIP: The following directions are intended for those of you installing a Frontier Technologies product for the first time. If you already have a product from Frontier Technologies, then during the installation, you will see a Type of Installation dialog box. Click the Install New button to install Intranet Genie Lite. If you have already installed either the Intranet Genie Lite clients or servers, go instead to the section "Installing Additional Components of Intranet Genie Lite."

B

1. Close all open applications. Do not exit Windows, or shut off your computer.

2. Remove the CD-ROM from the back of the book.

3. Open your computer's CD-ROM drive, insert the book's CD-ROM, and close the drive.

4. Do one of the following:

    ◆   The installation may begin immediately. If it does, you see a screen like the one shown in Figure B-1. You can then proceed to step 6.

    ◆   If the installation does not begin, go to step 5.

5. Do one of the following:

    ◆   Windows NT 3.51 users should select File, Run from Program Manager. In the displayed Run dialog box (shown here), enter **d:\setup**, where d:\ is your CD-ROM drive. Then click OK.

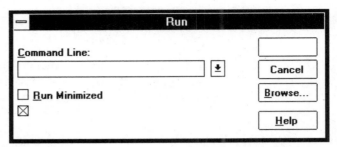

♦ Windows NT 4.0 users should click Start, Run from your Windows NT taskbar. In the displayed Run dialog box (shown here), enter **d:\setup**, where d:\ is your CD-ROM drive. Then click OK.

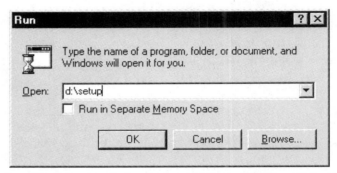

6. On the On the Frontier dialog box, as shown in Figure B-1, click on the drop-down menu, and highlight the Intranet Genie Lite Clients

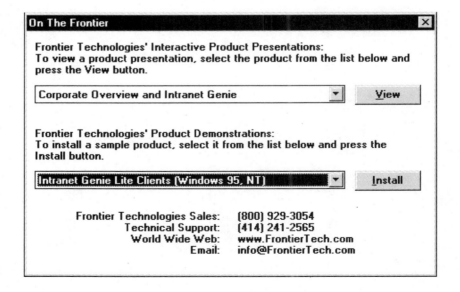

On the
Frontier
dialog box
Figure B-1.

(Windows 95, NT) or the Intranet Genie Lite Servers (Windows NT) option.

TIP: You can also select a product name from the Presentations drop-down list to first view a slide presentation of Frontier products. Once you have selected the product, click the View button to view the presentation. If this is the first demonstration you are viewing, you will be prompted to perform a short install of DemoShield.

7. On the Intranet Genie dialog box, shown next, click the Install Intranet Genie button to begin your installation.

TIP: If you would first like to see a slide presentation of Intranet Genie, click the View the Intranet Genie Overview Slide Presentation button.

B

8. In the Destination Directory dialog box, specify the directory where Intranet Genie Lite should be installed, or click OK to install in the default directory, SUPERTCP.

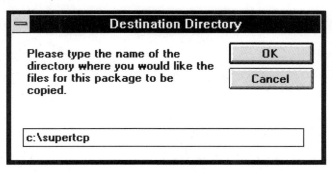

9. If the directory you choose to install Intranet Genie on doesn't exist, you are shown the following message. Click Yes to allow the installation program to create the directory for you.

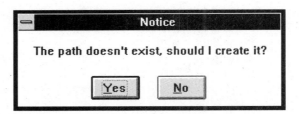

10. The following dialog box appears to remind you to shut down any open applications. This dialog box appears whether or not you have other applications open. If you do have applications open, shut them down. When you click OK, the Installer initializes.

11. In the User Identification dialog box, shown here, enter your name and the name of your company. This information is for use by your software. Click OK to continue.

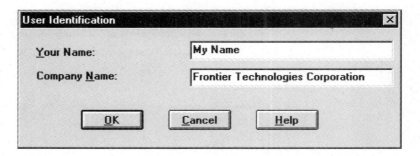

12. The Windows NT Privileges Warning dialog box displays, as shown here:

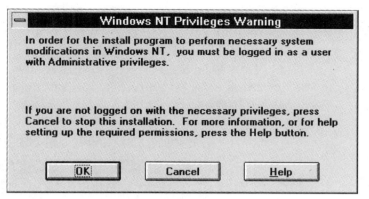

♦ If you are installing only the clients, click OK.

♦ If you are installing the servers, you need to create a Windows NT account with **administrator privileges** and "**Log on as a Service**" and "**Log on Locally**" user rights, as the Caution stated at the beginning of this section. If you forgot to do so, click the Cancel button to exit the installation and create the account, and log in with the new account. If you are already logged in with the correct account, click the OK button to continue your installation.

B

13. In the Intranet Genie Lite Edition dialog box, be sure to select the box for the application set you intend to install. You can select both the client and server sets. Click Install to continue.

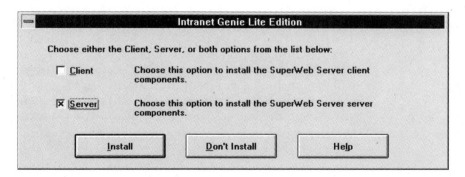

14. You then see the files for Intranet Genie Lite being installed, and your system is updated. You may also be told that your AUTOEXEC.BAT was altered. Then do one of the following:

♦ If you only installed the client applications, you may be asked if you want to reboot your computer. Please do so. Once your computer has restarted, you are ready to use Intranet Genie Lite!

♦ If you installed the servers, go on to the next step.

15. The Intranet Genie Setup Wizards: Information dialog box appears, as shown here:

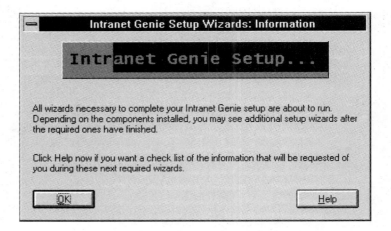

If you want to see what required wizards you are going to go through, click the Help button. Otherwise, click OK to continue.

NOTE: The only wizards that you must go through are the SuperWeb Server wizard and the Serial Number Setup wizard. Without running through these wizards, your Web server will not function properly and your clients will see error messages from the Serial Server when they attempt to run their applications. Later in the setup, you can choose whether or not you want to go through the User, Group, and Folder Setup wizards.

16. You are then greeted by the SuperWeb Server Setup Wizard dialog box, shown in Figure B-2. Click Next to move to the next wizard page.

17. The SuperWeb Server Setup wizard page, shown in Figure B-3, first asks you to enter the name you want to give your SuperWeb Server. Enter a specific name that you can easily recognize, in case more than one SuperWeb Server is installed on your network.

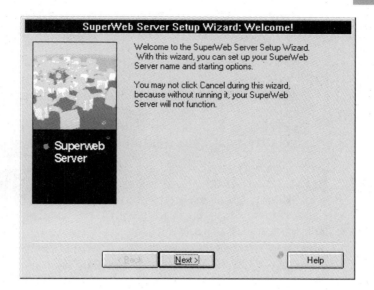

SuperWeb
Server Setup
Wizard:
Welcome!
page
Figure B-2.

18. You can select how to start your SuperWeb Server. If you are not familiar with Windows NT, you might want to leave the default value of Automatic. This means that SuperWeb Server will automatically start whenever you restart your computer. Click the Help button on the wizard page for more information about your starting options.

 B

Initial steps on
the SuperWeb
Server Setup
Wizard
dialog box
Figure B-3.

19. Click Next to continue your configuration.

20. On the Finished! dialog, shown in Figure B-4, click the Finish button to accept your changes and move to the next dialog box.

21. The SuperWeb Account dialog box, shown in Figure B-5, appears and asks you for a Windows NT account name and password. You *must* enter the username and password of an account with **administrator privileges** and the user rights **"Log on as a Service"** and **"Log on Locally."** Click the Continue button to move to the next wizard.

CAUTION: If the account you enter does not have these specific rights, you will encounter problems starting your SuperWeb Server. If you don't know how to set up such an account, see the Caution at the beginning of this section for information.

NOTE: If you created an account with these rights before you began the installation or during the installation, be sure to enter this account's information here. If you have not created such an account, you need to exit the installation and create the account now.

SuperWeb
Server Setup
Wizard:
Finished! page
Figure B-4.

SuperWeb Server Setup Wizard: Finished!

Congratulations! You have finished setting up your SuperWeb Server.

Note that when you log on to the Windows NT computer, you will need to log on as a user with Log on as a Service rights. If you do not, the SuperWeb Server will not start.

If you are not sure how to set up this account, run the installation again, and click the Help button on the dialog that tells you that you need Administartive privileges to install the Servers.

• Superweb Server

< Back   Finish   Help

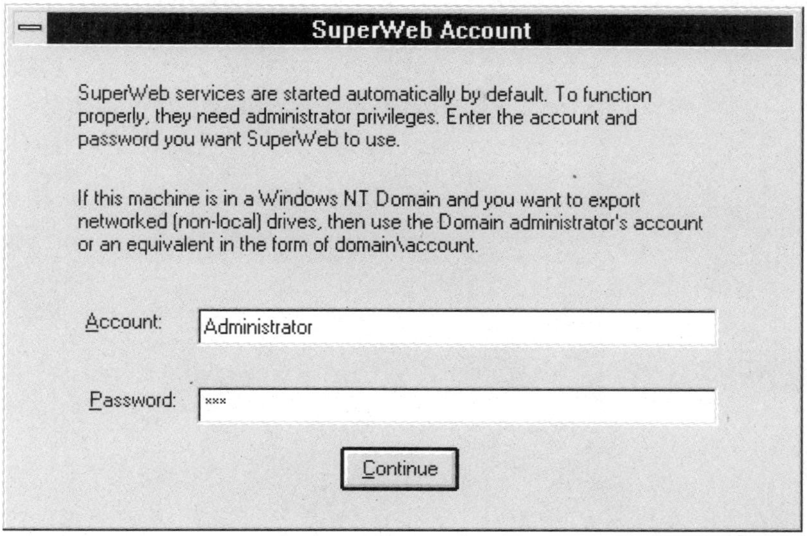

SuperWeb
Account
dialog box
Figure B-5.

22. The Serial Number Server wizard appears, as shown in Figure B-6. In this dialog box, click the Browse button to find the file on your CD-ROM that has a .FSN extension, such as LITE.FSN. This file contains the three client serial numbers that you are authorized to use. After you install one to three clients, they connect to the Serial Number Server to obtain their serial numbers.

FTC Serial
Number
Server Setup
Wizard:
Welcome!
page
Figure B-6.

23. Once you have found the file in the Browse dialog box, click OK.

24. Click Next on the Serial Number Server wizard page.

25. On the Finished! dialog box, shown in Figure B-7, click the Finish button.

26. The following dialog box displays to tell you that your serial numbers were successfully imported. Click OK.

27. In the Intranet Genie Setup Wizard dialog box, be sure that the User, Group, and Folder wizards are checked, as shown in Figure B-8. Then click Next.

TIP: To learn about each of these wizards, click once on the name of the wizard you are interested in to highlight it. Then click the Help on Selected Wizard button.

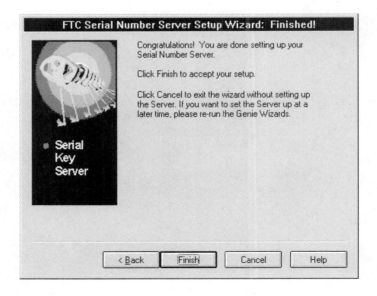

FTC Serial
Number
Server Setup
Wizard:
Finished! page
Figure B-7.

Intranet Genie
Setup Wizard:
Welcome!
page
Figure B-8.

28. On the initial User Setup wizard page, shown in Figure B-9, click the Next button to begin setting up your users. These are the people you are going to allow to connect to your SuperWeb Server and administer it.

 TIP: You can enter as many users as you want, as long as they are all logging in using one of your four (one server and three client) licenses.

 B

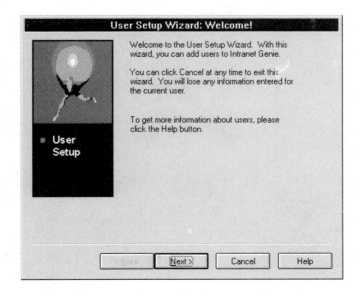

User Setup
Wizard:
Welcome!
page
Figure B-9.

NOTE: An account is automatically created on the Web server for a main administrator. The login name is Webmaster, with no password. The person with this login name, normally referred to as the SuperWeb Master, has control over every aspect of the SuperWeb Server. You should, therefore, be sure to place a password on this account when you have finished with the installation. Log in to the WebMaster application to add a password.

29. Enter a username on the next User Setup wizard page, shown in Figure B-10. This name can contain spaces. You might want to use first and last names to make identifying users easier.

30. You can either leave the Password field blank or enter a password for the new user. If you think you will be able to remember the password, enter one and inform the user of the password. Otherwise, you can let the user change his or her own password once Intranet Genie Lite is set up. If you enter a password, be sure to reenter it in the Password Verification field. Click Next to continue.

31. On the Additional User Information page, shown in Figure B-11, enter a description of the user. For example, you could enter what the person's job responsibilities are, or his or her job title.

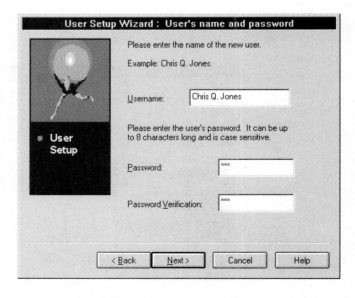

User Setup
Wizard:
User's Name
and Password
page
Figure B-10.

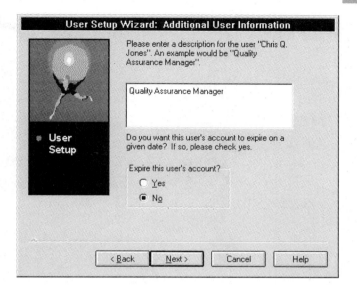

User Setup
Wizard:
Additional
User
Information
page
Figure B-11.

32. Do one of the following:

♦ If you want to set an expiration date for the user's account, select
the Yes radio button and click Next. You then see the User
Expiration Date page, shown in Figure B-12, where you can set the
time and date after which the account will no longer be valid. Click
Next on the User Expiration Date page to continue.

T IP: Setting expiration dates is really only necessary if you have
temporary help, such as consultants. Having their accounts expire
automatically means that no one needs to remember to remove the person
from the SuperWeb Server user list once that person is gone.

♦ If you don't see a need for setting an expiration date for the user's
account, select the No radio button and click Next.

33. On the Finished! page, shown in Figure B-13, you can decide whether or
not you want to add another user. Do one of the following:

♦ If you want to add another user, select the Yes radio button, click
Next, and repeat the steps starting at number 29.

♦ If you don't want to add another user, select the No radio button,
and click Finish to start the next wizard.

B

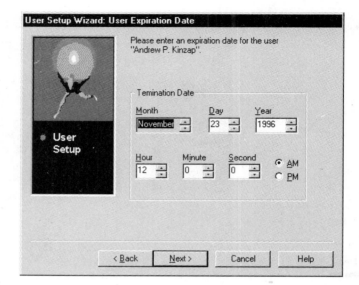

34. On the first page of the Group Setup wizard, shown in Figure B-14, click Next to begin setting up groups.

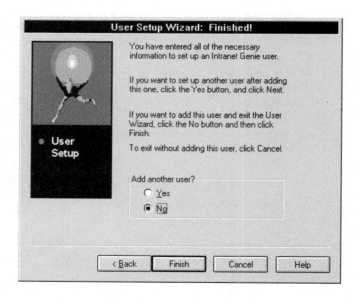

User Setup
Wizard:
Finished! page
Figure B-13.

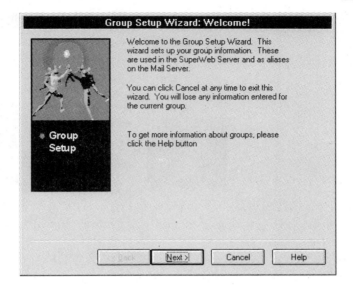

Group Setup
Wizard:
Welcome!
page
Figure B-14.

TIP: Rights to the folders you will create are set by groups. For example, the Engineering group may have access to a folder that the Marketing group does not. An easy way to set up groups is to set one up for each department. If you need to add more later, the SuperWeb Master can do so through the WebMaster application.

35. On the Group Name and Description page, shown in Figure B-15, first enter a descriptive name for the group. The name can contain spaces.

36. Enter a description of the group. For example, you might describe the criteria you used to determine who would be a group member. Click Next when you have finished.

37. On the Group Owner page, shown in Figure B-16, select the person you want to be the group's owner. This person would be responsible for adding and removing users from the group. If you want to make the owner someone who is not in the list, click the Add New User button and follow steps 29 through 33 to add the user.

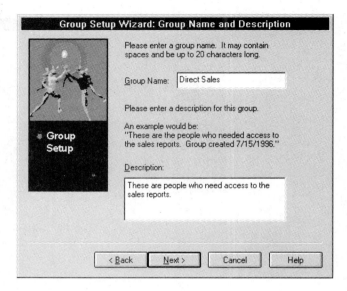

Group Setup
Wizard:
Group Name
and
Description
page
Figure B-15.

TIP: The group owner could be the head of the department, or an employee in the department who is interested in Web servers. However, if you aren't sure who should be the group owner, you can make the SuperWeb Master, identified by the login name Webmaster in this wizard, the owner.

Group Setup
Wizard:
Group Owner
page
Figure B-16.

38. On the Group Members page, shown in Figure B-17, you can select which users you want to add to your group. You can do the following on this page:

♦ To add one or more users in the Available Users list, highlight the names and click the Add Users button.

♦ If you want to add a user not currently in the Available Users list, click the New User button, and follow steps 29 through 33 to add the user.

♦ If you add someone to the group, but decide you don't want the person to be a member, highlight the name in the Currently in Group list, and click the Remove Users button.

 Tɪᴘ: To highlight more than one user at a time, hold down the CTRL key as you click your left mouse button.

39. When you have finished adding users to the group, click the Next button to continue.

40. On the Finished! page, shown in Figure B-18, you can decide whether or not you want to add another group. Do one of the following:

♦ If you want to add another group, select the Yes radio button, click Next, and repeat the steps starting at number 35.

♦ If you don't want to add another group, select the No radio button, and click Finish.

41. On the first page of the Folder Setup wizard, shown in Figure B-19, click the Next button to begin setting up your folders. All of the files that you store on your SuperWeb Server are stored in folders.

 Tɪᴘ: An easy way to set up folders is to create one for each department. If you later need to add more folders, folder owners or the SuperWeb Master can do so.

42. On the Name page, shown in Figure B-20, enter a descriptive name of the folder. The name can contain spaces.

43. Select where you want to place the folder. You need to highlight the folder name under which you want to add your new folder. Click Next when you have selected the location.

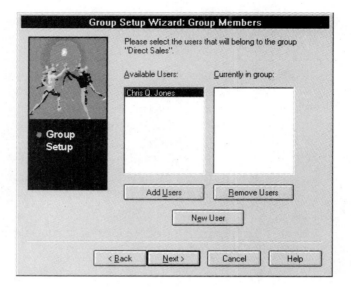

Group Setup
Wizard:
Group
Members page
Figure B-17.

TIP: To expand the directory structure, click on the plus sign (+) to the left of the folder name.

44. On the Information page, shown in Figure B-21, enter a title. This field is mainly for folders for which you had to use abbreviated names.

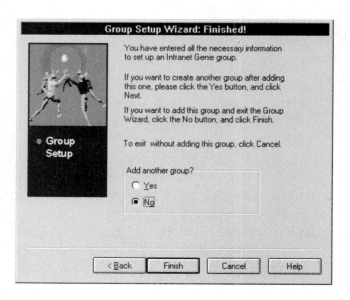

Group Setup
Wizard:
Finished! page
Figure B-18.

Folder Setup
Wizard:
Welcome!
page
Figure B-19.

45. In the Overview field, enter a description of the folder, so that you know what types of files should be stored in it. Click Next to continue.

46. On the Owner page, shown in Figure B-22, select the folder owner from the Owner list. This person is the only one (except the SuperWeb Master) who can add subfolders to this folder. This person is also responsible for making any changes to the access rights that groups have to the folder. Click Next to continue.

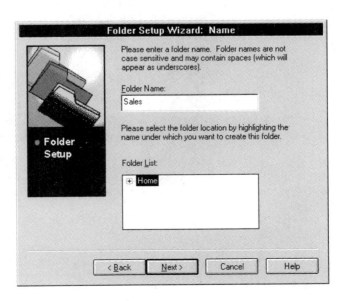

Folder Setup
Wizard:
Name page
Figure B-20.

Folder Setup
Wizard:
Information
page
Figure B-21.

T IP: If you want to assign a folder to someone whose name is not in the
Owner list, you can click the Add a New User button and follow steps 29
through 33 to add the person.

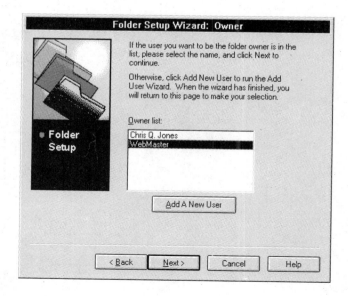

Folder Setup
Wizard:
Owner page
Figure B-22.

47. On the Group Access Rights page, shown in Figure B-23, you can select the type of access each group will have to the new folder when they access the folder through the Intranet Genie Lite applications. To set the access, highlight the group name in the Group list. Click on the button corresponding to the access you want to give the group. Click Next when you have finished.

 TIP: Deny All means that the group will not be able to open any files in the folder. Read Only means that the group can open any files, but not modify them. Modify means that the group can read or modify any of the folder's contents.

 TIP: If you want to add a group, click the Add New Group button, and repeat steps 35 through 40. You can then set the access rights for the new group.

B

48. On the Allow Operations page, shown in Figure B-24, you can determine what rights people have to a folder's content when they access it through a browser. Click Next when you have finished.

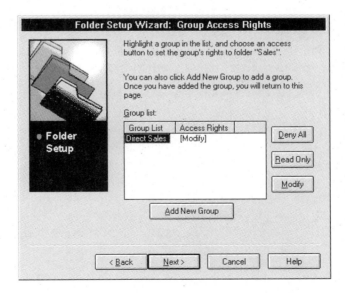

Folder Setup
Wizard:
Group Access
Rights page
Figure B-23.

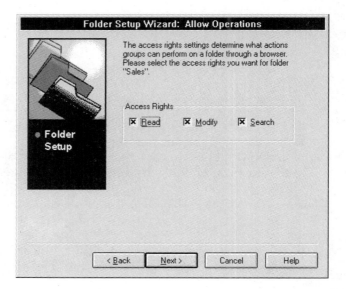

Folder Setup
Wizard: Allow
Operations
page
Figure B-24.

49. On the Authenticate page, shown in Figure B-25, select the operations for which you want to require people to log in. The information you set on this page only applies when the folder is accessed through a browser. For example, if you set Read access to require a login, then when a person attempts to access the page through a browser, that person must enter his or her username and password for Intranet Genie Lite (the username and password were set in the User Setup wizard). Click Next to continue.

T IP: The Read option means that people can open any file through a browser. Modify rights are not currently supported by many browsers. Search means that people can search the contents of the folder.

50. On the Subfolder Searchable page, shown in Figure B-26, check the box if you want users to automatically have access to search subfolders when they search main folders. Click Next to continue.

51. On the Finished! page, shown in Figure B-27, you can decide whether or not you want to add another folder. Do one of the following:

   ♦ If you want to add another folder, select the Yes radio button, click Next, and repeat the steps starting at number 42.

   ♦ If you don't want to add another folder, select the No radio button, and click Finish.

52. On the Finished! page of the Intranet Genie Setup Wizards dialog box, shown in Figure B-28, click the Finish button to complete your setup and exit the wizards.

B

 TIP: If you would like to reconfigure any component, click the Back button.

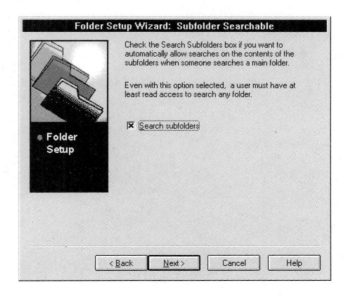

Folder Setup
Wizard:
Subfolder
Searchable
page
Figure B-26.

Folder Setup
Wizard:
Finished! page
Figure B-27.

53. You are told that you need to restart your computer before your changes can take effect, as shown here. Click Yes to restart your computer.

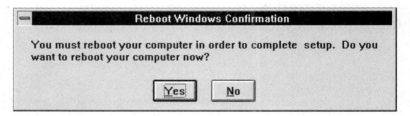

 TIP: For step-by-step tutorials about Intranet Genie Lite, you can open the Tutorial Help, represented by the icon shown here:

SuperWeb
Tutorial

Reference help, or the help files that can also be accessed through the applications, is found under the Reference Help icon, shown here:

SuperWeb
Reference

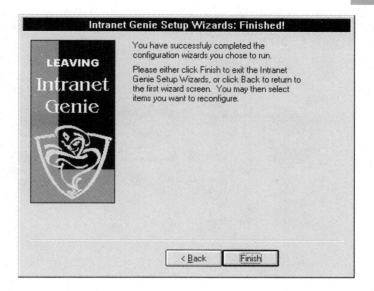

B

CAUTION: You may receive the error message "At least one service or drive failed during system startup. Use Event Viewer to examine the event log for details." If so, you did not properly configure your NT account before installing your software. You must configure the account you entered on the SuperWeb Server Setup wizard as described at the beginning of this section (give the account **administrator privileges** and "**Log on as a Service**" and "**Log on Locally**" user rights), and restart your computer. You should no longer get this error message.

Installing Additional Components of Intranet Genie Lite

If you have already installed either the client or server components on your Windows NT computer, and you now want to add the other components, you need to do the following during your installation:

1. Start your installation as you did previously (see the section "Installing Intranet Genie Lite for the First Time" if you have forgotten).

2. You will see a Type of Installation dialog box, as shown here. Click the Update button.

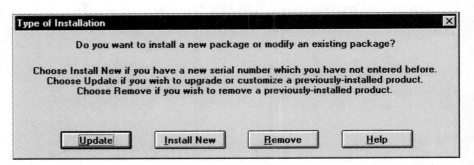

3. The Windows NT Privileges Warning dialog box displays, as shown here:

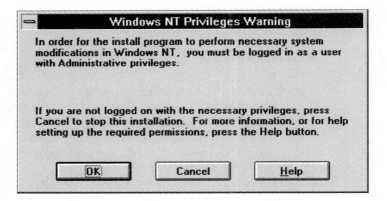

♦ If you are installing only the clients, click OK.

♦ If you are installing the servers, you need to create a Windows NT account with **administrator privileges** and "**Log on as a Service**" and "**Log on Locally**" user rights, as the Caution stated at the beginning of the previous section. If you forgot to do so, click the Cancel button to exit the installation and create the account, and log in with the new account. If you are already logged in to the correct account, click the OK button to continue your installation.

4. You then see a Module Selection dialog box, where you can select the components you want to install. For example, you could select SuperWeb Server Client if you have already installed the servers and you now want to install the clients. Click the Install button.

5. Once the files are installed, you are returned to the Module Selection screen. Click Done.
6. Follow the remaining prompts to complete your installation.

Installing Intranet Genie Lite on Windows 95

What follows are the directions for installing Intranet Genie Lite on a computer running Windows 95. On a Windows 95 computer, only the client applications are available. These include Tapestry Browser, WebMaster, WebDesigner, HyperCheck, and ImageMaster. See the section at the beginning of the chapter, "What's in Intranet Genie Lite?," for a description of the applications.

 CAUTION: You need to install the server applications on one Windows NT computer so that your client computers have something to connect to. You should do this before installing any clients. You can install the client applications up to three times. You can place one, two, or all three of the client sets on a Windows 95 computer.

B

System Requirements

Before you install Intranet Genie Lite, be sure your personal computer meets the following criteria:

◆ Windows 95 installed and running properly
◆ 486/66 or higher processor
◆ 8MB of memory (RAM)
◆ 35MB of hard drive space
◆ TCP/IP stack installed and running (consult your Windows 95 documentation if you are not sure if you have a TCP/IP stack)
◆ CD-ROM drive

Installation Directions

 TIP: The following directions are intended for those of you installing a Frontier Technologies product for the first time. If you already have a product from Frontier Technologies, then during the installation, you will see a Type of Installation dialog box. Click the Install New button to install Intranet Genie Lite.

1. Close all open applications. Do not exit Windows, or shut off your computer.

2. Remove the CD-ROM from the back of the book.

3. Open your computer's CD-ROM drive, insert the book's CD-ROM, and close the drive.

4. Do one of the following:

   ♦ The installation may begin immediately. If it does, you see a screen like the one shown earlier in Figure B-1. You can then proceed to step 7.

   ♦ If the installation does not begin, go to step 5.

5. Click Start, Run from your Windows 95 taskbar.

6. In the Run dialog box, enter **d:\setup**, where d:\ is your CD-ROM drive, as shown here. Click OK.

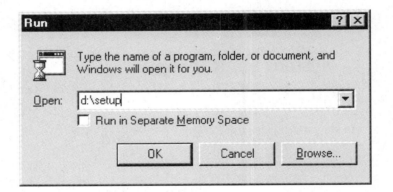

7. In the On the Frontier dialog box (Figure B-1), click on the drop-down menu, and highlight the Intranet Genie Lite Clients (Windows 95, NT) option.

TIP: You can also select a product name from the Presentations drop-down list to first view a slide presentation of Frontier products. Once you have selected the product, click the View button to view the presentation. If this is the first demonstration you are viewing, you will be prompted to perform a short install of DemoShield.

8. In the Intranet Genie dialog box, click the Install Intranet Genie button to begin your installation.

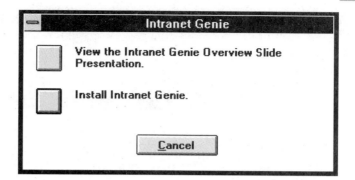

TIP: If you would first like to see a slide presentation of Intranet Genie, click the View the Intranet Genie Overview Slide Presentation button.

9. In the Destination Directory dialog box, specify the directory to which Intranet Genie Lite should be installed, or click OK to install in the default directory, SUPERTCP.

B

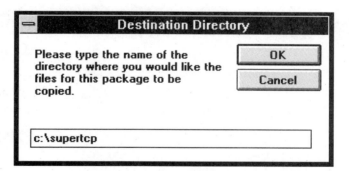

10. If the directory you choose to install Intranet Genie on doesn't exist, you are shown the following message. Click Yes to allow the installation program to create the directory for you.

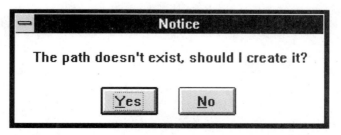

11. The following dialog box appears to remind you to shut down any open applications. This dialog box appears whether or not you have other applications open. If you do have applications open, shut them down. When you click OK, the Installer initializes.

12. In the User Identification dialog box, enter your name and the name of your company. This information is for use by your software. Click OK to continue.

13. In the Intranet Genie Lite Edition dialog box, you can only select Client because you are installing on a Windows 95 computer. Click Install to continue.

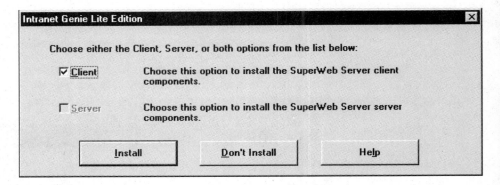

14. You then see the files for Intranet Genie Lite being installed. Once they are completely installed, you may be asked if you want to reboot your computer. Please do so.

15. Once your computer has restarted, you are ready to use Intranet Genie Lite, assuming that your computer is connected to a network with the Intranet Genie Lite servers installed and running.

T IP: For step-by-step tutorials about Intranet Genie Lite, you can open the Tutorial Help, represented by the icon shown here:

SuperWeb
Tutorial

Reference help, or the help files that can also be accessed through the applications, is found under the Reference Help icon, shown here:

SuperWeb
Reference

B

Uninstalling Intranet Genie Lite

If you want to remove Intranet Genie Lite from your computer, follow these directions:

1. Close all open applications. Do not exit Windows, or shut off your computer.
2. Remove the CD-ROM from the back of the book.
3. Open your computer's CD-ROM drive, insert the book's CD-ROM, and close the drive.
4. If the installation doesn't begin immediately, start the installation as has been previously explained in the section for your operating system. Be sure to enter **d:\setup** in the Run dialog box.
5. In the On the Frontier dialog box (Figure B-1), click on the drop-down menu, and highlight the product you previously installed.
6. Click the Install button.
7. In the Intranet Genie dialog box, click the Install Intranet Genie button.

8. The dialog box reminding you to shut down any open applications appears. This dialog box appears whether or not you have other applications open. If you do have applications open, shut them down. When you click OK, the Installer initializes.

9. In the User Identification dialog box, the username and company name that you have already entered appears. Click OK to continue.

10. The Type of Installation dialog box appears. Click the Remove button.

11. You are asked if you are sure you want to remove Intranet Genie Lite Edition. Click Yes.

12. The files are removed. If you have shared files, you might see a dialog box like the following. If these are files that you are sure you don't need again, click the Yes button. If you are not sure, click the No button.

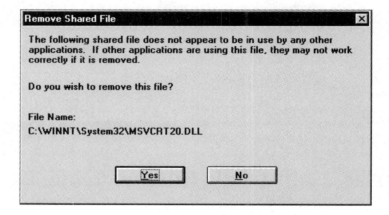

13. You are then asked, in the Confirm Removal dialog box shown here, if you want to clean off all user accounts. If you don't want to save any of the Web server accounts, click the Yes button. Otherwise, click No.

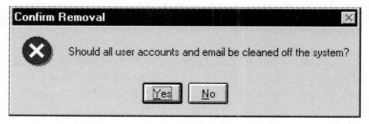

14. You are then told that Intranet Genie Lite has been removed from your computer, as shown here. Click OK.

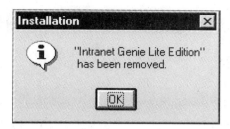

15. You may be told that your AUTOEXEC.BAT file was changed, as shown here. Click OK.

16. You may see an error message like the one shown here. Note what the message says, and click OK.

TIP: If your installation directory couldn't be deleted, and you no longer want to use Intranet Genie, you can delete your installation directory by hand (using Windows Explorer, for example) after the removal of Intranet Genie is complete.

17. You then see the message shown here, telling you that removal is complete. Click OK.

Thank You ☒

You have successfully installed or removed your Frontier applications.

OK

18. Restart your computer before starting other applications. You have then finished uninstalling Intranet Genie.

Installing Internet Explorer

Microsoft's Internet Explorer is also included on your CD-ROM. The version you use depends on your operating system. If you would like more information about Internet Explorer, please visit Microsoft's Web site at http://www.microsoft.com.

CAUTION: If you are installing Internet Explorer on Windows NT 3.51, you need to have Service Pack 4 on your computer. This is an update for your NT 3.51 operating system that you must get from Microsoft.

NOTE: The screens shown in this section are for the Windows NT 4.0 installation. You may see different dialog boxes for different platform installations.

1. Close all open applications. Do not exit Windows, or shut off your computer.

2. Remove the CD-ROM from the back of the book.

3. Open your computer's CD-ROM drive, insert the book's CD-ROM, and close the drive.

4. If the installation doesn't begin immediately, start the installation as has been previously explained in the section for your operating system. Be sure to enter **d:\setup** in the Run dialog box.

5. In the On the Frontier dialog box (Figure B-1), click on the drop-down menu, and highlight one of the following, depending on your operating system: Internet Explorer (Windows 95), Internet Explorer (Windows NT 3.51), or Internet Explorer (Windows NT 4.0).

6. Click the Install button.

7. Some of the installation files are extracted.

8. You then see a dialog box similar to the following that lets you know Internet Explorer is going to be installed. Click Yes.

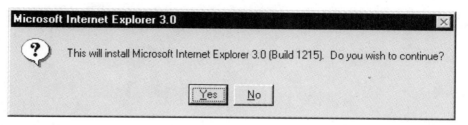

9. Microsoft's licensing agreement is displayed. Read it carefully. If you decide you accept the agreement, click the I Agree button. If you don't agree, click the I Disagree button to end the installation.

10. The files are then copied to your computer. When the copy is complete, you see a dialog box asking if you want to restart your computer. Click Yes to restart your computer so that you can begin using Internet Explorer.

B

Contact Information for Frontier Technologies

♦ Sales: (800) 929-3054

♦ Web home page: www.frontiertech.com

♦ E-mail for technical support: support@frontiertech.com

♦ E-mail for other information: info@frontiertech.com

♦ Telephone for general information: (414) 241-4555, Monday through Friday, 8 A.M.–5 P.M. CST

♦ FTP: ftp.frontiertech.com

♦ Log in as Anonymous using your full Internet address as a password. An example of a full Internet address is user@system.com.

♦ BBS via Modem (414) 241-7083

♦ CompuServe: 70274,2771

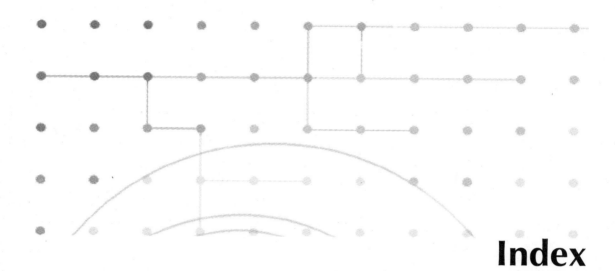

Index

Y

The Books to Use When There'

Save Time and Get

the Information You

Need with this Critically

Acclaimed Series from

Osborne/McGraw-Hill.

**The Internet
for Busy People**
by Christian Crumlish
$22.95 USA
ISBN: 0-07-882108-8

**Windows 95
for Busy People**
by Ron Mansfield
$22.95 USA
ISBN: 0-07-882110-X

**Word for Windows 95
for Busy People**
by Christian Crumlish
$22.95 USA
ISBN: 0-07-882109-6

**Excel for Windows 95
for Busy People**
by Ron Mansfield
$22.95 USA
ISBN: 0-07-882111-8

To Order, Call 1-800-262-4729